The Politics of Culture

Naoki Sakai is a controversial and influential thinker in Asian and cultural studies and his work continues to make itself felt across a broad range of both national and disciplinary borders. Originally finding a home in the otherwise circumscribed field of Japan studies, Sakai's writings have succeeded in destabilizing that home, exposing the fragility of its boundaries to an outside that threatens constantly to overwhelm it.

Bringing together contributors from North America, Europe, and Russia, this volume takes the groundbreaking work of Naoki Sakai as its starting point and broadens the scope of cultural studies to bridge across philosophy and critical theory. At the same time it explicitly problematizes the putative divide between "Asian" and "Western" research objects and methodologies, and the link between culture and the nation.

The Politics of Culture will appeal to upper level undergraduates and graduates in Asian studies, cultural studies, comparative literature and philosophy.

Richard F. Calichman is Associate Professor of the City College of New York, CUNY, USA.

John Namjun Kim is Assistant Professor at the University of California, Riverside, USA.

Routledge/Leiden Series in Modern East Asian Politics and History

Series editors: Rikki Kersten, Christopher Goto-Jones and Axel Schneider.

Through addressing ideas about history and politics in the modern period, and by encouraging comparative and inter-disciplinary work amongst East Asian specialists, the Leiden Series on Modern East Asian History and Politics seeks to combine area studies' focus on primary sources in the vernacular, with a distinct disciplinary edge.

The Leiden Series focuses on philosophy, politics, political thought, history, the history of ideas, and foreign policy as they relate to modern East Asia, and will emphasise theoretical approaches in all of these fields. As well as single-authored volumes, edited or multi-authored submissions that bring together a range of country specialisations and disciplines are welcome.

The Politics of Culture

Around the work of Naoki Sakai

Edited by
Richard F. Calichman and
John Namjun Kim

Routledge
Taylor & Francis Group

LONDON AND NEW YORK

First published 2010
by Routledge
2 Park Square, Milton Park, Abingdon, Oxon OX14 4RN

Simultaneously published in the USA and Canada
by Routledge
711 Third Ave, New York, NY 10017

Routledge is an imprint of the Taylor & Francis Group, an Informa business

© 2010 Editorial Selection and matter, Richard F. Calichman and John
Namjun Kim. Individual chapters, the contributors.

Typeset in Times New Roman by Newgen Imaging Systems Pvt. Ltd

First issued in paperback 2013

British Library Cataloguing in Publication Data

A catalogue record for this book is available from the British Library

Library of Congress Cataloging-in-Publication Data
  The politics of culture : around the work of Naoki Sakai / edited by
  Richard Calichman and John Namjun Kim.
  p. cm. – (Routledge/Leiden series in modern East Asian politics and
  history)
  Includes bibliographical references and index.
  1. Politics and culture–Japan. 2. Japan – Politics and government.
  3. Sakai, Naoki, 1946 – Criticism and interpretation. I. Calichman,
  Richard. II. Kim, John Namjun.
  JA75.7.P664 2010
  306.20952–dc22
                                                            2009050229

ISBN 13: 978-0-415-56216-4 (hbk)
ISBN 13: 978-0-415-85494-8 (pbk)

Contents

List of Contributors

Michael K. Bourdaghs teaches modern Japanese literature at the University of Chicago. He is the author of *The Dawn That Never Comes: Shimazaki Tōson and Japanese Nationalism* (2003) and the translation editor of Kamei Hideo, *Transformations of Sensibility: The Phenomenology of Meiji Literature* (2002). He received his Ph.D. in East Asian Literature from Cornell University in 1996.

Richard F. Calichman is Associate Professor of Japan Studies and Chair of the Department of Foreign Languages and Literatures at the City College of New York. His publications include: *Takeuchi Yoshimi: Displacing the West* (2004), *Contemporary Japanese Thought* (2005), *What is Modernity? Writings of Takeuchi Yoshimi* (2005), and *Overcoming Modernity: Cultural Identity in Wartime Japan* (2008).

Brett de Bary is Professor of Asian Studies and Comparative Literature at Cornell University and an Associate Editor of *Traces: A Multilingual Series of Cultural Theory and Translation*. She is editor of the most recent volume in the *Traces* series, *Universities in Translation: The Mental Labor of Globalization* (2009). She has published criticism and translation in the areas of Japanese fiction, film, literary and gender theory, and directed Cornell's Society for the Humanities from 2003 to 2008.

William Haver is Associate Professor of Comparative Literature at Binghamton University and author of *The Body of This Death: Historicty and Sociality in the Time of AIDS* (1996).

John Namjun Kim is Assistant Professor of Comparative Literature at the University of California, Riverside, and serves on the editorial collective of *Traces: A Multilingual Series of Cultural Theory and Translation*. His essays have appeared in such journals as *positions: east asia cultures critique* and *The Germanic Review: Literature, Culture, Theory*.

J. Victor Koschmann is Professor in the Department of History at Cornell University. His publications include *Conflict in Modern Japanese History: The Neglected Tradition* (1982), *The Mito Ideology: Discourse, Reform and*

Insurrection in Late Tokugawa Japan, 1790–1864 (1987), *Revolution and Subjectivity in Postwar Japan* (1996), *Total War and "Modernization"* (1998), and *Pan-Asianism in Modern Japanese History: Colonialism, Regionalism and Borders* (2007).

Andreas Langenohl is the director of the research group "Idioms of Social Analysis" at the Center of Excellence "Cultural Foundations of Integration," University of Konstanz. He is the author of *Tradition und Gesellschaftskritik. Eine Rekonstruktion der Modernisierungstheorie* (2007).

Thomas Lamarre teaches East Asian Studies and Art History and Communications Studies at McGill University. His books include *The Anime Machine: A Media Theory of Animation* (2009), *Shadows on the Screen: Tanizaki Jun'ichirô on Cinema and Oriental Aesthetics* (2005), and *Uncovering Heian Japan: An Archaeology of Sensation and Inscription* (2000).

Sandro Mezzadra is Associate Professor of the History of Political Thought in the Department of Politics, Institutions, and History at the University of Bologna. He has served as a research fellow at the Centre for Cultural Research at the University of Western Sydney, Australia (2006–8). His publications include *La costituzione del sociale. Il pensiero politico e giuridico di Hugo Preuss* (1999), *Diritto di fuga. Migrazioni, cittadinanza, globalizzazione* (2001), and *La condizione postcoloniale. Storia e politica nel mondo globale* (2008).

Alberto Moreiras is Sixth Century Professor of Modern Thought and Hispanic Studies at the University of Aberdeen in Scotland. He is also a regular visiting professor at the University of Buffalo in New York. He has published *Linea de sombra. El no sujeto de lo politico* (2007), *The Exhaustion of Difference. The Politics of Latin American Cultural Studies* (2001), *Tercer espacio: Duelo y literatura en America Latina* (1999), and *Interpretacion y diferencia* (1993), among other books.

Frédéric Neyrat is Professor of Philosophy at Lycee Charlie Chaplin (Lyon, France) and the former program director at the College International de Philosophie (2001–7). He is a member of the editorial board of the journal *Multitudes* and a contributor to the journals *Rue Descartes* and *Lignes*. His publications include *Le terrorisme* (2009), *Biopolitique des catastrophes* (2008), and *L'indemne. Heidegger et la destruction du monde* (2008).

Helen Petrovsky is Senior Research Associate at the Institute of Philosophy, Russian Academy of Sciences. Her major fields of interest are contemporary philosophy, visual studies, and North American literature and culture. She is author of *The Unapparent. Essays on the Philosophy of Photography* (2002), *Anti-photography* (2003), and *Theory of the Image* (forthcoming). She is compiler, editor and co-translator of Jean-Luc

Nancy's *Corpus* (1999) and Gertrude Stein's selected writings. Since 2002 she has been editor-in-chief of the biannual theoretical journal *Sinij Divan*.

Naoki Sakai is Professor of Comparative Literature and Asian Studies at Cornell University. He has published in the fields of comparative literature, comparative intellectual history, translation studies, studies of racism and nationalism, and comparative colonialism. His publications include *Translation and Subjectivity* (in English, Japanese and Korean); *Voices of the Past* (in English and Japanese; Korean forthcoming); *Japan/Image/the United States: The Community of Sympathy and Imperial Nationalisms* (in Japanese and Korean); *Hope and the Constitution* (in Japanese; Korean forthcoming). He is the founding senior editor of *Traces; a multi-lingual series of cultural theory and translation*, which is published in Chinese, Korean, Japanese, English, and German.

Jon Solomon is a professor in the Institute of Arts and Humanities, Shanghai Jiaotong University. He recently co-edited with Naoki Sakai Vol. 4 of the *Traces* series, titled, "Translation, Biopolitics and Colonial Difference" (2005). His essays have been published in various journals such as *Transversal, Transeuropéenes, Multitudes, Router, Transtext(e)s, The Journal of Future Studies, positions: east asia critique, Refengxueshu*, and *Dangdai (Con-temporary)*. He writes in Chinese as well as in English, and has published a Chinese translation of Jean-Luc Nancy's landmark essay on sovereignty, "La communauté désœuvrée".

Acknowledgements

We are extremely grateful to Jon Solomon for his assistance in soliciting essays from contributors. We also thank Flannery Wilson and Bryan Ziadie, doctoral students in Comparative Literature at the University of California, Riverside, and Dexter Thomas, a doctoral student in Asian studies at Cornell University, for proofreading and reformatting these essays as well as transcribing the interview with Naoki Sakai. We are especially grateful to Stephanie Rogers, Senior Editor of Asian Studies at Routledge, and Christopher S. Goto-Jones, an editor of the series in which this volume appears, for their encouragement. Our gratitude also goes out to two anonymous reviewers for their insightful comments and criticisms.

This project was made possible by a Regents Faculty Fellowship from the University of California, Riverside, and a research residency at the Institute for Advanced Study, University of Konstanz. We would like to express our appreciation to these institutions for their support.

Richard F. Calichman and John Namjun Kim
Konstanz – New York – Riverside, August 2009

Introduction

The work of Naoki Sakai continues to make itself felt across a broad range of both national and disciplinary borders. Originally finding a home in the otherwise circumscribed field of Japan studies, Sakai's writings have succeeded in large part in destabilizing that home, exposing the fragility of its boundaries to an outside world that threatens constantly to overwhelm it. Beyond Japan studies, then, these writings have come to produce powerful effects in such diverse disciplines as postcolonial studies, ethnic studies, philosophy, literary theory, film studies, intellectual history, cultural studies, political science, comparative literature, translation studies, anthropology, and linguistics. Yet it is perhaps the problematic of culture that has most centrally informed Sakai's work from its beginnings, in *Voices of the Past: The Status of Language in Eighteenth-Century Japanese Discourse* (1991), to his most recent *Kibō to kenpō: Nihon-koku kenpō no hatsuwa shutai to ōtō* (Hope and the Constitution: The Subject of Utterance of the Japanese Constitution and its Response, 2008). Typically, the notion of culture is conceived in strictly empiricist or positivist terms, such that discrete cultural entities are believed to exist in more or less selfsame form, with their own proper customs, practices, and traditions. These cultures are the ones that are encountered in everyday experience, and whose preeminent modern form is national culture. Despite the fact that such a particularist conception of culture appears inherently at odds with the universal mission of the university, its resiliency can be seen in the institutional framework of the latter, whereby such fields as literature, history, and philosophy, etc. come to be organized on the basis of the national culture unit (e.g., *Italian* literature, *Korean* history). Sakai's response to this view of culture takes the form of an intervention that is guided by both historical and theoretical concerns. He draws attention to the fact that everyday experience consists of encounters with objects that derive less from individual national cultures than from movements *between* cultures, and that, far more radically, such movements actually precede and are thus constitutive of these individual cultures themselves. This double move, it should be noted, lies at the core of much of Sakai's thought. As an initial step of his analysis, Sakai's concern is to historicize experience, thereby showing that what appears at first glance to be natural or in any way fixed exists most originally as the result of a dynamic interaction of larger, geopolitical forces, which must in turn be investigated in order to better grasp the nature of experience.[1] This move is consistent with much of cultural studies discourse today, which appeals to history as part of its critique of the static understanding of everyday reality. The second, more explicitly theoretical step Sakai takes goes beyond the limitations of historical inquiry to touch upon certain general or formal principles. Here what is at issue is nothing less than the status of the individual unit, without which all notions of national culture must necessarily collapse. For Sakai, the unit as such can never be found to exist in its wholeness or integrity, or rather such attributes—and so the unit itself—come into being only retrospectively, at the level of ideation and the imaginary. As a general principle, this insight informs Sakai's thinking on a number of very different topics, as for example those of subjectivity and translation.[2] In respect to the notion of culture, however, the need to think the ultimate impossibility of the unit arises out of a sensitivity to the insufficiencies of historicization. For if the project of historicizing culture succeeds in disclosing the otherwise concealed presence of the artificial (or institutional) in the natural, just as it exposes the workings of the dynamic within the apparently static and fixed, its status as an empirical discourse nevertheless prevents it from adequately interrogating the legitimacy of the unit. Because of this inability, historicization (and the discourse of cultural studies which grounds itself upon it) always risks being incorporated or subsumed by the very historical unities it sets out to critique, its work of dissolution undermined by the reconstitution of those units at a later, displaced level.

The refusal to accept the empirical integrity of the cultural unit as a departure point for his examination of cultural phenomena distinguishes Sakai from the lion's share of cultural studies research being done today, and places him, along with such scholars as Gayatri Spivak and Homi Bhabha, at the very forefront of cultural analysis—a position achieved, it must be emphasized, partly through recognition of the inherent limitations of this field. Following Sakai, the still widespread notion that cultural objects are traceable back to discrete cultures, typically figured along national lines, must yield to the historicist understanding that situates these objects in more dynamic and fluid interstitial zones. Were the analysis to end at this point, however, one would find oneself strictly pursuing the movement of cultural objects on the basis of cultural units conceivable in ever more molecular terms. Hence the necessity to break with the very notion of the unit, since the conception of cultural interstices or between-spaces ends in reifying precisely those boundaries of culture it seeks to critique. The between, that is to say, is still understood in historical inquiry along the fixed lines of intercultural space, and in this sense merely displaces the traditional focus on cultural interiority to that of cultural exteriority without apparently realizing that the latter remains wholly dependant upon the former. In contrast, problematizing the status of the unit allows one to conceive of cultural forces beyond the restricted economy (from the Greek *oikos*, or "house") of inside and outside.

This view better enables an understanding that the determination of cultural objects on the basis of *either* cultural entities *or* the movements between cultural entities remains similarly beholden to an underlying conception of culture as itself an object. Such objectification reduces the enormously complex problematic of cultural transmission or dissemination to one of more or less regulated exchange, and it is only by calling into question the dominant status of the unit that this issue can begin to be addressed.

As we indicated, the notion of translation is conceived by Sakai in strikingly similar terms. Here Sakai wishes to effect a kind of reversal in the dominant understanding of this notion, according to which, as for example he explains in *'Sekaishi' no kaitai: honyaku shutai rekishi* (The Dissolution of "World History": Translation, Subjectivity, History), two particular languages are originally posed against one another on the basis of specific difference, a difference which is then traversed by the operation of translation as conducted by the translator, who appears to exist to some degree in both language communities.[3] Sakai's determination of this understanding as false, or at the very least derivative, is aided by his previous study of eighteenth-century Japanese discourse, in which he traced this view back to the specifically modern formation of Japan as a nation-state and Japanese as a national language. Prior to this time, no consciousness existed with which to distinguish spoken Japanese from spoken Chinese, as the linguistic differences that were to be found on the Japanese archipelago then were of such immensity as to render impossible any attempt to conceive of Japanese as a comprehensive unity. Active negotiation of these differences was frequently unavoidable as a part of everyday life, but this took place in more or less extemporary or improvisational fashion, without recourse to any binary framework according to which discrete languages are posited strictly in opposition to one another. Historical research thus reveals that translation takes place primordially as a practical act, a concrete way to negotiate difference, but that upon the advent of modernity and the incipient formation of the nation-state a theoretical conception of linguistic difference—i.e., *specific* difference, the difference between species that fall under the same class or genus—came into being, what Sakai articulates under the heading of the representation of translation. In this way, the relation between theory and praxis is mapped by Sakai according to two distinct temporal frameworks: 1. chronological history, given that it is modernity and the massively organizing device that is nation-state discourse that sets in motion the transition from the "act of translation" to the representational doubling of that act; and 2. the instant of translation itself, which takes place, following Sakai, in *all* attempts at communication regardless of what national languages are being deployed or of the linguistic facility of the speakers involved, and which is subsequently abstracted in the form of representation as a tool to organize and make sense of the original translational experience.

It is in order to explain this transition, in both its historical and more general sense, that Sakai formulates the concept of the schema of cofiguration.

Kant's notion of the schema is invoked here because it is a question precisely of bringing together concepts and intuition in such a way that the otherwise empty formalism of the former can be reconciled with, or as it were fulfilled by, the concrete sensibility of the latter. Again one finds Sakai recognizing the limits of empirically-based discourse to grasp everyday experience, since the apprehended content of sensible intuition is, thanks to the schema, directly shaped or organized by concepts that are irreducible to experience itself (and rather which, according to Kant, derive from the understanding, or *Verstand*). Hence experience is lifted from the level of immediacy and sub-mitted to a kind of filtering process by which external objects are rendered less foreign or threatening because viewed as more consonant with the cog-nitive workings of the subject itself. This is perhaps especially true in the case of the schema of cofiguration, for this notion is designed specifically to address the subject's tendency to organize its experience of the world on the basis of an imaginary figure with which it identifies, or which rather actively creates that sense of identification in the subject, by virtue of the subject's complimentary disidentification with or exclusion of a contrasting figure. The schema of cofiguration attempts to take into account how the desire for subjective identity comes to be produced and modulated. This desire expresses itself not simply through an enclosed or hermetic self-relation; rather the subject must ecstatically go beyond itself and enter into relation with external objects *in terms of which* it then defines itself, in ricochet fashion as it were. Far from being given or pre-constituted, subjective identity instead comes to be formed by the movement in which the self departs from itself into the world, which is thereupon marked *subjectively* at the same time that the self finds itself marked *objectively*,[4] only to then return to itself equipped with the consciousness of what it is and is not. Alterity lies at the heart of the self-relation, clearly enough, but the return from the world to the self takes place strictly by negating that alterity, neutralizing it in the process of interioriza-tion. Just as the self-relation presupposes interaction with external objects, so too does the desire for subjective identity involve alignment with a figure that is imagined to exist strictly in opposition to another figure, and in that sense paradoxically *requires* this other as other. In Sakai's work, cofiguration is typically conceived in terms of the discursive binary between East and West, but it should be emphasized that this notion answers first of all to a formal or logical need, and as such constitutes a valuable tool whose application is in no way limited to cultural analysis.

Sakai underscores that the schema of cofiguration must be considered in terms of its productive aspect, or what he calls its "poietic function." What is produced is the subject's desire for identity, and it is for this reason that the dynamics of translation are to be understood less in terms of the regulated transfer of meaning from one language unity to another than the formation of subjectivity vis-à-vis objects that are figured oppositionally. Let us examine this process more concretely in order to grasp what is most directly at stake for Sakai. At the site of translation, a language that is known by some exists alongside another language that is unknown, and it is the task of the translator to negotiate this difference. At the instant of this negotiation, the translator finds himself bereft of any guarantee that the translations he proposes are correct. No rules exist to which he could refer that would fully eliminate the possibility of mistranslation, that would in other words transform the act or decision of translation, taken in all its contingency, into a matter of knowledge. The absence of any translational blueprint that could simply be applied to this situation means that all judgments concerning the accuracy of the translation are invariably also translations. Such judgments are not unimportant, but it is crucial to bear in mind that the notion of interlingual equivalence or symmetry they presuppose in their conception of translation is necessarily derivative of the original act of translation itself. It is on the basis of this retrospective position that the originally practical nature of translation—the active encounter with difference that cannot be reduced to specific difference—comes to be effaced, and in its stead arises a purely representational accounting of what occurred. This repetition of the past, however, since it is conducted from the deferred and so abstract viewpoint of the present, artificially fabricates the past; in other words, it *creates* it when it claims to be doing nothing more than recreating it or seamlessly returning to it.[5] Here we see very clearly that this representational "translation" of the original site of translation does more than simply reflect the latter. Two erasures are taking place, in effect: the first appears in the absorption of the original act of translation by its representation, while the second emerges in the pretense that this representation transparently presents the act—that is, the erasure consists in nothing other than the disavowal of representation's own status as act.

The passage from the act of translation to its representation provides the ground upon which the schema of cofiguration will assert its claims by governing the particular form that representation will take. It is here that Sakai introduces into this matrix not only the question of subjective identity but also the equally crucial problematic of community, although these two are for him necessarily interrelated. Translation as it is represented poses two language unities against one another, and these unities are typically understood to coincide with distinct national-cultural entities whose external heterogeneity vis-à-vis one another is conditioned by their own putative internal homogeneity. Translating between Swedish and Vietnamese, for example, appears to involve not simply the linguistic difference between these two entities but also the national-cultural difference between Sweden and Vietnam. (This direct coincidence between language and national-cultural entity is naturally rendered more complicated in the case of so-called "imperial languages"—English, French, Spanish, Chinese, etc.—but the imaginary cofiguration of such unities as existing in two separate and autonomous domains remains no less operative.) Faced with this binary, the subject finds itself seduced into identifying with one or the other of these given coordinates, and through this process of individual subject formation the community, understood as the sphere of collective subjectivity, comes to be constituted.

Here one must rigorously avoid any understanding that depicts the subject's identification with the figure of a language unity alongside that of a national-cultural community as taking place autonomously, motivated by nothing other than the subject's own activity or spontaneity. Such a conception in its abstraction utterly fails to take into account the pivotal role played by ideology in subject formation. Rather, subjective identification necessarily contains both active and passive moments, given that these figures, although grounded in the subject's imagination, nevertheless also possess the ability to manipulate subjective desire.[6] This is the strange nature of the figure: lacking any material existence in and of itself, it is yet capable of creating material effects in the world; and although originally produced by the subject, it yet succeeds in reversing that hierarchy and achieving sufficient independence to in turn create its creator.

Sakai illustrates this usurpation of the subject's sovereignty by its own figuration through his conception of the subject as that which is *subjected* to (or subjugated by) not only the desire for identification, but also to those diverse social institutions that prey upon this desire, and without which they would have no reason for being. This emphasis on the subject's subjection clearly represents a critique of the classical notion of subjectivity, in which the foregrounding of such attributes as autonomy, mastery and free will is rendered possible by the disavowal of its sociality and exposure to alterity. For Sakai, passivity is primary, but this passivity refers strictly to man's situatedness in a world of other things and other people that precede him, that have a material existence outside him and so cannot be reduced to his own cognitive interiority and powers of constitution. Such passivity, however, must in no way be confused with the submission or acquiescence demanded by the various social mechanisms of identification, whose true force appears only at the moment when they transcend their objective status and become internalized by the subject. This moment of internalization represents a kind of response on the part of the subject, and as such can be understood as an opportunity for activity (or consciousness) to assert itself in relation to those forces that it otherwise passively receives. In this regard, Sakai's conception of subjective identification can be said to bear a strong resemblance to the Althusserian notion of interpellation. To recall, Althusser formulated this notion in order to comprehend the process of subject formation—i.e., the transformation of concrete individuals into subjects—specifically as an internalization of ideology. Significantly, an external moment is set forth in distinction from an internal moment. In Althusser's famous example, a policeman hails someone on the street, "Hey, you there!," and, as he writes, "the hailed individual will turn around. By this mere one-hundred-and-eighty-degree physical conversion, he becomes a *subject*."[7] At this initial, external moment, a form or image of subjective identity presents itself in purely virtual terms since it is as yet unclear if any affinity exists between it and the individual in question. In a movement of call and response, the individual then confirms this otherwise empty hailing, he assumes and makes his own the identity that is offered him, and it is only at this point that subjectivity passes from the virtual to the actual. For Sakai, similarly, the suturing of subjective identity takes place through the subject's commitment to, or act of affiliation with, such figured objects as, for example, linguistic unities and national-cultural communities. Although figured by the subject, these entities nevertheless ideologically hail or interpellate it in an attempt to claim this subject as their own, and this is achieved by the latter's signaling its recognition of itself through the physical act of turning around. Sakai understands this act of turning as the mobilization of the body, since, as he insists, subjective identity can only be sustained by concretely acting upon and transforming the world through participation in social institutions. The assumption of identity takes place *theoretically* through specular identification with an image, as for instance when the subject sees itself as belonging to a particular national language and national-cultural community. However, those acts that consolidate belonging and determine the subject as part of a community (whether defined in terms of language, ethnicity, religion, nationality, race, gender, sexual orientation, etc.) reveal the eminently *practical* nature of identificatory existence, which has nothing abstract about it except for the fact that it originates in the illusory desire to secure one's own self-image.

This complex interweaving of the theoretical and practical can also be grasped in terms of the relation between form and content. For the subject prior to its relation with the world of objects can only be conceived as a kind of empty form, as yet undetermined. Interaction with objects on both an epistemological and practical level provides content to this subject, thereby enabling its formation. In the scene of translation previously discussed, for example, subjective identification with particular or specific languages to the exclusion of others typically occurs alongside the related identification with particular cultures, with the result that the subject now defines itself in those objective terms. ("Who am I? I am a speaker of English, as opposed to Swahili or Chinese, and I am American, as opposed to Kenyan or Chinese.") If these objects fulfill or lend substance to the subject, however, it is nevertheless also true that the subject has no choice but to reciprocate in kind, for particular languages and cultures are likewise empty shells without the active participation of subjects who, through this activity, endow these objects with content and life. This explains the tremendous force of ideology, since the consolidation and constant safeguarding of its bond with subjects is necessary in order to prevent its own desiccation. In this conception, the relation between subject and object is defined in terms of their mutually parasitic existence whereby each draws life and sustains itself strictly through dependence on the other. Here we might point out that Sakai's notion of the schema of cofiguration requires, at an even deeper level, the original co-determination of subject by object and object by subject, which is implicit in his conception of subject formation. Understood as the unchanging or selfsame substratum of its various properties, the subject must undergo the journey that is its experience of the world and external objects in order to determine itself.

Through this fulfillment of internal form by external content, the enriched subject passes beyond what Hegel called abstract universality to achieve concrete universality. In so doing, Sakai reminds us, the various social institutions of identification find themselves enriched as well.

Given the force of its logic and the wide array of social resources at its disposal, how then is one to resist this trap of identification? It is beyond the scope of this introduction to analyze in any depth Sakai's powerful response to this question, but let us conclude by sketching at least the beginning of such a reading. As we have seen, Sakai interprets the scene of translation as a profoundly ideological site in which identificatory mechanisms in the form of linguistic and cultural unities ideologically lure the subject into a sense of belonging by establishing relations of affiliation with certain of these objects at the exclusion of other, comparable objects. In the passage from the bare *act* of translation, understood here as an extemporary negotiation with difference, to the deferred and abstracted *representation* of translation, however, a space is opened up in which such identification can be resisted and the promise of subjectivity declined. For Sakai, this threshold between praxis and theory must be thought in all its fragility and elusiveness, since it is in fact the same space claimed by the subject's desire for identity. Nothing, or almost nothing, separates these two, which is why the moment of disidentification must not be confused with liberation;[8] rather it must be thought as a kind of task or ethical responsibility over which one must maintain constant vigilance. The original, disorienting practice of translation, conceived ultimately in its most general terms as a synecdoche for *all* practical activity, is invariably sublated or lifted up to the level of representation, where it is asked to organize and retrospectively make sense of this initial experience. In this sublation, however, a remainder emerges that functions to undermine the organization of experience by exposing its derivative and ideological nature. Sakai refuses the empirical trap of claiming that it is possible to simply remain at this level of praxis, for he realizes that the theoretical doubling of experience cannot not take place. If he thus acknowledges the powerful claims of representational knowledge, he nonetheless believes it is possible to effectively disturb and displace this latter by scrutinizing its logic and calling attention to its limitations. By challenging the legitimacy of identification, Sakai points the way to an experience of difference that is far more unsettling and yet far more expansive because it is released from the constraints of subjective desire.

The problem of identification and translation brings together the first section of this collection of essays dealing either directly with Sakai's work or using his work as a point of departure for continued theoretical reflection. Michael Bourdaghs's contribution exemplifies the combination of approaches through a sustained close reading of *Sanshirō* by Natsume Sôseki, widely considered the first modern novelist in Japan. Whereas Sôseki has been commonly read in terms of the psychological interiority he confers to his characters and, hence, also as the literary representative of Japan's putatively mimetic relation to the West, Bourdaghs distances himself from such readings, focusing instead on the "anti-humanist" aspects of Sôseki's *Sanshirō*. In contrast to Sôseki's other works that are organized around triangles of desire, Bourdaghs argues that *Sanshirō* repeatedly breaks from this triangular logic not only at the order of the narrative but also on that of the linguistic signifier. In the name of the eponymous figure Sanshirō, the word "san" or "three" in Japanese is followed by "shi" or four(23), Bourdaghs notes. Reading Sôseki in the light of Sakai's work on translation, Bourdaghs argues that the text's oscillation among various languages, e.g. French, Latin, Classical Chinese and Japanese, challenges the normative conception of translation as a mere transfer of meaning between languages. Contrary to this representation, the novel contains intentional acts of mistranslation or, more precisely, misidentification of the languages involved in a translation, for instance the portrayal of Latin as Greek. Bourdaghs proposes that such instances in the novel perform the epistemology of translation as analyzed by Sakai. Namely, if one does not understand a language and is in need of translation, one does not even know how to know if what is said is indeed an instance of language or non-sense. Translation retroactively confers identity upon a language. However, Bourdaghs goes yet further by turning also to how *Sanshirō* deals with translation at the level of the script in the figure of "stray sheep," oscillating between Chinese, *katakana* and the Roman alphabet(33). Such moments of heteroglossia, Bourdaghs suggests, break from the schema of cofiguration that represents translation as a transfer of meaning between linguistic unities.

Continuing this focus on the nexus of literary language and translation, Brett de Bary's contribution extends it by raising the question of gender and ethnicity in theoretical discourses on translation in general and in the work of Japanese-German literary writer Tawada Yôko in particular. While de Bary welcomes the current upsurge in interest in translation theory, she critiques current discussions on translation for widely ignoring the question of gender in the representation and practice of translation. In this sense, de Bary argues that to the extent that gender is raised in discourses on translation, it is generally subordinated to the category of national or cultural difference. De Bary therefore contends that, contrary to the express aspirations of contemporary discourses on translation, current treatments of translation might "reenact the divisions implemented by the modern state"(44). This condition is particularly evident, de Bary suggests, in the trope of "boundary crossing" frequently invoked in readings of Tawada's *The Bath*, which was originally written in Japanese but published only in German and English translations. Though invoked in a celebratory mode, this trope threatens to reinscribe the East–West boundary that Tawada is lauded as crossing and may testify to the assimilationist drive of Eurocentric frames of reference. Reading Tawada in the light of Judith Butler's *Antigone's Claim*, de Bary argues that greater attention should be paid to how Tawada's texts dislocate the national and cultural frames through which gendered and minority subjects are rendered intelligible. Throughout *The Bath*, as de Bary contends, Tawada's narrator refuses to follow the pronominal conventions of being addressed in the second person and hence also the normative regimes of identification. For de Bary, the instability of the pronominal system in Tawada's work suggests that characters are subjects of "suspended deixis" and thus irreducible to categories of individuation such as national or cultural identity.

The question of translation and its relation to politics also is the focus of John Namjun Kim's contribution to this volume. At the center of Kim's concerns is the conservative politics that hermeneutic approaches to translation perpetuate by framing translation in terms of the self/other opposition. Through a critical reconstruction of Sakai's work on translation, Kim argues that Sakai's non- or anti-hermeneutic approach to translation exposes the limits of the self/other trope found in Hans-Georg Gadamer's and Paul Ricœur's writings on translation. Though they both invoke translation as a propaedeutic into hermeneutics, their work on translation performatively effects a refutation of translation and an entrenchment of a conservative politics of maintaining "tradition." Reformulating Gayatri Spivak's notion of the "politics of translation" in terms of politics *as* translation, Kim reexamines Sakai's work to show that, just as translation is essentially political as a practice, politics too is always translational(54). In this sense, Kim emphasizes Sakai's constrasting notions of the homolingual versus heterolingual modes of address to underscore the mutual implication of politics and translation. Whereas the homolingual address describes a hermeneutic attitude that posits the addresser and addressee as members of a homogeneous, if distinct, linguistic community, the heterolingual address describes the attitude of the translator who, essentially, does not belong to any particular linguistic community and is thus the site of politics *per se*, as a discontinuity. However, as Kim also argues, translation itself is a term of ambivalence, for it is the translator's practice of rendering linguistic discontinuity continuous that allows for the constitution of the hermeneutic attitude, which posits the unity of language and hence also the self/other opposition as given. Translation is the condition of possibility for the image of distinct languages as systematic unities that can be "named," such as "German" or "Japanese."

Introducing the question of visual culture into this volume, Thomas Lamarre's essay draws our attention to animal figures in Japanese wartime animation and the imperial politics at work in representations of ethnic subjects within the empire as animals. Reading films such as Seo Mitsuyo's *Momotarô: Umi no shinpei* (Momotarô's Divine Soldiers at Sea) through Sakai's analysis of Tanabe Hajime's *Shu no ronri* (Logic of Species), Lamarre critiques prior readings of Japanese wartime representations of humans as animals, or sub-humans, for focusing exclusively on the Japanese representation of Americans in films and for overlooking the representation of peoples within the Japanese imperial state. Lamarre argues that such readings perpetuate the view of imperial Japan as driven by a mono-ethnic nationalism and, in turn, reinforce the logic of American multi-ethnic nationalism as a more universalistic position capable of subsuming "mono-ethnic" Japan in the postwar era. Read in terms of Sakai's analysis of Tanabe, Lamarre contends, the Japanese cinematic representation of colonized peoples variously as elephants, leopards, apes or tigers working together with the Japanese, who too are often represented in animal form, does not so much naturalize the races or ethnicities within the empire as it *mediates* them into an image of the empire as a multi-ethnic state of putative "co-prosperity"(80). While these representations juvenilize the peoples within the empire by portraying them as companion species to the Japanese, Lamarre argues that these animal representations are not to be read as a de-humanization of the human as though the figure of the human were the universal and that of the animal the particular. It is rather the other way around. In transforming ethnicities into animals, Japanese wartime animation abstracts and hence negates the human as a particular and elevates the animal to the status of a universal so as to suggest the assimilatory "inclusiveness" of Japanese multi-ethnic nationalism in contrast to the mono-ethnic nationalism, or white racism, that many Japanese perceived in Western discourses of political modernity.

Helen Petrovsky's contribution expands upon the theme of visual culture through a philosophical meditation on the ontology of images. What is it, Petrovsky asks, that makes an image possible qua image? Opposing the concept of the image to that of the visual insofar as the visual deals with sensorial reality, Petrovsky proposes that the notion of the image must be understood as standing on the side of the invisible, rather than on that of the visible. By this, she means that the "invisible is the condition for the circulation of images; it stands for their essential communicability." The invisible, in other words, is the background against which something can appear, such as an image. Petrovsky cites as an example the dual nature of the photograph. A photograph is not just a representational image; it is also a material thing that supports the image. This relation thus implicates the photograph in a complex play between ideality and materiality. Yet, Petrovsky also adds that the image is the "other" of representation and is rather the condition for a representation's appearance, which she understands to mean a figure that oscillates between the visible and the invisible. Its oscillation, she contends, is dependent on the community that recognizes itself within it. That is to say, the representational quality of a representation is predicated on a prior discursive matrix according to which a community reads representations as representations. Hence, she argues, "The image comes in full view when the preceding generations are reborn through the affective lives of the communities existing in the present"(97). Petrovsky extends her meditation on the invisible to Walter Benjamin's theses on history, proposing that the invisible image is the subject of history, which she links in turn to Antonio Negri and Michael Hardt's notion of the multitude.

Opening the second section of this volume "Economies of Difference," William Haver's essay "For a Communist Ontology" addresses what is arguably the most widely noted source of bewilderment and frustration for readers of Karl Marx, namely, his nearly complete silence on what "communism" would or should look like. Haver argues that Marx's relative silence on communism does not mean that Marx lacks a concept of communism. On the contrary, Haver contends that the concept of communism is everywhere in Marx's writings as their principal problematic. Contravening the conventional reading of Marx's notion of communism as a telos achieved upon the withering of capitalism, Haver proposes that we think of the historical temporality of communism as an orientation toward the future, a "futurity," that points not to an infinitely deferred end but to the present. The concept of communism, Haver suggests, is essentially experimental or, more precisely, speculative with respect to the workings of capitalism. What capitalism occults and the epistemological standpoint that communism takes are captured in the idea of the common, which Haver stresses is not a concept of division and distribution but of circulation. Conceived in terms of circulation rather than division and distribution, the common is thus not a substance but a matrix of relations perpetually in flux. In a vivid example of the common as a concept of circulation, Haver cites Marx's analysis of money showing that money when removed from circulation ceases to be "money." Circulation is money's ontology. In this sense, Haver argues that Marx's notion of the mode of production applies also to human ontology to the extent that human subjectivity just consists in the tools humans use, that is, as prostheses that allow for a metabolic or circulatory relation with their environment. Or, as Haver illustrates it, "The slave is an effect of slavery, the serf of serfdom, the artisan her craft" (109). Insofar as the communist ontology mode of production is driven by circulation, it is sharply distinguished from the capitalist mode of production, which is driven not by the circulation of capital but toward its acceleration to the point of annihilation through its accumulation.

Resonating with Haver's concern for the conjunction of Marxian political economy and the question of the common, Sandro Mezzadra's contribution brings this conjunction to bear directly on Sakai's analysis of translation in a hitherto unexpected but extremely compelling way. Mezzadra argues that Sakai's distinction between the homolingual and heterolingual modes of address provide a new ground for a critical theory of politics in the context of the global dimension of capital. Contrary to the view that this dimension is characterized by homogeneity, Mezzadra observes that it is "deeply heterogeneous as far as both its spatial and temporal constitution is concerned" (121). Hence, he argues that the site for analyzing capital in the global dimension is less its flows than its articulation, the nodal points that force homogeneity out of the living heterogeneity encountered by capital. Reading the concept of articulation as essentially a process of translation, Mezzadra contends that global capital operates according to the stance of the homolingual address, in which the speaker posits him or herself as a member of a homogeneous linguistic community. Capital essentially interpellates subjects through the language of "value" as it encounters heterogeneous forms of life and social relations, or "cultures," and in so doing compels them to conform to the language of value. Mezzadra thus critiques dominant approaches to cultural studies and postcolonial studies for emphasizing the analysis of power over that of exploitation. If the analysis of power can account for the production of subjectivities, the analysis of exploitation shows how antagonisms reduce—or homolingually translate—subjectivities to the norm of abstract labor intelligible only to capital. By emphasizing exploitation, Mezzadra foregrounds all labor as *living* labor fundamentally heterogeneous to the language of value. He thus argues for the multitude as a collective subject capable of transforming this relation through resistance, and proposes that Sakai's notion of the "heterolingual address" provides the means for forming a new common. The common, Mezzadra contends citing Sakai, consists in the multitude as "a non-aggregate community of foreigners" (135).

Continuing themes raised by Mezzadra, Jon Solomon poses the question of global culture in the era of post-Fordism. Solomon foregrounds the point of antagonism between contemporary regimes of labor across the globe and the diversity of human life across its populations. This antagonism, Solomon argues, compels subjects to conform to an imperative of "communication" to mitigate such diversity while simultaneously generating an "ideology of anthropological difference" (138). Solomon proposes that this ideology is to be located in the idea of "culture" and, in a manner resonant with de Bary's contribution, identifies translation as the regime that manages the representation of differences among "cultures." In this sense, Solomon explains his Foucauldian formulation of "the biopolitics of translation" as the regime by which the image of "originary difference ... is segmented and organized according to the various classificatory schemes of biologico-sociological knowledge emerging out of the colonial encounter" (139). That is to say, translation is a social practice that assigns social identities according to schemata generated by colonialism. By the same token, Solomon stresses, the translational perspective also discloses such relations as thoroughly political, as constituted in relations of address. Yet, while drawing upon Sakai's work on translation, Solomon also critiques Sakai's notion of the heterolingual address for its overemphasis on the "distance" between addresser and addressee, submitting instead that it should be complemented with a notion of "intimacy" between them. Turning to a critique of Giorgio Agamben's work, Solomon questions why Agamben repeatedly frames his *Homo Sacer* in terms of the West alone while admitting that the paradigm of the "camp" upon which he draws historically originates in the colonial periphery. Using Agamben's earlier work on shifters in *Language and Death*, Solomon argues that, in spite of his profound analysis of deixis, Agamben fails to recognize that the concept of the "West" is also a shifter.

J. Victor Koschmann's contribution concludes this section's themes of economics and antagonisms of difference with a turn to the intellectual history of the debates on *shutaisei* (active subjectivity) in wartime Japan. While intellectual historians have conventionally framed the debates on *shutaisei* strictly in relation to the contemporaneous discussions of technology, Koschmann argues that a related but distinct discussion of "economic ethics" and *shutaisei* is critical for understanding postwar debates concerning labor management and productivity. The wartime discussion on "economic ethics" arose out of the wartime *shutaisei* debates from a constellation of concerns going beyond the merely economic, among them the philosophical, the political and the pragmatic. As Koschmann explains, the wartime intellectuals faced a twofold problem presented by the wartime situation. On the one hand, the war required the imposition of economic controls at the national level and thus some form of large-scale planning and management. On the other hand, human beings would have to be mobilized to meet the demands of the wartime economy, and hence their subjective intentions and motivations would need to be appealed to. The result, Koschmann argues, was a discourse on "economic ethics" that sought to theorize subjective ethics and interest together. Koschmann contrasts in particular "rationalist" with "Japanist" approaches to economic ethics. Among the rationalists, Koschmann focuses on the members of the Shôwa Kenkyûkai (Shôwa Research Association) Miki Kiyoshi and Ryû Shintarô, who proposed "cooperativism" as a new economic system(158). Miki and Ryû envisioned an ethical economic order replacing liberalism and placing primacy on the whole over individual subjects. As such, economic production would be driven by public interest over profit-making. Control over industrial and commercial firms would devolve from capitalists to their managers who were committed to central planning and public interest. By contrast, the "Japanist" Nanihata Haruo, as Koschmann explains, argued for a view of the Japanese economy centered on the emperor as a putatively purely public being. As Koschmann's analysis shows, Nanihata's views joined economics with ethics in a tenuous manner. If the emperor is a purely public being, he cannot be motivated by private interest; thus, if national subjects are to serve the emperor, they serve only themselves as the public; hence public interest and self-interest are one and the same.

This volume's concluding section brings together three essays dealing with one of the most enduring themes in Sakai's work: the images of the West and its outside. Engaging directly with Sakai's critique of the West, Frédéric Neyrat directs our attention to the West's discursive emergence in terms of a *relation*. Reading Sakai in conjunction with Claude Lévi-Strauss and Edward W. Said, Neyrat proposes that any attempt to critique the West necessarily results in an epistemic double-bind specific to this concept as a discursive formation. Whereas the mere act of defining the "West" participates in its self-affirmation as an *exception*, the act of refusing to define the West and denying it an "essence" also participates in the West's "scheme of exploitation and destruction" by masking its real effects in the global, postcolonial scene. Neyrat argues not only that this double-bind can be avoided by focusing on the relational character of the West's discursive emergence, but also that the West is characterized by the avoidance, or denial, of its relational character. That is to say, the West emerges only in a relation to its others but denies its relational character. Reading Claude Lévi-Strauss on the Western exportation of "development" as a form of exploitation leading to destruction, Neyrat proposes that the Western relation is principally a relation in reverse. The destructive effects of the Western relation often take place at a distance and in advance of direct contact with the non-West. In this way, Neyrat argues, "The West devours the similar other and transforms it into the same." Following Edward Said, Neyrat argues that this distal relation prepares the way for "the installation of imperialism at a distance" in the form of imperial knowledge production about the similar other, i.e. those who are to be colonized. It is this epistemic relation combined with actual imperial practice then that installs a radical separation between center and periphery, a separation so fundamental that it allows for a denial of a mutually constitutive relation between the two. Tracing this separation as a denied relation, Neyrat thus expands upon Sakai's analysis of the West's relation to the Rest, glossing it as a "subjective-discursive double formation" (182). This double formation, Neyrat argues, is necessarily asymmetrical by virtue of the logic of the universal and the particular governing it. Namely, neither a territory nor a cultural formation, the West proves to be a conceptual place that excepts itself from the relation through which it emerges, masking as it does so its racializing effects in the form of "national humanism." Moving beyond Sakai's critique of national humanism, Neyrat argues that the logic of "national humanism" extends also to France's "republican humanism," whose principal pretense is the formal equality of all citizens yet which accretes in the form of racialized exclusion of minorities in France.

Reflecting similar concerns as Neyrat but from a sociological point of view, Andreas Langenohl's contribution offers a meta-discursive critique of sociology's Multiple Modernities (MM) paradigm as a means of forgoing the concept of "modernization," which has undergone extensive criticism for its reliance on a narrative of historical development rooted in European colonization. In turning to the MM paradigm, macro-sociology acknowledges, as the name suggests, that there are many ways of being "modern," that culture plays a decisive role in modernity and that the methodological nationalism underwriting prior forms of modernization theory must be abandoned in favor of "civilizations" as the basic frame of analysis. However, as Langenohl argues, this is where the problems of the MM paradigm begin. By proclaiming modernity common but plural in form, the MM paradigm in macro-sociology unwittingly surrenders the analysis of "totalizing forces and processes" (Lamarre) of modernization in favor of comparative sociological history tracing the emergence of "other" modernities. In so doing, another concept moves to the center in the MM paradigm to explain the differences among modernities, namely "tradition." Hence, Langenohl muses, just as modernity has been characterized as issuing "promissory notes" (in the form of promises of greater autonomy, economic prosperity and the like) that serve regulative rather than constitutive ends, the MM paradigm too has issued promissory notes with respect to the "totalizing forces and processes" that it promises to explain but cannot due to its turn to the historical analysis of multiple "traditions" producing multiple modernities (194). Yet, the MM paradigm's conception of "tradition" is itself problematic in that it remains, in Langenohl's words, "traditional." Langenohl proposes to rescue the project of explaining the "totalizing forces" of modernization by examining the notion of "tradition" not as a substance but as a process of "handing over" an imagined substance. In releasing the concept of "tradition" from its traditional understanding, Langenohl argues that it is the processes of handing over an imagined "tradition" that explains the "totalizing forces" with which the processes of modernization as "rationalization" are characterized. Modernity, as it were, has always been traditional. By turning to a processual understanding of "tradition," Langenohl does away not only with the conceptual frame of "civilizations" embraced by the MM paradigm but also the long-standing narrative of modernity's putative beginnings in Europe.

Completing this section's focus on the constitution of the West, Alberto Moreiras examines the theologico-political implications of Naoki Sakai's work through a reading of Ignacio de Loyola's *Ejercicios espirituales*, a founding set of texts of the Jesuit order. Taking Sakai's critique of the theological universalism of Christian missionaries and colonizers as his point of departure, Moreiras focuses on how this form of universalism, according to which the world is viewed as emanating from a single center, still organizes political modernity in the form of the interstate system. Moreiras argues that Sakai's notion of the schema of cofiguration, i.e. the mimetic logic structuring the interstate system, criticizes what is essentially a remnant of theological universalism of both the West and non-West. However, Moreiras discerns nuances within the genealogy of theological universalism, in particular in Jesuit thought, that approximate the ethics of the heterolingual address in Sakai's work. Though Jesuit religious consciousness remains committed to theocentric conceptions of truth, it nevertheless admits another principle, *composición de lugar*, which Moreiras translates as "situational consciousness" (212). Situational consciousness, Moreiras contends, permits political decision-making at a local level, based on local conditions, and hence bears directly on the question of political authority within the church hierarchy. Reading Ignacio's dealings with the Patriarch of Ethiopia, Moreiras identifies a conception of political authority by which political autonomy and heteronomy are mixed. Ignacio, in effect, conceived of his authority such that he could issue orders to local church leaders *not* to feel bound by his orders and to decide in local matters in a manner appropriate to the demands of the situation in order to fulfill the ends of "truth."

Bibliography

Althusser, L. (2001). *Lenin and Philosophy and Other Essays*. Trans. Ben Brewster. New York, Monthly Review Press.

Sakai, N. (1991). *Voices of the Past: The Status of Language in Eighteenth-Century Japanese Discourse*. Ithaca, Cornell University Press.

——. (1996). *Shizan sareru Nihongo Nihonjin: 'Nihon' no rekishi-chiseiteki haichi*. Tokyo, Shinyōsha.

——. (1997). *Translation and Subjectivity: On "Japan" and Cultural Nationalism.* Minnesota, University of Minnesota Press.

——. (1999). *'Sekaishi' no kaitai: honyaku shutai rekishi.* Tokyo, Ibunsha.

——. (2008). *Kibō to kenpō: Nihon-koku kenpō no hatsuwa shutai to ōtō.* Tokyo, Ibunsha.

Notes

1 As Sakai declares in a footnote in *Voices of the Past*, "Of course, there was no national language equivalent to today's *hyojun kogo* (standard spoken Japanese, or NHK Japanese). Motoori translated the *Kokinshu* into a dialect probably unintelligible to Japanese living in other remote regions. State intervention in everyday culture since the Meiji period is just astounding – and probably an inescapable aspect of the modern nation-state – and it has been changing the cultural features of Japan fundamentally. We must constantly remind ourselves that what now seems 'natural' is a very recent historical construct. 'Always historicize!'" (264, n. 27).

2 The reference here is of course to Sakai's *Translation and Subjectivity: On "Japan" and Cultural Nationalism*. It is no exaggeration to claim that this insight ties together at its most vital point the many different issues at stake in this text, from the problematic of national language unity in Theresa Hak Kyung Cha's *Dictée* to that of subject identification in the philosopher Watsuji Tetsurō. This same insight also governs the careful dismantling of such cultural categories as the Japanese language and Japanese people, thereby rendering them, in Sakai's noteworthy phrase, "stillborn." See *Shizan sareru Nihongo Nihonjin: 'Nihon' no rekishi-chiseiteki haichi* (The Stillbirth of Japanese as Language and Ethnos: The Historical and Geopolitical Configuration of "Japan"), esp. 166–210.

3 *'Sekaishi' no kaitai: honyaku shutai rekishi*, 118–20. In this passage, Sakai attempts to work out the relation between specific difference and generality insofar as both presuppose, while nevertheless concealing, the practical act of translation.

4 "Those speech acts change the world systematically through the transformation of her relations to it; slowly but irreparably they inscribe a regime … on the speaker's body. In this respect, translation is a *subjective* or *shutai-teki* technology that transforms the world by transforming the speaker." *Translation and Subjectivity*, 28.

5 This is partly why the notion of return in Sakai typically designates an impossibility that the subject attempts to conceal, or rather of which it is in denial. The force of this denial manifests itself in direct proportion to the degree to which the subject senses a threat to its identity.

6 Sakai underlines this dual aspect of the figure as follows: "[T]he figure in cofiguration is imaginary in the sense that it is a sensible image on the one hand, and practical in its ability to evoke one to act toward the future on the other." *Translation and Subjectivity*, 52.

7 Althusser, *Lenin and Philosophy and Other Essays*, 118.

8 As Sakai writes of the postwar critic and China scholar Takeuchi Yoshimi, "Above all, resistance is that which disturbs the possible representational relationship between the self and its image. It is something that resists the formation of those identities that subject people to various institutions. Yet this does not liberate them; this does not lead to emancipation because people are often subject to what they fear most through the words of emancipation." *Translation and Subjectivity*, 175–76.

Part I

Translation and its effects

1 Novelistic desire, theoretical attitude, and translating heteroglossia

Reading Natsume Sōseki's *Sanshirō* with Naoki Sakai

Michael K. Bourdaghs (Natsume Sōseki, 1899)[1]

Novelistic desire

> ... the process of learning does not necessarily lead to the inauguration of the initial project. The learning does not actually take us to the destination that was indicated at the moment of departure, of the initial investment of our desire to know. [...] Instead of edging toward the promised goal, we may be overwhelmed and made erratic by the sight of many different social relations that have been made available through the work and labor of languages. We may begin to lose ourselves and the sight of our destination. [...] In that sense, it does not produce a 'work.' It resembles the 'work' of making a product according to a preconceived plan much less than a failure in the execution of such a plan. Therefore, what this 'unwork' accomplishes is the dispersion, displacement, and fragmentation of the core of desire itself. Desire to arrive at the destination is displaced by many different desires for different relations; the desire to know an unknown language decomposes and multiplies into many heterogeneous desires.
>
> (Sakai 1997: 35–36)[2]

Natsume Sōseki (1867–1916) is frequently hailed as Japan's greatest modern novelist. His major works are customarily grouped into threesomes: the first trilogy, consisting of *Sanshirō* (1908), *And Then. ...* (*Sore kara*, 1909) and *The Gate* (*Mon*, 1910); and the second trilogy, consisting of *Until After the Spring Equinox* (*Higan sugi made*, 1912), *The Wayfarer* (*Kōjin*, 1913) and *Kokoro* (1914). It is a remarkable body of work, especially given Sōseki's relatively short career: he wrote fiction only during the last twelve years of his life. Moreover, there are many other brilliant stories, novellas, and novels that so far elude capture into this triangulating schema.

But the critics (myself included) keep trying, of course, because that is what critics do. Literally hundreds of books and thousands of articles have been written on Sōseki in Japanese: he has remained a figure of fascination over the century since he published his first stories. A number of themes have been proposed as the key to his oeuvre. One widely held version is that Sōseki is the great Japanese novelist of psychological interiority, the first writer to capture the inner life of the modern subject. The *Encyclopedia of Japan* entry on the author gives the standard line: "At first his style was florid and pedantic, combining the traditional *haibun* (essay style employed by haiku poets, usually studded with haiku) and *kambun* (Chinese prose) styles with European modes of expression. Eventually he developed a more colloquial and flexible prose style better suited to examining the depths of human psychology."[3] In this version of modernization theory, Sōseki marks the success of Japan's mimetic identification with the West, so that his mature style of narrating individual interiority provides one benchmark for measuring the Japanese nation's emergence as a modern national subject.

Even critics of modernization theory tend to accept this definition of Sōseki. The respected Japanese scholar Kamei Hideo, for example, in an extended critique of the ideologies of interiority that have defined "modernity" in Japanese literary discourse since the 1880s, argues that:

> Among the modern novelists of Japan, the most vigorous producer of the image of the human as burdened with an "interior," embedded within the family, was Natsume Sōseki. It is not without reason that Sōseki studies have concentrated on this, cranking out author studies that forcibly project this "interiority" onto Sōseki's own life.
>
> (Kamei 1999: 237–38)[4]

Here, Sōseki is critiqued as one of the ideologues of modern humanism and Civilization and Enlightenment in Japan. This view is not necessarily mistaken, but for various reasons I want to map out another line of reading here. I want to focus on a different, more explicitly anti-humanist dimension in Sōseki's works; one that undermines both the "objective and subjective fallacies" shared across even putatively opposed schools of thought such as romanticism and realism (Girard 1965: 16). This version of Sōseki lays stress on his early aesthetic of *hininjō* (non-human), derived from the detached practices of *haikai* sketching, or *shaseibun* (Turney 1978: 285–97). It also focuses on his explicitly theoretical writings, which are often dismissed as secondary to the fiction.

It is hardly an original gesture in reading Sōseki to point out the relevance of René Girard's theory of imitative, triangular desire. Under this form, the third-party mediator – the rival whose model ignites the subject's desire for the object – must be excluded in order for the subject's sense of autonomy to be sustained. Karatani Kōjin, for example, notes that in *Kokoro* the character Sensei's desire for the daughter of his landlord only appears after his friend K falls in love with her, setting up an ambivalent love/hate relationship between the two men. The novel reveals how our "consciousness and desire, which appear to us as immediate (or unmediated), are already mediated by the other," so that our own interiority only reaches us at some delay (Calichman 2005: 126).[5] Karatani in turn cites Sakuta Keiichi, a sociologist who tried to retheorize his own discipline, shifting it from a predominately binary mode of thought to one based on the intersubjective triangle. Sakuta too employs Sōseki's *Kokoro* as a key text (Sakuta 1981: 134–47). Stephen Dodd has drawn persuasive connections between the triangles depicted in *Kokoro* and the emergence in Meiji Japan of "homosocial" forms of desire (Dodd 1998: 473–98). The triangular logic in *Kokoro* is so powerful that a major debate was set off in the 1980s when a new generation of critics began filling in missing angles and sides, carrying the novel's abruptly suspended storyline forward to what they believed were its implicit trigonometric resolutions.[6]

We can find many obvious instances of imitative desire in other works by Sōseki: *The Gate, The Wayfarer, Grass Pillow, Until the Spring Equinox and Beyond,* and *And Then* … all revolve around romantic triangles, and I am still barely scratching the surface. If Sōseki can be called a novelist of psychological interiority, then, we must note that he never fails to explore how the desires of the interior are intersubjective, how that desire is actually desire for the desire of the other – that of the third-party mediator. Moreover, as in Girard, characters caught up in these triangles generally get trapped under the crushing demands for infinite sacrifice that such an Oedipal structure invokes: both K and Sensei in *Kokoro* commit suicide, Daisuke in *And Then* … suffers a nervous breakdown, and Sōsuke in *The Gate* finds himself utterly desiccated, refused even the solace of religious salvation.

In order that my own reading here not seem too obviously imitative of previous scholarship, I want to focus on a work that does not so easily reduce to triangular logic: *Sanshirō*. I have to begin by confessing that the first character in the eponymous hero's name (*san*:三) means "three." The second character in that name (*shi*:四), though, complicates matters, because it means "four," and in fact this hints at the nature of this work, or unwork. Nihei Michiaki states the problem succinctly: "Here we have three men and one woman: Ninomiya, Sanshirō, and 'the handsome young man who came and took Mineko away,' and, on the other hand, Mineko" (Nihei 2001: 84).[7] We might also throw in Haraguchi the painter, Yōjirō the classmate, Hirota the professor, and Nonomiya's sister Yoshiko. In other words, too many sides for a proper triangle, echoing the hint embedded in the hero's given name, which might be translated "third or fourth son."[8]

This does not mean that *Sanshirō* sidesteps the problems of desire. In the first chapter, Sanshirō rides the train that carries him from rural Kyushu to Tokyo, where he will enroll in the university. He engages in a conversation with a fellow passenger, a man Sanshirō will later learn is none other than Hirota, a professor at the university. After discussing the appetite for peaches of the famous poet Masaoka Shiki (in real life, a close friend of Sōseki's), Hirota declares:

> You know, our hands reach out naturally for things we like. There's no way to stop them. A pig hasn't got hands, so his nose reaches out instead.

I've heard that if you tie a pig down and put food in front of him, the tip of his snout will grow longer. It grows and grows until it reaches the food. Single-mindedness is an awesome thing. [...] It's lucky for us we're not pigs. Think what would happen if our noses kept stretching toward all the things we wanted. By now they'd be so long we couldn't get on a train.
(Rubin 1977: 13; translation slightly modified)

Unbeknownst to Hirota, this remark serves as an ironic commentary on what happened to Sanshirō the previous night: an older married woman, one whose dark skin reminds him of his rural hometown and whose husband is away working in semi-colonial Dairen, has seemingly tried to seduce the youth. Sanshirō clearly felt a charge of interest: she repeatedly captured his gaze. But he was ultimately unable, or unwilling, to act on her apparent availability. Her parting words the following morning echo painfully in Sanshirō's ears: "*Anata wa yoppodo mune no nai kata desu ne*" (*SZ* 5: 282), or, in Jay Rubin's translation "You're quite a coward, aren't you?" (Rubin 1977: 9). Depending on how we translate *mune* here, though, she could also be accusing Sanshirō of lacking heart, passion, or even breasts. One is tempted to translate her dismissal as "You really don't have any balls, do you?"

This bothers Sanshirō. Not just because the woman seems to be laughing at him, but also because he is sure he does have *mune*. That is to say, he wants things: women, learning, the city, modernity, everything. "He was going to Tokyo. He would enter the University. He would meet famous scholars, associate with students of taste and breeding, do research in the library, write books. Society would acclaim him, his mother would be over-joyed" (Rubin 1977: 19). Sanshirō gets onto that train because he believes that what he desires lies at the other end of the line. But does he ever reach his destination?

In fact, what Sanshirō mostly does in Tokyo is get lost, as he follows the dictates of his "light, airy restlessness" (Rubin 1977: 52). Another driving force seems to be an adversity to triangles: it is in large part to escape the triangle formed between himself, his mother, and the odious Miwata Omitsu back home – a triangle seemingly determined to trap Sanshirō into marriage – that he sets into motion. Here, the object of triangular desire evades both the subject and the mediator. In Tokyo, too, he sometimes finds himself caught up unwillingly in the machinations of triangular desire. For instance, at the university track meet, Sanshirō at first thinks the runners are foolish to participate, but then notices that among the other spectators "the ladies were watching with great enthusiasm, and Mineko and Yoshiko more so than any. Sanshirō suddenly wanted to start galloping" (Rubin 1977: 111). When Nonomiya wins the race and is congratulated by Mineko, Sanshirō cannot help but stare in jealousy, but once again his response is to set into motion and he flees the scene.

But while Sanshirō feels powerfully attracted to Mineko, he never makes his move – in part because he is unable to figure out who his true rival might be. He mainly suspects Nonomiya, but in the end Mineko chooses to marry a man Sanshirō has never even met – again, the object runs away from both the subject and the mediator (whomever he may be). The object of desire turns out, after all, to retain the status of being other – another subject, that is, one whose possession of money she can loan to Sanshirō, a problematic issue under Meiji legal codes, already suggests the shake-up she will bring to Sanshirō's worldview (Komori 1995: 141–55). The key term used throughout the novel to describe Sanshirō (and Mineko) is "stray sheep." I will return to this phrase again below, but for now let me point out that it indicates that Sanshirō does not know his place in the trigonometry of desire.

At one point in the novel, Sanshirō comes close to defining the three angles of a triangle that might provide direction to his desire. The life he leads in Tokyo, he decides, can be classified into three "worlds."[9] The first is the tranquil and drowsy past, the world prior to the 1880s, the world of San-shirō's rural hometown and his mother. The second is that of the university and scholars – the world of Nonomiya and Hirota, peaceful and unworldly.

> Sanshirō's third world was as radiant and fluid as spring, a world of electric lights, of silver spoons, of cheers and laughter, of glasses bubbling over with champagne. And crowning everything were beautiful women. Sanshirō had spoken to one of them, he had seen another twice. This world was for him the most profound. This world was just in front of him, but it was unapproachable, like a shaft of lightning in the farthest heavens. Sanshirō gazed at it from afar and found it baffling. He seemed to possess the qualifications to be the master of some part of this world; without him a void would open up in it somewhere. It should have wanted to fill that void and develop to perfection, but for some reason this world closed itself to him and blocked the route by which he might attain free access.
>
> (Rubin 1977: 63–64)

All the elements are in place for triangular desire: Sanshirō (first world) should outrival Nonomiya (second world) to win Mineko (third world). Instead of rivalry, though, Sanshirō decides the best thing would be to com-bine the three into a new, heterogeneous assemblage: "Then he mixed the three together and from the mixture obtained a conclusion. The best thing would be to bring his mother from the country, marry a beautiful woman, and devote himself to learning." The narrator chides Sanshirō for reaching such "a terribly mediocre conclusion," and even Sanshirō seems dissatisfied and begins to "translate" its terms: rather than stick to one beautiful woman, he dreams about coming "into contact with as many beautiful women as possible to enlarge the scope of the influence derived from the translation and to perfect his own individuality" (Rubin 1977: 64).

In sum, *Sanshirō* is the comedy of a man, a "stray sheep" who cannot find a mediator. To borrow Girard's language, he has passions but not desires.

Sanshirō is sometimes called a *Bildungsroman*, a novel of sentimental education. And yet, much like the eponymous protagonist of Sōseki's earlier *Botchan* (1906), Sanshirō does not mature, does not grow up into a socialized ego. Faced with a lecture comparing "Kant's transcendental idealism versus Berkeley's transcendental realism," he can only cover his notebooks with the words "stray sheep" (Rubin 1977: 96). In the anti-Oedipal formation that emerges (here, as in so much of Sōseki's fiction, fathers are conspicuously absent), Sanshirō remains a "stray sheep" to the very end. Rather than an ego driven by desire to fill a perceived lack in himself, Sanshirō is more a desiring machine, deterritorializing and reterritorializing the boundaries of his three worlds to cobble together new circuits and mappings by which to follow his passions – and thereby derail his desire.

At least, that is how I, as a reader of Naoki Sakai's work on desire, want to read it.

The theoretical attitude

> In other words, what characterizes translation from ordinary speech is that it gives rise to an attitude or stance that is neither that of the addresser nor the addressee. […] In the enunciation of translation, the subject of the enunciation and the subject of the enunciated are not expected to coincide with one another. The translator's desire must be at least displaced, if not entirely dissipated, in translational enunciation […] At best, she can be a subject in transit, first because the translator cannot be an 'individual' in the sense of individuum in order to perform translation and second because she is a singular that marks an elusive point of discontinuity in the social, whereas translation is the practice of creating continuity at that singular point of discontinuity.
>
> (Sakai 1997: 12, 13, 53)

In addition to his fiction, Sōseki was also an extraordinary literary theorist. In 1907, he published his most important theoretical work, the massive *Theory of Literature* (*Bungakuron*). Begun during his stay as a research exchange student in London from 1900–1902, *Theory of Literature* represents an audacious refraction of the existing discourse of literature that Sōseki encountered in England. In it, he attempted to produce a universal, scientific theory, one that could encompass both European and Asian forms of writing. Sōseki relied in particular on two cutting-edge modern disciplines: psychology and sociology. He would continue to develop his theoretical project in a series of lectures and essays up until his death in 1916.

One issue Sōseki repeatedly raised in his theoretical works was imitative desire. In Book Five of *Theory of Literature*, Sōseki attempts to explain the dynamics of the fluidity of shared social consciousness, particularly with respect to literary taste. He distinguishes between three modes of consciousness that he believes are present in all ages. The vast majority of people are characterized by a mode of imitative consciousness (*mogiteki ishiki*): their attention focuses on the same objects as does that of everyone around them, and they likewise acquire their tastes and desires through mimesis of their peers (*SZ* 14: 421–23).

This imitation is necessary and good: without it, no social order could be sustained. But it is not the mode of consciousness that characterizes the production of literature, nor that which gives shape to trends in literary taste. That role belongs to two other modes: the consciousness of talent, which is able to anticipate the next focal point of shared communal consciousness, and hence arrives there ahead of the masses; and (more crucially) the consciousness of genius, which leaps from focal point to focal point on a trajectory completely out of synch with that of imitative consciousness. The genius's appearance is a matter of sheer contingency, rather than historical necessity (*SZ* 14: 423–36). Hence, Sōseki argues, while we see development in literary taste from one age to the next, that development does not follow any necessary pattern or logic – an explicit rejection of the evolutionary Civilization and Enlightenment model, at least in the realm of literature.

In a 1908 lecture, "The Attitudes of the Creative Writer" ("Sōsakka no taido"), Sōseki again took up the relation between literature and imitation. Here, the geopolitical dimensions of the issue emerge more fully. Rehearsing his critique of the notion that there is a progressive linear structure to literary history, Sōseki attacks those who believe that an age of Naturalism should follow that of Romanticism in contemporary Japanese literature because that is the order in which those movements appeared in the West. In the realms of science and technology, imitation may be justified, because in those fields, new really is better.

> Depending on the time and circumstances, engaging in imitation [*monomane*] can be extremely useful and convenient, because it allows one immediately to apply the end results, skipping past the trials and procedures and troublesome processes required to get to that point. In fact, each of the so-called conveniences of modern civilization currently used in our country – beginning with the telegraph, the telephone, the steam locomotive and the steamship – are the products of imitation. That is completely fine.

In literature, however, this does not apply.

> Many people say that Japan's literature is immature. Sadly, I must agree. Yet to admit that the literature of our own county is immature does not mean that we take today's literature in the West as our standard. [...] Unless one can prove logically that the development of immature literatures necessarily follows a single path and necessarily reaches a single destination point, it is too hasty to conclude that the historical tendencies

of contemporary Western literature must become those of the immature Japanese literature.

(*SZ* 16:167)

While literature may depict imitative desire, in itself it should not be the product of imitative desire.

In *Sanshirō*, we encounter a similar sequence in which individual imitative desire is mapped onto a broader geopolitical field, in which Japan is engaged in a tense, ambiguous relation of mimetic desire with the West. Sanshirō reluctantly decides to visit Mineko to borrow twenty yen from her. Mostly, though, Sanshirō just wants to see her again, as his head fills "with images of Mineko – her face, her hands, her neckline, the obi and kimono she wore" (Rubin 1977: 137). All the while, he tries to imagine Mineko's attitude toward himself: until she reveals this, he will not know how he should act or think. As he waits in Mineko's parlor for his audience with her, he finds himself staring at his own reflection in a long mirror in the room. "He looked at the mirror and candlesticks. They had a strangely Western air about them that he associated with Catholicism, though why Catholicism he himself did not know" (Rubin 1977: 138–39). From elsewhere in the house, he hears someone (probably Yoshiko) practice violin, Western music that he does not understand but that seems to echo his own emotions.

Finally, Mineko appears before him – not in person but via reflection. "Sanshirō moved half-seeing eyes to the mirror, and there stood Mineko. [...] Mineko was reflected clearly from the chest upward, holding aside the curtain that hung beyond the door. In the mirror, she looked at Sanshirō. Sanshirō looked at Mineko in the mirror. She smiled" (Rubin 1977: 139). Sanshirō's whole being comes to him by way of reflection here: he cannot figure out who he is, or what he feels, unless Mineko, who is associated repeatedly with things Western, first reveals her attitude toward him:

> She looked straight at him, saying nothing, a smile about her eyes and lips, and the sight of her thus filled Sanshirō with a sweet agony. Sweet as it was, he began to feel almost from the moment she sat down that he could not endure being looked at this way.
>
> (Rubin 1977: 139)

Despite her remarkably familiar tone, Sanshirō still cannot figure out where he stands with her. He concludes, echoing what Yōjirō has told him earlier, that there is something Western about her: "she was an Ibsen woman. But was it only her disregard for the conventional that made her an Ibsen woman, or did it involve her deepest thoughts and feelings? He did not know" (Rubin 1977: 141–42). The other here is mysterious, Western, unfathomable, and the self cannot become a unified ego until it can figure out precisely how it is reflected in the desire of that other – a position that could become fixed only through the presence of a mediator.

Another key issue in Sōseki's theory – perhaps the central question – is the relationship between literature and science. The characters in *Sanshirō* are fascinated by this problem. At a dinner of scholars and artists, for example, conversation turns to the topic of whether scientists are better compared to naturalists or romantics. Do they rely on direct observation of reality, or instead on imagination and fantastic artifice? Both, it turns out: Nonomiya's scientific experiments require the creation of an artificial laboratory environment to produce the conditions under which his object, the pressure of light, finally becomes visible for observation. "Then physicists are romantic naturalists," one of the company declares. Professor Hirota responds to this by insisting on a distinction between literature and the natural sciences:

> But there is one thing we ought to keep in mind in the study of man. Namely, that a human being placed in particular circumstances has the ability and the right to do just the opposite of what the circumstances dictate. The trouble is, we have this odd habit of thinking that men and light both act according to mechanical laws. This leads to some stunning errors. We set things up to make a man angry, and he laughs. We try to make him laugh, and again he does just the opposite, he gets angry.
>
> (Rubin 1977: 153)

In this neo-Kantian mode, literature becomes the realm for exploring the unpredictable, the otherness that distinguishes the human being from other objects of scientific query.

Sōseki himself theorized the distinction between scientist and literary writer in terms of "attitude" or "stance" (*taido*). In the abovementioned 1908 lecture, Sōseki defines "attitude" as "a way of holding the mind, a way of looking at things" (*kokoro no mochikata, mono no mikata*); such attitudes are, he argues, the product of "education" and "habit" (*SZ* 16: 161). In distinguishing a scientific attitude from a literary one, emotions or feelings emerge as central. In *Theory of Literature*, it is the active role played by the emotional fringes to our conscious focal point that distinguishes literature from science, where only the focal point itself is relevant. This is the crux of the famous F+f formula, by which Sōseki attempted to define literature (*SZ* 14: 27–28). Sōseki uses contemporary psychological studies to explicate the waveform of consciousness, whereby F sits atop the crest of the wave as the focal point, while f lies at the lower fringes of consciousness, only imperfectly in focus. These lower fringes are also the site of operation of poetic language: Sōseki uses a catalog of rhetorical tropes to explicate how continuity is achieved between different moments of consciousness.

Book Three of *Theory of Literature* is devoted to an extended comparison of literature and science as forms of practice. Faced with a given phenomenon, science needs to unpack the "how" behind it, which inevitably includes a temporal dimension: the scientist maps out the timeline of causal factors that led to the appearance of the phenomenon. Literature, on the other hand, is relatively free from the obligation to explain "how" or to trace through all of the temporal lines of causality. Instead, Sōseki argues, literature cuts the phenomenon out of the complex interweaving of temporal development to focus on a single, simple segment of time. Some works, such as haiku, are nearly static and bereft of temporal development altogether, like a sculpture or still-life painting.

This difference in approaches is paralleled in different "attitudes." A scientist's attitude is, according to Sōseki, ruthlessly analytical: given a phenomenon, the scientist wants to break it down into its composite elements. Any analysis that a literary writer performs, on the other hand, is secondary to his or her primary purpose: producing wholes that give a vivid impression of the depicted object. Hence, a writer is satisfied with the naked eye and does not need a microscope, nor does he need to carry out laboratory experiments to dissect his object. Scientists also sometimes deal in wholes, but in such instances we again find a crucial distinction between their attitude and that of literary writers. The scientist grasps a whole via abstract concepts and as a means to explain the phenomenon's form and mechanical structure. Ultimately, the goal is classification: a stripping away of inessential singularities from the phenomenon in order to locate it on a grid of abstract categories. The goal is generalization: to compile individual instances into abstract "isms." Hence, numbers and mathematical formulas are the preferred language.

For literature, on the other hand, what is crucial is to give a picture of the whole. Rather than attempt to locate the object's position within an abstract system, the literary writer attempts to convey an impression of its essence as a singular thing, including its emotional resonance. In place of abstract numbers, literature uses analogy and symbolism to convey what is difficult to express explicitly.

> The literary writer gives fragrance to that which is without fragrance, form to that which is formless. In contrast, the scientist strips away the form from that which has form, the flavor from that which has flavor. In this regard, the literary writer and the scientist carry out their translation [*honyaku*] of things in completely opposite directions, one going left, the other right, each carrying out [his/her] allotted duties indifferent to the other. Accordingly, literary writers use the technique of symbolism in order to express sensations and emotions, while scientists record things using their own particular set of signs without any regard for sensation or emotion.
>
> (*SZ* 14: 251)

Ultimately, Sōseki concludes, there are different modes of "truth" in science and literature. While scientific truth might at times be useful to literary writers, there are other times when writers must turn their backs on scientific truth and create via imagination something that cannot exist in real life. Literary truth has been achieved when the depicted object directly summons up its feeling as if it were necessarily true – when what we read feels exactly like the depicted object, even if this means violating reality. Hence, to reach literary truth a writer uses techniques that would be anathema to a scientist. Sōseki explicates, in particular, the techniques of exaggeration, abbreviation or selectivity, and imaginative combination. This also means, Sōseki notes, that unlike scientific truth, literary truth shifts with time. What is perceived as truth by one generation may not be accepted as such by a subsequent generation.

But from what "stance" or "attitude" does Sōseki carry out his own theoretical practice? Is the *Theory of Literature* a scientific project or a literary one? As Joseph Murphy has demonstrated, there are good historical and cultural reasons that help explain why an intellectual trained in Meiji Japan would not only feel compelled to explore the boundary between literature and science, but also enjoy literacy in the languages of both (Murphy 2004). As Murphy points out, what is crucial here is that Sōseki did not attempt to collapse the domains of literature and science, but rather used a kind of transversal strategy to both distinguish and connect the two.

It seems that the attitude through which Sōseki approaches his theoretical project might best be compared to that of the translator, as defined by Naoki Sakai: a singular "subject in transit." Thomas Lamarre, in exploring the tensions between empiricism and positivism in Sōseki's theory, argues that "rather than postulate a simple and maybe inevitable *collapse* of empiricism into positivism (or of science into scientism), the important task is to attend to the *translation* that inevitably occurs between empiricism and positivism" (Lamarre 2008: 53). Sticking with this act of translation might, Lamarre argues, direct us toward an interruption, an ethical openness to the world that would avoid a simple consolidation of knowledge into discrete disciplines.

This interruption jams up what Sakai calls the schema of cofiguration, a conceptual apparatus that functions to reproduce the mimetic desire for homogeneous identification. In its place, we should consider the attitude of Sōseki the translator as that of one who stands in the gap between "the difference of attitudes and stances," a site of "essential linguistic hybridity inherent in the position of the translator" (Sakai 1997: 53, 67). In this interruptive practice, the translator's desire for identification is displaced by his or her practice: translators are unable to identify with either the "I" or the "you" in the enunciation, so that the translation becomes "an instance of *continuity in discontinuity* and a poietic social practice that institutes a relation at the site of incommensurability" (Sakai 1997: 13). Sōseki's theoretical practice distinguishes science and literature precisely so that he, as translator, can sidestep the desire to identify with either one, becoming in the process a kind of stray sheep, guided only by his passions.

Translating heteroglossia

> Paradoxically, the distinctive trait of the Japanese language is its capacity
> to absorb foreign elements so thoroughly as to obliterate the distinction
> between itself and Chinese; heterogeneity – the absence of a coherent
> writing system and the copresence of different inscriptional principles –
> defined the identity of the Japanese language. Of course, every writing
> system is in one way or another "contaminated" by heterogeneity just as
> Japanese has been. Every language originates essentially as a creole. […]
> We must caution ourselves against the commonsensical notion that writ-
> ing systems like the Japanese are abnormal; as a matter of fact, the
> Japanese system is perhaps a very accurate representation of the nature of
> writing itself.
>
> (Sakai 1991: 13)

Let me return again to the *Encyclopedia of Japan* entry: "At first his style was
florid and pedantic, combining the traditional *haibun* (essay style employed
by haiku poets, usually studded with haiku) and *kambun* (Chinese prose)
styles with European modes of expression. Eventually he developed a more
colloquial and flexible prose style better suited to examining the depths of
human psychology." This description suggests a progressive evolution from
hybridity to homogeneity. In fact, when we look at Sōseki's fiction, we do
find a stylistic transformation from the early stories, written in a variety of
styles, including various forms of classical Japanese, to the language used in
the later novels, which employ a more standardized form of the *genbun itchi*
(unification of spoken and written languages) style that became the norm in
modern fiction. But this narrative of maturing style holds together only at the
expense of erasing much heterogeneity: it is a representation of translation
that effaces the productivity of translation – the *"oscilliation or indeterminacy
of personality in translation"* (Sakai 1991: 266–67). It effaces, that is, how
Sōseki, like Sanshirō, may not after all have arrived at his presumed destination.
   Sōseki's education and early career precede the emergence of the standardized modern form of Japanese as a national language. He was raised, that is,
to write in a "blur of languages, and not at all a system of languages"
(Deleuze and Guattari 1986: 24). As a glance at the marginalia in the books
from his own library, and at his own notes taken during his research for the
Theory of Literature project indicate, Sōseki was equally comfortable in jot-
ting notes to himself in the scripts we identify as Chinese, English, and Japanese. *Theory of Literature* presumes a similar heterogeneity on the part of its
reader: the main body of the argument is written in a form of classical Japanese, but the work is studded with untranslated quotations from English literature, and even some from classical Chinese, so that a single page in the
work might include Sōseki's own scientific analysis written in Japanese,
extended English quotations from poems by Spenser and Byron, and lines
from an anonymous classical Chinese poem (e.g. *SZ* 14: 38). The text is a blur

of inscription styles, one that – as Sakai suggests – is not so much a marker of historical particularity, a trait that distinguishes Meiji Japan from other cultures or eras, as it is a potential site for approaching broader questions about the heterogeneity of writing and language in general.

Early in his career, Sōseki was also an English teacher, a translator, and a scholar of classical Chinese. Moreover, in his novels – even the later, supposedly mature novels – he practices various forms of translation, and in *Sanshirō*, as Dennis Washburn has argued, translation becomes a central trope organizing the work (Washburn 2007: 71–106). As Sanshirō the stray sheep follows his restless wanderings, he continually bumps into the problem of translation. Translation in typical representations promises to cross a boundary between two supposedly distinct and homogeneous national languages, to bring them into communication, but the novel demonstrates that translation in its actual practice is much more complex.

At another dinner party, for example, Sanshirō repeatedly hears foreign words. One of the guests speaks a line of French: "Il a le diable corps" is transcribed in roman letters, with a *katakana* pronunciation gloss provided in superscript, followed immediately by a parenthetical translation into Japanese, presumably for the novel reader's benefit. Yōjirō, on the other hand, repeatedly uses the phrase "*de te fabula*," presented to the reader of the novel in the *katakana* script often used to transcribe words from foreign languages, with no translation provided. After the dinner, Sanshirō privately asks Yōjirō, "What is *de te fabula*?" The response he gets to his query: "It's Greek" (Rubin 1977: 107–10; *SZ* 5: 439–43).

Sanshirō here is placed in a situation that Sakai has analyzed in detail. A Japanese reader presented with an article that he or she is told is written in Swahili likely cannot read Swahili.

> The readers who need translation do not know the language to translate from; it follows that, in principle, they should not be able to know how to identify that language which they do not know. If I were to give them a piece of translation from the original in Hattari and tell them it is from Swahili, therefore, they would never be able to tell if I were lying. [...] Nevertheless, the readers would not dare to doubt that it was from Swahili. This is simply because they do not know how to doubt it, just as we do not doubt that many unknown languages. ... exist in this world.
>
> (Sakai 1997: 55)

The representation of translation via the schema of cofiguration disguises our inability to even recognize a language in the absence of an *a priori* Regulative Idea, an imaginary being that has a poetic function: we lose ability to see that "my ignorance of a language must necessarily be my ignorance of the fact that I do not know it" (Sakai 1997: 56). "*De te fabula*," after all, is not Greek, but Latin. Moreover, we might translate it into English as meaning "this fable concerns you": in other words, it means something like "this is not foreign to you."[10] Perhaps Sōseki means to poke fun at Yōjirō's pretentiousness, or perhaps it is Yōjirō who is playing a joke at the expense of Sanshirō's ignorance. More likely, this slippage is symptomatic of the way translation, writing, and heteroglossia are used throughout the novel. As Sanshirō later repeats the phrase "*de te fabula*" to himself, still ignorant of its meaning, he decides that it "was a phrase that called for dancing" (Rubin 1977: 187; *SZ* 5: 567).[11]

Let me return here to the problem of stray sheep in the novel and see if I can map out some of their lines of wandering, especially in terms of language, writing, and translation.[12] The stray sheep wander into the novel as a problem of translation. After a sequence in which they encounter a lost child, Mineko and Sanshirō drift away from their friends, and Sanshirō becomes anxious that the others may think that they have become lost. Mineko asks Sanshirō, "Do you know how to translate *maigo* into English?" Sanshirō cannot answer, and so Mineko supplies the answer: "'Stray sheep.' Do you understand?" a query that again leaves Sanshirō speechless: "He thought he understood the meaning of 'stray sheep,' but then again perhaps he did not." In terms of script, we move here from 「迷子」(まひご) (lost child), written with Chinese characters and a hiragana superscript pronunciation gloss, indicating a Japanese word, to 「迷へる子」(ストレイ、シープ), the same Chinese characters albeit conjugated with Japanese hiragana differently, and a katakana superscript pronunciation gloss tell us to read this hybrid Japanese/Chinese phrase as the English words "stray sheep" (Rubin 1977: 94, translation modified; *SZ* 5: 417–18).

The next sighting of a stray sheep in the novel are in Sanshirō's notes from the philosophy class, already mentioned above. Here, we get the phrase in the form "stray sheep" (ストレイシープ), both when the narrator describes the words jotted down in the notebook and when Yōjirō is quoted reading the notes aloud (Rubin 1977: 96; *SZ* 5: 420–21). In other words, we get English written in roman letters, with a katakana superscript pronunciation gloss, indicating that we should pronounce the English as English. The subsequent appearance comes in a hand-painted postcard that Sanshirō receives, he supposes, from Mineko:

The sender had drawn a picture on one side of the card. It showed a little stream with shaggy grass on its banks and two sheep lying at the end of the grass. Across the stream stood a large man with a walking stick. He had a ferocious-looking face modeled closely on the devil in Western paintings, and he had been carefully labeled, "Devil," so as to preclude any error. The card's only return address was "Lost Child." Sanshirō knew immediately who that was. And he was greatly pleased that she had put two stray sheep in the picture, suggesting that he was the other one. Mineko had included him from the beginning, it seemed. Now at last he understood what she had meant by "Stray sheep".

(Rubin 1977: 99–100; *SZ* 5: 426)

This postcard, with its suggestion of a triangular relationship, pleases Sanshirō because Mineko seems to be expressing desire for him – but it again renders him speechless, as he finds himself unable to send the expected response to the missive. In terms of drifting script and languages, the passage here is attempting to translate a visual image of sheep into written language. In the description of the painting, the figures are called 「羊」 (ひつじ): the standard Chinese character meaning sheep, with a hiragana pronunciation gloss giving the standard Japanese name for the animal. Several of the words in this passage use Chinese characters given katakana pronunciation glosses ("stick," "devil"), and in the end the phrase that Sanshirō believes he has finally grasped is rendered again as "stray sheep" (ストレイシープ), English in roman letters with a katakana pronunciation gloss.

As the novel nears its climax, after Sanshirō learns Mineko will marry another man, he waits outside a church on Sunday morning for Mineko to emerge. As he waits, we get a sentence fragment that seems to represent Sanshirō's thoughts, though the attribution of speaker could also be the narrator: "Stray sheep. Stray sheep. The cloud looked like a sheep" (Rubin 1977: 208; *SZ* 5: 602). Here, Sōseki apparently invents a neologism, a phrase that looks like but is not a Chinese word: 「迷羊」 (ストレイシープ), the characters bearing a meaning like "stray sheep" and again the katakana gloss assigning an English pronunciation. The clouds have the shape of 「羊」 (ひつじ): presumably, of the animal, but then again, perhaps of the Chinese character. The line Mineko utters to herself after emerging, "For I acknowledge my transgressions, and my sin is ever before me," comes, as Nihei notes, from Psalms 51, a song of confession of triangular desire, in which David repents for having stolen Bathsheba from her husband Uriah. In the biblical story (2 Samuel 12), the prophet Nathan uses a proverb about sheep to confront David with his wrongdoing. In other words, in Mineko's utterance the sheep derive from the Word of God, with all the issues of script and translation that this entails. Finally, the last words of the novel, Sanshirō confronts a painting of Mineko and is asked what the title of the painting should be. Again, Sanshirō is struck dumb: "Sanshirō did not answer him, but to himself he muttered over and over, 'Stray sheep. Stray sheep'" (Rubin 1977: 212). The form of script in which Sanshirō speaks to himself (there are no quotation marks setting off the phrase in the original Japanese): 「迷羊、迷羊」 (ストレイシープストレイシープ). Here again we find an attempt to translate from visual image to written script, and we learn that Sanshirō thinks in Chinese neologisms accompanied by a Japanese script that instructs him how to pronounce the Chinese as if it were English. Stray sheep, indeed.

In this blur of languages and scripts that we find in Sōseki's writings, can we find patterns of usage? Should we be attentive to how what "can be said in one language cannot be said in another," and with how "the totality of what can and can't be said varies necessarily with each language and with the connections between these languages" (Deleuze and Guattari 1986: 24)? Do, for example, Chinese, Japanese and English form a linguistic triangle for Sōseki, and if so, what desires does this triangle produce?

Much has been written about the role Sōseki played in the formation of the modern vernacular Japanese writing style, *genbun itchi*, forging new practices for linking voice to written text.[13] Likewise, there are multiple studies connecting Sōseki's fiction to such pre-modern Japanese cultural forms as haiku poetry, haikai prose sketches, Noh chanting, etc. Likewise, there is a substantial body of scholarship on Sōseki's relationship to classical Chinese, both as reader and poet. Karatani Kōjin argues, for example, that Sōseki's relation to the classical Chinese literary tradition was primarily political: for him, this lineage was associated with the possibilities for social revolution that early Meiji had contained but that had been suppressed with the rise of the various systems that constituted the modern Japanese nation-state, as well as with a resistance to the supposed universality of Western forms of thought (Karatani 1993: 40–44). Clearly, the *bunjin* (literati) tradition and its stance of withdrawal from the mundane world also appealed strongly to Sōseki, especially in his later years (Yiu 1998: 182–96).[14]

What about Sōseki's relationship to English? When queried about the possibility of bringing out an American edition of his works, Soseki responded, "Sorry. There is none of my works I wish to be read by Americans" (Yu 1969: 8).[15] That message was written in Japanese, but we find a similar message in another note, this one written in English, that Sōseki sent along with a copy of his first novel, *Wagahai wa neko de aru* (I am a cat) to a Mr. Young (apparently, an American) in 1908:

> Herein, a cat speaks in the first person plural, we. Whether regal or editorial, it is beyond the ken of the author to see. Gargantua, Quixote, and Tristram Shandy, each has had his day. It is high time this feline King lay in peace upon a shelf in Mr Young's library. And may all his catspaw-philosophy as well as his quaint language, ever remain hieroglyphic in the eyes of the occidentals!
>
> (*SZ* 26: 284)

We find a similar thematic focus in "We Live in Different Worlds" (1904), one of the twelve poems Sōseki is known to have written in English that survive today:

> We live in different worlds, you and I.
> Try what means you will,
> We cannot meet, you and I.
> You live in your world and are happy;
> I in mine and am contented.
> Then let us understand better
> Not to interfere with each other's lot.
> We break an ox's horn by bending it;
> We are not meant to be broken like that!
> Your world is far away from me.

It is veiled with miles of mist and haze.
It is in vain that I should strain my eyes
To catch glimpses of your abode.
Flowers may there be; and lots of things pretty,
Yet never in a dream I wished to be there.
For I am here and not there;
And I am forever mine and not yours!

(*SZ* 13: 185–86)

Neither of the above works in English were intended for publication, a significant fact. It seems that for Sōseki, English functioned as a kind of linguistic panopticon: it was the language in which he desired to see without being seen in return.

If that is so, what business does this American English-speaker have in reading Sōseki by way of the theoretical writings of Naoki Sakai? What are, that is, the ethics of the reading or translation attitude I am adopting here? In fact, the ethics of heteroglossia, translation, and passion that I have argued characterize Sōseki's work seem to define ethics in terms of a relation to the other that is not immediately defined by the schema of cofiguration, in which the practice of translation does not aim to produce two distinct, homogeneous identities. Frederic Jameson, even as he addresses the potential pitfalls of reading Sōseki by way of translation, discusses the "modern irony" that characterizes Sōseki's fiction, "one of inner comfort and familiarity with which, on the inside, each is deeply comfortable; the self as the old clothes we wear around the home – which, however, looks different and unfamiliar, somehow shocking, from the outside" (Jameson 1991: 124). It is the shock that breaks through the illusion of familiarity, a shock available only to someone "outside." This irony "can essentially be described as a brusque movement in which the inside becomes aware ... that it has an outside in the first place" (Jameson 1991: 138). There is a sense of an unknowable outside that haunts the interiors here, a kind of unintelligible noise of language that derails any desire for identification. The relation to this external other is enacted through script and through "a pure and intense sonorous material that is always connected to *its own abolition* – a deterritorialized musical sound, a cry that escapes signification, composition, song, words – a sonority that ruptures in order to break away from a chain that is still all too signifying" (Deleuze and Guattari 1986: 6). *De te fabula*, a phrase that calls for dancing.

There is a noise in *Sanshirō*, a scribbling that gestures toward an exterior reader, a reader who is other, who approaches the text through the attitude of a translator. Such a reader finds in these texts not identity but, as Karatani suggests, "diversity," or to use Sanshirō's vocabulary, stray sheep.[16] The reader should, like Sanshirō, produce his translation not by choosing between one of the three worlds (or languages), but rather by mixing them together.

38   *Michael K. Bourdaghs*

Bibliography

Bourdaghs, M. K. (Forthcoming). Introduction: Overthrowing the Emperor in Japanese Literary Studies. *The Linguistic Turn in Contemporary Japanese Literary Studies: Politics, Language, Textuality.* M. K. Bourdaghs (Ed.). Ann Arbor, University of Michigan Center for Japanese Studies Publications.

Calichman, R. F. (Ed.) (2005). *Contemporary Japanese Thought.* New York, Columbia University Press.

Deleuze, G. and Guattari, F. (1986). *Kafka: Toward a Minor Literature.* Minneapolis, University of Minnesota Press.

Dodd, S. (1998). The Significance of Bodies in Sōseki's Kokoro. *Monumenta Nipponica* 53(4): 473–98.

Girard, R. (1965). *Deceit, Desire & the Novel: Self and Other in Literary Structure.* Baltimore, Johns Hopkins University Press.

Hoye, T. (unpublished work). Politics, Philosophy and Myth in Natsume Sōseki's First Trilogy. Chicago, presented at the 20th Annual Meeting of the Eric Voegelin Society, Sept. 2–4, 2004.

Iijima T. and Vardaman Jr., James M. (Ed.) (1987). *The World of Natsume Sōseki.* Tokyo, Kinseidō.

Ishihara Chiaki (1999). *Sōseki no kigōgaku.* Tokyo, Kōdansha.

Jameson, F. R. (1991). Sōseki and Western Modernism. *boundary 2* 18 (3): 123–41.

Kamei Hideo (1999). *Shōsetsu ron: Shōsetsu shinzui to kindai.* Tokyo, Iwanami Shoten.

Karatani, K. (1993). *Origins of Modern Japanese Literature.* Durham, Duke University Press.

Komori Yōichi (1995). *Sōseki wo yominaosu.* Tokyo, Chikuma Shobō.

Lamarre, T. (2008). Expanded Empiricism: Natsume Sōseki with William James. *Japan Forum* 20 (1): 47–77.

Nihei Michiaki (2001). Nanji no me no mae ni totte: Sanshirō no kōzu. *Kokubungaku* 46 (1): 78–84.

Murphy, J. A. (2004). *Metaphorical Circuit: Negotiations Between Literature and Science in 20th Century Japan.* Ithaca, New York, Cornell University East Asia Program.

Oshino Takeshi (1994). Kokoro ronsō no yukue. *Sōryoku tôron: Sōseki no Kokoro.* N. M. Komori Yōichi, and Miyagawa Takeo. Tokyo, Kanrin Shobō: 12–27.

Sakai, N. (1991). *Voices of the Past: The Status of Language in Eighteenth-Century Japanese Discourse.* Ithaca, Cornell University Press.

——. (1997). *Translation and Subjectivity: On 'Japan' and Cultural Nationalism.* Minneapolis, University of Minnesota Press.

Sakaki, A. (1999). *Recontextualizing Texts: Narrative Performance in Modern Japanese Fiction.* Cambridge, Harvard University Asia Center.

Sakuta Keiichi (1981). *Kojinshugi no unmei: kindai shōsetsu to shakaigaku.* Tokyo, Iwanami Shoten.

Seki N. (1977). *Sanshirō: A Novel.* Tokyo, University of Tokyo Press.

——. (1993–99). *Sōseki zenshū.* Tokyo, Iwanami Shoten.

Turney, A. (1978). A Feeling of Beauty: Natsume Sōseki's Ichiya. *Monumenta Nipponica* 33 (3): 285–97.

Washburn, D. (2007). *Translating Mount Fuji: Modern Japanese Fiction and the Ethics of Identity.* New York, Columbia University Press.

Yiu, A. (1998). *Chaos and Order in the Works of Natsume Sōseki.* Honolulu, University of Hawaii Press.

Yu, B. (1969). *Natsume Sōseki.* New York, Twayne Publishers.

Notes

1 The opening lines of a *kanshi* (Chinese poem) (Sōseki 1993–99: 18:25) (hereafter by abbreviated in citations as SZ), 29 volumes. All citations from Sōseki's works are taken from this edition; translations are mine, except where otherwise noted. Maria Flutsch translates these lines: "Mastering Eastern and Western scripts:/My heart is burdened with ancient and modern sorrows." See her "An Introduction to Sōseki's Chinese Poetry," (Takehisa and Vardaman, Jr. 1987: 1–15).

2 Here, Sakai is discussing in specific the desires that are elicited in the process of language learning.

3 "Natsume Sōseki" entry (Uchida Michio) (*Kodansha Encyclopedia* 1983: 5:349–51).

4 Translations of all quotations from Japanese sources are mine, except where otherwise noted.

5 In Calichman, by Karatani Kōjin, "Sōseki's Diversity: On Kokoro," 119–29.

6 The so-called "Kokoro debate" is summarized in English (Sakaki 1999: 29–53); and in my "Introduction: Overthrowing the Emperor in Japanese Literary Studies." (Bourdaghs forthcoming). In Japanese, see Oshino Takeshi (Oshino 1994: 12–27).

7 The embedded quotation is modified slightly from Jay Rubin's translation (Sōseki 1977: 186). All subsequent quotations from *Sanshirō* will use this edition, abbreviated as "Rubin" in citations as opposed to "Sōseki."

8 It could also mean "the fourth son of a man who was himself a third son," though Sanshirō in fact clearly seems to be a first son (Ishihara 1999: 240n19).

9 For alternate readings of the triangular logic behind this passage, see Stephen Dodd (Dodd 1998: 482–90) and Dennis Washburn (Washburn 2007: 97–98).

10 Sōseki probably knew the phrase from the closing line of Robert Browning's "The Statue and the Bust."

11 "De te fabula" has a counterpart, "hydriotaphia," another word that Sanshirō associates with Professor Hirota. When Sanshirō asks the latter what it means, he is told "I don't know myself. I suppose it's Greek" (Rubin 1977: 190).

12 Many previous critics have explored the implications of "stray sheep" and translation in the novel (Washburn 2007: 101–5). Also see Timothy Hoye's unpublished work (Hoye 2004).

13 For example, see Ishihara (Ishihara 1999: 29–42).

14 See also Flutsch, "An Introduction to Sōseki's Chinese Poetry" in Takehisa and Vardaman, Jr.

15 See SZ 24:544 for the original 1916 letter.

16 In Karatani "Sōseki's Diversity: On *Kokoro*," from Calichman's book.

2 Deixis, dislocation, and suspense in translation

Tawada Yôko's "The Bath"

Brett de Bary[1]

When asked, "Are you Japanese?" I would answer, "Yes, you are Japanese." The trick in this game was to change "you" into "I," but I didn't yet realize it.

Tawada Yôko, "Urokomochi," tr. Yumi Selden, 2002

(*Das Bad*, 1989)[2]

Over the past two decades, a surge in translation studies and the ongoing elaboration of translation theory have vibrantly reshaped scholarship in more traditional areas of literature, language, and culture. Destabilizing the hierarchized distinction between "original" and "translation" has proven an apt means for dismantling power relations inherent in Eurocentric notions of modernity, bringing rich new vistas into view. Studies of translation have greatly added to the complexity and rigor with which critical work on the nation, nationalism, colonialism, and racism may be conducted. For an emerging global studies, they have also enabled more nuanced conceptualizations of diasporic and creolized subjectivities and texts.

Yet often enough, a new valorization of translation and celebration of linguistic hybridity in North American literary studies has been accompanied by a puzzling relapse into reliance on the same notions of linguistic borders and territorialized language and cultural unities that have been made obsolete by recent translation studies. A sophisticated argument for the teaching of world literature in translation unhesitatingly asserts, for example, that a text translated from another language can serve as a "window on the world," and that such texts deserve close reading because "world literature is constituted differently in different cultures," and "much can be learned from close attention to the working of a given cultural system" (Damrosch 2003: 26). The lapse, here, back into the commonsensical assumption of isomorphism among text, language, culture, and geography offers surprising evidence of the continued resilience of Roman Jakobson's notion of "translation proper," a privileging of "inter-lingual" translation subjected to extended critique in Naoki Sakai's formidable study, *Translation and Subjectivity* (Sakai 1997). Jakobson's awarding of recognition, from among the three classes of intralingual, inter-semiotic, and inter-lingual translation ("the interpretation of verbal signs by means of some other language"), to inter-lingual translation alone as "translation proper" assumes the existence of distinguishable borders between one language and "some other language" (Jakobson 1971: 261). Yet, as Sakai argues, such comparison of "two" languages cannot take place without the process of translation itself, which precedes, rather than follows, our being able to distinguish between them. Like the movement of a pencil tracing a line, or border, on a page of paper, translation is precisely the *movement* of creating the border, and must not be confused with the static (and arbitrary) *representation of difference* that is its after-effect. Only under the specific schema of translation whose historical emergence was co-terminous with that of modern nationalism, Sakai notes, do we "displace translation with the representation of translation." This displacement "also enables the representation of ethnic or national subjects" – for by erasing the process of translation and the presence of "the translator who is always in-between," the representation of translation is made to "discriminatorily posit one language unity against another (and one 'cultural' unity against another)" (Sakai 1997: 15).

Its continued haunting by the notion of "translation proper" offers striking evidence that what is at stake in contemporary translation studies is far more than the extension of a linguistic metaphor, as some would describe it. That the elaboration of the generative possibilities of translation can easily falter, retracing subjective and territorial boundaries naturalized through modernity's violence, only attests to the durability of the modern *representation* of translation as it has been implicated in maintaining the division into geopolitical units of the modern (colonial and post-colonial) world. As Sakai and Solomon have asserted, translation should be understood as a "subjective technology," which "actually produces differentially coded subjects, typically national ones" (Sakai and Solomon 2006: 27). Translation's close association with the subjective technology of the national, moreover, may explain why the study of translation and gender has tended to become elided, or underrepresented, in translation studies, as we shall discuss below. In the following pages I will examine some of these issues in the reception of the highly acclaimed, "boundary-crossing" writer of German and Japanese texts, Tawada Yôko (b. 1960). By reading Tawada's work in relation to a little noticed linking of translation and gender in Judith Butler's *Antigone's Claim* (2000), I suggest how Tawada's texts themselves may offer alternative perspectives.

Tawada and questions for translation studies

A small scholarly literature engaging the works of Tawada Yôko is emerging. Granted some of the most prestigious awards in the German and Japanese publishing worlds, Tawada's literary texts have increasingly become the focus of conference panels and symposia in the U.S., Germany, and Japan. Aspects of her writing appear tailored for consideration under the rubric of transnational/translation studies that have become preoccupations of contemporary cultural criticism, and interest in the two has grown in tandem. Consonant with her distinguished prizes, appointments, and invitations, Tawada's work is frequently analyzed with reference to the writings of Benjamin and Derrida, surrealist poetry, or the conceptualist art of Joseph Beuys – that is, to what might still be called a certain genealogy of European high modernism. In Japan, dust jackets and critical essays alike prominently feature the keyword *ekkyô*, or "boundary crossing," in relation to Tawada. While elaborating the formal inventiveness of Tawada's exploration of the intercultural and the multilingual, however, few have problematized the dominant construction, in critical discourse, of Tawada's "boundary crossing" along an East–West axis.[3] Could the self-congratulatory tone of her work's reception in the "East" (Japan) and "West" (Germany, the U.S.) be just another testament to Eurocentrism's undiminished capacity for assimilation? Has Tawada's "boundary-crossing" been read as a kind of racial and cultural "passing," in a manner which privileges and perpetuates notions of a hegemonic West? If such is the case, of course, this would not imply that Eurocentrism and "the West" are entities to be attributed a certain geographic fixity.

Such suspicions might be intensified by some observations about the positioning, classification, and marketing of Tawada's works within the Japanese literary world. While Tawada's language experiments have been linked to Gilles Deleuze's notions of minoritarian writing, for example, she is not generally studied as a "minority" writer, or linked to the politics of ethnicity within Japan. Rather, characterizations of her literary contributions seem to conform to a pattern observed in the United States in the late 1980s and early 1990s by Rey Chow. As Chow has noted, at the same time that notions of fragmented subjectivity, decentering, and the fluidity of the signifier came to dominate academic literary discourse, the "ideological burden of humanity" and "truth" was shifted to texts by emerging ethnic writers. As the very boundary between text and context was being destabilized, texts by ethnic writers were nevertheless tied closely to context and required to faithfully offer up historical and ethnographic truths.[4] Japanese criticism of Tawada has tended to conform to this pattern, and has resisted comparing her uses of language to those of minority writers within Japan.

I call attention to these aspects of the critical reception of Tawada Yôko's work not to diminish in any way its merit. In fact, I will suggest that Tawada's writing contains radical dimensions which the reading strategies above seek, precisely, to contain. I am using Tawada's texts and their reception, rather, to intervene in contemporary discussions of translation on several counts. First, Tawada's reception suggests that the current embrace of translation studies by many critics continues to rely, for its articulation of difference, on the same modern regulatory schema of translation that distributes difference as national, cultural, and ethnic difference. The representation of Tawada as boundary-crossing obviously construes this "boundary" as that between Germany and Japan, making Tawada a representative of Japan while erasing heterogeneity within.

Moreover, in Tawada's case it becomes clear that the radical potential of, say, Benjaminian or Derridean notions of translation to emancipate language from meaning (by refusing to see translation as communication, as *Übersetzung* or "transfer" of meaning from one language to another) can lead to a celebration of "translatability" that voids it of consideration of history. Under the banner of "translatability" the complex politics of the international translation market are often obfuscated, guaranteeing visibility for a few "representative" writers in ways that corroborate existing ethnocentric biases. This phenomenon is diagnosed in the contribution to a recent volume on translation by Latin Americanist Sylvia Molloy, humorously entitled "Postcolonial Latin American and the Magical Realist Imperative: A Report to an Academy." Molloy recounts her experience, as an Argentine doctoral candidate studying French literature in Paris, of being told to abandon her initial plans in favor of writing a dissertation about the reception of Latin American literature in France. At that moment, she writes, "I knew that I was being assigned the role of the native informant," but also "that the native was spoken for," since only a limited range of writers (typically "magical realists") met the French demand for Latin American specificity (Molloy 2005: 370–71). Not only has the construct of Latin American literature in the metropolitan "West" been based on a narrow band of translated writers, but the impressive work of Latin American critical theorists is generally excluded from American academic studies of translation itself. Unlike the English that Morinaka Takaaki has called the "money" or "general form of value" of contemporary language exchange (Morinaka 2006: 44), Spanish is not viewed as a "language of authority or of intellectual exchange" (Molloy 2005: 373). The same, of course, is true of writings by Asian critics.[5] As an increasingly favored mode of intercultural knowledge mediation, Molloy warns, translation studies risks propagating a misleading trope of "translatability" as the West's "easy familiarity" with the Rest. The literary heterogeneity, pertinent social asymmetries, and, in many cases, well-established transculturated Westernism that characterize these sites are overlooked (Molloy 2005: 374–75). Tawada, as an emblem of translation that may slip into "translatability," is often read in ways that divorce her writings from the more intractable tensions of multicultural politics.

Finally, a consideration of Tawada's texts and reception prompts an observation about the tendency for gender difference to be subsumed under questions of national and ethnic difference in translation studies. In North America, at least, the boom in translation studies since the early 1990s has occurred in tandem with a conspicuous retreat of feminist criticism (particularly) in academic work and cultural theory, in the context of a powerful backlash orchestrated by evangelical and right-wing political forces. While theorists like Lawrence Venuti have sought to define translation studies in opposition to the ideological erasure of translation, then, the *invisibility* of both the translator and her gender (still predominantly female) persists. This is evident even in Venuti's influential *Translation Studies Reader*, where only

3 of 30 essays deal explicitly with gender politics. The ratio is characteristic of many recent volumes on translation.

One may ponder why recent translation studies, with the notable exception of persistent concerns articulated by theorists like Sherry Simon and Gayatri Spivak, have so avoided addressing gender politics. Nearly two decades ago, Lori Chamberlain pointed out that the very language we use to speak of translation, whether literary or legal, is gendered and thus implicated in the negotiation of power. Around the concepts of copy and original, fidelity and faithlessness, processes of production and reproduction (historically them-selves gendered as a fundamental social division of labor) are controlled, and categories of propriety and identity regulated (Chamberlain 2000).[6] Do the contours of contemporary translation studies reenact the divisions imple-mented by the modern state, clearly subordinating gender identity to the national? Has a certain aporia around gender in Benjamin's influential essay gone unproblematized? If not, when we posit that Benjamin's "pure lan-guage" is an element (even if not given in the mode of presence) "in which languages encounter each other only in their differences," why are these dif-ferences invariably coded as national and ethnic (Morinaka 2006: 49)?[7]

Antigone, translation, and the post-Oedipal subject

With the publication of her book, *Antigone's Claim: Kinship Between Life and Death*, Judith Butler addressed a text with iconic status in modern debates over translation and philosophy.[8] Interestingly, while Butler herself gives scant attention to an explicit problematics of translation in her book, a few key points in her argument turn on matters of translation. Early on, for example, Butler is at pains to remind us of a double meaning of Antigone's name that is lost in translation to English. Citing a scholar of Greek literature who has explicated the "rich polyvalence of Antigone's name" in Greek, Butler points out that it can be construed as "anti-generation (*gonê* [generation])"(Butler 2000: 88).[9]

By mobilizing a typical example of how language may exceed translation, Butler in fact links Antigone's name to the dominant gendered tropes for translation, since "generation" refers to offspring, and thus to processes of production and reproduction. But Butler clarifies that in Sophocles' play Antigone is named "anti-generation" because she will have, in fact, no off-spring. She carries a curse, as the offspring of the incestuous union which made Oedipus simultaneously her father and her brother. As the product of incest, Antigone can maintain no stable identity within her family. Butler writes:

> In other words, Antigone is one for whom symbolic positions have become incoherent, confounding as she does brother and father, emerging as she does not as a mother but – as one etymology suggests – "in place of a mother." [...] [I]f the stability of the maternal place cannot be secured, and neither can the stability of the paternal, what happens to

Oedipus and the interdiction for which he stands? What has Oedipus engendered?

(Butler 2000: 22)

Bound to live through this curse, Antigone, in Butler's eyes, is fated not to have a life to live, to be condemned, literally, to a living death.

The practical political context of Butler's reading of *Antigone*, published in 2000, was the struggle for recognition of new, "fragile, porous, and expansive" modalities of kin relationships, including those of same-sex parents and same-sex partners. The legally ambiguous kinship status of partners of those dying of AIDS resonated particularly closely with the story of Antigone. Invoking Antigone's fate of living entombment, Butler makes an argument she has continued to develop in the past several years about a kind of death in life of subjects who have "no place in the terms that confer intelligibility on life."

The verb "translate" appears just once more in Butler's book, but it is again at a crucial point in the argument, where gender, substitutability, and language are brought together. Following, but taking issue with Hegel's argument that Antigone represents the conflict between one kind of law (kinship) and another (the laws of the state), Butler argues rather that Antigone's "claim" when she buries her brother Polyneices situates her "at the very limit of legal conceptualization." Declaring that she can "never have another brother," Antigone defines this act as a *singular* one. It can have only *one* possible instance of application; it cannot be "transposed from context to context." Butler therefore asks if this law that defies conceptualization "stands as an epistemic scandal within the realm of law, a law that cannot be *translated* ... ?" (Butler 2000: 33). The impossibility of translation marks a limit of intelligibility, the intelligibility of the terms that define the human subject.

The question of translatability thus becomes the vehicle for Butler's challenge to the structural inevitability of the Oedipal complex. By emphasizing the doubled and ambiguous nature of Antigone's relations to her kin, she casts Antigone, not in a role of pure opposition to the patriarchal power of the state, but as situated in a sliding and unstable position within the Oedipal family drama. Butler's targets here are Lévi-Strauss and Lacan, and the central place they still hold in contemporary theories of culture and the symbolic. As she points out, for Lévi-Strauss, the incest taboo is neither nature nor culture but the "threshold" that supports the distinction between them. The Oedipal prohibition is not, strictly speaking, universal, for Lévi-Strauss, but has a "universalizing function." But this very move may be symptomatic of a kind of ethnocentrism. As Butler notes, "no exception can call this universalizing into question precisely because it does not rely on empirical instantiation" (Butler 2000: 45).

Butler is equally challenging of Lacan's use of the Oedipus complex to ground the symbolic in the words of the father, making it "structured by a kinship that has assumed the form of a linguistic structure" (Butler 2000: 54). Again turning to questions of translation and translatability, she calls attention to work of feminist anthropologists who have challenged purely functionalist and structuralist accounts of kinship which "privilege symbolic relations at the expense of social action" (Butler 2000: 93). By shifting the status of the Oedipus complex from that which is universalizing to that which is contingent, Butler has sought to dislodge the Lacanian phallus from its role in the constitution of the totality of the symbolic, and to envision different terms of intelligibility for emerging new subjects. Formulated in its most dramatic terms, this critique might be seen as effecting a dislocation in the very deictic structures that orient us in language. For Butler, "the very possibility of a pronomial reference, of an 'I,' a 'you,' a 'we' and 'they' appears to rely on this mode of kinship that operates as language" (Butler 2000: 19).

"Suspending the cathexis: the post-Oedipal subject in 'The Bath'" (original title: "Urokomochi", 1989, tr. Yumi Selden, 2002)

While many valuable analyses have focused on issues of bilingualism, translation, linguistic alterity, defamiliarization, and word play in Tawada Yôko's writing, critics have tended to recuperate these "in-between spaces" explored in her texts as at the boundary of the German and the Japanese. Conventional notions of national language, thus, undergird these descriptions of the aesthetics opened up in her texts. Gender politics are often elided in these commentaries, and Tawada's status as a minority writer in the German context passes without mention. As I have suggested, in the Japanese context, such a separation of Tawada's language experiments from those of, say, resident Korean writers reinforces the idea that minority writers are trapped by narcissism of content and a referential style that narrates their "own" histories.[10] In the German context, those who emphasize linguistic and physical mobility in Tawada's work often do not address contradictory aspects of its reception in Germany. Included among the prizes awarded to Tawada in Germany, for example, is the Chamisso prize for a "foreign writer." And, as Bettina Brandt has pointed out,

> When describing the writings of Yôko Tawada, journalists and critics alike have tended to include in the characterization of these works that they are "somehow surreal," and, in the same breath to flippantly dismiss them. When used in this, rather common ... way, the word "surreal" is emptied of any specific meaning and has become an interchangeable synonym for a whole host of other words: "eccentric," "out-dated," in some way "non-German," "strange," or simply "incomprehensible."
> (Brandt 2004)[11]

I would like to suggest that significant dimensions of Tawada's texts remain unexplored if we do not give greater attention to ways in which they locate themselves within the dynamics of gendered and minority subject formation.

Far from being merely a sign of the eccentric or the foreign, the dream-like "surrealism" of her texts strives to perform a dislocation of the existing "terms of intelligibility" through which we have access to a social "life." The surprising and unsettling features of Tawada's texts are often those which produce in the reader an affect suggestive of the costs of such incorporation (and, indeed, its dislocation), as a violence done to psychic life.

Tawada's short story, "The Bath," for example, is told by a female Japanese narrator living in a place which vaguely resembles a German city. In one scene, she uses the mimeticism involved in foreign language acquisition to playfully resist her (male) German instructor's efforts to interpellate her in the position of the Japanese subject. In the passage cited at the opening of the essay, the narrator explains that, according to this "pedagogical method ... the student repeats everything the teacher says until she's memorized it." The narrator at first carries out these practices enthusiastically, simultaneously falling in love with her instructor. This transference soon ceases to work smoothly, however.

> The second class, however, did not go so easily. My happiness, which consisted of repeating everything I heard, was destroyed all too soon.
>
> When asked, "Are you Japanese?" I would answer, "Yes, you are Japanese." The trick in this game was to change "you" into "I", but I didn't yet realize it.
>
> (Tawada 2002: 28)

A similar refusal of address in the second person occurs elsewhere in the story. When she answers the phone and a caller says, "It's you," the narrator says, "I thought about this for a moment and said, 'It isn't'" (Tawada 2002: 5). Toward the end of the tale, this alienation from pronouns is enacted in a telling scene, when the narrator, on a visit to Japan, tells her mother she will never return to live there.

> "I'm not coming back. Even if I came back, I would be somebody else already."
>
> "Who are you?"
>
> "What are you talking about? It's me."
>
> (Tawada 2002: 45)

The refusal of second person address leads to a further development in the narrator's mode of speech with her partner. On the day of her unsuccessful language lesson, she and her teacher/partner buy a Japanese doll and a "blond violinist marionette" and from this point on ventriloquize their conversations through these puppets, referring to each other as "he" and "she." When the violinist puppet attempts to initiate sex with the Japanese doll, however, it is revealed that "he has no sex organ, just two spindly legs." He refuses the narrator's offer to sew one for him, or have it carved out of wood.

The resonance of these developments with Butler's suggestion of the instability of pronominal references – the "I" and "you" and "we" and "they" – taken to be anchored in kinship is too close to be missed. In fact, one might suggest that Tawada's characters here are trying to "suspend" a certain economy of kinship and language centered on the phallus as a symbol of lack.

Seen in their similarity to Butler's proposals, moreover, the narrator and her partner might be seen as "subjects in translation," as Morinaka Takaaki has defined it in a recent article on "Translation as Dissemination." In language that converges strikingly with Butler's, he states

> What dissemination problematizes ... is the singularity of that kind of signifier of lack, and the *totality* (emphasis mine) of the linguistic system structured with it as its center. ... Therefore dissemination neither presupposes nor posits a symbolic order.
>
> (Morinaka 2006: 48)

But Morinaka notes that to live as a "subject in translation" has a cost. The libido must "de-cathect" from a specific language and live in a "state of suspension." He admits, "this state of indeterminacy is difficult to sustain indefinitely" (Morinaka 2006: 51). To be sure, in a thematization of violence that is often underemphasized in constructions of Tawada's "border-crossing," the narrator of "The Bath" soon has her tongue torn out of her mouth and becomes mute for the duration of the tale. The narrator has been robbed of her tongue by the vengeful spirit of a dead woman and, at the end of the story, she herself is consigned to a phantasmagorial, flying sarcophagus which metamorphoses into a "transparent coffin," consigning her to the status of a living dead.

The surreal texture of Tawada's writing has sometimes been linked to a fascination with the single word and its materiality, which Tawada, as a reader of Benjamin, has explored. In Tawada's work, Christina Kraenzle writes, "language takes on the qualities of space, and it is the experience of linguistic, not physical, mobility that has the most radical effect on subjectivity and embodiment" (Kraenzle 2006). Yet Tawada's surrealism cannot be seen as a matter of spatialization alone. It is precisely the simultaneous unmooring of spatiality and temporality that disorients Tawada's texts, from beginning to end, and makes of them a surreal world. In their dream-like quality, her narratives are not motivated by discrete events – "movement," whether of plot or as change of setting may be triggered by the slightest association or resonance between words and images rather than by naturalistic causes. The sense of a dream-scape, where distortions of time and space fuse, is reminiscent of the visual effect of a Dali canvas. This, too, may be related to the "subject of translation." For, as Morinaka suggests, once language is granted autonomy from the symbolic, it loses its linear order and must be decoded as we interpret dreams.

Here, too, critics' commentary on what appear to be the conspicuous motifs of embodiment in Tawada's writing must be qualified. Calling attention to the corporeality of perception has been seen as an aspect of the literary technique of synaesthesia deployed by Japanese writers like Tanizaki. Yet these processes of decomposition and recombination so striking in Tawada's work seem to work differently from the technique of synaesthesia Thomas Lamarre has perceptively linked to imperialist questions of race in Tanizaki's work. Tanizaki's synaesthesia, in fact, seems staid compared to Tawada's, for it consists largely of defining nouns in terms of sensuous adverbs ("poets seek out beautiful characters, just as a beautiful woman desires to adorn her body with rare gems," is an example Lamarre cites from Tanizaki's "Poetry and Characters") (Lamarre 1999: 23).

While Tanizaki's prose admittedly evokes a combination of corporeal sensations, the relationship between objects and sensations is constructed as causal, and naturalistically linked. If Lamarre helpfully associates this with techniques of Symbolism, the kineticism and "unnatural" fusions of time and space in Tawada's text are definitely closer to surrealist styles. The following describes the scene in which the narrator loses her tongue to the ghost:

> In each of the woman's eyes reflected the flame of a candle. The flames wavered and swam out of her eyes like red tropical fish and began to dance around her ears. ... When the tropical fish glittered, they were reflected in the skin of her face and divided into drops of light. One of the fish slid down her shoulder and began to run about on the table. I screamed soundlessly. But it was only a rat that had stolen the earring and was running away. Dragged along by the rat, the earring got caught in a candlestick and knocked it over.
>
> (Tawada 2002: 24)

Writing as a "subject of translation," I would suggest, Tawada Yôko conveys to the reader affects of disorientation and dislocation that characterize the world of "suspended deixis." Read in this way, her work can become a more powerful critique of globalization and "linguistic imperialism." Her "new" world, that is, is not as effortlessly utopian as some have made it appear, and also requires bravery.

Bibliography

Brandt, B. (March 13, 2004) The Tea Ceremony of Marquis de Sade: Yôko Tawada and the Surreal. *Working Papers Symposium*. University of Kentucky.

Butler, J. (2000) *Antigone's Claim: Kinship Between Life and Death*. New York, Columbia University Press.

Chamberlain, L. (2000) Gender and Metaphorics of Translation. In Venuti, L. (Ed.) *Translation Studies Reader*. New York and London, Routledge.

Chow, R. (1998) *Ethics After Idealism*. Bloomington and Indianapolis, University of Indianapolis Press.

——. (2001) The Secrets of Ethnic Abjection. In Morris, M. and De Bary, B. (Ed.) *'Race' Panic and the Memory of Migration*. Hong Kong, Hong Kong University Press.

——. (November 8, 2002) The Interruption of Referentiality: Poststructuralist Theory and the Conundrum of Critical Multiculturalism. Cornell University.

Damrosch, D. (2003) *What is World Literature?* Princeton: Princeton University Press.

Gougouris, S. (2003) Philosophy's Need for Antigone. *Does Literature Think?* Stanford, Stanford University Press.

Jakobson, R. (1971) On Linguistic Aspects of Translation. In *Selected Writings*. vol. 2. The Hague and Paris, Mouton.

Kraenzle, C. (2006) Traveling Without Moving: Physical and Linguistic Mobility in Yôko Tawada's *Uberseezungen* in 'Translation and Mobility.' *Transit*, 2.

Lamarre, T. (1999) The Deformation of the Modern Spectator: Synaesthesia, Cinema, and the Spectre of Race in Tanizaki. *Japan Forum*, 11.

Molloy, S. (2005) Postcolonial Latin America and the Magical Realist Imperative: A Report to an Academy. In Wood, M. and Berman, S. (Eds.) *Nation, Language, and the Ethics of Translation*. Princeton, Princeton University Press.

Morinaka Takaaki. (2006) Translation as Dissemination: Multilinguality and De-Cathexis. In Sakai, N. and Solomon, J. (Eds.) *Traces 4: Translation, Biopolitics, Colonial Difference*. Hong Kong, Hong Kong University Press.

Sakai, N. (1997) *Translation and Subjectivity: On Japan and Cultural Nationalism*. Minneapolis, University of Minnesota Press.

Sakai, N. and Solomon, J. (Eds.) (2006) *Traces 4: Translation, Biopolitics, Colonial Difference*. Hong Kong, Hong Kong University Press.

Tawada, Y. (2002) The Bath. *Where Europe Begins*. Bernofsky, S. and Selden, Y. (Trans.) New York, New Directions.

Weber, S. (2005) The Touch of Translation. In Berman, S. and Wood, M. (Ed.) *Nation, Language, and the Ethics of Translation*. Princeton, Princeton University Press.

Yildiz, Y. (March 13, 2004) Beyond Organic Belonging: Multilingual Writing and Transnational Imaginaries. *Working Papers Symposium*. University of Kentucky.

Notes

1 Many thanks to Professor Shuling Stéphanie Tsai for organizing productive discussions of translation at the conference, "La Traduction et le sens du MO(N)DE" at Tamkang University, June 16–18, 2006. An earlier version of this paper was published in *Tamkang Studies of Foreign Languages and Literatures*, No. 9, 2007.

2 "The Bath" was first published as *Das Bad*, Peter Pörtner, (Trans.) Tubingen: Konkurshbuch Verlag Claudia Gehrke, 2004. Yumi Selden's translation is based on the original Japanese text, *"Urokomochi (Scales),"* which remains unpublished. My citations are based on the Selden translation from Japanese.

3 The "dominant East-West axis" characterizing Tawada's writings throughout the 1990s is remarked by Yasmin Yildiz (Yildiz 2004).

4 Chow discussed this phenomenon in her appropriately entitled paper (Chow 2002). The phrase "the ideological burden of 'humanity'" occurs in her discussion of "Women in the Holocene" (Chow 1998: 108).

5 Indeed, the growing number of edited collections on translation being published by American university presses is overwhelmingly dominated by essays written in English by American academics, and contains few translations!

6 Lori Chamberlain's article was first published in *Signs* in 1989 and later reprinted in her book in 2000.

7 A more incisive interpretation of Benjamin's "pure language" is offered in Morinaka Takaaki's "Translation as Dissemination" in *Translation, Biopolitics, and Colonial Difference*, p. 49. See also the excellent discussion in Samuel Weber's "The Touch of Translation" in Sandra Berman and Michael Wood, ed., *Nation, Language, and the Ethics of Translation* (Princeton: Princeton University Press, 2005).

8 On the history of these commentaries, see Statis Gougouris' essay (Gougouris 2003).

9 Butler cites Gougouris here.

10 On the perceived narcissism of the ethnic writers see Rey Chow's essay (Chow 2002).

11 In op. cit., "Tawada Yôko: Voices from Everywhere," *Working Papers Symposium*, University of Kentucky, March 13, 2004.

3 Politics as translation
Naoki Sakai and the critique of hermeneutics

John Namjun Kim

The exterior

The discourse on translation is haunted by hermeneutics. Positing the possibility of understanding linguistic statements as their end, hermeneutic approaches to language represent the practice of translation as an exemplary instance of the communicative transfer of "meaning" between two imagined consciousnesses: a "self" and an "other." Each with its own "horizon of understanding" is imagined to approach the other in a dialog and come to understanding through an ongoing "fusion of horizons."[1] The difference in languages in the scene of translation is imagined to illustrate this process of the "self" confronting not only the "meaning" of the "other" but also the "otherness" of the "other." What haunts theoretical approaches to translation is this representation of translation as an encounter between the language of the "self" and the language of the "other," as if languages were systematic unities subject to such representation. Indeed, it is as though the self/other opposition, without which philosophical hermeneutics would cease, were so self-evidently "applicable" to the scene of translation that even those who refute hermeneutics might accept this opposition as empirically given.

However, the commonsensicality of this representation of translation should suffice to provoke one's doubt. Naoki Sakai argues that the actual practice of translation is radically heterogeneous to its representation as an encounter between two linguistic unities imagined as "self" and "other" (Sakai 1997: 54). The practice of translation is heterogeneous to its representation to the extent that languages too are heterogeneous to their representation as systematic unities. Both translation and language manifest themselves as temporal events incommensurate to the spatiality of representation. Nevertheless, the self/other opposition persists as a governing paradigm in theoretical discussions on translation. If this persistence is not simply the result of a simple theoretical "mistake," as it very well may be, then might it have another function in these discussions? What does it license in these arguments? To what does its recurrence testify about translation? The short answer, which will require further complication, is the imagination and politics of the cultural "exterior" upon which hermeneutic approaches to translation depend in denial.

In his *Sur la traduction* (On Translation), Paul Ricœur argues that "[t]wo partners are in effect placed in a relation by the act of translation, the stranger – a term covering the work, the author, his language – and the reader of the translated work. And, between the two, the translator who transmits, passes on the entire message from one idiom into the other. The ordeal [*épreuve*] in question resides in this uncomfortable situation of the mediator" (Ricœur 2004:8–9). Ricœur's tripartite representation of the scene of translation appears straightforward enough: there is a "self" trying to understand an "other" with the assistance of a third party, the translator, who is presumably the sole party to share the languages of the other two. This tripartite relation would appear to complicate the hermeneutics of the self/other opposition, but it does not. For, since the "reader" (self) is unable to understand the language of the "stranger" (other), the opposition shifts to the axis between the translator (self) and the language of the "stranger," which for the translator is not entirely "other." Yet, even this opposition will be reduced, though unwittingly, leaving only one figure standing: the translator.

Though Ricœur embraces translation for its potential to "deprovincialize the mother language" (17), he maintains the self/other opposition by recasting it in the "ethical" terms of "linguistic hospitality." The translator, for him, establishes an ethical relation to the other in which " ... the pleasure of inhabiting the language of the other is compensated by the pleasure of receiving the speech [*parole*] of the stranger in one's home, in one's *own* [*propre*] abode of welcome" (20; my emphasis). However, the ethical language of hospitality masks the fundamental non-ethical structure of Ricœur's notion of translation: the translator and the stranger remain atomistically self and other, even as each is said to be "welcomed" to dwell in the other's language in a relation of the "guest" and "host." This putatively "ethical" representation of translation as a reciprocal exchange of "pleasure" harbors the self's unilateral vision upon the other, its exterior limit.

If translation promises a certain "pleasure" derived from engaging with the "other" in Ricœur's work, it promises a recursion to the self's putative "traditions" in Hans-Georg Gadamer's. For Gadamer, the self/other relation is not just taken as given but as *handed down* by "tradition."[2] Unlike Ricœur, Gadamer considers translation only to the extent that it reconfirms his views on interpretation and the historical character of understanding. In *Wahrheit und Methode* (Truth and Method), Gadamer points to translation as an "extreme case" of communicative activity, in which "understanding [*Verständigung*]" takes place, not among the "partners of a conversation, but between the simultaneous interpreters," on the one hand, and between the translator (or interpreter) and the text he or she translates, on the other (Gadamer 1975: 362–63). More explicitly than Ricœur, Gadamer centers the self/other opposition around the imagination of one consciousness communing with another around the "meaning" of an agreed upon common object. Yet, in spite of the frequency with which he insists upon the "commonness" between consciousnesses, Gadamer's use of the self/other opposition is predicated on the imagination of linguistic distance in which languages appear as given and mutually exclusive unities.

Though he cites translation as an example in which interpretation closes the metaphorical "gap" in understanding, he paradoxically uses it to stress the role of cultural traditions in the process of interpretation (Gadamer 1975: 367–73). His consciousness-centered notion of the "horizon of under-standing," which first appears in his argument as a description of how one consciousness enters a conversation with a set of assumptions, necessitates an explanation of how this "horizon" is formed, and this in turn necessitates the imagination of a tradition in whose conceptual terms consciousness is caught in the present (Gadamer 1975: 275). Thus, the self/other opposition, which begins as an opposition between human consciousnesses or languages as dis-crete unities, extends to the circumscription of cultural traditions as if they too were bounded unities. In other words, Gadamer uses the concept of translation to inscribe an image of the cultural interior by introducing the image of the exterior from the perspective of the "self," namely, its "horizon" toward the "other."

However, the imagination of the self/other opposition is not restricted to hermeneutics. Gayatri Chakravorty Spivak's work on translation is emphati-cally non-hermeneutic yet, nevertheless, draws upon it in modified form. Whereas hermeneutic approaches to translation use this opposition to situate the "self," Spivak's work on translation uses the figure of the "other" as a liminal moment that discloses social power relations in language. In her "Politics of Translation," Spivak argues for a mode of translation that attends to the rhetoricity of the languages from and into which one translates. Arguing through a three-part model of translation distinguishing rhetoric, logic and silence (Spivak 1993: 181), she draws an analogical relationship between logic/rhetoric and social logic/social practice (Spivak 1993: 187). A translator's attentiveness to the rhetoricity of the languages involved in a translation amounts to the attentiveness to the unpredictability of social practice. How one translates, implies how one works with one's "other." The task of translation is, in other words, the task of working with the contingency of the "other" and all of its figurations. Arguing for an intimate grasp of the language from which one translates, Spivak conceives of translation as a task with real political implications, in particular, for languages that are dying out (Spivak 2005: 95).

This task, Spivak emphasizes, is a particularly fraught challenge for the "Third World" feminist translating into the hegemonic language of English (Spivak 1993: 182). That is to say, the self/other opposition in her politics of translation is an opposition that she does not take as given but as *imposed* by post-colonial logic and global capital. She works within its terms but does so in order to disrupt the socio-political legacy left by a particular configuration of this opposition. This politics of translation as a politics of disruption retains the figure of the "other" in order to make real disparities of social power clear. It takes the politically given – the global social hegemony of the

Euro-American Anglophone – as its point of methodological departure and object of critique. Indeed, to the extent that a remnant of the self/other opposition remains in her work, it remains as a "trace." She argues, "The impossibility of translation is what puts its necessity in a double bind. It is an active site of conflict, not an irreducible guarantee. If we are thinking defini-tions, I should suggest the thinking of trace rather than that of achieved translation: the trace of the other, trace of history, even cultural traces ... " (Spivak 2005: 105). The trace is, in other words, that which marks but does not signify, and therefore is not subject to semantic economization. Unlike the hermeneuts, Spivak conceives of translation not as a practice situating a "self" within a given community, but a striation the "self," the metropole, with the trace of the "other," the exterior called the global South (Spivak 2005: 95).

Though the imagination of the exterior in no way shares the same political function in the works of Ricœur, Gadamer and Spivak, it nevertheless persists in their distinct views on translation and enables the political significance that translation accrues in each. Translation is thought to be necessitated by the fact of this exterior, that is, by the "fact" of something not understood. What Ricœur, Gadamer and Spivak share in their views on translation, *pace* of their vast differences, is a phenomenological perspectivalism in which a subject's non-understanding is viewed as the precondition for translation.

Yet, might not this relation between non-understanding and translation in fact be reversed? That is to say, might it not be the case, as Sakai argues, that translation is the precondition for knowing that one does not know? If so, the imagination of the exterior – and the self/other opposition – would prove to be, not the precondition for translation, but its effect. But, if this is the case, would it not suggest that one could reformulate Spivak's term "the politics *of* translation" as "politics *as* translation," that is, take "politics" and "transla-tion" out of a genitive relation and into a relation of equivalence? It is this question that organizes my reading of Sakai's non-hermeneutic approach to translation. The equivalence of politics and translation is nowhere explicitly made in his work. Yet, the two are always thought of together, as his work returns repeatedly to the problem of how social discontinuities are ren-dered continuous by the creation and exclusion of social excess, the image of the exterior. In rereading his work in terms of politics *as* translation, my aim is to show that neither politics nor translation is predicated on the image of the exterior and, in so doing, make way for thinking the social without a concept of the "enemy" or the "camp" in which to confine thought.[3] It is rather the case that politics and translation produce the image of the exterior.

The scene of address

The point of departure for Naoki Sakai's work on translation is not transla-tion itself, but the scene of address as the site of social practice. This unlikely methodological point of departure is explained by the epistemological obser-vation that addressing precedes translation. Prior to the scene of the address, it is impossible to know if translation is called for. But deciding on whether a translation is called for, even if the address is made in a language "common" to both the addresser and the addressee, is itself part of the practice of translation. In other words, the address precedes translation but its articulation is contingent upon translation. How does this differ from the hermeneutic approach to translation grounded on the self/other opposition?

Unlike the self/other opposition, upon which hermeneutics relies, the addresser/addressee relation is strictly temporal and impersonal, emerging only at the scene of address. Prior to the scene of address, neither addresser nor addressee can be said to "exist," for these terms are indices of a *relation*, not of given positions. And because the scene of address is strictly temporal, the address cannot be confused with the hermeneutics of "communication," which presupposes a spatial separation, or "gap," between two "consciousnesses." In *Translation and Subjectivity*, Sakai writes,

> The two verbal designations "to address" and "to communicate" can be distinguished from one another precisely because the former precludes the description of what it accomplishes, as a performative, whereas the latter anticipates its accomplishment, just as "aiming" and "striking" can be distinguished in the contrasting phrases "aiming at a target" and "striking a target." In order to "strike a target" one first has to "aim at it." Unless one aims first, one cannot even "fail to strike it." In this sense, just as "aiming" is prior to "striking," so "addressing" is anterior to "communicating." And "addressing" is distinguished from "communicating" because an addressing does not guarantee the message's arrival at the destination.
> (Sakai 1997: 4)

An address "precludes the description of what it accomplishes" in the sense that, unlike communication, an address does not presuppose it will arrive at its addressee or even that its addressee will recognize itself as the addressee. In this sense, the address "aims" without the promise of "striking." It is the address that articulates the relation in which the positionalities called the "addresser" and "addressee" emerge, whereas "communication" presupposes the givenness of the "self" and an "other."

In other words, the notion of the address complements Louis Althusser's concept of interpellation, the process by which an addressee undergoes subjectivization in being ideologically "hailed" (Althusser 2001: 174–75). As a complement to interpellation, the address is constitutive of the imagination of social collectivities, such as one's imaginary belonging to a "nation" or "racial" group. One's belonging is "imaginary" not in the sense that it does not exist or is merely a "psychological state," rather in the sense that the reality of one's belonging is the reality of an image. An image is itself real as an image, but its representational content conceals its reality as an image. The address "my fellow Americans," for instance, is real in that it consists of three words, or 17 letters and two spaces. Yet, its representational content – a first

personal appropriative address to a very real multiethnic imperialist col-
lectivity bound together not by a state, military or economy but ultimately by
the semiotic circulation of their aesthetic emblems – elides the address's
material reality as a text.

If the relationship between the addressee and the address is that of possible
interpellation, what is the relation between the addresser and the address?
Were the address to be confused with communication, the relation could be
described simply as the relation between a speaker and an expression of his or
her "intention." By contrast, such reduction to intention is impossible when
this relationship is posed in terms of the address. The address gives birth to
the addresser, rather than the addresser to its address. Just as the address does
not guarantee that it will arrive at its destination, it also does not secure
the identity of the addresser. It, in fact, introduces a radical separation
between what is said and who said it, as shown in Sakai's analysis of the first
personal utterance "I," the word thought to assure seamless self-reference.

Drawing upon but critiquing Emile Benveniste's work on first personal
utterances, Sakai agrees with Benveniste that "I" refers to the "reality of discourse," rather than to its speaker, as well as with his insistence that the "I" is
temporal. But, Sakai critiques Benveniste on the extent to which the "I" is
empty as well as the structure of its temporality. Sakai detects an inconsistency where Benveniste claims,

> There is no concept "I" that incorporates all the *I*'s that are uttered at
> every moment in the mouths of all speakers, in the sense that there is a
> concept "tree" to which all the individual uses of *tree* refer. The "*I*," then,
> does not denominate any lexical entity. Could it then be said that *I* refers
> to a particular individual? If that were the case, a permanent contra-
> diction would be admitted into language and anarchy into its use. How
> could the same term refer indifferently to any individual whatsoever and
> still at the same time identify him in his individuality? We are in the
> presence of a class of words, the "personal pronouns," that escape the
> status of all the other signs of language. Then, what does *I* refer to? To
> something very peculiar which is exclusively linguistic: *I* refers to the act
> of individual discourse in which it is pronounced, and by this it desig-
> nates the speaker. It is a term that cannot be identified except in what we
> have called elsewhere an instance of discourse and that has only a
> momentary reference. The reality to which it refers is the reality of the
> discourse. It is in the instance of discourse in which *I* designates the
> speaker that the speaker proclaims himself as the "subject."
>
> (Benveniste 1971: 226).

For Benveniste, the "I" as a pronoun is neither universal nor particular with
respect to its "referent." Unlike a noun, the "I" is not a concept and, hence,
not a universal. Though it can be universally appropriated – anyone can say it
with or without the "intention" of self-reference – it remains conceptually

empty and anonymous by necessity. It also does not refer to its particular speaker, such as a proper name, for if it did a particular "permanent contradiction would be admitted" in that each speaker would appropriate the name of the other and, as Benveniste imagines, "anarchy" would break out. It functions, instead, as a shifter, a deictic marker that "shifts" in relation to an address. Hence, Benveniste concludes, "*I* refers to the act of individual discourse in which it is pronounced, and by this it designates the speaker." "I" refers not to its speaker but to the instance of discourse, or address, in which it appears. And insofar as its reference is specific to the instance of discourse in which it appears, it is strictly temporal.

Sakai's critique turns on a conceptual slippage in Benveniste's formulation on the referentiality of the "I." Though Benveniste concludes that the "I" refers to the reality of discourse in which it is spoken, he undermines this conclusion by also claiming that this referential relation allows the "I" to "designate the speaker" within an utterance. The distinction between "to refer" and "to designate" is left unexplained, and a trace of the empirical speaker is left behind in the "I." Sakai critiques Benveniste for this remnant of personhood in the "I." Whereas Benveniste elsewhere excludes the third person from personhood insofar as it stands outside of the field of address – i.e. the third person is spoken about but is neither the addresser nor addressee – he reserves personhood to the first and second persons. However, Sakai points out that what is said in language cannot be confused with who said it, especially in the case of self-reference (Sakai 1991: 67). As Sakai observes, all pronominal positions must be impersonal in order for language to signify. Persons exist, but not in language.

In other words, the "I" uttered in discourse indeed refers to the reality of a discourse as discourse but remains radically heterogeneous to its speaker. The speaker who marks him or herself in an address with an "I" is nowhere in the "I", and is not even designated by the "I." However, if this were so, one might ask, how could Sakai's view of the address and translation ever engage in any politics whatsoever? If I cannot say "I" and mean "me," would that not end the possibility of "my" political engagement?

Sakai's seemingly counterintuitive critique of Benveniste could be taken as a part of his larger anti-humanist project to disclose the inhuman, or non-human, elements of language and the politics left concealed by an eighteenth-century humanist aestheticism that continue today in placing "Man" at the center of language and politics (Sakai and Solomon 2004: 1–35).[4] However, his critique of Benveniste is not based upon this aspect of his work – his critique of humanism is rather based on his reflections on language. Instead, his critique of Benveniste is based on a philosophical observation drawn from a distinction between the "subject of enunciation" and the "subject of the enunciated;" that is, the subject posited as the source of the enunciation, or "speaker," and the subject posited within the enunciated, the "I." It is this distinction that allows Sakai to raise his second critique of Benveniste's view of the "I," namely, regarding its temporal structure. His critique of its temporal structure in turn discloses the politics with which Sakai is most concerned in his work on translation, the political agency of the letter once released from "personal" intention and the linguistic deconstruction of nationalism.

Whereas Benveniste insists that the "presence of the speaker to his enunciation makes it necessary for *each instance of discourse to constitute a center of internal reference*" and that this situation requires "specific forms whose function is *to put the speaker in a constant and necessary relation with his enunciation*" (Benveniste 1974: 82; emphasis in the original), Sakai argues that such self-centering forms are by necessity irrelevant to the signification of the enunciated. In *Voices of the Past*, Sakai argues,

> Any utterance must be produced at a certain place, a certain time, but an utterance, once produced, gains a relative autonomy and becomes independent of its origin. Regardless of whether one knows who first enunciated or not, one can understand what the utterance signifies. Insofar as what it says is at issue, one does not need to know and is never able to tell who spoke it or where and when it was uttered. The same utterance can be repeated "in principle" by anybody anywhere. And if it cannot be repeated, then it will not be the same utterance. What constitutes the identity of an utterance is what it says, the enunciated (énoncé). ... Yet, that any person can say it without identifying her- or himself with "I" is the necessary condition for such an utterance to be communicable. The anonymity of the enunciated is, I must repeat, the very possibility of utterance. A particular "I" transforms itself into an anonymous "I" in the enunciated, and an ideal or imaginary state in which *a subject of a speech act must be coincidental with the subject of an enunciation* is called the enunciation. Supposedly the enunciated is a product of the enunciation. It should be emphasized, however, that it is impossible to recover from an enunciated the originary enunciation, in which the subject, situation, and intention are all integrated into a single occurrence of speech.
>
> (Sakai 1991: 67; emphasis in the original)

Two seemingly non-political linguistic issues are at work here dealing with the temporality of the "I," yet both have political implications. The first is repetition. The repeatability of an enunciated is the precondition for its signification. Anyone must be able to say the same utterance for it to signify. If the subject of the enunciation and the subject of the enunciated are not rigorously differentiated – a situation that would leave the subject of the enunciated essentially tied to a particular individual – it would be impossible to repeat the utterance with the same signification or with any signification whatsoever. An utterance would apply to only one subject and be unrepeatable by anyone else. But if it is unrepeatable by anyone else, it would be in a language so private to the subject of enunciation that it would cease to be an instance of language. Language presupposes alterity, an addressee, who in principle is as anonymous as the addresser and who can also in principle repeat whatever has been said.

The second issue dealing with temporality in Sakai's critique of Benveniste is the rupture between the subject of the enunciation and the subject of the enunciated. Insofar as the two are not identical and must be kept distinct for signification to occur, the subject of enunciation can appear in language only in the form of what it is not, the subject of the enunciated. Indeed, to the extent that the subject of the enunciation can be represented at all, it is only as a "subject that is to be represented," as the subject of the enunciated (Sakai 1991:70). Illustrating this rupture, Sakai turns to a problem that emerges in Immanuel Kant's analysis of the transcendental subject in the *Critique of Pure Reason* (Sakai 1991: 329–33): the subject uttering "I think" is posited but found nowhere within the field of representation, in this case between the enframing quotation marks (cf., Kant 1911 AK 3:B429–30). If it were represented, another enframing "I think" would have to accompany the representation of the initial "I think," or "I think, 'I think'," and another transcendental subject would be posited outside of the utterance as its subject of enunciation. This foreclosure to representation, however, does not mean that the subject of enunciation is radically alienated to its own speech. Rather, it means that the subject of the enunciated is the condition of possibility for the emergence of the subject of the enunciation. Hence, Sakai concludes, the "subject is possible only with this separation" (Sakai 1991: 71). The subject of enunciation marks only a theoretical possibility that attains the contours of lived reality as a subject of the enunciated, as a representation. One might then conclude that the subject of the enunciation emerges only with its subjectivization, or subjection to the protocols of social intelligibility, and that it is foreclosed from the outset from social or political practice. However, Sakai argues that just as one must maintain a rigorous distinction between the subject of the enunciation and the subject of the enunciated, one must also distinguish two temporalities where Benveniste recognizes only one:

> In utterance, one lives two different temporalities that never meet: the time in which what one means to say is presented, and the time of the actual speech in which saying is actually executed. By virtue of the fact that somebody must enunciate it for an event to be registered as such, an event insofar as it is identified and memorized in the text is inevitably also a discursive event, an image retained in and by discourse. An event that is described in a statement precedes and succeeds other events in actuality, so that it should be justifiable to say that the event took, takes, or will take place in time. Yet the statement can be repeatedly uttered. What puzzles us here is that an enunciation in which an event is described is also an event. The event described in many different enunciations can be the same, whereas none of these enunciations can be the same.

> Therefore, I must conclude that the "present" of the enunciation and the "now" of the enunciated cannot coincide with each other and that the antinomy that exists between the two terms, as a matter of fact, makes up the very possibility of verbalization and of linguistic expression in general.
>
> (Sakai 1991: 68–69)

The temporality of the enunciation cannot be confused with the temporality of the enunciated, just as the temporality of writing or reading cannot be confused with the temporality represented in a novel. As an event, an enunciation cannot be repeated and be the same enunciation, for enunciation is fundamentally a performance. It is always singular. But, the events described within the enunciation must be able to maintain their identity over repetition in order for it to be an instance of language. This is to say, because Benveniste confuses the temporality articulating the sound "I" with the temporality within the utterance, in which the "I" can be situated in any number of times, he also undermines the distinction between the subject of the enunciation and the subject of the enunciated. He undermines the distinction that, he maintains, keeps "permanent contradiction and anarchy" from arising if all were to appropriate the "I" for their particular selves. Indeed, were it not for this difference in temporalities, utterances such as "I am a cat" could only count as nonsense or a lie, but never as the first line of a novel by Natsume Sôseki. By the same token, political speech about what "I will do" or what "we could have done" would also be foreclosed from the outset. Contrary to the conclusion, then, that the separation of the subject of enunciation from the subject of the enunciated forecloses political engagement, it makes such engagement possible in language. But, how an utterance will function politically cannot be anticipated in advance.

The scene of translation

Just as the subject of enunciation remains other to its representation as the subject of the enunciated, the practice of translation remains other to its representation. And how it is represented is fraught with the political imagination of the location of cultures and those imagined to constitute them. The representation of translation that Sakai critiques is by Roman Jakobson, who distinguishes three forms of translation: "1) Intralingual translation or *rewording* is an interpretation of verbal signs by means of other signs of the same language. 2) Interlingual translation or *translation proper* is an interpretation of verbal signs by means of some other language. 3) Intersemiotic translation or *transmutation* is an interpretation of verbal signs by means of signs of nonverbal sign systems" (Jakobson 1971: 261; emphasis in the original). Though all three representations of translation come under question in Sakai's work on translation, the representation which he principally critiques is the second, "Interlingual translation or translation proper." Calling into question the propriety claim in the formulation "translation proper," Sakai argues that " ... viewed from the position of the translator, neither the unitary unity of a language nor the plurality of language unities can be taken for granted" (Sakai 1997: 10). The problem, in other words, with Jakobson's view of translation is the assumption it makes about language. Sakai calls the assumption that leads to this representation the "regime of translation," or an ideology by which translators "imagine their relationship to what they do in translation as the symmetrical exchange between two languages" (Sakai 1997: 51). However, as Sakai argues, languages are not systematic unities with discernible boundaries. They are subject neither to boundedness nor even to systematization, though the representation of languages presented in dictionaries and grammar textbooks portray them as though they were. Once again, as in the self/other opposition, a spatial metaphor governs the representation of languages as bounded unities. By contrast, the actual practice of enunciation in language, such as in translation, is fundamentally temporal or, more precisely, temporalizing. Language "happens" and cannot be circumscribed.

Sakai's claim should not be taken as resting on an empirical observation that some languages, such as Indo-European languages, are related and have some vocabulary in common making the rigorous distinction between languages difficult or impossible. It should also not be taken as a denial of the existence of grammar in languages. Rather, it should be taken as an epistemological observation: Just as the linguistic performance of an address distributes the relation of the addresser and the addressee, translation distributes the relation of the languages involved in the translation and creates the image of their systematic unity, or grammar. Prior to the moment of translation, as Sakai argues, the representation of the difference between languages cannot emerge. Even the figure of the untranslatable, which is often used to espouse the particularity of a language and the cultural "tradition" it is imagined to inform, emerges only with the practice of translation:

> What makes it possible to represent the initial difference as an already determined difference between one language unity and another is the work of translation itself. This is why we always have to remind ourselves that the untranslatable, or what can never be appropriated by the economy of translational communication, cannot exist prior to the enunciation of translation. It is translation that gives birth to the untranslatable. Thus, the untranslatable is as much a testimony to the sociality of the translator, whose figure exposes the presence of a non-aggregate community between the addresser and the addressee, as to the translatable itself.
> (Sakai 1997: 14)

Both the translatable and the untranslatable emerge as knowable only after translation in the sense that, prior to translation, it is impossible to know what can and cannot be translated. Moreover, in the case in which a language is completely unfamiliar to a translator, the translator cannot tell if what appears as an instance of language is indeed an instance of language rather than nonsense made to sound and look as if it were language.

Complementing the notion of the regime of translation, Sakai offers a second term to describe how the regime of translation structures the epistemological desire of those caught within it. What Sakai calls the "schema of cofiguration" functions as a "discursive apparatus that makes it possible to represent translation" (Sakai 1997: 15). Whereas the regime of translation is the imaginary rule that the translator follows in the process of translating from an "other" language, the schema of cofiguration is a rule by which a "self" is posited as standing in symmetry with this "other" language. This applies not only to the case of a linguistic "self," e.g. one's self-conception as a speaker of a particular language, but also to the image of one's membership in a "cultural community". Sakai argues,

> As the practice of translation remains radically heterogeneous to the representation of translation, translation need not be represented as a communication between two clearly delineated linguistic communities. There should be many different ways to apprehend translation in which the subjectivity of a community does not necessarily constitute itself in terms of language unity or the homogeneous sphere of ethnic or national culture. The particular representation of translation in which translation is understood to be communication between two particular languages is, no doubt, a historical construct. And it is this particular representation of translation that gave rise to the possibility of figuring out the unity of ethnic or national language together with another language unity. Indeed, this is one of the reasons for which I have claimed that the Japanese language was born, or stillborn, in the eighteenth century among a very small portion of literary people, when the schema of cofiguration came into being. This is to say that the schema of cofiguration is a means by which a national community represents itself to itself, thereby constituting itself as a subject. But it seemed to me that this autoconstitution of the national subject would not proceed unitarily; on the contrary, it would constitute itself only by making visible the figure of an other with which it engages in a translational relationship.
>
> (Sakai 1997: 15–16)

The "schema of cofiguration" designates a rule of self-location in symmetrical order, such that if an "other" were posited as a systematic unity, so too would a "self" in one-to-one correspondence. Sakai's claim that the Japanese language was "still born" is thus an epistemological, and not historical, claim. It was "still born" in the sense that it became an epistemological object of cultural reflection the moment when translation became a question for intellectuals in eighteenth century "Japan." Prior to this moment of confronting a language incommensurable to their own, the inhabitants of the Japanese archipelago spoke and wrote, but the self-representation of this speaking and writing was neither unified nor legible as a unity by any name, least of all "Japanese." The schema of cofiguration enables the positing of not just a self, but a collective "self" regardless of the actual heterogeneity of the signifying practices, or "languages," that can be found within any circumscribed territory. The schema of cofiguration is explicitly political in the case of Japan in particular, in that the representation of the Japanese language as a systematic unity was metaleptically used to posit the existence of a Japanese "ethnos" distinct from others. If the regime of translation names the ideology of how to translate the image of the "other," the schema of cofiguration names the mechanism by which the "self" comes to appear to "itself."

Politics as translation

Unlike Ricœur, Gadamer and Spivak, Sakai's reflections on the task of translation do not begin with the premise that there are different languages. Instead, it begins with the premise that there must first be translation in order to recognize a discontinuity among languages. The labor of translation is the *a priori* condition for the epistemological representation of the difference between languages.

But, what is the practice of translation prior to its representation? If translation is not the transfer of "meaning" across two languages imagined as systematic unities but the condition of possibility for this imagination, then what is it that happens in translation? Hermeneutic approaches to translation view translation as a process of consciousness that, in essence, does not distinguish itself from any other situation of interpretation according to one's "horizon of understanding." Yet, this image of translation remains centered on a view of the constitution of the "human" that simply cannot be known. By contrast, Sakai's analysis of translation does not make any reference to subjective intention, reflection or will, and instead reads the translator's labor from the perspective of its doing:

> Through the labor of the translator, the incommensurability as difference that calls for the service of the translator in the first place is negotiated and worked on. In other words, the work of translation is a practice by which the initial discontinuity between the addresser and the addressee is made continuous and recognizable. In this respect, translation is just like other social practices that render the points of discontinuity in social formation continuous. Only retrospectively and after translation, therefore, can we recognize the initial incommensurability as a gap, crevice, or border. But when represented as a gap, it is no longer incommensurate.
>
> (Sakai 1997: 14)

Though Sakai borrows from the language of subjective metaphysics, his argument should be taken as strictly epistemological and ethical yet without reference to the "subject." Namely, the activity of the translator is to render the "discontinuity" between addresser and addressee "continuous." Describing translation in these terms is distinct from describing it as a communicative transfer of meaning between "self" and "other," for whereas the self/other opposition is imagined as spatially given, the addresser/addressee relation is temporally constituted at the moment of the address. Moreover, what the translator works upon is not a predetermined "gap" between languages, but an "incommensurability" that becomes recognizable as an incommensurability "retrospectively after translation" in the sense that translation articulates the specific differences of the incommensurable and, in so doing, also renders differences commensurable, hence, representable. Therefore, he also claims if such differences are represented as a "gap," they are no longer incommensurate, because the image of a "gap" between languages provides a frame for rendering an unintelligibility intelligible. The difference between languages is now a known difference, and the image of the gap makes this difference repeatable as an utterance.

Sakai calls translation an instance of "continuity in discontinuity" in the social (Sakai 1997: 13), drawing upon Nishida Kitarô in his analysis of the subjective formation of spatio-temporal reality (Nishida 1966 8:7–106). It makes the discontinuous continuous in the sense that it draws a relation between social beings where previously there was none. Here, the ethical dimensions of Sakai's analysis come to the fore when considering the stance of the translator in the scene of address. The translator is neither the addresser nor the addressee, neither the first nor second person. She, in the strict scene of translation, cannot say "I" and "mean" herself as the subject of enunciation. The "I" that she translates must refer to the addresser as he or she addresses the addressee. The translator thus occupies a position akin to the rupture between the subject of the enunciation and the subject of the enunciated when writing the word "I." The translator stands at a distance to the "I" that she translates not as the subject of enunciation but as a point of discontinuity, who is not even a third person in the scene of address. Sakai argues,

> In respect to personal relationality as well as to the addresser/addressee structure, the translator must be internally split and multiple, and devoid of a stable positionality. At best, she can be a *subject in transit*, first because the translator cannot be an "individual" in the sense of *individuum* in order to perform translation, and second because she is a singular that marks an elusive point of discontinuity in the social, whereas translation is the practice of creating continuity at that singular point of discontinuity, and a poietic social practice that institutes a relation at the site of incommensurability. This is why the aspect of discontinuity inherent in translation would be completely repressed if we were to determine translation to be a form of communication.
>
> (Sakai 1997: 13; emphasis in the original)

In an everyday sense, the translator stands in an "ethical" relation insofar as she negotiates the terms of the addresser into those continuous, or intelligible, to the addressee. However, she is "ethical" in another sense. Insofar as she occupies a social position in the scene of the address that is not the first, second or third person and her enunciation is not "her own," her presence at the scene of translation discloses the discontinuity of any enunciation and any enunciative position. Her invisibility at the scene of the address is belied by her physical presence at the scene of translation. She cannot be held responsible for what is said in the address but only for her translation. Thus, she occupies an ethically precarious position of being socially discontinuous to the scene of address but socially continuous with the scene of translation. Her enunciative activity oscillates her between both. That is, her presence reminds us that the social is constituted by practices of articulation that produce such oscillating enunciative positions forcing those who occupy them to speak, as it were, with a "forked-tongue." Her situation is essentially that of an ethnic minority.

It is here then that politics can begin to be thought of as translation. The political is the site at which discontinuity in the social is rendered continuous, but only with respect to those standing within the scene of the address. Those who must translate the address by performing the labor for its enunciation remain continuous, or accountable, only to the labor they perform. This oscillation of the enunciative position of the translator takes its most politically concrete form in Sakai's critique of area studies and the West.

Sakai's critique of area studies cannot be separated from his critique of the West, for the creation of the idea of "areas" external to the "West" is the condition upon which the latter comes to represent itself to itself through the former as its mirror (Sakai 2001:74–91). That is to say, the institutional apparatus through which "other" cultures, languages and societies are studied is itself not an apolitical apparatus for the "objective" production of knowledge about a given "area." Rather, it is the apparatus that makes the "area," the object of knowledge against which the "West" can appear to itself as the subject of knowledge whose objective reality is taken as given. Needless to say, the "area" that comes under the purview of a specific area studies program and the enunciative position called the "West" are not given realities, but discursive formations organized around the logic of the universal and the particular. In other words, the relation between an area and the West is not one of predetermined difference. Rather, it is a relation that determines the difference between the two.

> It is a name for a subject that gathers itself in discourse but is also an object constituted discursively; it is, evidently, a name always associating itself with those regions, communities, and peoples that appear politically or economically superior to other regions, communities, and peoples. Basically, it is just like the name "Japan," which reputedly designates a geographic area, a tradition, a national identity, a culture, an ethnos,

a market, and so on, yet, unlike all the other names associated with geographic particularities, it [the West] also implies the refusal of its self-delimitation; it claims that it is capable of sustaining, if not actually transcending, an impulse to transcend all the particularizations.

(Sakai 1997:154)

Sakai's claim is not that Japan is part of the West or that Japan is the same as the West as discursive formations. Rather, his claim is they are the "same" with respect to their position relative to the particulars they subsume: Just as the "West" posits itself as a universal with respect to many particulars subsumed under this name, so too does "Japan." A universal is "universal" only in respect to the particulars it subsumes, which is to say that a "universal" is always subject to particularization to another universal subsuming it as a particular. The universal and the particular reinforce one another.

However, what distinguishes the concept of the West is the kind of universality it claims, absolute universality, or universality without delimitation. It is a discursive formation that refuses particularization as an "area." What makes area studies political is that it is grounded in a cultural power relation constituted by the knowledge it produces about other "areas":

... the West is never content with what it is recognized as by others; it is always urged to approach others in order to ceaselessly transform its self-image; it continually seeks itself in the midst of interaction with the Other; it would never be satisfied with being recognized, but would wish to recognize others; it would rather be a supplier of recognition than a receiver thereof. In short, the West must represent the moment of the universal under which particulars are subsumed. Indeed, the West is particular in itself, but it also constitutes the universal point of reference in relation to which others recognize themselves as particularities. In this regard, the West thinks itself to be ubiquitous.

(Sakai 1997:154–55)

The Hegelian economy of recognition in which subjects emerge through the reciprocal exchange of recognition is in the West's relation to its others, which are left unrecognized by the West. In Hegelian terms, the universality claimed by the West is the kind of universality claimed by the "master" in the dialectic of self-consciousness, a failed position for Hegel. However, the force of Sakai's critique is not, ultimately, Hegelian. Rather, the force of his critique lies in an asymmetrical relation in the flow of knowledge production that is installed in the humanities between the West and its others. Institutionally, the humanities have made a fundamental distinction in the image of "Man" according to which it organizes the knowledge produced about this image. A basic distinction is made between two images of "Man" and the kind of knowledge production organized around each: *anthropos* and *humanitas* (Nishitani 2006). The first pertains to the extraction of general principles from the various ways this image manifests itself through case studies; the second pertains to the self-reflective production of knowledge about "man" setting new conditions for knowledge (Sakai 2001:74). This division is not just academic, it is thoroughly political, for whereas *humanitas* designates self-reflective knowledge by and about the West, or Europe, *anthropos* designates "man" pictured as the West's others. *Anthropos* can be studied, but does not study itself (Sakai 2001:74).[5]

This asymmetrical relation is not to be explained in economic terms, i.e. by the fact that "Western" economies can support academic research projects about the non-West. Rather, it has to do with the enunciative position of area studies as "Western." Conventionally, the study of an "area" is thought to be unproblematically predicated on a predetermined cultural difference between the area and the so-called West. To study an area then would mean to determine those differences and rearticulate them to an addressee, i.e. one's students and colleagues, who are predetermined as "Western." The possibility of addressing one's work to addressees in the "area" one studies is excluded from the outset in area studies – it would be a self-defeating exercise exposing the colonial economy of knowledge at the core of area studies. And, yet, it is because area studies cannot happen in isolation from the "area" in question that the condition upon which area studies first became possible, the assumption of predetermined cultural difference, becomes exposed as the instituting of cultural difference:

> ... the description of cultural difference is always the acknowledgment and endorsement of a particular enunciative positionality in the student's relationship to the object of study. To describe cultural difference is to establish a specific enunciative position from which the student is to observe it. But we cannot emphasize too much that one cannot encounter cultural difference without encountering other people; one never experiences it in a social vacuum; to encounter other people is to be engaged in some social relation with them. Thus, the description of cultural difference is always correlative with an act of inscribing and instituting specific social relations that necessarily involve the student himself or herself.
>
> (Sakai 1997:120)

The teacher of area studies finds him or herself implicated in a translational situation suturing the student into an enunciative position, a standpoint from which he or she makes her address to an audience – which is to say that, he or she is in a practical situation of recasting knowledge into terms that his or her audience will recognize *as* knowledge. The expectation of area studies is that this enunciative position is continuous with the enunciative position of the audience, namely, "Western." In other words, the address is expected to take place "homolingually," meaning not that the address takes place in a language common to both addresser and addressee but that the enunciative positions of both are continuous with one another. In the homolingual address, Sakai argues, "the addresser adopts the position representative of a putatively homogeneous language society and relates to the general addressees, who are also representative of an equally homogeneous language community" (Sakai 1997:4). The stance of addressing one's audience "homolingually" is that of the hermeneutic attitude, which attempts to recover "meaning" for an "us" as representatives of a circumscribed language community.

However, what area studies could not anticipate and struggles to deny is that students of area studies, who constitute its primary audience, are brought into a practical situation in which they are simultaneously brought to identify with and yet disavow the "area" they study. They are asked to be both "of" the area, by producing intimate knowledge of it, and also not "of" it by determining its cultural differences from the West and communicating them to a "Western" audience. Yet, it should be noted that this is the very process by which the "area" and the "West" emerge as a determined difference and by which the activity of the student becomes "political," yet political in a manner that area studies disavows. Its disavowal takes place by masking the area studies practitioner's scene of address as a scene of communication between two continuous positions, between the sender (the practitioner) and the recipient (the Western audience) as members of the same "community."

The politics of area studies come to the fore when it is recognized that the audience of area studies is not, and was never, homogeneous. For not only were those who hail from the "area" in question always active in the production of area studies – as students, researchers, teachers – but also those who have become *de facto* members of the "area" by virtue of the practical relation they established with the "area" they might have once "studied" in contemplative detachment. In other words, area studies – if not the entirety of the humanities – presupposes what was never the case, the unity of the "we" with which it makes its address. It is in this sense then that Sakai insists upon a mode of address radically distinct from the hermeneutic attitude of the homolingual address, which assumes that every message will arrive at its destination and thus asks nothing of the addressee.

In contrast to the homolingual address, Sakai proposes the "heterolingual" address, in which the addressee is never assumed to be continuous with the enunciative position of the address and is asked to participate in its translation. Sakai writes, "in the heterolingual address, addressing in enunciation is not supposed to coincide with eventual communication, so that it is demanded of the addressee to act to incept or receive what is offered by the addresser. ... In the heterolingual address, therefore, the act of inception or reception occurs as the act of translation, and translation takes place at every listening or reading" (Sakai 1997:8). The heterolingual implicates the addressee in the making of the address, by *asking* the addressee to countertranslate it.

It is here that the formulation "politics as translation" I have sought to specify through a close reading of Sakai's work on translation accrues a sense distinct from the politics of translation. Considering politics *as* translation

70   *John Namjun Kim*

would be to take the political as a site in which a non-aggregate community is constituted through translation and countertranslation. It is a site in which it is never assumed that the temporality of what is said is coextensive with who said it or to whom it is said, and thus it is a site in which all remain foreigners, whose politics is, by necessity, to translate without assuming that the message will arrive at its destination.

Bibiliography

Agamben, G. (1998) *Homo Sacer: Sovereign Power and Bare Life.* Stanford University Press, Stanford.

Althusser, L. (2001) Ideology and Ideological State Apparatuses. In *Lenin and Philosophy and Other Essays*, Monthly Review Press, New York, pp. 127–86.

Benveniste, E. (1971) *Problems in General Linguistics.* University of Miami Press, Coral Gables, Fla.

——. (1974) *Problèmes de linguistique générale.* Gallimard, Paris.

Foucault, M. (2002) *The Order of Things: An Archaeology of the Human Sciences.* Routledge, London.

Gadamer, H.-G. (1975) *Wahrheit und Methode.* Mohr, Tübingen.

Jakobson, R. (1971) On Linguistic Aspects of Translation. In *Selected Writings, vol. 2. Word and Language*, Mouton, The Hague and Paris, pp. 260–66.

Kant, I. (1903) *Kritik der reinen Vernunft.* Bruno Cassirer, Berlin.

——. (1911) Kritik der reinen Vernunft. Kant's gesammelte Schriften, ed. Königlich Preußischen Akademie der Wissenschaften (AK), Vol. 3 Bruno Cassirer, Berlin.

Langenohl, A. (2007) *Tradition und Gesellschaftskritik. Eine Rekonstruktion der Modernisierungstheorie.* Campus, Frankfurt am Main and New York.

Nishida Kitarô (1947) Sekai no jiko doitsu to renzoku. In *Nishida Kitarô Zenshû, vol. 8*, Iwanami Shoten, Tokyo, pp. 7–106.

Nishitani Osamu (2006) Anthropos and Humanitas: Two Western Concepts of 'Human Being'. In *Traces 4: Translation, Biopolitics, Colonial Difference*, (Eds, Sakai, N. and Solomon, J.) Hong Kong University Press, Hong Kong, pp. 259–73.

Ricœur, P. (2004) *Sur la traduction.* Bayard, Paris.

Sakai, N. (1991) *Voices of the Past: The Status of Language in Eighteenth-Century Japanese Discourse.* Cornell University Press, Ithaca.

——. (1997) *Translation and Subjectivity: On "Japan" and Cultural Nationalism.* University of Minnesota Press, Minneapolis.

——. (2001) Dislocation of the West and the Status of the Humanities. *Traces 1: A Multilingual Journal of Cultural Theory and Translation*, Specters of the West and Politics of Translation, 71–94.

Sakai, N. and Solomon, J. (2006) Addressing the Multitude. In *Traces: 4. Translation, Biopolitics, Colonial Difference*, (Eds, Sakai, N. and Solomon, J.) Hong Kong University Press, Hong Kong and London.

Schmitt, C. (1996) *The Concept of the Political.* University of Chicago Press, Chicago, Ill.

Spivak, G.C. (2005) Translating into English. In *Nation, Language, and the Ethics of Translation*, (Eds, Bermann, S. and Wood, M.) Princeton University Press, Princeton, pp. 93–110.

——. (1993) The Politics of Translation. In *Outside the Teaching Machine*, Routledge, New York, pp. 179–200.

Notes

1 The notions of the "horizon of understanding" and the "fusion of horizons" belong to Hans-Georg Gadamer. See Gadamer 1975: 275–90.
2 For a comprehensive critique of "tradition" in relation to modernity, see Langenohl 2008.
3 For the concept of the "enemy," see Schmitt 1996. For the concept of the "camp," see Agamben 1998.
4 For the critique of humanism which informs Sakai's work, see Foucault 1994.
5 For a detailed analysis of the distinction between *anthropos* and *humanitas* and, see Nishitani 2006.

4 The biopolitics of companion species

Wartime animation and multi-ethnic nationalism

Thomas Lamarre

In Japanese wartime animation, Japan's enemies and colonized peoples frequently appear in animal form.[1] In animated versions of the manga *Norakuro* (Stray Black) produced in the 1930s, for instance, there is a dog regiment that stands in for Japanese soldiers, and the dogs do battle with tigers, monkeys, and pigs who apparently represent peoples, races, or nations within the Japanese empire. In animated films based on the folklore character Momotarô (Peach Boy) produced between 1931 and 1945, animals common to Japan (monkeys, dogs, pheasants) serve as Japanese soldiers, while peoples of Japan's conquered territories take the form of animals indigenous to those regions.

At first glance, such an association of peoples with animal species seems to present nothing more than a naturalization of ethnos, race, or nation. After all, insofar as a dog does not choose to be a dog, depictions of the Japanese regiment as a dog regiment would seem to naturalize Japaneseness, to make it appear as a natural classification, a given, an ontological condition or empirical fact. As such, the transformation of peoples into animal species in wartime animation seems designed to avoid a confrontation with the *negativity* and *mediation* inherent in nationalism that Naoki Sakai has repeatedly shown to be one of the central concerns of Kyoto School Philosophy of roughly the same period, particularly in his discussion of the essays of Tanabe Hajime gathered in a volume entitled *Shu no ronri* or "The Logic of Species" (Sakai 2000). Animal species in wartime animation might appear to imply an immediate, unmediated, positivistic belonging to an ethnos, race, or nation.

There is nonetheless a sort of negativity at work in the dynamics of animal species in wartime animations. There is mediation of ethnos or nation. But such negativity is not apparent if we read these animations exclusively at the level of representation, if we assume that dogs unambiguously represent the Japanese, for instance, and completely ignore the specificity of animation. This is where Sakai's work on Tanabe Hajime and "The Logic of Species" proves crucial, not because it addresses the specificity of animation per se, but because it forces us to move beyond a simplistic analysis of representation and to take a closer look at mediation, which in turn leads to a consideration of media (animation).

Philosophy and animation differ profoundly in their treatment of species, and I will gradually draw a contrast between them at the level of their political implications. Where Sakai carefully excavates a politics of national subjectivity and sovereignty from Kyoto School Philosophy, I find in wartime animation something closer to Michel Foucault's discussion of security and biopolitics. Which is to say, in animation, mediation is not so much a matter of the negation of the subject (that produces and promises to stabilize the national subject), but of a "spacing" or material interval that tends to act at the level of the circulation of images and the distribution of populations.

The logic of species

One of the hallmarks of Naoki Sakai's work is a sustained critique of the postwar myth of Japan as a mono-ethnic society, a myth that finds popular expression in *Nihonjinron* or discourses on Japaneseness, discourses that stress the uniqueness of being Japanese. Unlike most critics of *Nihonjinron*, who are content to signal the excesses and exclusionary tendencies of Japanese cultural nationalism as mono-ethnic nationalism, Sakai deliberately avoids and directly challenges the received critiques. His work shows how the received critiques remain content to take issue with mono-ethnic nationalism, that is, particularism, while accepting universalism, typically in the form of Western or American multi-ethnic nationalism. In other words, the received critiques rely on an opposition between particularism and universalism, in a variety of forms. In one of his key essays, for instance, a study of Kyoto School philosopher Tanabe Hajime, Sakai writes, "I refuse to address the problem of the Kyoto School Philosophy and nationalism within the framework of either the West vs the East or the United States vs Japan, multi-ethnic universalism vs mono-ethnic particularism, Christianity vs Asiatic religions, while at the same time I do not hesitate to deal with issues coming out of the fact that many intellectuals and political agents in the West or the East, Europe and North America or East Asia, could not and cannot think of their positionality without reference to such crude binaries" (2000: 466).

In other words, Sakai does not see different kinds of nationalism (say, multi-ethnic versus mono-ethnic) but detects a sort of dialectical tension within nationalism, an unrelenting co-figuration of the particular and the universal, which makes nationalism exceedingly productive and compelling, and impossible to contest simply by attacking particularism. To address nationalism in the register of universalism, Sakai turns primarily to Kyoto School Philosophy of interwar and wartime Japan. At that time philosophers directly engaged questions about multi-ethnic nationalism, precisely because Japanese imperial nationalism had forced some manner of a confrontation with questions about ethnos, races, folks, or peoples. These philosophers could not treat mono-ethnic society as a given. As Sakai points out, the difficulty that such philosophers experienced in their attempts to provide empirical definitions for such terms as *minshu* or *minzoku* (people, folk, ethnos, race, nation) betrays the instability inherent in particularistic or mono-ethnic nationalism. Ultimately, Sakai shows, certain Kyoto School philosophers came to recognize that particularism can only ground and sustain itself through some relation to universalism. To use a turn of phrase that Sakai develops at length in his work on translation (Sakai 1997), Kyoto School Philosophy of prewar Japan demonstrates how mono-ethnic nationalisms (particularisms) become *co-figured* within multi-ethnic nationalism through the work of the universal. The question then is not *whether* one will engage with multi-ethnic nationalism but *how* one will engage with it. It is matter of negotiation (thrownness, or a schema), not of rejection or acceptance (rational choice).

The interest of Tanabe for Sakai lies in Tanabe's turn to the terms of formal logic – *ko* or "individual," *shu* or "species," and *rui* or "genus" – in order to expose the instability and ambivalence inherent in concepts of ethnicity and nationality. Sakai argues that Tanabe's use of such terms does not follow from the formal logic of Aristotle or the taxonomies of Linnaeus. In contrast with Aristotle and Linnaeus, for Tanabe, individuals do not unambiguously belong to a species, nor do species fit into a genus in a positive or natural way. Rather, Sakai argues, Tanabe's use of species and genus recalls Hegel's dialectic of the particular and universal. The individual (subject) only belongs fully (that is, self-consciously) to a species insofar as the individual *negates* the species and thus gains freedom from it. It is the genus that mediates the individual's self-aware negation of the species. Tanabe's logic of species, as Sakai deftly unravels it, takes a Hegelian turn wherein the individual (subject) only belongs to the species (particular: ethnos, race, or nation) by self-consciously negating it through the mediation of the genus (universal: State, empire, or God). It is in this sense that Sakai sees Tanabe's logic of species offering a metaphysical foundation for Japanese imperial nationalism and for the idea of the Greater East Asia Co-Prosperity Sphere.

Now, because the individual cannot belong to a species unless the individual is *aware* of belonging, the logical is the ethical in Tanabe (480). It demands a mode of praxis. You must to some degree consciously resist your species to belong to it. But what actual practices might afford an ethical awareness of belonging to a species through its negation? The prime example in Sakai's account of Tanabe comes from Tanabe's lecture "Shi Sei" or "Death and Life," delivered in 1943 as the first in a series of lectures organized to deal with anxiety about death on the part of volunteer student soldiers or draftees about to leave for the front (469). Here Tanabe calls on the readiness to die for the State as an ethical practice of negation of the species mediated by the genus or universal. Interestingly enough, Tanabe says that by risking his life, a man acquires the right to rebel against the State. This proposition may seem to contradict Tanabe's claim that the genus mediates the individual's negation of the species. Isn't the State the universal? How can you negate the universal?

In fact, you cannot negate the genus or the universal. You can only do its work. In Tanabe's "Death and Life," the species is still the nation or ethnos, but the genus is now both the State and God. To sustain the universality of the State, Tanabe exhorts his audience to devote themselves to the continued perfection of the universality inherent in the existing State, and he calls on God as that universal principle.

Readers of Robert Heinlein will probably note that Tanabe's proposal recalls the basic conceit of *Starship Troopers* (1959): to become a citizen, you must enlist, which means you must be prepared to die. It is this readiness to die for the State that gives you the right to vote, that is, to question and thus to take responsibility for and improve the State. What is more, in Heinlein's novel, as in Tanabe's logic of species, ethnicity is at once acknowledged and negated: the novel includes a cast of multi-ethnic names, but you would be hard pressed to find actual ethnic practices. Readiness for death ethically trumps all other modes of practice. The State trumps other forms of belonging and identification by mediating them.

In Heinlein's novel, the military actively discourages enlistment, and you can drop out at any time without penalty (except that you will not gain the rights of a citizen). This is unlike Tanabe's historical situation, in which recruitment was a pressing concern for the Japanese State, leading to conscription not only of younger and younger men but also of ethnic nationals residing with the Japanese empire (both men as soldiers and women as military sexual slaves or "comfort women"). Nonetheless, if I draw out the analogy between Tanabe Hajime's philosophy and Robert Heinlein's novel, two points can be made. First, in keeping with Sakai's critical project, such an analogy discourages us from positing an opposition between Japan and the West on the basis of Japanese mono-ethnic nationalism (particularism) versus American multi-ethnic nationalism (universalism).

Second, I have slipped a science fiction writer into the discussion because it is above all in the world of science fiction that the Japanese conceptualization of multi-ethnic social formations persisted in the postwar era, even as the American Occupation and subsequent domination of parts of East Asia made the Japanese nation appear as a species of mono-ethnic nationalism to be negated and "sublated" within the genus of the Pax Americana. We might note, for instance, that *Starship Troopers* would have a profound impact on Japanese science fiction, and the cover illustration of the Japanese translation would provide the major inspiration for anime mecha designs. But the persistence of the imaginary of multi-ethnic empire in Japanese science fiction is not merely a matter of coincidental influences between American and Japanese science fictions.

As the above excursus through Tanabe's logic of species makes clear, the analogy with science fiction runs deeper: once we adopt a formal logic of species to address questions of ethnicity and nationality that cannot be resolved via positivistic inquiry and strict definitions, we open the door to the evaluation and integration not only of other humans (species as ethnos, race, people) but also of non-human species (non-human animals, non-animal terrestrials, and extraterrestrial or alien species). The evaluation and potential integration of other species is, needless to say, one of the domains of certain fictions that today we generally group under the rubric of science fiction. Science fictions that explore relations between humans and non-humans also entail a sort of "formal logic of species" whose implications can be effectively opened to discussion by reference to Tanabe's Hegelian twist on the formal logic of species.

The same is true of Japanese wartime animations in which animal species do battle and form alliances: there is in such animations a formal logic of species in which the translation of peoples into species allows for evaluation and integration of them. The very process of depicting nationality (say, Korean) in terms of animal species (tiger) already implies some degree of negative mediation of ethnicity or nationality by means of a "formalization" of a nation as a species. There are precedents for the use of animals in wartime animations. Conventions of national animal heraldry had become widespread in newspapers and comics in the late nineteenth and early twentieth centuries: the Russian bear, the American eagle, the British bulldog, and a range of other animals that were designed to convey national characteristics. The political cartoons of *Tokyo Puck* or *Tôkyô Pakku* provide numerous instances. Or we might take the tradition of fables and folktales as a point of departure. Nonetheless, in keeping with Sakai's analysis of Tanabe, we need to ask how the universal mediates, and what kind of universalism is at stake. In the case of *Tokyo Puck*, for instance, should we address internationalism, cosmopolitanism, the State, or national Empire? But then, precisely because the boundaries between internationalism, cosmopolitanism, and imperialism are not clear and distinct, we need to ask what kind of material configuration (or more precisely, spacing or interval) grounds or sustains a historically specific "co-figuration" of the particular and universal.

Let me begin with an account, however brief, of the historical context for Japanese wartime animations. Such contextualization is not intended as an explanation of these animations. Instead, I wish to move from historical contextualization to *historicity*, that is, to what is historically new about animal species in animation, which allows them to open beyond their historical context and extend into other historical formations. At the level of historicity, we can then address mediation and negativity of animation's animals with greater historical specificity.

Yellow peril and companion species

In *War without Mercy*, John Dower contrasts images of the Japanese enemy in American wartime propaganda with images of Americans and Westerners in Japanese wartime propaganda. He finds that Americans tended to dehumanize their Japanese enemies, and one strategy involved bestializing them by representing them as animals: "A characteristic feature of this level of anti-Japanese sentiment was the resort to nonhuman or subhuman representation, in which the Japanese were perceived as animals, reptiles, or insects (monkeys, baboons, gorillas, dogs, mice and rats, vipers and rattlesnakes, cockroaches, vermin, or more indirectly, 'the Japanese herd' and the like)" (Dower 1986: 81). And yet, "without question ... the most common caricature of the Japanese by Westerners, writers and cartoonists alike, was the monkey or ape" (84). Such depictions reinforced a sense that the Japanese were not humans but animals to be hunted down and exterminated.

In contrast, even though the Japanese war media also tended to dehumanize the enemy, its strategy was not to bestialize the American enemy. Dower stresses how Japanese tended to depict the American enemy as failed humans: as demons, ogres, or fiends. Crucial to his assessment is the representation of English and American enemies in Seo Mitsuyo's 1945 animated film *Momotarô: Umi no shinpei* (Momotarô's Divine Soldiers of the Sea), the last in a series of wartime animated adaptations of the Momotarô folktale intended to reflect national military values (Seo 1945). In one of the climatic scenes in this film, Japan's English-speaking enemies appear in human form but with horns on their head, reflecting their degraded and demonic stature. Facing them is Momotarô, whose spiritual purity and youthful vigor intimidates and overpowers them (Figure 4.1).

Dower concludes, "the depiction of the enemy as demons, devils, or ogres permitted the rise of an exterminationist rhetoric in Japan comparable to the metaphors of the hunt or of exterminating vermin in the West" (255). Nonetheless, in the context of this particular film, he argues that, "Momotarô and

Figure 4.1 The English commander, sporting a horn on his head, nervously addresses Momotarô (flanked by his companion animals) in English to the effect that "...you're placing us in a difficult situation," which is translated into Japanese in the accompanying title.

the Caucasians thus confronted each other as figures who partook of supra-national as well as human qualities; and in this regard they were actually closer to each other than was apparent at first glance" (255). In these Japa-nese depictions of American and English enemies, Dower sees "symbolic ruptures" that "helped prepare the ground for discarding the antipodal ste-reotypes of pure Self and incorrigibly evil Other once Japan had acknowl-edged its defeat" (255).

It is telling that Dower ignores the other conspicuous characters in this scene: Momotarô's animal helpers, who play a larger role in the film than the Caucasians. Dower's attention falls almost exclusively on how the Japanese see Caucasians. He largely ignores the animals in the film, not only Momo-tarô's Japanese animal helpers (rabbits, bears, monkeys, pheasants) but also the film's depiction of non-Japanese nations and peoples included in Japan's empire. While Dower is aware of the Japanese empire, he tends to assume that a distinction between humans and animals always amounts to bes-tialization and thus to categorical dehumanization. He assumes that there is nothing at stake in these animal depictions but an unrelenting degradation and oppression of non-Japanese ethnicities and nationalities. In other words, Dower refuses to acknowledge exactly what Sakai highlights: the work of the universal in nationalism, and specifically in the instance of Japanese multi-ethnic nationalism. Dower reduces the Japanese empire to mono-ethnic nationalism, which then requires American multi-ethnic nationalism to bring out the humanism that lies encrypted in the "symbolic ruptures" appearing in Japanese representations of Caucasians – as if the failed or lacking expression of universalism in the Japanese empire left it primed to "embrace defeat," that is, to embrace American universalism.

The animals in the Momotarô film tell a different story. To the traditional animals of the folktale (dog, monkey, pheasant), the film adds rabbits and bears, and rather than one animal of each species, there are platoons and squadrons of them. Figure 4.1 includes a monkey seated on Momotarô's left, a bear standing at attention behind the monkey, a rabbit seated on his left (only the ear is visible in the image), and if you look closely, the head of a pheasant to the right. In addition, leading up to the confrontation with the Caucasian enemy, Momotarô's animal platoons and squadrons construct an airbase on an island, with the eager assistance of animals apparently indi-genous to the island. (There is a generic quality to the elephants, leopards, apes, and other animals that raises doubts about the degree to which these animals are based on actual indigenous animals or on other animations.) The scenes of animals working together are among the longer and happier scenes in the film, and in keeping with the film's address to children or general audiences, the animals are above all cute, receptive, and winsome. They fairly cry out for nurture, charming us with their gentle open faces, energetic movements, and willingness. Of course, we should not conclude that such a strategy of using cute little animal helpers is somehow innocent of power relations, especially in light of their childlike qualities. But we do need to acknowledge two major omissions in Dower's account of Japan's wartime media that come of his omission of these animals: Japanese multi-ethnic nationalism and the materiality of media. I will address questions of media and historical materiality in the next section. Let me here continue with the discussion of the consequences of ignoring Japan's multi-ethnic nationalism.

The omission of Japan's multi-ethnic nationalism allows Dower to embrace the American multi-ethnic order and Japan's integration into it. The implications of his gesture can be better understood by looking from a different angle, that of the prehistory of science fiction. In effect, *War without Mercy* depends on an opposition between two streams or lineages of fictionalized encounters with non-human others that today constitute a tension within many science fictions – eradication of the alien other in contrast to integration.

When Dower wishes to underscore the ideological effects of American or Japanese wartime representations of the enemy, he speaks of how they tend to encourage a complete extermination of the non-animal other. This scenario recalls yellow peril fiction, in which non-white nationalities and ethnicities (frequently a generalized Oriental) threaten to invade and conquer Caucasian lands. Because these non-white or yellow peoples were dehumanized and de-differentiated in what Peter Button calls the "para-human" (Button 2003), they entered directly into early science fictions in the form of alien swarms attacking Earth (Tatsumi 2006: 63–70). It is precisely this sort of scenario that Dower detects at work in both American and Japanese wartime media: "the depiction of the enemy as demons, devils, or ogres permitted the rise of an exterminationist rhetoric in Japan comparable to the metaphors of the hunt or of exterminating vermin in the West" (255). Dower tends to find clearer expression of this impulse to exterminate others on the American side, however, in his examples and conclusions: "No side had a monopoly on attributing 'beastliness' to the other, although the Westerners possessed a more intricate web of metaphors with which to convey this" (11).

In contrast to the evils of "exterminationist rhetoric," which entails evaluation without integration, Dower holds out the possibility for a friendlier assimilatory encounter with the foreign or ethnic other. Oddly enough, Dower even attributes assimilation in the form of a "cutification" of conquered peoples to the American order, highlighting the postwar American transformation of the ugly simian Japanese into a cute little chimp: "to the victors, the simian became a pet, the child a pupil, the madman a patient" (13). Such a cutification and juvenilization of ethnic others is not exclusively American, as Japan's wartime animation attests. This imaginary of integration of others grows out of a different lineage of fictionalized encounters with non-human others, that of the animal helper of folktales, which gradually transforms into the companion animals or companion species that became prevalent in children's literature, comics, films, and animation from the 1920s, and becoming something of a cultural dominant in family entertainment today. The Momotarô films and much of Japanese wartime animation belong to this lineage.

Expressions of multi-ethnic nationalism derive in part from Japan's conscious evocation of, and resistance to, American racism. The Japanese war was couched as one of racial liberation, emancipating "Asians" or "people of color" from "white demons" or Western imperialists. As Dower points out, the Japanese media consistently expressed indignation over how Westerners looked upon colored people in general as simply "races who should serve them like domestic animals" (248). In addition to concern about the instability of mono-ethnic nationalism and its threat to the stability of the Japanese empire, which Sakai highlights in his account of Tanabe, there was a general recognition of the danger of mono-ethnic nationalism as a mode of racism. Such concerns entered into Japanese diplomacy as well. For instance, the Japanese delegation to the Paris Peace Conference of 1919 demanded not only territorial control over former German colonies in East Asia and the South Pacific but also made a proposal for racial equality, which mandated equal and just treatment for all alien nationals of states without distinction on the basis of race or nationality. The rejection of both demands confirmed the impression among many Japanese that Western modernity was predicated on racism, that is, mono-ethnic (white) nationalism that merely pretended to endorse multi-ethnicity. Thus the Japanese bid to "overcome modernity," that is, to overcome Western modernity, also included resistance to both racial prejudice and mono-ethnic nationalism (see Calichman 2008). This is why Japan's Fifteen-Year Asia-Pacific War could be couched as a war of racial liberation, of freeing peoples and nations of Asia from Western domination, and offering the vision of a new sphere of non-racial, that is, non-hierarchal "co-prosperity."

Dower ignores these concerns in Japanese wartime media and seems intent on reading them in terms of an impulse toward mono-ethnic nationalism, as if Japanese multi-ethnic nationalism, which expressed such modes as Pan-Asianism and the Greater East Asia Co-Prosperity Sphere, were discredited due the defeat of Japan and thus not worthy of critical attention. But, in the context of wartime animation at least, we cannot in good conscience reduce the transformation of peoples into cute little animals to an expression of mono-ethnic nationalism. There is in wartime animations a sort of formal logic of species that evaluates peoples in order to integrate them into a multi-ethnic order (or more precisely, a multi-species order). Put another way, the translation of peoples into cute little animals entails a mediation of mono-ethnicity that at once negates and "elevates" it to produce a sense of multi-species cooperation and, if you will, co-prosperity – as with the productivity of cooperation among animals in *Momotarô: Umi no shinpei*. Maybe Dower omits such concerns because, once we acknowledge them, we begin to look differently at the apparent friendliness and co-prosperity of postwar American expressions of multi-ethnic nationalism and multi-species universalism.

In any event, following Sakai, we would have to reject an opposition between yellow peril and companion species. Yellow peril scenarios (mono-ethnic nationalism) readily serve as the negative condition for the production of companion species (multi-ethnic empire). This does not mean that we must abandon companion species (if that were in fact possible). But we do need to take a closer look at their operations.

The life of animal characters

The vitality of animation is most palpable in its animal characters. Even though we are aware of forms of animation that deliberately avoid cute little non-humans, animation commonly brings to mind images of cute little animals frolicking, dancing, leaping, and cavorting, as well as being stretched, squashed, and otherwise deformed, only to bounce back. Historically, it was largely in the form of children's films (or family or general audience films) that animation reached wider audiences, and typically such films centered on, or called attention to, cute little animals. We have only to think of Felix the Cat, Bugs Bunny, Oswald the Rabbit, Cubby Bear, Mickey Mouse, or Tom and Jerry; or in Japan, Norakuro the Stray Black, Songoku the monkey, Dankichi's monkey in the *Bôken Dankichi* animations, Maabo's animal friends, or the diverse animal helpers in Momotarô animations.

Such animal characters evoke a sort of "kinetophilia," a delight in movement and a fascination with plasticity and elasticity, which Sergei Eisenstein (1988) called "plasmaticness," and which we might also call plasmaticity. The deformation and reformation of characters – stretching, squashing, flattening, and inflating – provides a major source of pleasure in animation. Years later, Disney animators Ollie Johnson and Frank Thomas (1981) outlined the various techniques that emerged in the 1930s, which gradually became associated with Disney, among them the famous "squash and stretch" that today plays a central role in Pixar's vision of computer animation.[2] Ôtsuka Eiji notes that the elasticity associated with animated characters imparts a sense of their invulnerability and even immortality: they appear resilient and resistant to injury and death (2008). Theirs is a fascinatingly deathless vitality.

But the characters do not actually have to be violently stretched, squashed, or otherwise deformed to convey this sense of plasticity and thus vitality. Animated animals seem to channel an almost supernatural force of movement, evident in the dynamism of their actions, especially when leaping and frolicking but even in mundane activities like walking. There are a number of technical reasons for this plasticity, and a number of reasons why it tends to settle on animal characters. Let me speak first to the technical reasons.

Animated characters show a fluidity of line and contour that imparts a sense of heightened energy and vitality. This stems in part from new styles of drawing characters that became prevalent in the 1920s, which is as apparent in comics as in cartoons. The contours of characters became more rounded, and their composition based on round or spherical elements. Such a style appeared youthful and well suited to the younger readers and viewers who were a newly targeted audience for comics and cartoons. It originated largely in the United States and became associated primarily with Walt Disney. With the cinema emerging as distinctive art with a global reach and nearly synchronous reception and production, however, Japanese comics and cartoons, or manga and *manga-eiga* (manga films), did not lag in implementing these features.

Many of the animations or manga films in Japan were adapted from popular manga for boys, as in the instances of *Norakuro* and *Bôken Dankichi*, originally serialized in *Shônen kurabu*. But animation introduces something new to the manga, something already implicit in comics but which emerges through the interrelation of comics and cartoons, manga and animation: this something is what Miyamoto Hirohito, in his discussion of prewar manga, calls the tendency toward a sense of the life and autonomous existence of the character (2003: 47–48). As for the relation of manga to animation, while we tend to think of media mix or media convergence as a phenomenon of the 1990s, such cross-over and convergence effects had already begun in earnest in the 1930s, at the level of establishing what contemporary manga critic Itô Gô calls the "sense of existence" (*sonzaikan*) and "sense of life" (*seimeikan*) of the character (2005: 94–95) in his discussion of transmedial worlds centered on manga characters.[3] Animation contributes directly to the sense of the life, vitality, and autonomous existence of characters due to a specific technical array that channels the force of the moving image into character animation. With the continued crossover between manga, animation, and cinema, these effects become integral to manga expression as well.

In animation production, with the introduction of layers of celluloid and the animation stand, which gradually became standard practice in the 1930s, the camera was fixed (on a rostrum), and so, to impart a sense of motion, animators had the choice of moving the sheets, or animating the characters, or both. In the 1930s and 1940s, the emphasis fell on character animation, to the point that character animation appeared to be *the* art of animation, taking precedence over camera movement and editing (animation is largely pre-edited). While the art of painting backgrounds received attention, this was a matter of art, not of animation per se.[4]

It was not until the 1950s, when animators explicitly developed procedures of limited animation, deemphasizing character animation and playing with iconic expression, that moving the celluloid sheets became an appealing option for imparting a sense of movement. Tezuka Osamu played an integral role in this transformation with the television animation for *Tetsuwan Atomu* in the early 1960s, for which his team used techniques for dramatically limiting character animation and shifting the experience of movement into other registers of the moving image. Nonetheless, such techniques are still frequently disparaged today, and the bias toward character animation as *the* art of animation remains.

In the 1930s and 1940s, the animation stand, with its fixed camera and celluloid layers, encouraged an emphasis on character animation. Thus the force of the moving image, which comes of the mechanical succession of images, became channeled into characters, whose plasticity embodies that force, at once folding it into their bodies and releasing it. Needless to say, this is not a matter of representation. Plasticity does not represent the force of the mechanical succession of images. It affords an actual experience of it. The animated character summons and channels a technical force. As a consequence, a technical force is now experienced as plasmaticity, as vitality, as life itself.

Such an experience is not, as so many commentators would have it, an illusion of life. It is a real experience of a force wherein the technical and the vital appear inseparable. We might call this techno-animism or techno-vitalism, provided we do not take the "ism" to imply that this is an idealist construction or illusion. It is a new experience of life. But why does this experience gravitate toward, or settle on, the animation of animal characters, especially cute little animals?

Animal characters presented certain advantages, both for perceptual and socioeconomic reasons. It is a commonplace of animation that the human eye is less finicky about accuracy of movement with animal characters than with human characters. Humans apparently subject human figures to greater scrutiny and demand a higher degree of verisimilitude. Surely, such expectations are as much learned as innate, but in any event, what matters is that conventions in cinema and animation gradually introduced a rough separation into the moving image, whereby animation tended toward animal energies, and cinema toward human verisimilitude. In addition, as Jonathan Burt (2002) discusses at length, images of animals in cinema have historically evoked a great deal of concern about violence to animals, to the point where we accept truly gruesome violence to humans on film (understanding it as staged) while balking at the least violence to animals (because we tend not to perceive it as staged).[5] In contrast, although animation, like cinema, has its conventions, codes, and limits for violence, it allows for greater violence to and more violent deformation of animal characters, surely because we perceive them as deathless and invulnerable embodiments of a techno-vital force.

In addition to these perceptual considerations that affected the development of conventions for animals in animation, two other factors had a major impact on animation animals: the emergence of folklore studies and children's culture. In the 1920s and 1930s, in Japan as in other parts of the world, the emergence of mass culture brought with it a new sense of distinct markets and audiences. This era saw, for instance, the mass production of cultural materials for women (women's journals and other female-directed commodities), as well as the mass production of a children's culture, with new journals and books intended for children, which would increasingly include manga. This process was not merely a matter of discovering and developing new markets or niche audiences, but of actively isolating and shaping them, economically, legally and politically. As early as the Film Laws of 1917, for instance, the Japanese government displayed a concern for segregating audiences by gender (mandating separate seating for men and women). Furthermore, particularly in the course of the 1920s, certain films raised questions in the popular imagination about the impact of cinema on juvenile delinquency, which contributed to new regulations and new entertainments to produce what was deemed child-appropriate material. Consequently, from the mid-1910s through the

1920s, as cinema emerged as a form of entertainment distinctive from other entertainments, such developments led to the delineation of children as a distinct population, audience, and market, to be cultivated as such. Not surprisingly, this newly delineated children's culture emphasized animal characters, in illustrated books, manga, animation, and in magazines stressing the importance of nature skills as the basis for a scientific appreciation of things.

While there are strong associations between children and animals in many cultures (children show a liking for animals, and children are often seen as akin to animals), the invention of folklore or ethnography played an important role in mediating the relation between Japanese children and animal characters by drawing animal helpers out of traditional tales, which could be repackaged in a more cosmopolitan form in children's entertainments. It is surely not a coincidence that Yanagita Kunio, the "father" of Japanese ethnography, published a major book on Momotarô (*Momotarô no tanjô*, 1931) at the same time that the first Momotarô cartoons were being produced, for instance, *Nippon ichi Momotarô* (Momotarô of Japan supreme, 1928) and *Sora no Momotarô* (Momotarô of the skies, 1931). Yanagita not only devoted himself to collecting folktales as an effort to protect the strangeness and diversity of rural Japan, which he saw vanishing in the light of a rationalist modernity (Ivy 1995), but he also contributed to destabilizing the idea of a mono-ethnic Japan by calling attention to the strange characters and cultures inhabiting the lore gathered in remote areas, which he sometimes interpreted as lingering signs of an ancient and authentic population driven into obscurity with the emergence of another dominant population. In other words, his folklore studies undermined the notion of an ancient and immutable mono-ethnicity, for it unearthed different populations in Japan.

The emergence of folklore in combination with the development of children's culture thus led to the establishment of a nexus conjoining children, folktales, and animals in popular entertainments. It is not surprising then that when critics as different as Sergei Einstein and Ôtsuka Eiji consider the plasmaticity and vitality of animation characters, they turn simultaneously to the realm of folklore and children. All these factors – the technical tendencies of animation; perceptions about violence and verisimilitude in film; the establishment of children as a population, audience, and market through government regulation and cultural industries; and the invention of folklore – contributed to making the cute little animated animal not only integral to children's culture but also the nodal point (or attractor) producing connections across distinct social domains or activities (law, modes of production, art, and knowledge production). The vitality of these new entities is not a mere illusion of life. It marks the point of entry of life into the political and the social where it will at once produce new connections across domains and ground them. This is a lot of work for a little animal, and so we have steadily produced legions of them over the past hundred odd years.

In sum, to understand how the life of animated animals works, we need to consider two levels or registers: that of plasmaticity or techno-vitality, and that of representation. But, as Sakai's account of Tanabe shows, we must not read representation in terms of a mere re-presentation in which the animal character is an immediate or unmediated stand-in for something else (say, a dog soldier standing for a Japanese soldier). Instead we need to attend to representation as mediation, and to the work of negativity. To give a more concrete sense of what is at stake, by way of conclusion, I will turn to the example of Norakuro. I will show how the register of plasmaticity implies a kind of biopolitics (governance of populations), while that of representation implies a politics of sovereignty (formation of subjectivity).

The biopolitics of species

Created by Tagawa Suiho, Norakuro the Stray Black Dog first appeared in print in *Shônen kurabu* in 1931, the year in which the rigged Manchurian Incident gave the Japanese government its excuse to begin a full-scale invasion of, and war against, China. Norakuro begins his adventures as an accident-prone soldier in a dog regiment under the command of Buru the Bulldog. The character enjoyed such popularity that animation adaptations soon followed, with some episodes adapted repeatedly. There are, for instance, two extant versions of Norakuro's first adventure in the army entitled *Norakuro nitôhei* (Norakuro, Private Second Class). Murata Yasuji directed a version in 1933 (1993a), and Seo Mitsuyo directed another in 1935 (2004a).

In Murata's version, Norakuro stands out from the other dogs in the dog regiment on the basis of his color (the other dogs are white), and he constantly stumbles and bumbles through his duties. In one scene, as the dog soldiers smartly salute their commander, Norakuro throws both hands in the air in a moment of irrepressible enthusiasm. Or, in another scene, as the other dog soldiers march crisply, Norakuro plods glumly and without conviction (Figure 4.2).

Norakuro's unruly and lazy behavior is striking in comparison with the general insistence in national policy films on regimentation and synchronization of soldierly activities, which reached new aesthetic heights in films like *Hawai Mare oki kaisen* (War at sea from Hawaii to Malaysia, 1945). In Seo's 1935 production of Norakuro as a private second class, Norakuro lazily sleeps on after the other soldiers are already at their calisthenics. Fortunately, Norakuro's bed comes to life, and when the bed is unable to awaken him, it runs him out to join the squad of soldiers.

Despite his lack of discipline and coordination, the Stray Black shows unusual spirit on the battlefield – he runs headlong to face the enemy when other dogs of regiment hesitate. He also has dumb luck in spades, and frequently produces a victory through some sort of ruse. As a result of his spirit, ingenuity, and good fortune, Norakuro leads the dog regiment to victory after victory against its enemies. With each victory, Norakuro rises in rank, and consequently there are a series of animated shorts based on the manga episodes that track Norakuro's climb through the military ranks. The episodes begin with "private second-class" (*Norakuro nitôhei*), and Stray Black

Figure 4.2 In Murata's 1933 version of Norakuro's adventures as a private second class, the stray dog frequently finds it difficult to stay in formation with the other dog soldiers.

gradually rises from "private first-class" (*Norakuro ittōhei*, 1935) (Seo 2004b) to "corporal" (*Norakuro gochô*, 1934) (Murata 1993b) and "minor company officer" (*Norakuro shôjô*, director and date unknown). Because Norakuro made his appearance in 1931 at the start of Japan's war against China, his rise through the ranks corresponds with Japan's movement deeper and deeper into its "war of liberation."

Now, Norakuro and the dogs are clearly Japanese. In *Norakuro gochô* (Corporal Norakuro, 1934), for instance, Japanese flags stand at the gate to the dogs' military encampment. But what do the animal enemies stand for? In Seo Mitsuyo's 1935 version of *Norakuro nitôhei*, for instance, the dog regiment encounters a ferocious tiger. Because national animal heraldry retained some importance in the 1930s, and because Korea commonly designated itself as a tiger, it is tempting to construe Norakuro's battle against the tiger as a representation of Japan versus Korea: dog versus tiger is Japan versus Korea. Such reading certainly proves interesting. In Seo's film, Norakuro accidentally paints himself with tiger stripes and confronts the adult tiger as if he were a cub of the same species. Norakuro's little tiger disguise allows him to immobilize the larger tiger (among other things his proximity allows him to toss laughing gas down the tiger's throat), and in the end, the Japanese dog regiment cages and merrily drags off the tiger (Figure 4.3).

Read allegorically, the Japanese dog in Seo's *Norakuro Nitôhei* who acts as a friendly little benefactor of the same species in order to cage the tiger and

Figure 4.3 In the 1935 animated installment of Norakuro's adventures as private second class, the stray dog succeeds in capturing the enemy tiger, and the dog regiment merrily leads off the caged tiger with Norakuro dancing on the tank.

drag it home is evocative of the dupery and force involved in Japan's mass importation of Korean labor into Japanese factories during the war, and also recalls the "recruitment" of "comfort women" (Korean women were especially numerous among the women drafted by the Japanese army into military sexual slavery, by force or by ruse).

Similarly, other animals in the Norakuro series can also be read as allegorical representations of Japan's colonized peoples and enemies. The pigs, for instance, are usually read as Chinese, and there is cause to do so.[6] But there are many possible readings for the gorillas or apes in *Norakuro ittōhei* (who are frightened into submission by a jack-in-the-box tiger head) or monkeys in *Norakuro gochô* (who are apparently proving difficult to assimilate into the dog army).[7]

But there is a problem with reading such animations in terms of a one-to-one correspondence between animal and nation, that is, in terms of direct and unmediated representation. We then completely ignore the process of mediation at work in the animations. Even if we wish to insist that the dogs are Japanese and the tiger Korean, we have to acknowledge that, in the transformation of a nation into a species, there is a process of abstraction and thus of negation. There is a negation of mono-ethnic nationalism, reminiscent of Tanabe's logic of species. It is this negation of mono-ethnic nationalism that imparts an aura of merriness and playfulness to these animations. We are not just seeing a battle between nations. We are also seeing cute little animals at play. Even though the tiger looks glum, he retains his plasmaticity and vitality. He exists and acts on the same field of techno-vitality, which in the register of representation is that of multi-ethnic nationalism. Put another way, with reference to Sakai's account of Tanabe, there is a universal at work under these particularisms (animal species as peoples, ethnos, or nations). This is not about a mono-ethnic Japan conquering a mono-ethnic Korea. It is about a multi-ethnic Japanese evaluating and integrating peoples, ethnicities, or nationalities.

Yet, although it is appropriate to speak, as Sakai and Tanabe do, of the Japanese State or empire embodying and mediating, that is, carrying out the work of the universal at the level of representation, animation adds something to the dynamics of representation. It introduces life itself, in the mediation of plasmaticity or techno-vitality. This is another kind of negativity, a very specific co-figuration of the particular and universal, as it were.

In accordance with the conventions of animation animals, these are bipedal animals, with paw-like hands, often with the trappings of human attire, and acting rather human. Norakuro the Stray Black Dog is like so many other animated animals in this respect, like Oswald the Rabbit, Felix the Cat, Cubby Bear, and Momotarô's companion animals. Initially we might conclude that the human functions as the universal here, mediating – that is, negating and elevating – animal species. Yet we cannot say whether these characters are humanized animals or animalized humans. We cannot determine if the human mediates the animal or the animal mediates the human. Sergei Eisenstein is insightful here. He notes of animated figures, "here we have a being represented in drawing, a being of definite form, a being which has attained a definite appearance, and which behaves like the primal protoplasm, not yet possessing a stable form, but capable of assuming any form and which skipping along the rungs of the evolutionary ladder, attaches itself to any and all forms of animal existence" (1988: 21). In other words, it is ultimately the animal or animality that does the work of the universal. The human and humanity are at the level of the particular, of the species.

When animality (or more broadly, vitality) becomes the site of negativity spurring mediation, the political implications are very different from Tanabe's logic of species. While an analysis of representation as mediation can allow us to detect this "animal negativity" at work, this is no longer a politics of representation, of sovereignty and subjectivity. Once the human becomes a species or a particular, politics becomes governance articulated at the level of populations, in the form of security.

Sakai indicates something analogous at the end of his essay on Tanabe when he associates it with pastoral power (2000: 515). But his remarks are fleeting, and given his overall emphasis on sovereignty and subjectivity, it is not clear how Sakai sees Tanabe's discussion leading from a politics directed toward the imaginary at the level of subject formation to a politics directed at populations rather than individuals. Here we need to differentiate sovereignty, discipline, and security, as Foucault does in the first lecture in *Security, Population, Territory* (2007). This politics of animality and vitality is not directed at the imaginary (sovereignty, ideology, or subjectivity), nor is it a discipline directed at the bodies of individuals entailing segregations and divisions among them. It is a biopolitics related to the governance of populations, predicated on security. Once we acknowledge this politics of animality in animation, we see how the translation of peoples into cute little animals (companion species) in Japanese wartime animation extends into contemporary animation and science fiction, in which love and war between species is predicated upon a negation of the human via the "negativity" of animality and vitality, which transforms the politics of national sovereignty into a concern for security and governance of populations that is articulated in the form of interplanetary warfare and annihilation of life forms, species, and worlds. And the very thing that promises to save us – our fascination with cute little animals and alien others – is inextricably meshed with regimes of security and total war.

Bibliography

Akiyama M. (1998) *Maboroshi no sensô manga no sekai*. Natsume shobô, Tokyo.
Burt, J. (2002) *Animals in Film*. Reaktion Books, London.
Button, P. (2006) (Para-)Humanity, Yellow Peril, and the postcolonial (arche-) type. Postcolonial Studies (4): 421–47.
Calichman, R. (Ed. and trans.) (2008) *Overcoming Modernity: Cultural Identity in Wartime Japan*. Columbia University Press, New York.
Dower, J. (1986) *War without Mercy: Race and Power in the Pacific War*. Pantheon Books, New York.
Eisenstein, S. (1988) *Eisenstein on Disney*. Methuen, London.
Foucault, M. (2007) *Security, Population, Territory: Lectures at the Collège de France 1977–78*. Palgrave Macmillan, New York.
Heinlein, R. (1959) *Starship Troopers*. Putnam, New York.
Itô G. (2005) *Tezuka izu deddo: hirakareta hyôgenron e*. NTT shuppan, Tokyo.
Ivy, M. (1995) *Discourses of the Vanishing: Modernity, Phantasm, Japan*. University of Chicago Press, Chicago.
Iwerks, L. (Dir.) (2007) *The Pixar Story*. Leslie Iwerks Productions.
Lamarre, T. (2009a) *The Anime Machine: A Media Theory of Animation*. University of Minnesota Press, Minneapolis.
——(2009b) Speciesism Part 1: Translating Races into Animals in Wartime Animation, *Mechademia 3: Limits of the Human*. 75–95.
Miyamoto H. (2003) Manga ni oite kyarakutaa ga 'tatsu' to wa dô iu koto ka, *Nihon jidô bungaku* (March–April), 47–48.
Murata, Y. (Dir.) (1993a) *Norakuro nitôhei*. In *Shôwa manga eiga daikôshin* [videorecording] 5 vols. Victor Entertainment, Tokyo, vol. 1, title 1.
——. (Dir.) (1993b) *Norakuro gôchô*. In *Shôwa manga eiga daikôshin* [videorecording] 5 vols. Victor Entertainment, Tokyo, vol. 2, title 1.
Norakuro shôjô. In *Shôwa manga eiga daikôshin* [videorecording] 5 vols. Victor Entertainment, Tokyo, vol. 2, title 2.

Nippon ichi Momotarô. In *Shôwa manga eiga daikôshin* [videorecording] 5 vols. Victor Entertainment, Tokyo, vol. 3, title 3.

Ôtsuka, E. (2008) Disarming Atom: Tezuka Osamu's Manga at War and Peace, *Mechademia 3: The Limits of the Human*, 111–26.

Sakai, N. (1997) *Translation and Subjectivity: On 'Japan' and Cultural Nationalism*, University of Minnesota Press, Minneapolis.

——. (2000) Subject and Substratum: On Japanese Imperial Nationalism. *Cultural Studies*, 14 (3/4), 432–530.

Seo, M. (Dir.) (1945) *Momotaro: Umi no shinpei* Shôchiku hoomu bideo, Tokyo.

——. (Dir.) (2004a) *Norakuro nitôhei in Nihon aato animeeshon eiga senshû* [DVD] 12 vols. Kinokuniya Company, Tokyo, vol. 3, title 3.

——. (Dir.) (2004b) *Norakuro ittôhei in Nihon aato animeeshon eiga senshû* [DVD] 12 vols. Kinokuniya Company, Tokyo, vol. 3, title 4.

Sora no Momotarô. In *Shôwa manga eiga daikôshin* [videorecording] 5 vols. Victor Entertainment, Tokyo, vol. 1, title 3.

Tatsumi, T. (2006). Introduction. In *Full Metal Apache: Transactions between Cyberpunk Japan and Avant-Pop America* Duke University Press, Durham.

Thomas, F. and Johnson, O. (1981) *The Illusion of Life: Disney Animation*. Abbeville Press, New York.

Yanagita, K. (1951) *Momotarô no tanjô*. Kadokawa bunko 19. Kadokawa shoten, Tokyo.

Notes

1 This chapter constitutes a bridge between a recently published essay (Lamarre 2009b) and forthcoming essays on animals in Japanese manga and animation, forthcoming in *Mechademia* 5 and 6. My thanks to Rich Calichman for providing this opportunity to spell out the theoretical basis for this project through a dialogue with Naoki Sakai's work.

2 For Pixar's indebtedness to such techniques, see Leslie Iwerks's documentary *The Pixar Story* (2007).

3 Itô's project entails a distinction between *kyarakutaa* and *kyara* as a new paradigm for the analysis of manga expression. The term *kyarakutaa*, which derives from the Japanese pronunciation for the English word character, can be used to refer to characters in manga and anime, yet the abbreviated pronunciation *kyara* or "chara" has come into common use in talking about character more broadly, including character figurines and model kits (garage kits) for anime, manga and game characters. For Itô, *kyarakutaa* is the limited term, while *kyara* implies something that is not only larger but also ontologically prior to *kyarakutaa*.

4 See Chapter 2 of Thomas Lamarre (2009a) for a fuller account of the animation stand, and chapters six and fifteen for an account of full and limited animation.

5 See Lamarre 2009b: 80–83 for further discussion of these two points.

6 Akiyama Masami (1998) makes this point in a presentation and commentary on the manga of Norakuro's dog regiment versus the pigs.

7 Note that, in Japanese, dogs and monkeys are considered natural enemies, and instead of "like cat and dog," in Japanese one says "like dog and monkey."

5 Translating the image

Helen Petrovsky

I met Naoki Sakai in 2002 at Cornell, at a seminar on visual culture. He was then member of a group of scholars discussing the object of a new discipline as well as the possibility of introducing it in the academic curriculum. A year and a half later I had the privilege of attending another ongoing seminar at the same University sponsored by the Society for the Humanities, its topic this time being translation. Again Professor Sakai was closely involved in its work. I have learned much from those extensive and animated discussions and, to my delight, have discovered things that, I dare say, point to a certain commonality, to what we seem to share. This is all the more exciting as we come from different cultural and academic backgrounds and as Professor Sakai's experience, both professional and personal, is absolutely unique. What distinguishes him, however, is an inherent loyalty to the Other – be it another language, discourse or a different form of experience. Naoki Sakai is always willing to translate – and is engaged in this complicated activity. It is from him that we learn what translation implies – not as a technical or semiotic procedure, but as the very condition for retaining the trace of the Other. Professor Sakai's seminal theory of translation is helpful in understanding non-linguistic phenomena, including the image. In the notes that follow I will try to combine the two themes that have initially brought us together, namely, visuality and translation, while sketching out a way of reading present-day visual data. I would like to offer these thoughts to Naoki Sakai.

1.

In trying to approach the problematic of images today one should take into account the impact of a changed reality. The transformations themselves can be defined in very broad terms: politically they are often alluded to as "globalization," while theoretically they are accompanied with the denial of any access to reality whatever – a seemingly rival idea. In both cases, however, what is at issue is indeed a changed world as well as the changed conditions of its perception and representation. The humanities respond to the pressure coming from the outside world by introducing new disciplines, such as visual studies or media theory which is increasingly popular these days.

Let us begin with the simplest thing possible, that is, with the pair "image – visuality." In this scheme the image appears as a unit of the visual – in other words, the visual is posited by means of an image – in and through it. Indeed, how can we conceive of the visual without establishing its basic support, without singling out its elementary unit? In this perspective the image will be no less saturated and spectacular than visuality itself. It will appear as a kind of sedimentation or a minimal, distinct element of that which lends itself to the eye.

However, I would like to embark on a different path by opposing the image to the visual. If we accept that the visual has to do with the external traits of the reality in question (does one have to be reminded of the so-called pre-valence of images, the "society of the spectacle," etc.?), then the image, this object of the newest disciplines, will call for a consistent conceptual elabora-tion. Our task here is to sketch out ways of approaching the image under the conditions of total "visualization."

I shall begin by stating that the image is on the side of the invisible. This has nothing to do with any mystical properties or the assumption that beyond visibility there is either an underlying depth or a gap. The invisible is the condition for the circulation of images: it stands for their essential commu-nicability. Invisibility is where the "visual" is generated in all the mediatized collectives known to us. It is that sort of relationality – and likewise relatedness – which ensures the initial interconnection of all image flows. In the language of media theory this can be presented as "distribution channels" which affect the very content of the information that is transmitted through them. In the lan-guage of philosophy it can be understood as a passage or transition whereby corporeal contact between the human being and the world is achieved. It is in this transitory zone that the world and open singularities touch upon each other, and it is here that sense and image are born.

Let us linger on the invisible. It is not just an abstract scheme of some initial connectedness or communication posited as a condition of representa-tion – a communication, let it be noted, which *renders apparent*, develops (as in the photograph), allowing for an image to find itself on the hither side of visibility. Two things should be mentioned here. The invisible has to do with materiality, being part and parcel of it. Different analyses of the photograph, for example, have testified to the duality of representation itself: the photo-graph is implicated, in a complex manner, in its own material support. It is both thing and representation proper. Moreover, it is a kind of representation that keeps pushing the viewer out and carrying him/her away: be it the need to supply an image with an interpretation – only not an arbitrary one, but one that is dictated by the ripeness of the historical moment, that is, by its "recognizability" (W. Benjamin) (Cadava 1997: 64), or the exploration of the limits of both subjectivity and the modes of representation proper to it (R. Barthes, J. Derrida). Embedded in "matter," the photograph seems to exist only by way of extension: as "technical image" it loses its independent value related to a thing or an object (Flusser 2000: 14ff.; 51–52); as a special kind of representation it establishes "a new space-time category" (Barthes 1980: 278) when the past resides in the present, being its effect. Thus, whatever the interpretations offered, it is important to understand that representation is material; however, materiality has a special relationship to "ideality", which depends on the former.

My second observation concerns the fact that the invisible is located in the horizon of history (something that can already be inferred from Walter Benjamin's reflections). I would like to unite the idea of an invisible image with that of the subject of history – historical action included – which is presently being revised. Without going into details, I will point to the duality of the notion of multitude, which is known to us first of all through the writings of A. Negri and M. Hardt. What is it – a truly acting subject, initi-ally multiple, with no steady contours, or a kind of potentiality which awaits its actualization? Or – another possibility – is it not a *subject in transition*, one that is denied the possibility of presenting itself in fixed or definitive forms by social reality proper? (Suffice it to think of the numerous migrants and settlers in both the traditional and metaphorical sense.) To summarize my second thesis is as follows: the image also touches upon the "invisible" in social experience, i.e., it addresses not so much what remains hidden or concealed as what is untranslatable into the language of social identifications. In another place I have spoken of this in terms of anonymity, implying the essential incompleteness of all manifestations of the social (Petrovsky 2009: 1–9).[1] It will not be difficult to conclude that in both cases – of the image and the subject socially defined – the *limits of representation* are examined.

Thus, materiality and anonymity. Let us remember these as the two aspects which have to do with the invisible. This summation should free the invisible from its slightly outdated tint (at least from the point of view of terminology). The invisible is not a constant – its modifications are measured by the fact that it is inscribed in the historical horizon. (On the other hand, one can say that a renewed interest in the invisible is similarly a sign of a certain historical turn.)

Let us now dwell on the image and its properties. The image can be understood as dreamlike (pertaining to dreams), parasitic or rhizomatic, as image-*punctum* or singular image. A brief explanation of these terms is required. Initially multiple, images that appear in dreams while a person is asleep are connected in ways which are different from logical or perceptual ties. The logic at work here is best conveyed by the copulative "and." This means that images, without ever forming a finished whole, keep ramifying and spreading out in all directions with equal necessity and probability. In describing such images in his "Interpretation of Dreams", Freud resorts to the metaphor of the mycelium (Freud 1953: 525) (which, in the old Russian translations, is replaced with "netlike interlacement"). Emerging, but never advancing into the foreground, images vibrate; it is that ground, to use Jean-Luc Nancy's word, which entirely constitutes a surface (in a dream) (Nancy 8). Images are superficial. Dream images do not end up being either identity or representation, which means that they do not derive from a subject and are not in the least under its control. What is rather implied is the border or limit of subjectivity as such – in other words, the test to which it is put.

In Freud we come across the notion of the so-called hypnagogic image. Such hallucinations are immediately prior to dream images and persist for a while upon awakening. Firstly, they emerge in a state of psychic passivity which, just like sleep, is marked by an absent state of mind – or, we might add, an "empty" consciousness. Secondly, they are simply diagrams or outlines of the figures which appear in dreams themselves.[2] Such, in general, is the work of the dream-imagination: it does not create complete figures but instead sketches out the free contours of objects. It should be emphasized that images are relational, only they are related after the model of an epidemic. An image is the direct effect of "unpredictable, erratic and parasitic growth" (Nancy). Such an image indeed becomes "disembodied" (to recall the key word of visual studies). It points to the essential retreat of the subject, which, however, might be understood in different terms: it is here that the encounter between the world and singularities occurs.

This takes us directly to image-singularity. We are well aware of Roland Barthes' definition of singularity: it is the image-*punctum* or image-affect (Barthes 1981: 26–27).[3] Despite the rich interpretations of this notion, one has to admit that the image-*punctum* is a solitary entity which is posited at the brink of individuality. Singularity, however, might be seen in a broader light. I would suggest that today the image-*punctum* is a form of multiplicity and that the diagram it traces is that of images and communities, of images *as* communities. Such communities are no less parasitic, which is not to say that they are secondary or that they depend, directly and reprehensibly, on others. Emerging in the same spontaneous fashion, they keep condensing and dissolving and are beyond every stable social definition. In his late reflections Jean Baudrillard highlighted molecular or "rogue" events – precisely the events of the kind that can shake the symbolic closure of the system (Baudrillard 2006: 13). These events come from the outskirts – they are contagious and *infect* with themselves. They are event-viruses, if you will. Eventuality thus described directly bears on the image: the image is its invisible accomplice.

Prompted by this purely linguistic tip, then, let us continue discussing the image in terms of communicability. Communicability, however, has very little to do with communication in its semiotic understanding, for communicability here is obviously non-linguistic and does not imply transparency in the transmission of a message. (Nor does it necessarily imply the two basic poles within which such messages are bound to circulate; I am speaking of the pair formed by the addressee and the addressor.) If we speak of communicability in terms of communication, then its model will hinge on translation. This is a translation whose ambiguity is perhaps best reflected in the position of the translator: he or she always speaks in another person's name, being not so much a mediator as an instance which constitutes discourse in the form of something "natural" and continuous. The "empty" place of the translator is the condition for the emergence of communication and meaning (it should be noted that the translator is often referred to in terms of a "fractured I"). "Translation," concludes its leading theorist Naoki Sakai, "is a *poietic* social practice that institutes a relation at the site of incommensurability" (Sakai 2005: 15). However, translation is always a displacement. It is that shift whereby every single original exists, be it the relation to an other in the original itself or to the living language whose differences and tensions it happens to assimilate.

Thus, the communication of images takes the form of translation. This is how their multiplicity "sprouts," how it is engendered and "transmitted." And this is how their complex interrelation is accomplished – bypassing communication in its traditional guise.

In the same way as we are forced to redefine the notion of communication when approaching it anew, the concept of memory, from the perspective of images, becomes necessarily reversed. If we choose to speak of the latter concerning images in the sense outlined above, we have to give up the interpretation of memory as a social institution (although this interpretation, I must admit, is quite sophisticated, especially if it is based on the type of analysis elaborated by Michel Foucault). The memory of images is nothing but their very movement which gives rise to a perceiving collective. Such memory belongs neither to individuals nor special institutions. Yet it is material – a chain of images, which allows for figures to appear. Generally speaking, figures and figuration are precisely "the visual," as we have come to understand it. All the figures known to us are in one way or another linked to the act of cognition. Therefore, they are associated with the cognizing subject and the work of representation. The image, as I previously suggested, belongs to a different domain. It articulates one single thing: it is the world entering into communication, and it is memory that is restored to us.

So "we" herein is a special kind of entity. Instead of consuming images and depending on them, "we" are involved in a relationship of co-becoming. Properly speaking, this is the space of "our" freedom. Lack of freedom, on the contrary, is on the side of figuration; it is the space where the individual, society, the mass, and undoubtedly, signs have appeared and developed (in the chemical sense of the word), including so many visible – visual – signs. But in this nondescript molecular dredge, which is the object of our study, there exist relations without relations – this should be understood as an initial opening onto the others, as the *possibility* of all forms of unification to come.

The relationship between the image and the visual may be schematically presented as follows: ordinary visual images or, to be more exact, representations, are supported by the flow of invisible images which are essentially material. The task of the scholar of the visual, as I understand it, is nothing other than to uncover, under the veil of "hypervisuality," such implicit connections and flows.

Finally, I would like to touch on the question of whether images thus approached may be historically grounded. One might think that the invisible has existed for ages: from the "emptiness" of Byzantine icons, which is filled in only due to incarnation – the grandiose economy of God's presence in the profane and the historical, through the category of the sublime, which takes one out to the limit of representation as such, to the almost banal post-industrial "simulacra," those copies of copies deprived of any original what-ever. One might also be led to think that a certain analytic apparatus, privileged in our own time, is attuned to disclosing the invisible. However, if we assume that the understanding of the image is an abstraction embedded in the present time and dependent on the visual practices of our entirely media-tized world, then its application – its scope – stops being both timeless and dubiously universal.

Let us say a few words about the time in question. If an image is seen as inscribed in the plane of the historical, what is implied then is most likely a trace. This could be accounted for by the fact that, unlike representation, the image does not reduce to a set of visual signs. I will take the liberty of saying that the image is *the other* of representation. The image is the condition for its appearance under certain circumstances. By "appearance" I understand a twofold procedure: on the one hand, the image allows for the figure to take shape, while on the other, the figure itself appears only when a certain com-munity comes to recognize itself in it. The figure here is endowed with a changeable contour: it keeps oscillating between the visible and the invisible. Likewise, "community" is not a collective that is institutionally understood. One may speak of recognition, of the event of recognition, which renders something apparent (visible), but does so only in a partial way. This would stand for the pre-semantic recognition of a community that might fail to be a full-fledged historical subject. Or, more precisely, what is recognized is a community that has not yet been objectified into the social forms known to us and that ostensibly avoids them – either on account of its short-term existence or because of the fuzziness of its external bounds. It may be characterized only by some shared "structures of feeling" (Williams 1977: 128ff.), which do not "complete" it into a finished whole, a procedure required by the tra-ditional analysis of social forms. Recognition, therefore, resembles a flash: in its light a community, leaving its faint imprint, comes into view for the very first time.

I have mentioned earlier that images are initially multiple. And now let me expand on this by adding that they are *a priori* social. They are social in the sense that they postulate the connectedness of those whom they make appar-ent. If it is at all possible to speak of the subject of the image, each time it is a community: perceiving collectives, dreaming collectives, those that are implied by images and are implicated in them. It is a sort of connectedness that escapes analysis; yet such connectedness is quite fundamental (but without resting upon a foundation, as Nancy would have said). Without this con-nectedness one cannot conceive of life in the postindustrial society, of the power of the "society of the spectacle" or, even more so, of freedom from it. Moreover, it is only now that we are beginning to see things this way.

If I were to describe the task for the discipline of visual studies, I would confine myself to the following brief formulation: it is necessary to study image – history – affect in their openness to what we, not unjustifiably, consider our own time. It may well be that it is precisely this constellation that makes the image – and along with it the invisible – so significant to us. Indeed, the mentioned categories are equal insofar as they do not produce a closure of meaning: the image is the other of representation and as such it does not coincide with itself, while history is the dwelling-place of the affective lives of so many collectives. There are whole generations that have been doomed to oblivion for one reason or another. How can one liberate them from the non-being that was imposed on them, from the anonymity which in our present time appears as sinister? How can one remember without remembering? It turns out that the forgotten generations themselves return this memory in the form of traces. These traces, however, resemble neither archaeological sites nor the fragments of a material life which was spared by time. They are images that reach us from the past, presenting us with the memory of what we never knew. They make a present of themselves to us. There is nothing mysterious or mystical about it. The image comes into full view when preceding generations are reborn through the affective lives of communities existing in the present. Let us repeat and underscore: the image is an encounter.

2.

In the last part of his trilogy depicting the fate of the three famous twentieth century rulers (Lenin, Hitler and Hirohito), the Russian filmmaker Alexander Sokurov is more than ever engaged in translation.[4] This is not to say that he is adapting his cinematic or personal perception to a culture whose language and traditions are markedly different from his own, although he does carefully collect historical data and thus gives an almost documentary account of the days immediately preceding and following the Japanese Emperor's surrender to General MacArthur at the end of World War Two. But despite the obvious and even tragic political context, the film alludes to external reality only in passing. Moreover, this reality is presented as a *hallucination*: it appears in the distorted form of Hirohito's nightmare, lingering upon his awakening from an afternoon nap. This is the only instance when the viewer is introduced to the devastating scenes of the war. This episode underscores the leitmotif of the entire filmic project: the three leaders are shown in a radically – if not offensively – private space, devoid of all their power.

Lenin, who is hardly his former self – losing his senses as well as control over his physical body – is confined to a country house and is kept there under Stalin's supervision. Hitler idles at his Bavarian retreat in the company of Eva Braun and his close associates in the summer of 1942 – nothing but a private get-together. Hirohito indulges in his daily habits, which remain strangely unaffected by his imminent demise. The pattern of political impotence seems to be recurrent. Likewise, in all the three films very little is shown of the actual historical setting. A newsreel reproduced in *Moloch*, the opening film of the trilogy, is perhaps the only definite reference to time and place (i.e., the Nazi offensive on the Eastern Front leading to the battle of Stalingrad). We can therefore conclude that Sokurov performs a series of stunning reductions: no historicity (except for the telling details) and no impact of political power. In fact, no power at all.

I will not analyze the different ways in which Sokurov depicts his impotent dictators.[5] Indeed, the emphases vary. Instead, I will return to *The Sun* in order to concentrate on its message as well as the cinematic makeup it assumes. This film is even more "private" than the preceding ones, to the point of being voyeuristic. To be more exact, such is the sensation that the viewer develops when introduced to the hidden life of a godlike figure. For what we see is concealed from us by definition – if we are still dealing with the Emperor. The tension, however, is outlined from the very beginning: not only do we anticipate Hirohito's final transformation into a mere mortal (for such is the course of actual historical events), but his pending abdication has an ironic double in the movie: in a mildly playful manner the Emperor tries to convince his terrified valets that his body is no different from their own. Yet the words he pronounces on most occasions are registered "for history." And the political decisions that he makes are prompted by the people's love of his divine descendance (" ... Because of this love, I could not stop the war," confesses Hirohito). The two other sequences that highlight the transformation in question are the one depicting Emperor's negotiations with the American victor who at first appears arrogant and governed by contempt (this attitude is counterpoised by that of the Japanese military translator – for him, even in defeat, Hirohito remains a descendant of the sun) and the concluding scene of the Emperor's reunion with his wife right after his abdication from power: he tells her, not without amusement, that from now on he is an ordinary man, while the woman is both incredulous and happy to see her husband alive.

To be sure, Sokurov does not explore the role of the Japanese Emperor in issues of war and peace. In a way Hirohito is doomed to defeat from the outset. Indeed, he is shown like one of those exotic species which fascinate him so much: even in wartime the Emperor does not give up his studies of marine biology. Scientist, poet, polyglot, husband and father – such are the aspects of his personality that are gradually revealed before the viewer's eyes. As Susan Buck-Morss shrewdly remarks, "The figure of Hirohito transcends national type *and* allegorical meaning. His humanity is overwhelmingly present" (Buck-Morss). His humanity is in stark contrast to his divinity. And it is for this reason that the viewer is led to empathetic identification with the character's human part.

Empathy is a prelude to taking sides. If we do take sides, it is with the man and not the sovereign. In Sokurov's films politics becomes radically suspended. This suspension may be read as a critique of sovereignty calling for an affective investment on the part of the subjects. Devoid of such investment, the institute transforms into an empty shell and finally collapses. Indeed, Sokurov seems to be interested in life as such, before it assumes any of the forms known to us through inherently social experience. And he does everything to break the continuity of this sort of experience. We – the viewers, the subjects – are normally denied access to a time which destabilizes the movement of grand historical narratives. In a review of *Taurus*, the film about Lenin, I have called it the "time of private life" (Petrovsky 2003: 340–44). Indeed, it is a private time within history, an elusive, impalpable substance. Now, the question is: can it at all be represented? And, if yes, then how? Sokurov seems to have found purely cinematic means of rendering what remains essentially invisible. Such empty spaces of life are not merely instances of failure, although failure would already be a way of announcing liberation – first of all from the icons of power. (In the films political failure is accompanied with physical weakness, as if the discarding of an image or the ripping of a mask caused real physical suffering.) In fact, failure here is both cinematic narrative and trace. However, it is the filmic texture itself that induces changes in the viewer's optics. In *Moloch* it is boredom as the side-effect of Hitler's increasingly disorganized and hideous behavior. In *Taurus* a greenish curtain seems to hover over the entire screen, at once establishing and removing distance. Finally, *The Sun* penetrates our memory with its meticulously filmed details as well as long close-ups that create the effect of real time.

Boredom; a shifting distance suggesting something like uncertain implication; time that goes beyond the limits are normally ascribed to it in fiction and reality alike – such are the main cinematic effects in Sokurov's trilogy, which contribute to changing the viewer's perception. One can speak of those effects in terms of atmosphere, if atmosphere implies not only a certain mood or affective state shared by the audience, but also, within the film itself, that which subverts the narrative, initiating a supplementary – i.e., vertical – reading.[6] It is very difficult to formalize and even name these effects. However, their very indeterminacy proves to be more powerful than any bluntly formulated proposition.

This is not merely to say that form is content. Rather, on both the formal *and* conceptual levels, Sokurov refrains from making a judgment. I would suggest that he is involved in the work of translation, if the latter is redefined in terms of what Naoki Sakai calls "the heterolingual address": " … the heterolingual address does not abide by the normalcy of reciprocal and transparent communication, but instead assumes that *every utterance can fail to communicate* because heterogeneity is inherent in any medium, linguistic or otherwise. Every translation calls for a countertranslation … " (italics added) (Sakai 1997: 8). If there is no Orientalism in *The Sun*, as has been noted by critics, it is because Sokurov's translational project is at odds with a purely semiotic transposition, although his accuracy in treating historical and cultural material is well established. It is neither the Japanese Emperor nor General MacArthur who are addressed as foreigners par excellence (a different time, two different cultures), but the contemporary viewer. Indeed, to translate politics – or history – is to address without any guarantee of comprehension. For the delivery to reach its destination, the addressee should act by engaging anew in translation. We are used to the representation of translation that covers up the very mechanism by which discontinuity in the social fabric is rendered continuous. But this is how *every* representation comes to replace initial difference broadly understood (Sakai 1997: 14).[7]

It is thus quite clear that only the viewer can complete the cinematic message by engaging in "counter-translation," that is, reacting to what is being shown. The viewer is both implied and implicated in the message. Unlike so many films which are essentially adaptations of an historical narrative, Sokurov's trilogy pretends neither to illustrate nor to recount historical facts. Instead, it opens up a problematic space where definitions are suspended and the moral of the story remains uncomfortably open. (Identification with the characters is next to impossible, if only because they are "tyrants," while their condemnation is not in the least Sokurov's concern.) It is for the audience to judge what it sees, but then it would first have to decide on what is actually being shown. This space of free choice regarding the visual image is what Sokurov so successfully conveys. If we are translating, meanings are multiple and frail, and there is a chance of reaching out to the Other. But if translation stops, it is immediately replaced with one-dimensional representations. Sokurov seems to be saying: representation always plays into the hands of power, even if it is not necessarily a ruler who is being portrayed.

Bibliography

Barthes, R. (1980) Rhetoric of the Image. In Trachtenberg, A. (Ed.) *Classic Essays on Photography*. New Haven, Conn., Leete's Island Books.
——. (1981) *Camera Lucida. Reflections on Photography*, New York, Hill and Wang [Farrar, Straus and Giroux].
——. (1983) The Third Meaning. In Sontag, S. (Ed.) *Barthes: Selected Writings*. New York, Fontana/Collins.
Baudrillard, J. (2006) Les exilés du dialogue. *Culture of the Differences in Eurasia: Azerbaijan – Past and Present in the Dialogue of Civilizations. 13th International Conference.* Baku, Azerbaijan, Académie de la Latinité, Rio de Janiero, Educam.
Buck-Morss, S. (2006) *Sokurov's Sovereign Trinity: The Visual Economy of Power* (Lecture). San Francisco, MoMA.
Cadava, E. (1997) *Words of Light. Theses on the Photography of History*, Princeton, N.J., Princeton University Press.
Flusser, V. (2000) *Towards a Philosophy of Photography*, London, Reaktion Books.
Freud, S. (1953) The Interpretation of Dreams. In Strachey, J., Freud, A. Strachey, A. & Tyson, A. (Eds.) *The Standard Edition of the Complete Psychological Works of Sigmund Freud*. London, The Hogarth Press and the Insitute of Psycho-Analysis.
Nancy, J.-L. L'Image: mimesis & methexis (Electronic manuscript).
Petrovsky, H. (2003) Visions of the Past: Mediated and Unmediated History. *Third Text 65*, 17, 340–44.
——. (2009) The Anonymous Community. *Diogenes 222*, 1–9.

Sakai, N. (1997) *Translation and Subjectivity. On "Japan" and Cultural Nationalism*, Minneapolis, London, University of Minnesota Press.

——. (2005) Dislocation in Translation. *Sinij Divan 7*, 15.

Williams, R. (1977) *Marxism and Literature*, New York, Oxford, Oxford University Press.

Notes

1 Also as: http://kogni.narod.ru/community.htm.
2 See: Freud. Op. cit., vol. IV, esp. chapter 1 (e), (c). However, recent English translations may be more striking with respect to terminology.
3 Unlike the *studium* – this "*average* affect" prompted by innumerable photographs – the *punctum* (literally: "sting, speck, cut, little hole") is an "element which rises from the scene, shoots out of it like an arrow, and pierces me." Only some of the photographs are punctuated with such "sensitive points."
4 *The Sun* was released in 2005 with Japanese actor Issey Ogata impressively performing the role of the Emperor.
5 For a brilliant analysis of Sokurov's trilogy in terms of sovereign power, its icons and cinematic demystification, see: (Buck-Morss 2006).
6 The idea of a vertical or disjunctive reading of images belongs to Sergei Eisenstein. For a further elaboration of his thoughts related to the "accentuation within the fragment", see: Roland Barthes' "The Third Meaning" (Barthes 1983: 317–33). It should be said that Barthes' "third meaning" is nothing other than the photographic *punctum* applied to the film still.
7 For Naoki Sakai such difference is synonymous with "incommensurability."

Part II
Economies of difference

6　For a communist ontology

William Haver

The reader may well wonder at the fact that this chapter, which is concerned with Karl Marx's concept of communism, is offered as a contribution to a volume devoted to considerations of the work of Naoki Sakai. I would respond to any such bewilderment with three observations. First, rather obviously, I would simply note that Marx has been one of the canonical thinkers of Japanese intellectual life for more than one hundred years. This means that when one is talking about Marx, one is never just talking about "Marx"; and, conversely, that sometimes one is talking most seriously about Marx precisely when one avoids all mention of "Marx." Second, this chapter argues that Marx's concept of the common – the communist common – is a concept of circulation, rather than of the division and distribution of wealth. To conceive the common to be constituted in, and as, circulation necessarily implies that "communism" is a force, rather than a political form. Third, and concomitantly, this implies (again, necessarily) a conception of the relation of particular and universal radically other than the ("modern") concept of that relation, a concept that has been one of the principal objects of Sakai's critique for thirty years or more. In this modern conception, the particular can only ever be an example of the universal; the relation of particular and universal can only ever be a synechdoche. And it is on that basis that the universal, in itself and as such, can become the object of a possible knowledge. No one has traced the political effects of such a conception more patiently than has Sakai. But there is a radically other conception of the relation of particular to universal, which in order to avoid confusion we might designate as the relation between singularities and totality. This is a relation we find articulated in Spinoza, Deleuze, Marx, Nishida, and Balibar; and it is of course a commonplace in Buddhist cosmologies. Its current nickname is multiplicity, and its political expression is "multitude." Here, the relation between singularities and totality is one of radical immanence: the relation of singularity and totality is immediate. Within this relation, totality is always that which necessarily exceeds any possibility of the totality (in itself and as such). Spinoza articulated this relation with "*sive*," Dōgen with "*soku*," which as a graduate student Sakai once translated as "disjunct simultaneity." This chapter, then, is an attempt to decipher – that is, to invent – the politics of that translation.

It is sometimes said, in frustration perhaps, that Marx has relatively little to say about communism. True, one admits, there is the *Communist Manifesto* and the study of the Paris Commune, and certainly there are famous but merely suggestive fragments in *The German Ideology*, the *Grundrisse*, and *Capital*. But there is certainly nothing like the exhaustive analyses and descriptions of capitalism that are the constant preoccupation of the bulk of Marx's work. There is nothing like a sociology, or a political science, or even an economics of communism in Marx; we have nothing but a few suggestions of an anthropology, and a merely philosophical anthropology at that. But all this does not mean that Marx does not produce the *concept* of communism. On the contrary, Marx's concept of communism, which nowhere in his work finds an exhaustive formal theoretical exposition, is a concept without which his extended critical analyses of the capitalist mode of production would make neither philosophical nor political sense; there are few explicit discussions of the communist mode of production because the *concept* of communism is everywhere in his work. In other words, the concept is the object of sense, a problem, rather than a question which would be merely the object of knowledge. The concept of communism in Marx is an acknowledgment that we can only ever have a para-epistemological sense of communism.

Marx's concept of communism is therefore, as Peter Osborne has recently observed, speculative (Osborne 2005: 66–80). The concept is experimental. That is to say, the concept of communism is essentially, *as concept*, a certain orientation to "futurity" as a future that would be something essentially other than an extension of the present, but also an essential difference that is nowhere else than in the present. Communism in this concept is something other than a mere *telos*, the object of an infinitely deferred aspiration: the revolution is either here, now, or it is nothing. Which is to say, the concept of communism in Marx is a political concept. The social content of the communist mode of production is the object of political negotiation and struggle, which in fact *constitutes* communism as such. To the extent that the content of the communist mode of production is given by – or might be deduced from – its concept, the concept is neither philosophical nor political, neither theoretical nor practical. The concept of communism is thus essentially speculative, essentially experimental. As such, and *only* as such, is it a *provocation*. The speculative, experimental concept of communism in Marx, an orientation toward the essentially strange futurity that is nowhere but in the present, provokes and articulates a *sense* of the common and of communism as *also* something other than the mere negation of the capitalist mode of production. Politically, on the ground, this provocation is necessarily negative with respect to capital, to be sure; but it is also the case that communism is not merely the absence of capitalism.

The theme of my contribution is "communist ontology." I might as well have written "communist mode of production." I do not mean that a mode of production – in this case, communist – looks like ontology, or conversely that ontology – again in this case, communist – resembles a mode of production, or even that the status of a given mode of production is "ontological." I mean that, in Marx, the mode of production *is* ontology. There is nothing outside a mode of production (although of course there can be concurrent, contradictory modes of production). The concept of a mode of production specifies the technological essence of the human species, the different ways in which we appropriate nature; what Marx called the metabolism (*Stoffwechsel*) that is the human relation to something called "nature" is essentially and at all points mediated by our tools, including human bodies (our own and others). The tool is therefore not merely a means to an end, not merely instrumental in the ordinary sense of the term, but is prosthetic; this prosthesis is in fact *what we are.* There is no human being (or subject) outside of this prosthesis that is our metabolic relation with nature. Our species is nothing apart from our prosthetic technologies (including, again, our bodies) (Marx 1976: 285).[1] We have always already been cyborgs. In other, slightly more theoretical terms, there is no outside of mediation: we are not mediated *by* our relation to the tool, we *are* that mediation. But if the concept of a mode of production says there is no "outside" of mediation, then nothing transcends a mode of production. No more intimidating majescules, for being or for history. For Marx, the dialectic is first of all this non-transcendence which is always articulated as non-neutrality, the constitutive antagonism of class struggle. The Marxist dialectic is thus a thought of immanence, not as the immanence of essence in existence, but as the identity of essence and existence. A communist ontology cannot be conceived therefore, apart from this immanence.

Nor, therefore, can one posit that individual human beings either exist before or survive the social relation that determines their individuation. The relation, Marx repeatedly insists, determines the relata. Indeed, it would make no sense to appeal to the dialectic, any dialectic, if it were not to claim the priority of relation over relata. The Marxist dialectic is precisely an insistence upon the absolute priority of relation as differential articulation. Modes of production – ontologies – are therefore nothing other than the differential articulations that *are* the constitutive technological relation. The communist mode of production, then, is an other metabolism, an other mode of appropriation and production, an other technology.

Appropriation and production can never be confused with creation *ex nihilo.* Whatever counts for us as the world, whatever constitutes our mode of production, our ontology, is always already worked on. Appropriation and production always find their condition of possibility, their presuppositions, in what has been made; it is always a question of a movement from the made to the making, a movement Marx nicknamed "negation." The essential strangeness of futurity, the strangeness of the future in the present, cannot therefore be confused with a fanciful utopia; the strangeness of futurity lies not in its openness to anything at all (*liberté, egalité*, whoopee, as a famous cartoon once had it), but in its unpredictability, in its negotiability, its politics. In other words, what is "given" as what has been made constitutes condition or presupposition, the fact of being situated. It is in this sense that the capitalist mode of production is the condition for the communist mode of production. Marx's determinism, so-called, refers only to condition and situation, rather than to any guarantee. It is only because capitalism is our condition, the situation in which we find ourselves, that there is the possibility of communism (and its concept), rather than because there is some metahistorical necessity that decrees capitalism to be the prerequisite for communism. But it also means that it is within the capitalist mode of production that the conditions for the strangeness of the communist future must be sought.

These, then, are the three presuppositions for any concept of communism or communist ontology. First, there is no outside of mediation, no transcendence, no being outside of the technological metabolism – appropriation and production – that constitutes human being in its entirety: in a word, immanence. Second, the absolute priority of relation as differential articulation. Third, for us, here, now, capitalism is the condition for communism. If communism is *post*-capitalist, it is so because it is for us necessarily post-*capitalist*: no nostalgia, no utopias. With these presuppositions in mind, I want to approach Marx's concept of communist ontology, in a necessarily schematic and sketchy way, with a brief preliminary look at his consideration of precapitalist ontologies (economic formations, modes of production) in order to try to grasp something of what is at stake in a *sense* of the common. Then I want to take up Marx's consideration of the vicissitudes of the sense of the common within the capitalist mode of production. Finally, and this last point is the point of the exercise of course: I want to think about what, within capitalism, constitutes the common as problem; I want to think about what is essential to the capitalist mode of production but nevertheless belongs to the dissolution or "supersession" of capitalism.

One undoubtedly recalls that Marx's discussion of pre-capitalist economic formations in the *Grundrisse* serves most generally as a foil to bring the specificity of the capitalist mode of production into relief (Marx 1973: 471–514).[2] He is concerned in particular with the status of the so-called free worker ("free," that is, of every relation of dependency that would constrain the appropriation of the worker's labor power, and "free" of any access, other than the exchange of her labor power for a wage, to the commodities necessary to sustain life) (*G*, 471, 503). On Marx's account, it is one of the abiding myths of bourgeois political economy that worker and capitalist encounter each other as free, independent agents in the marketplace, and that therefore the constitutive relation between them – the arrangement that makes the capitalist in fact a "capitalist," and the worker in fact a "worker" – is contractual: a strange freedom, of course, founded in the worker's necessity. How this came to be so will receive its elaboration in the chapter on "So-Called Primitive Accumulation" in volume 1 of *Capital* (*C*, 871–940). What is important for us here is that, insofar as every economic formation is essentially and originally a social, political relation, all pre-capitalist economic formations are relations of dependency, relations that are prior to, and in fact constitute as such, the beings who articulate that relation. The slave is an effect of slavery, the serf of serfdom, the artisan of her craft.

It is first of all a question of a relation to the land, and of its uses and the ways in which it is appropriated by the community. Marx had obviously been reading Deleuze and Guattari when he remarked parenthetically that the nomad's relation to the land is a relation to the land's "elemental limit-lessness": "They relate to it as their property, although they never stabilize this property" (*G*, 491); the land is subject to a constant and simultaneous deterritorialization and reterritorialization (Deleuze and Guattari 1987: 351–423; 26–38). It is the herd rather than the land that is the object of appropriation; the land is the "in common" as such, an inexhaustible resource. In the Asiatic mode of production, land becomes a stabilized terri-tory – property – which is nevertheless the property of the entire community, and only of the community in its *Gemeinschaftlichkeit*, the community as such. The relation of the individual to the community is the strongest form of dependence, identity. The Asiatic peasant, as is also the case with the slave and the serf, belongs to the land; the land does not belong to peasant, serf, or slave. It is that relation of identity designated in the term autochthony; in the Asiatic mode of production, it is the community itself that is autochthonous. Marx had obviously been reading Rancière on *partage* in his considerations of the ancient (Roman) and Germanic (feudal) modes of production, for here it is a question of the division and distribution of the common (Rancière 1999). The Roman citizen is entitled to the appropriation and use of land only insofar as he is in fact a Roman citizen; it is his belonging to the com-munity of citizens that entitles him to a share of the land. Furthermore, it is precisely because land is subject to distribution at all that the distinction between public (land) and "private" land appears. Still, the common is prior because the citizen is entitled to a share in the distribution of land only because he is *of* the community; the "private," so-called, is thus only an articulation of the common. To that extent, even the richest of Roman citizens is absolutely dependent upon the community. In Germanic feudalism, however, the prior-ity is apparently reversed. It is the individual holding (comprised of extended family, retainers, and serfs) that is essential, and the coming-together, the *Vereinigung* or *Zusammenkommen*, that constitutes the common. The relation to the land is double. On the one hand, land subject to agricultural appro-priation is held individually; but land for hunting, grazing, and timber belongs to the common, and in large part constitutes the common as such. Here, the common is a matter of association, rather than "Asiatic" or "ancient" community. What bears emphasis is that, in all pre-capitalist eco-nomic formations, land as such is, first, *inalienable* (and it is by virtue of this inalienability that the relation to the land, in the Asiatic, ancient, and Ger-manic modes of production alike, defines "property" as dependency); second, land as such is *inexhaustible*. These two attributes of pre-capitalist land we will retain for a concept of communism. The common is what is as such inalienable: it belongs to no one (that is, cannot be subject to division and distribution) *because* it belongs to everyone. It is *res nullium* because it is *res omnium*.[3] And the common, for Marx, is in principle and in fact, inexhaustible: scarcity is only ever a category of bourgeois political science. In the course of one of his more spirited critiques of Malthus, for example, Marx argues that what is at stake in the question of over-population is not, as Malthus thinks, a natural scarcity; the scarcity that Malthus observes is in fact an effect of a given mode of production; the concept of an ahistorical ("natural") scarcity reduces a sense of the common to the administrative concept of distribution, and a sense of the economy to the banality of a mere budget (*G*, 604–8).

The pre-capitalist sense of "property," Marx claims, is logically (and etymologically, for all that) *original*:

> *Property* thus originally means no more than a human being's relation to his natural conditions of production as belonging to him as his, as *presupposed* along with *his own being*; relations to them as *natural presuppositions* of his self, which only form, so to speak, his extended body.
> (*G*, 491)

> *Property* therefore means *belonging to a clan* (community) having subjective-objective existence in it; and, by means of the relation of this community to the land and soil, [relating] to the earth as the individual's inorganic body; his relation to land and soil, to the external primary condition of production – since the earth is raw material, instrument and fruit all in one – as to a presupposition belonging to his individuality, as modes of his presence.
> (*G*, 492)

It is not only land that constitutes the substance of property, but the artisan's tools as well; what, among much else, will distinguish the worker under capitalism from the artisan (or, indeed, industrial capitalism from manufacture) is that the *craft* of the artisan resides in the fact that the tool is an inorganic extension of the artisan's being, and thereby belongs to the determination of that being. The artisan's relation to the tool is a singer's relation to "the voice," the absolutely impersonal determination of the singer's power-to-be (*potentia*). But in the capitalist mode of production, the relation of the worker to the tool is nothing more than a means to an end, merely accidental, merely instrumental. (Strictly speaking, this is true only in manufacture; a new, entirely other, relation of dependence arises with the machine: see *C*, 492–639). In any case, what is decisive as a presupposition of the capitalist mode of production is that the worker be freed from this social, technological, double relation to land and tool (*G*, 497). In pre-capitalist modes of production, then, what counts as "wealth" is either a concentration of use-values destined for more or less immediate consumption – land, livestock, for example – or it is merely barbarian bling, and thus must be strictly limited in one way or another *on behalf of the common*. Marx's immediate point is that the primitive accumulation that provides venture capital is not derived from land and its various implications in dependencies and the constitution of "property," but from usury and mercantile profits – from circulation, that is to say (*G*, 504–5).[4] I will return to this question of circulation.

Immediately following the section of the *Grundrisse* explicitly devoted to pre-capitalist modes of production, Marx turns to considerations of subjectification, the fact that the bourgeois capitalist revolution creates new subjects constituted in relations entirely other than pre-capitalist dependencies, and of the distinction he would later call that between formal and real subsumption. As defined in the text from the early 1860s entitled "Results of the Immediate Process of Production" (*C*, 948–1084), and in the chapter of *Capital* on "Absolute and Relative Surplus Value," formal subsumption consists simply of the formal inclusion of traditional modes of production (artisanal handicrafts, for example) within the capitalist enterprise. It is a transitional mode insofar as the worker's traditional relation to the objective conditions of labor – most conspicuously, the tool – appears to remain unchanged, yet that relation is now put in the service of the expropriation of labor power in order to produce absolute surplus value. In real subsumption, however,

> [t]he specifically capitalist mode of production ceases in general to be a mere means of producing relative surplus-value as soon as it has conquered an entire branch of production; this tendency is still more powerful when it has conquered all the important branches of production. It then becomes the universal, socially predominant form of the production process. It only continues to act as a special method of producing relative surplus-value in two respects: first, in so far as it seizes upon industries previously only formally subordinate to capital, that is, in so far as it continues to proselytize, and second, in so far as the industries already taken over continue to be revolutionized by changes in the methods of production.
>
> (*C*, 646; see also 1019–38)

Formal subsumption most often relies upon force or the threat of force to secure the cooperation of the workers; in real subsumption, the fact of subjectification means that the logic of capital has become the logic of all socio-economic relations, the sole possibility for relation altogether. In real subsumption, capitalism becomes ontology, outside of which there is nothing; capitalism has become in fact a mode of production.

Real subsumption achieves a kind of apotheosis, but also reaches its limit, in those few pages of the *Grundrisse* devoted to a speculative consideration of the capitalist road (*G*, 524–33). Marx's question in this fragment is deceptively straightforward: can road-building, or public works in general, become a capitalist enterprise, that is, can it be made to produce surplus-value? Marx's answer is a qualified affirmative; I will return to these qualifications momentarily. But to the extent that it is successful, it marks the triumph of capitalist ontology in, and as, real subsumption: "The separation of *public works* from the state, and their migration into the domain of the works undertaken by capital itself, indicates the degree to which the real community has constituted itself in the form of capital" (*G*, 531). All undertakings that have traditionally been public, work in common whether carried out under the aegis of the state or not, become capitalist ventures. This is real subsumption with a vengeance. The point hardly needs emphasis, perhaps, at a time – now, just for example – when all public institutions, all work-in-common, is becoming the work of the capitalist corporation, when the state itself and as such has become a capitalist enterprise. What does bear emphasis is a rather obvious logical conclusion: capitalism is in fact the annihilation of the common altogether, not merely of pre-capitalist communities constituted in relations of dependence, *Gemeinschaft*, but of the very possibility of association, *Gesellschaft*, altogether. Capital dreams of the identity of "public" and "private" by turning the common as such into a capitalist enterprise; the common would thus be no longer the limit of capitalist ambition, but merely one of its commodities. And few commodities sell quite as well as nostalgia for community.

But the closer capitalism comes to the realization of its dream of ontological totalitarianism, the more nearly it approaches its dissolution, its contradiction:

> There appears here the universalizing tendency of capital, which distinguishes it from all previous stages of production. Although limited by its very nature, it strives toward the universal development of the forces of production, and thus becomes the presupposition of a new mode of production, which is founded not on the development of the forces of production for the purpose of reproducing or at most expanding a given condition, but where the free, unobstructed, progressive and universal development of the forces of production is itself the presupposition of society and hence of its reproduction; where advance beyond the point of departure is the only presupposition. This tendency – which capital possesses, but which at the same time, since capital is a limited form of production, contradicts it and hence drives it towards dissolution – distinguishes capital from all earlier modes of production, and at the same time contains this element, that capital is posited as a mere point of transition. All previous forms of society – or, what is the same, of the forces of social production – foundered on the development of wealth. Those thinkers of antiquity who were possessed of consciousness therefore directly denounced wealth as the dissolution of the community.
> (*G*, 540)

It is a question of circulation and of wealth. Marx, of course, devotes extraordinary attention to questions of circulation, particularly in volume 2 of

Capital; here a very reductive, perhaps simplistic differentiation between the circulation of money and the circulation of capital will have to suffice (Marx 1978). The circulation of money is a presupposition of the capitalist mode of production, both historically (the original accumulation of capital is a transformation of the profits of usury and mercantile trade), and logically (because the circulation of money is in fact the abstract possibility of exchange beyond the immediate use-values exchanged in barter). But, Marx emphasizes, capital is not an effect of the circulation of money, or of exchange, because mere circulation can never, of itself, produce surplus-value. Indeed, capital is always both inside and outside circulation. Let us briefly first consider something Marx tells us about the circulation of money in the "Chapter on Money" in the *Grundrisse*:

> The circulation of money, like that of commodities, begins at an infinity of different points, and to an infinity of different points it returns. Departures from a single centre to the different points on the periphery and the return from all points of the periphery to a single centre do not take place in the circulatory process at the stage here being examined, i.e. its *direct* stage; they belong, rather, in a circulatory system *mediated* by a banking system. ... This much is clear from the outset: if money is a vehicle of circulation for the commodity, then the commodity is likewise a vehicle for the circulation of money. If money circulates commodities, then commodities circulate money. The circulation of commodities and the circulation of money thus determine one another.
>
> (*G*, 186; see also 195)

To belabor the obvious, perhaps, let me stress that the circulation of money and commodities (and money – gold and silver – is always itself a commodity for Marx) is an originally and essentially decentered system; multiplicity is its principle. In other words, there is no narrative of circulation, only a vast congeries of asymmetrical exchanges in a statistical system characterized by an essential disequilibrium. What matter in Marx's analyses of the circulation of money and commodities are the always uneven velocities of circulation and the fact that one can think of circulation as a system only in statistical averaging. In this respect, Marx clearly belongs in the genealogy of what the twentieth century came to know as chaos theory. Although the circulation of money and commodities is constantly interrupted by consumption, circulation as a decentered system is characterized by perpetual exchange: the system, as system, is perpetual flux. Now, because the system is decentered – originally multiple – and its principle is disequilibrium, the circulation of money and commodities is spatio-temporal. Indeed, Marx tells us that money is objectified circulation time. "Money is itself a product of circulation" (*G*, 659). It is not merely that circulation occurs within the putatively *a priori* coordinates of time and space; it is more radically the case that circulation *as such* (and not merely of money and commodities) determines the fact *that there is* time and space. Circulation, which is after all essentially nothing other than socio-political relationality, determines the existence of beings *as* "extension," as material resistance, separation, and articulation (recall that "extension" is precisely what "property" meant in pre-capitalist modes of production). Circulation is the material resistance that constitutes non-identity, an original separation of the mythical One from itself. For Marx, temporality and materiality are the same thing.

Furthermore, insofar as money is in circulation (and Marx has defined "money" as the *possibility* of circulation; money is not really money at all outside of the circulation of which it is the abstract possibility), money belongs to no one: *res nullium, res omnium*. Were money *as such* to become "private property," that is, once money is withdrawn from circulation in hoarding or *as capital*, it is in effect and in fact no longer "money." Whether as hoard or as capital, money withdrawn from circulation is alienated. Money in circulation is therefore a limit of capital. The logical figure for circulation is therefore not *partage*, the division, distribution, and consequent accumulation of wealth, of which private property is the capitalist apotheosis, but the essential disequilibrium of incessant theft, as the free appropriation of the common. Theft, after all, simply puts back into circulation what had been withdrawn from circulation; money is, as it were, reunited with its essence in theft. Let me offer yet another figure of circulation to juxtapose to the figure of division, distribution, and accumulation that constitutes bourgeois private property: circulation as contagion. Recall the consequences for the knowledge called epidemiology of the hard lessons of that absolutely steep learning curve called the AIDS pandemic. Early in the pandemic, epidemiology could only conceive transmission of HIV according to a model of the division and distribution of the virus as a kind of private property; it could only conceive the pandemic as a kind of simple exchange on the capitalist model. Before epidemiology could speak intelligibly about the pandemic, it had to learn, first, that the origin of the pandemic was only ever the multiplicity of a decentered systematicity; and second, that the affectivity in question – sex, drugs – is not a question of the inheritance of private property, but of a general, anonymous circulation of the affects. Had epidemiologists read Spinoza on the affects and Marx on circulation in 1981, the course of response to the pandemic might have been very different. Circulation, then, is a generalized contagion, the relationality in general that is the condition for every relation, and of which the relata are merely effects. Theft, contagion, and circulation are figures of a free appropriation of the common, in principle inexhaustible and inalienable; theft, contagion, and circulation are figures of communist ontology. The circulation of money is thus not only a presupposition of capitalism, but of communism.

The circulation of capital, however, is an entirely different matter. We know the essentially Hegelian story capitalism tells itself about itself according to Marx's account in the *Grundrisse*. From the perspective of the bourgeoisie, and in the vocabulary of bourgeois political economy, the narrative describes a movement that goes something like this: the original accumulation of money (as venture capital) is the result of the merchant's moral virtue of asceticism; this money is then invested in the raw materials, tools, and so forth that constitute the means of production, as well as in labor; the finished product (commodity) is exchanged for a price determined by the cunning of market forces; the difference between price and investment constitutes the reward for asceticism (delayed gratification), a narrative ever renewed in further investment. Value is nothing but virtue's reward as actualized by the cunning of the market. Such is the edifying tale capitalism tells itself about itself.

Marx's translation of the *capitalist* narrative in the *Grundrisse* goes something like this: capital takes the place of absolute abstraction, the Absolute Spirit (and capital does so insofar as the object of capitalist desire is *absolute* wealth, not only all the bright and shiny things, but money for the sake of money, wealth *as such*), which can only be a pure abstraction of which "money" is merely the manifest sign; money is withdrawn from circulation – alienated, negated – in the objectified, "dead" labor of the means of production, and in the living labor of the worker, which produces surplus-value (absolute and relative), subsequently realized in the price of the commodity exchanged on the market; at which point, as money, wealth returns to itself, only bigger, in the infinity of its abstraction. The circulation of capital (and it is only *as* this process begins that money in fact becomes "capital") is precisely the alienation or negation of wealth in materiality, that is to say, in the *temporality* of production. Capital as such is nothing but the process of this temporo-spatial material mediation (*G*, 255, 620). Capital, then, is nothing other than a kind of eternal restlessness which nevertheless still dreams of an entropic reunion with itself in and as absolute wealth. Capital is always on the verge of this unattainable absolute wealth (as private property), but in order to achieve it (as "surplus accumulation" in David Harvey's terms) must always alienate itself yet once again in time and space (the materiality of raw materials, the means of production, labor, and commodities). Capital is nothing but that always-renewed alienation in materiality (that is, in temporality). On the brink of Nirvana, the Bodhisattva of Infinite Wealth keeps coming back for more.

But even from the perspective of capitalism, this uplifting tale of the circulation of capital is not without its vicissitudes, vicissitudes that still constitute a clear and present danger for capital altogether. I will mention two, both of which constitute internal limits to capital, necessary presuppositions of capital capable of precipitating the dissolution of capital. The first is the problem of the capitalist road. One of the principal reasons enterprises such as road building, war, education – in short, public works – are undertaken in common (most often by the state) in a capitalist society is to avoid the problem of what Marx calls "sunk capital," capital sunk in the mediations of its alienation or negation. In other words, such enterprises can produce no surplus-value within the statistically average velocity of the circulation of capital;

in fact, they appear to bring the circulation of capital to a halt in the materiality of its constitutive mediations. We know, from Marx's extended consideration of cooperation, the machine, and the production of relative
surplus-value in volume 1 of *Capital*, of course, that capital always attempts
to reduce the time of production to the zero degree of production, to instan-
taneity; capital always strives to accelerate the circulation of capital to an
absolute velocity, which would mean the annihilation of the extension that
temporality – circulation – *is* (*G*, 629). Thus, it is circulation as such, trans-
portation and communication in the instance of Marx's consideration of the
capitalist road, that constitutes the sunk capital that would precipitate the
dissolution of capitalism.

The second internal limit of capitalism is constituted by the clear and present danger of surplus accumulation. The problem is straightforward,
although hardly simple. The capitalist cannot find ways to transform money
into capital, no ways to alienate money in the dialectical process that is the
production of commodities.[5] To be sure, money can still circulate, at times at
nearly absolute velocity, but it cannot circulate *as capital*. One can become
vastly richer, certainly – the case of George Soros is exemplary here – but
that is simply speculation, gambling; and speculation can never produce surplus-value. (This is why Marx was adamant that money, as gold and silver,
had to remain a commodity [that is, the material objectification of the labor
of its production]; otherwise, "value" becomes merely arbitrary, merely the
object of speculation, the world of Bernie Madoff and the Wall Street bank-
sters.) So here is the contradiction. Absolute wealth, as the realization of
surplus accumulation, is the abstract object of capitalist desire (as opposed to
mere barbarian bling or hoarding); but, like hoarding or luxury, its achieve-
ment would be the utter dissolution of the dialectical circulation of capital.
There are thus two limits to the circulation that constitutes capital as such:
the limit of a virtually absolute deceleration in sunk capital, and the limit of a
no less virtual absolute acceleration in speculation. At both extremes, however, albeit in contradictory ways, it is the fact of the very circulation that is a
presupposition of the capitalist mode of production, that threatens capital
with dissolution, because in the bipolar circulatory disorders of capitalism,
the mania of speculation, theft, and contagion at one extreme and the
depression of sunk capital at the other, what is called private property
becomes simply an anachronism, characteristic of a pre-communist mode of
production.

Of course it is not merely the bad infinities of circulation run amok that
interrupt the happy dialectical story of capital's reunion with itself in the
abstraction of absolute wealth, and thereby augur the dissolution of the
capitalist mode of production. The glad dialectical tidings of the consumma-
tion of capital are of course reserved exclusively for the bourgeoisie; from the
perspective of the worker, the process of the realization of capital as such in
the production of surplus-value is not only unhappy, it is not even a dialectical process at all. For the capitalist, alienation is merely the essential

negative moment in which money is transformed into capital; it is fraught with the risks of circulation, to be sure – sunk capital, speculation, theft – but it is only a moment, albeit ever renewed. For the worker, the capitalist mode of production is alienation as unsurpassable ontological condition. The worker's essential and definitive propertylessness is nothing less than her absolute alienation from "property" defined as her existential relation to the objective conditions of production, to "nature," raw materials, and the prosthetic tool, whether in agriculture or handicraft. But the worker is nothing outside those relations; they constitute her power-to-be, her *potentia*; her subjectivity is her *poiesis*. It is nothing less than all this that constitutes the proper, or the property that is alienated under capitalism. Nothing remains for the worker; she has become *nothing but* her capacity for labor (*Arbeitsvermögen*), her labor power (*Arbeitskraft*), which is not even hers, however.

In its objectified form (and labor is nothing but that process of objectification) as commodity, her labor power belongs to the capitalist.

The point at which the circulation of capital makes its dialectical turn for its return trip laden with surplus-value is the point of the expropriation of labor power, which for the worker is a point of absolute and pure loss: no supersession or sublation here, merely a *really* bad infinity that is therefore not dialectical at all. As Marx writes in the *Grundrisse*:

> The worker emerges not only not richer, but emerges rather poorer from the process than he entered. For not only has he produced the conditions of necessary labour as conditions belonging to capital; but also the value-creating possibility, the realization [*Verwertung*] which lies as a possibility within him, now likewise exists as surplus value, surplus product, in a word as capital, as master over living labour capacity, as value endowed with its own might and will, confronting him in his abstract, objectless, purely subjective poverty. He has produced not only the alien wealth and his own poverty, but also the relation of this wealth as independent, self-sufficient wealth, relative to himself as the poverty which this wealth consumes, and from which wealth thereby draws new vital spirits into itself, and realizes itself anew.   (*G*, 453)

There is nothing left for the worker save the minimum required to sustain and reproduce the working class in a zero-degree existence, "the penury which is living labour's sole possession" (*G*, 461). And if this is so, it is because,

> After constantly repeated labour, he always has *only* his living, direct labour itself to exchange. The repetition itself is in fact only apparent. *What he exchanges for capital is his entire labouring capacity, which he spends, say, in 20 years.* Instead of paying him for it in a lump sum, capital pays him in small doses, as he places it at capital's disposal, say weekly. This alters absolutely nothing in the nature of the thing and

gives no grounds whatsoever for concluding that ... labour forms *his*
capital.

(*G*, 293–94)

When the worker works, it is the entirety of her capacity for labor that is at
stake; every day that she works exhausts the whole of the possible, without
remainder. The temporality of labor is arhythmic precisely because all time, all
being, is concentrated – immanent – in the pure duration of the work. It is only
the mystifications of the putatively contractual exchange between capitalist and
worker that make it seem as if labor *power*, the *capacity* for labor, could be
subject to temporal division and distribution. Even if labor consists only of
speaking, it is my entire capacity or power to speak that is exercised in its totality
all at once. That the exercise of that labor power or capacity for labor is subject
to repetition is irrelevant; it simply means that the totality is at stake more than
once, not that it has been, or can be, subject to division and distribution. The
interruptions that separate repetitions of a singularity are not divisions.

The worker is nothing but labor power. As Marx argues in the chapter on
"The Working Day" in *Capital*,

[I]t is self-evident that the worker is nothing other than labour-power for
the duration of his whole life, and that therefore all his disposable time is
by nature and by right labour-time, to be devoted to the self-valorization
of capital.

(*C*, 375)

Capital asks no questions about the length of life of labour-power. What
interests it is purely and simply the maximum of labour-power that can
be set in motion in a working day. It attains this objective by shortening
the life of labour-power, in the same way as a greedy farmer snatches
more produce from the soil by robbing it of its fertility.

(*C*, 376)

In this respect, Marx continues, the worker is in fact a slave. What worker and
slave have in common is the fact of being *nothing but* labor power at the disposition of someone else. This constitutes the worker's *Lebensäußerung*, the
"externalization of her life" (*G*, 293). As sheer exteriority, "the worker is a
worker," the proposition of self-identity which, as Wittgenstein argued, is not
a philosophical argument, coupled to the indefinite pronoun, as "any worker
at all." This sheer exteriority means that the worker is nothing but predicate,
never a subject, logical, epistemological, or political. In passing, I would note
that it is around the question of this nothing-but and sheer exteriority that
Rancière constructs his compelling critique of Marx in *The Philosopher and
His Poor*; my wager is not that Rancière was wrong, but that this concept

of the worker's essential destitution also harbors possibilities other than those realized in Marx's practical political pronunciamentos (Rancière 2003: 55–124). If the absolute exposure or essential destitution leads on the one hand to the anonymity and interchangeability of workers, and thence to the constitution of the Industrial Reserve Army and the composition of the masses as the statistical object of knowledge, management, and control (what Foucault called a "population"), it nevertheless also leads, on the other hand but at the same time, and for the very same reasons, to a thought of the worker, the IRA, the masses, as the pure circulation of the common (what Rancière called the *dēmos*): on the one hand, immiseration; on the other, equality. This is not to say that immiseration is emancipation, far from it. It is to say that without this thought of pure circulation, this absolutely statistical figure of a common destitution (which can never be the object of division and distribution), there can be no concept of communism, no communist ontology. It is for this reason, after all, that it is the proletariat that bears the universal value of emancipation.

The figure of "the worker" is the figure of a *sense* of communist ontology; that is, the figure of the worker is the figure of necessary presuppositions of the communist mode of production (rather than of administrative programmatic pronouncements). I have attempted to identify four of these presuppositions. (1) In her propertylessness, the worker is the figure of alienation from relations of dependency. (2) Because the whole of her labor power or capacity for labor is at stake without reserve whenever she works, the worker is the figure of social being as indivisible multiplicity. (3) In her consequent destitution, exposure, and sheer exteriority, in her *Lebensäußerung*, the worker is the figure of ontology as immanence. (4) Insofar as she is the anonymous figure of non-dependence, the indivisible, and ontological immanence, the worker is thereby the object of a pure circulation, the figure of equality. This figure is an unavoidable consequence of capitalism, and thereby a presupposition of communist ontology. But the communist mode of production is neither the mere inversion, negation, or outside of the capitalist mode of production; communism does not turn the capitalist frown upside down. The point is to posit communism not as an infinitely deferred happy ending, for communism is neither necessarily happy nor an ending, but as the interruption, here and now, of the capitalist mode of production. Communism is the eruption of futurity in the present. The revolution is either here, now, or it is nothing. (On this point you will notice my sympathies are entirely with the *Rōnōha* and with Jacques Rancière.)

The task of communist philosophy now lies not in providing theoretical guidance for practice (for politics is never deduced from theory), nor simply in the work of critique (which is, nevertheless, absolutely essential), but in conceptualizing the sense of the communist ontology evoked by the figure of the worker. The task lies in thinking another sense of appropriation, another sense and experience of *aisthēsis*, another sense of *poiesis* and production, another sense of the common.[6]

Bibliography

Deleuze, G. and Guattari, F. (1987) *A Thousand Plateaus: Capitalism and Schizo-phrenia*. Minneapolis, University of Minnesota Press.
Hardt, M. and Negri, A. (2004) *Multitude: War and Democracy in the Age of Empire*. New York, Penguin.
Harvey, D. (2006) *The Limits to Capital*. London, Verso.
Marx, K. (1973) *Grundrisse: Foundations of the Critique of Political Economy* [G] *(Rough Draft)*. London, Penguin.
——. (1976) *Capital: A Critique of Political Economy*. [C] vol. 1, New York, Vintage.
——. (1978) *Capital: A Critique of Political Economy*. [C] vol. 2, New York, Vintage.
——. (1981) *Capital: A Critique of Political Economy*. [C] vol. 3, New York, Vintage.
Osborne, P. (2005) *How to Read Marx*. New York, Norton.
Rancière, J. (1999) *Disagreement: Politics and Philosophy*. Minneapolis, University of Minnesota Press.
——. (2003) *The Philosopher and His Poor*. Durham, Duke University Press.
Schmitt, C. (2003) *The Nomos of the Earth in the International Law of the Jus Publicum Europaeum*. New York, Telos.
Stiegler, B. (1998) *Technics and Time*. vol. 1, *The Fault of Epimetheus*, Stanford, Stanford University Press.

Notes

1 Hereafter cited parenthetically as *C*. For an extensive recent consideration of the priority of the prosthetic, by all means see Bernard Stiegler, *Technics and Time*, vol. 1, *The Fault of Epimetheus* (Stiegler 1998).
2 Hereafter cited parenthetically as *G*.
3 Carl Schmitt is a valuable guide here. For Schmitt, of course, any appropriation (or *nomos*) of the "earth" that does not immediately result in capital's version of private property, is merely barbaric; it is interesting to note how much of Schmitt's work constitutes a steadfast refusal to read Marx (Schmitt 2003).
4 See also volume 3 of Karl Marx's *Capital* translated by David Fernbach (Marx 1981: 728–48).
5 See the new updated edition of David Harvey (Harvey 2006); also pertinent is Michael Hardt and Antonio Negri, *Multitude: War and Democracy in the Age of Empire* (Hardt and Negri 2004: 3–95).
6 I read a slightly different version of this chapter to the Department of East Asian Studies at New York University on 24 April 2007; I am grateful to Yukiko Hanawa and Harry Harootunian for the invitation, and to the audience for their responses.

7 Living in transition

Toward a heterolingual theory of the multitude

Sandro Mezzadra

Capital as translation

"It is impossible to undo the consequences of the history of imperialism no matter how desperately one wishes that imperialism had never been effectuated" (Sakai 1997: 18). Let us start from this quite generic statement by Naoki Sakai in order to map the particular conditions under which his theory of translation can provide us useful tools in an attempt to establish a new ground for a critical theory of politics. I will look to these conditions first of all from the point of view of the meaning of the global dimension that is taking shape under our eyes – in a process of *transition* that does not seem to be close to its end. Far from being characterized by homogeneity, the global dimension is deeply heterogeneous as far as both its spatial and its temporal constitution is concerned. Problems of *articulation* of the multiplicity of spaces and times that make up the global dimension lie at the very core of the processes through which power relations are redefined in the present and global capital itself works.

In recent debates the concept of articulation has been widely used especially due to the interpretation of the concept proposed by Ernesto Laclau and Chantal Mouffe on the basis of their particular reading of Antonio Gramsci. According to Laclau and Mouffe (2001: 113), "the practice of articulation [...] consists in the construction of nodal points which partially fix meaning; and the partial character of this fixation proceeds from the openness of the social, a result, in its turn, of the constant overflowing of every discourse by the infinitude of the field of discursivity." Despite the critical remarks on this theory made by Stuart Hall (1986), Laclau and Mouffe's definition of articulation is quite consistent with his own use of the concept. Hall points to the emergence of a new historical force, or, more accurately, the emergence of a new series of political and social subjects through a "non-necessary connection" between this historical force and new ideological constellations. Through these influential theoretical positions, the concept of articulation has become a keyword in several proposals to rethink the politics of social movements: proposals that are often developed in the field of identity politics.

From my point of view the basic problem with this use of the concept lies in the fact that it does not seem to take into account the fact that articulation is a strategic moment in the notion of capital itself. While this is true at the very level of the *logical* notion of capital – we only need to remember the classical problem of the mediation of single fractions of capital in the unity of what Marx termed *Kapital im allgemeinen* ("capital in general") – the question of articulation becomes even more crucial in the contemporary global age. To articulate radically heterogeneous geographic, political, legal, social, and cultural scales in the global dimension of current accumulation circuits is one of the most important tasks that confronts contemporary capitalism. And also from the point of view of capital, articulation "consists in the construction of nodal points" that crisscross the heterogeneity of the global dimension. But the meaning of these capitalist nodal points (just to give a few examples: global stock exchange markets, rating and investors service companies such as Moody's, transnational legal firms, international and state agencies engaged in promoting neo-liberal globalization, and so on) is far from being "partially fixed." It is rather absolutely fixed and it radically limits what Laclau and Mouffe call the "openness of the social." Nonetheless, articulation, as Stuart Hall (1986) puts it, works as a language. To put it more precisely: it functions in the same way as a language functions when it is confronted with a plurality of other languages that have to be reduced to its code.

Articulation means therefore *translation*, and one of the key points I will make in this chapter is that translation is one of the fundamental modes of operation of global capital. *Capital as translation* is building up its own global dimension: the *language of value* (exchange value in its pure logical form) is the semantic structure, and above all the *grammar*, of this dimension, reproducing itself through an intensified version of what Naoki Sakai would call "homolingual address" (Sakai 1997: 3). It can be added that this address is at the same time an *interpellation*, to put it with Louis Althusser: the multiplicity of languages (that is, of forms of life, of social relations, of "cultures") that capital encounters in the deployment and codification of its heterogeneous "chains of value" (Spivak 1999: 99–111) are "addressed" according to the imperative of making themselves conform to the language of value.

A high degree of hybridism, as well as a multiplicity of differences, can be tolerated and even promoted by capital, as Hardt and Negri (2000: 137–46) have suggested: but its semantic structure remains "homolingual" insofar as the language of value dominates it. Nonetheless, again looking at this structure from the point of view suggested by the concept of translation, it remains deeply *antagonistic*. Translation itself can be a useful analytical tool in order to develop an analysis of the antagonisms that shape global capitalism. These antagonisms must be located at the very level of what we can call, along with the interpretation of Marx proposed by Jason Read, *production of subjectivity* (Read 2003: 153). Capital as translation addresses (interpellates) its subjects, at a very abstract level, prescribing a form of subjectivity that can be translated into the language of value.

Production of value, in the global age, is becoming more and more identified with this kind of translation. As Christian Marazzi has effectively shown,
in contemporary capitalist economy *language and communication* "structurally and at the same time shape both the production of goods and services
and the financial sphere" (Marazzi 2002: 10). The mediation (the articulation)
between the different levels of production of value in the unity of capital can
itself be conceived of as a linguistic mediation, basically consisting of a kind
of translation. From this point of view, it seems particularly important to
remember that, as Naoki Sakai and Jon Solomon put it, "translation names
primarily a *social* relationship whose forms permeate linguistic activity as a
whole, rather than simply comprising a secondary or exceptional situation"
(Sakai and Solomon 2006: 9).

The very concept of *exploitation* has to be redefined and deepened under
these conditions. And I think that such a reassessment of the concept of
exploitation is one of the basic tasks we are confronted with nowadays. Cultural studies and postcolonial studies, as has been clearly stated by Stuart
Hall (1992), have found it much easier to focus on *power* than on *exploitation*.
And they have tended therefore to articulate their political stance in terms of
a critique of power relations rather than in terms of a critique of exploitation,
which would imply a mapping of its geography as well as of its "intensive"
character. Although the Foucauldian emphasis on the productive nature of
power has played a crucial role in cultural and postcolonial studies, this unilateral emphasis on power has corresponded to the reproduction of a kind of
logical primacy (and of a kind of externality) of power with respect to the
movements and practices of subjects.

Going back to the point made by Jason Read, we must recall that "at the
foundations of the capitalist mode of production is the production of subjectivity in both senses of the genitive: the constitution of subjectivity, of a
particular subjective comportment, and in the turn the productive power of
subjectivity, its capacity to produce wealth" (Read 2003: 153). To put it in a
rather simplistic way, we can say that while the concept of power accounts for
the ways in which the "constitution of subjectivity" is produced, the concept
of exploitation points to the level of battles and clashes that shape the
reduction of the subjective "capacity of producing wealth" to the norm of
abstract labor, the condition of its translation into the language of value.
These clashes and these battles reproduce themselves not only in the production of "material" wealth, but also in the production of "immaterial" goods
such as culture, linguistic and symbolic structures, knowledge and imaginaries. They crisscross, as for instance Brett Neilson (2004) has very effectively
pointed out, the very production of the "real abstractions" that make the
"homolingual address" and the regime of translation of capital possible.

We must look at exploitation from the point of view of the *living labor* that
is invested and "captured" by capital through multiple modalities, all conver-
ging toward the production of its global dimension. The composition of contemporary living labor is crisscrossed by this multiplicity of the modalities of

its "capture" by capital. While capital articulates its global dimension through translation into the language of value, we need to think of the constitution of a collective subject capable of radical transformation starting from the antagonisms and conflicts that shape each moment of "capture." Needless to say, no one of these moments is individual, since they all invest networks of social cooperation that themselves produce forms of subjectivity. The attempt will be made in the last section of this chapter to apply the concept of "heterolingual address" proposed by Naoki Sakai to the problems of the constitution of a new political subject as a process through which the politics of liberation has to be rethought of today.

But first of all we need to make sense of the quotation from which we started. Why is the history of imperialism so important in order to understand our present situation? In the next section I will show how capital as translation reproduces – under postcolonial conditions – one of the main characteristics of the modern Western colonial project.

Capital and the West

Since its very inception, the history of capital has been world history. As Marx stated in the *Grundrisse*, "the tendency to create the world market is immediately given with the concept of capital. Every limit (*Grenze*) appears as an obstacle to be overcome" (Marx 1857–58: 311). The history of capital is not to be understood unless we conceive of it as the making of this unprecedented geographic scale (Guha 2002: 35, 43). The time and space of capital are structurally interwoven in the project of modernity. As Walter Mignolo and Anibal Quijano have stressed from a Latin American perspective, we need an account of this structural link between time and space within the history of capital capable of displacing the very imaginary produced by capital as a world system in the process of its development. The "split between the two distinct forms of modernity – imperial modernity and colonial modernity – is itself the very definition of something like Modernity in general in the constitution of the hierarchical, non-democratic world of Capital." Once again we are confronted with a problem of *articulation*. The history of capital is not to be separated from the fact that both forms of modernity "are bound to a common index, the normative value of the West" (Sakai and Solomon 2006: 21). This common index articulates both at the material and at the epistemic level the history of capital as a world history.

While we must acknowledge the effectiveness of this articulation, we also need to recall that it operated through violence and domination, and that resistance has been met with violence and domination since the beginning of modern history. The world history of capital is itself split by a kind of double movement, and we must reflect this double movement in any attempt to reconstruct it. On the one hand we have a process of expansion of capital that produces its particular geography, giving way to specific center – periphery relations; on the other hand we have processes of resistance that displace this very geography. On the one hand we have an imaginary constructed around the centrality of Europe and the West; on the other hand we have the "conflictive imaginary that emerges with and from the colonial difference" (Mignolo 2001: 57). This split inscribes itself within the very concept of the West, and must be highlighted when looking at the different series of oppositions that the West itself has produced in order to make sense of the colonial encounters that constitute modern history as world history: Asia and the West, the West and the Rest, etc.

It is from this point of view that, as Naoki Sakai has written, modernity "cannot be considered unless in reference to translation" (Sakai 2000a: 797). The unity of modern historical time (echoing in its "homogeneous and empty" structure what Marx has termed the "spectral objectivity" of capital) had always to be produced through a kind of violent synchronization of a multiplicity of heterogeneous times. And this violent synchronization is itself an act of translation. Let me point to the fact that this problem is particularly acute in the moment of *transition* to capitalism, in that process of "primitive accumulation" in which the conditions of capitalism have to be established. As Dipesh Chakrabarty writes, "the problem of capitalist modernity cannot any longer be seen simply as a sociological transition [...] but as a problem of translation, as well" (Chakrabarty 2000: 17). I would like to add that transition – as well as primitive accumulation (Perelman 2000; De Angelis 2007: 136–41) – is not only a historical category: it is at the same time a *logical* category that lies at the very core of the concept of capital.

We can put it this way: transition is equivalent to the establishment of the possibility of translation, through the regime of "homolingual address" that makes capital possible. Let me add that if we look at the concept of transition from this point of view, it is pretty clear that it is precisely transition in colonial contexts that most effectively reveals the main problem that lies at the very heart of transition to capitalism. Marx attempted to grasp this problem through the concept of "Asiatic mode of production," which precisely for this reason still deserves careful consideration despite all its well known shortcomings and pitfalls (Spivak 1999: 97): the particular kind of heterogeneity encountered by capitalism in non-European contexts made the general difficulty of establishing the conditions of its translation into the language of value even more acute than it was in Western Europe (where nonetheless, as we know from Marx's analysis of the "so called primitive accumulation," it required a dramatic employment of violence). What we need to add is that the problem of transition reemerges in each historical moment when the conditions of translation have to be established anew. My point is precisely that global capitalism is characterized by the fact that capital as translation is compelled to confront the problem of the establishment of the conditions of possibility of translation at the very level of its everyday operation. Primitive accumulation and transition (what Marx called the "prehistory of capital") are the ghosts that haunt capital at the highest level of its historical development.

Naoki Sakai has brilliantly pointed out how the concept of modernity "can never be understood without reference to [the] pairing of the pre-modern and the modern" (Sakai 1997: 154). And he has stressed the fact that this pairing is structurally linked to a geopolitical understanding of the West as the site of modernity and the non-West as the site of pre-modernity. Narratives of modernization have articulated the relation between the West and the non-West, taking the shape of different theories of the "stages" of historical development. The concept of the West itself historically emerged "in the midst of interaction with the Other," establishing itself as the common ground on which historical and cultural "differences" had to be made commensurable. Modern universalism is indeed unthinkable outside of this continuous translation: as Sakai writes, "the West is particular in itself, but it also constitutes the universal point of reference in relation to which others recognize themselves as particularities. In this regard, the West thinks itself to be ubiquitous" (Sakai 1997: 154–55). The colonial imprint of modern universalism lies precisely in this movement of translation, and there is a structural affinity between modern universalism and capital from this point of view.

It is important to stress, along with the development of postcolonial criticism, that this movement of translation has never been "smooth," since it has been interrupted, challenged and continuously hybridized by the multifarious intervention of non-Western subjects. But it is equally necessary to keep in mind the effectiveness of the Western "homolingual address" in its attempt to shape at the same time a topography of knowledge and a geopolitics of power. Naoki Sakai's emphasis on "demands for symmetry and equality," on the "imitative relation to "the West"" that has shaped through a logic of "cofiguration" the creation of the history of modern Japanese thought is a good exemplification of this effectiveness (Sakai 1997: 48, 68; see also Sakai 2000b). At the same time, his criticism of the rhetoric of "Asian values," in which he sees "a simple reversal of Eurocentric culturalism," reminds us that "the West" still holds its influence in the global present (Sakai 2000a: 800).

Nonetheless, it is worth considering the hypothesis that our time is characterized by the long crisis of the structures of power that historically articulated and channeled the Western "homolingual address" within an established regime of translation. The instability of global capital finds here one of its most important roots: to put it once again in a very abstract way, each act of capitalist translation is at least potentially confronted with the problem of establishing the conditions that make translation itself possible. Anti-colonial movements and struggles successfully disrupted the "metaborder" that distinguished the metropolitan from the colonial space and time, compelling capital and the West itself to come to terms with a much more complex, *postcolonial* geography of power (Mezzadra and Rahola 2006). It is a geography crisscrossed by lines of conflict and relations of power, by a multiplicity of borders to which huge divides in the distribution of wealth correspond. But its increasing complexity makes it more and more difficult to make sense of it using fixed categories of center and periphery, North and South. Modernity is not anymore synonymous with the West, and the defeat of the US unilateralism in Iraq has something to say about the crisis of old-style imperialism. Global capital itself is not necessarily Western in its composition. But what remains strong, and still needs to be provincialized and disrupted, is surely the West (not only Europe) as an "imaginary figure" that keeps on addressing and interpellating the subjects that inhabit the global present (Chakrabarty 2000: 4).

My point is that this enduring influence of the West as an "imaginary figure" is part and parcel of the enduring dominance of capital on a world scale. It is precisely the deep affinity between the "homolingual address" of the West and the regime of translation through which capital operates that ensures the reproduction of that "imaginary figure" well beyond the rhetoric of the "clash of civilizations" and the "war on terrorism." I agree with Naoki Sakai and Jon Solomon that under these conditions "the critique of Euro-centrism becomes a good rhetoric for the elite, whose subjectivity is partly formed in their systemic competition with 'the West' through the structural (class) accumulation of value by the labor of their social inferiors" (Sakai and Solomon 2006: 21). This is not the path we have to follow. In a way we have to accept the full deployment of the logic of capital on a world scale; we have even to accept – to put it provocatively – the becoming-world of the West under the dominance of capital, we have to carefully map the new antagonisms that crisscross this process. And we have to search for a different regime of translation, capable of interrupting and disrupting the "homolingual address" of capital and opening up new spaces of freedom and equality. Spaces in which a new world can be invented: beyond the West and beyond the Rest.

Space and time of global capitalism

Time and space have been indeed crucial to the discussion of globalization. The discourse of "time and space compression," first articulated by David Harvey (1989), has become a kind of cliché in current debates. I think we must go beyond this cliché and try to investigate much deeper transformations in the *articulation* of space and time that seem to announce a kind of political, economic, social, and cultural experience significantly different from the "chronotope," to put it with Michail Bakhtin, that has been characteristic of modernity. To put it simply: the rhetoric of "time and space compression" seems to take for granted the *unity* of time and space, and therefore produces an image of the contemporary global dimension of experience that is para-doxically a kind of mirror of the ways in which time and space are imagined by capital: that is, as "smooth," "homogeneous and void" coordinates of accumulation processes. And it does not address the crucial problem of the *production* of these coordinates.

Something similar can be said also about the use of the image of "flows" in order to describe the landscape of the global age: as Anna Tsing has effectively pointed out, this image too often leads us to ignore "the recarving of channels and the remapping of the possibilities of geography" that make these flows possible while limiting, stopping and "taming" other flows, most notably movements of migration (Tsing 2000: 327; see also Ferguson 2006: 47). While the image of flows tends to limit the analysis of the global condition to the level of circulation, what is urgently needed is once again a criticism of the "hidden relations of production" that lie beneath the "surface" of circulation, to use the metaphor suggested by Marx; however we must be aware of the fact that these relations of production have not to do merely with traditional labor relations, but refer more generally to "the making of the objects and subjects who circulate, the channels of circulation, and the landscape elements that enclose and frame those channels" (Tsing 2000: 337).

Let us look at the transformations of space from a political point of view. Sovereignty and law have been in modern times the two basic criteria of definition of a political space (Galli 2001): a territory was defined in its unity as the geographical sphere of validity of a particular State sovereignty and of a particular (national) legal system. Nowadays, while a global law is emerging as "centered on a multiplicity of global but partial regimes that address the needs of specialized sectors," sovereignty "remains a systemic property but its institutional insertion and its capacity to legitimate and absorb all legitimating power, to be the source of the law, have become unstable" (Sassen 2006: 242, 415). The image of a "mixed constitution" of Empire as proposed by Hardt and Negri is particularly effective in order to grasp the situation emerging from these complex transformations (2000: 3.5). But we must always remember that it makes sense to use the notion of "mixed constitution," as well the notion itself of Empire, only if we stress its character as a tendency and not as an already established and fixed model. This means to take seriously into consideration, as a defining element of the concept itself and not as occasional "perturbations," the possibility of conflicts and clashes on each layer of the multilevel articulation of the "mixed constitution." And at the same time it should imply the necessity of analyzing the production of the space corresponding to the "mixed constitution" as an ongoing and dynamic process.

From this point of view I find the notion of lateral spaces, or "latitudes," particularly thought provoking. This notion has been proposed by Aihwa Ong within a critical discussion of Hardt and Negri's *Empire*. While in my opinion she often tends to oversimplify Hardt and Negri's argument, I do think that her notion of "latitudes" can be very useful in order to further develop an analysis of the transformations that are reshaping political and economic geography under the sign of global capital. Put very shortly, Ong points to the fact that the stretching of market powers does not correspond to a homogenization of labor control and worker politics. "Striated spaces of production that combine different kinds of labor regimes" are emerging, and contrary to the idea of a linear transition from a disciplinary to regulatory mode of control, "contemporary transnational production networks are underpinned by carceral modes of labor discipline" (Ong 2006: 121, 124).

While the unity of national spaces in East and Southeast Asia is disrupted by "neoliberalism as exception" and by "zoning technologies" that open up the spaces in which "market-driven calculations are being introduced in the management of populations" (Ong 2006: 3), lateral spaces and enclaves are reproducing on a transnational scale conditions of labor segregation that tend to be ethnicized. This notion of "latitudes," which would deserve comparison with the analysis of "resource-extraction enclaves" in Africa recently provided by James Ferguson (2006: 13–14, 34–38, 194–210), helps us to deepen our knowledge of the heterogeneity of the global space of capitalism. But it also gives us a hint as to the complex structure of global time. Investigating the architecture of electronics-production systems run by Asian managers, which "displays a striking interpenetration of high-tech systems with migrant or ethnicized techniques of labor incarceration," she observes that "the "geographical stretching of network economies is often accompanied by a temporal stretching, a regression to 'older' forms of labor disciplining epitomized by the high-tech sweatshop" (Ong 2006: 125).

It is a problem we can frame in the terms suggested by the Marxian distinction between "formal" and "real subsumption of labor under capital" (along with the one between "absolute" and "relative" surplus value). At stake in that distinction is precisely a question of different historical times: not in the sense, as it is often misinterpreted, that they merely define two different "stages" in the development of the capitalist mode of production, but rather in the sense that they point to two different relations of capital with time. While real subsumption refers to a situation in which capital itself directly organizes the mode of labor and cooperation, producing a kind of synchronicity between the time of capitalist accumulation and the time of production, formal subsumption points to a different situation: to a situation in which capital encounters "*already* existing" (Marx uses the verb *vorfinden*) forms of labor organization and discipline, limiting itself to incorporate (and to exploit) them in the process of its development (Marx 1857–58: 405, emphasis added). Formal subsumption points therefore to a situation in which a peculiar temporal disjuncture inscribes itself in the structure of capital.

Far from being a relic of the past, formal subsumption reproduces itself and crisscrosses real subsumption in the age of global capital. Moreover, as the example of electronics-production systems proposed by Ong shows, we cannot take the distinction between formal and real subsumption as a key to map the geography of global capitalism, as though it were possible to think of the global "North" as the space of real subsumption and of the global "South" as the space of formal subsumption. Once again the problem we are confronted with is to make sense of the *articulation* between the two different forms of subsumption, of their *translation* into the unitary language of value.

More generally, it is the radical heterogeneity of global space and time that makes articulation and translation strategic moments in the concept itself of global capital, interpreting this concept as the hallmark of the capitalist determination of the world we live in. I would suggest that a basic logical operator of articulation and translation can be seen in the *border*. In several works Étienne Balibar has argued that far from being marginal, the border tends nowadays to inscribe itself at the very center of our political, social, and cultural experience. Europe itself is becoming in his opinion a "borderland" (Balibar 2005; Balibar and Mezzadra 2006). But we need to stress the fact that borders themselves are sites of deep transformations that are reshaping the very institution of border. To sum up a huge literature on the point using the recent important work of an Italian scholar, borders are becoming mobile without ceasing to produce fixed mechanisms of closure, they are becoming "deterritorialized" without ceasing to invest in particular places (Rigo 2007).

The European experience is in fact particularly interesting from this point of view. Looking at the so called enlargement process and at the new migration regime in the making, the mobility of borders can be traced both in its effect as strategic device that allows the articulation of European space with "neighboring" spaces (and the translation of European law into other legal orders), and as a biopolitical technology that inscribes within European citizenship "lateral spaces" around which labor markets can be reorganized (Walters 2002). Particularly investigating the position of migrants within European citizenship and labor markets, Enrica Rigo has effectively argued that new hierarchies are emerging at the very level of legal regulation, disrupting the traditional formal homogeneity of modern citizenship. And while these hierarchies are penetrating in the structure of European labor markets, tracing peculiar "borders of production" (Rigo 2007: 191–97), "temporal borders" are emerging as a result of the many "waiting rooms" designed for migrants both on their way to Europe and inside Europe, "legally defining the condition of migrants according to a rule of a temporary character which is bound to permanently reproduce itself" (Rigo 2007: 214).

I think it is worth linking this notion of "temporal borders" with the problems of articulation and translation between "formal" and "real subsumption of labor under capital" addressed above and thinking of "temporal borders" as key devices in producing junctures among different kinds of labor regimes and disciplines that seem indeed to belong to different historical times. If we tackle the notion of latitudes again from this point of view, we can make the point that latitudes are made up and "fenced" by a complex set of borders and boundaries: "geopolitical" borders that articulate their "transnational" character, legal borders that curtail migrants' mobility and rights, cultural and social boundaries produced by processes of ethnicization, borders of production, temporal borders that separate different historical times and make their translation into the unitary language of value possible. While these borders and boundaries are key to what Achille Mbembe has called "the domestication of world time" from the point of view of capital (Mbembe 2000: 260), we must think of them as constantly *in the making*, since they are confronted with a set of subjective practices, behaviors, and imaginaries that challenge them. It is this challenge that makes borders and boundaries social relations, crisscrossed by the multifarious tensions between "border reinforcing" and "border crossing" (Vila 2000): movements and struggles that develop around them, particularly involving migrants and issues of mobility, are key to the possibility of imagining and producing different modalities of "domestication of world time," different kinds of articulation and translation capable of disrupting capital's domination (Mezzadra 2006).

Living labor in transition

Movements of migration and practices of mobility are key to the transformations of the composition of contemporary living labor. I employ the concept of composition along the lines that have been developed since the 1960s by Italian "autonomist Marxism" (Wright 2002). But I am speaking of living labor particularly taking into account the reflections on this Marxian concept proposed by Dipesh Chakrabarty in a seminal chapter of *Provincializing Europe*. Chakrabarty looks in a very original way at the classical problem of the relation between "abstract" and "concrete" labor, in a way substituting this latter concept with the one of "living labor" that is particularly used by Marx in the *Grundrisse*. The critical point, Chakrabarty writes, "is that the labor that is abstracted in the capitalist's search for a common measure of human activity is *living*" (Chakrabarty 2000: 60). The very process of abstracting living labor from the multiplicity of differences that make up "life" is conceptualized by Chakrabarty as a process of *translation* (Chakrabarty 2000: 71): a process of translation that is at the same time a deeply antagonistic social relation.

Discipline, violence, and "despotism" are the key modalities through which capital addresses living labor in its attempt to translate it into the code of abstract labor. To be more precise: they are the key modalities that crisscross capital's relation with living labor especially in processes of *transition*, when the norm of abstract labor – that is, the "key to the hermeneutic grid through which capital requires us to read the world" (Chakrabarty 2000: 55) – has to be established in front of the radical heterogeneity of "life." One of the main problems implied by transition to capitalism is the political and legal constitution of the labor market. In order to make the labor market possible, a particular commodity has to be produced, that is, "labor power," a concept fully developed by Marx only in *Capital*. I think we have to take this concept into account in order to further develop Chakrabarty's analysis of the relation between abstract and living labor. The concept itself of labor power, as has been stressed by Paolo Virno (1999: 121–30), directly addresses life anyway, since it is defined by Marx as "the sum of all physical and intellectual attitudes contained by a living body" (Marx 1867: 181). What makes it particularly important in the context of our present discussion is that it points to the necessary process of *separation* (of abstraction) of these "attitudes" from their "container" (the "living body") that logically precedes the capitalist relation of production.

This process of separation *is* the production of labor power as a commodity – that is, the production of particular kinds of subjects who are *compelled* to sell their labor power in order to reproduce themselves. This was the main problem at stake in the scene of the "so-called primitive accumulation." From a series of recent historical works (see for instance Moulier Boutang 1998; Steinfeld 1991 and 2001) we know that the solution to this problem could not lie, contrary to many statements by Marx himself, in the smooth establishment of "free" wage labor as the "normal" modality of subsumption of labor under capital. Other modalities of "capture" of labor were (and are) rather structurally necessary in order to make labor power available as a commodity. A huge deal of violence (a series of "nonpecuniary" pressures to compel work, ranging from slavery to indenture to peculiar administrative statuses for migrant workers) had and has to be employed to ensure the continuity of capitalist accumulation – and the continuity of what Marx called the "encounter" between capital and labor power (Marx 1867: 181, 742; Althusser 1982: 584–87). This is the main reason why primitive accumulation cannot be considered to be only a historical moment: it is rather to be regarded as a kind of reservoir of potential "exceptions" (to what Marx called the "silent compulsion of economic relations" [Marx 1867: 765]) that can be activated at any "stage" of capitalist development when the ordinary functioning of the labor market appears to be interrupted.

I think it is worth considering the contemporary global situation from this point of view. The radical heterogeneity of labor regimes not only at the "global" but also at each "local" level, mobile and flexible labor relations, the problem itself of articulating what Ong calls lateral spaces of production with the global circuits of accumulation – all these continuously confront capital with the possibility of the refusal by living labor to subordinate itself to the norm of abstract labor. And let me add that this problem is crucial also in order to establish the "stability" that is needed in order to ensure the functioning of financial global markets; also the life of the inhabitants of the "planet of slums" so effectively described by Mike Davis (2006) is subject to the norm of abstract labor, independently of the fact that their labor power can remain outside of the labor market. It is precisely the production of the conditions of this subordination of living labor to abstract labor that constitutes one of the main problems of transition, not only at the point of production but also more generally as a societal problem.

This is the reason why we must take seriously the idea of *living labor in transition*. The very fact that the subordination to the norm of abstract labor cannot be taken for granted and must be reconstructed by capital along the entire deployment of its heterogeneous chains of value makes the traditional image of the working class, as a collective subject disciplined (and made political) by capital itself through its organization of labor cooperation, obsolete. This is not a kind of sociological statement, and it has nothing to do with the fact that factory workers continue to exist in huge masses. The crucial point rather consists in the fact that the constitution and composition of living labor are nowadays *open processes* both from the point of view of capital and from the point of view of the subjectivities that make up living labor itself. Since capital is compelled to impose abstract labor as a common measure of human activity, it needs a unitary figure of labor in general: but the radical heterogeneity of the modalities of contemporary "capture" of labor makes this capitalist representation of the unity of labor problematic, an *ongoing process of translation* much more than a stable presupposition of development – a process of translation moving back and forth from production to circulation to finance itself, where, as stated above, the appearance of the exchange of capital with capital cannot get rid of the necessary continuous reproduction on a global scale of social relations shaped by the norm of abstract labor. On the other hand, from the point of view of what Jason Read calls "the productive power of subjectivity," the heterogeneity of labor does not only correspond to a multiplicity of hierarchies that crisscross its composition. It also expresses the diversity of human faculties, of practices of cooperation often developing outside the direct command of capital, of "forms of life" that make up that productive power.

Toward a heterolingual theory of the multitude

In this diversity we must be able to acknowledge the imprint of a complex history of struggles and movements of labor that blew up the traditional notion of working class and its political representations. Among other things, it is in order to grasp this complex "genealogy" of contemporary living labor that the concept of *multitude* has been introduced in recent years within the tradition of Italian autonomist Marxism (Hardt and Negri 2000, 2004; Virno 2004). There are at least two current misunderstandings of this concept that must be avoided. Firstly, the concept of multitude doesn't aim at opposing labor as multiplicity against capital as One. It rather attempts to focus on the particular kind of articulation between unity and multiplicity that lives at the heart of capital and tries to imagine a different kind of articulation between the two elements, starting from the construction of a new common ground (of a new One) capable of sustaining a different regime of cooperation and production. Secondly, although the concept of multitude is critical of the traditional representations of the working class, it is not a kind of mystical or merely aesthetic icon. It is – and maybe this aspect has not been stressed enough in the debate – a *concept of class*. This means that it is a determined concept, constructed around the manifold forms of exploitation that characterize contemporary capitalism and retaining the *partial* nature of the notion of class.

The concept of multitude tries to acknowledge the fact that the heterogeneity of labor corresponds to a multiplicity of struggles, practices of resistance and refusal that cannot be linearly unified and represented by traditional political organizations as parties and unions. The problem of the communicability and translatability of these necessarily partial struggles and practices becomes therefore the central problem of a political theory of the multitude. To put it rather schematically, while capital posits its element of unity (the language of value) as a presupposition of its "homo-lingual address," to imagine a process of political subjectivation of the multi-tude means to think of the production of the *common* as a work in progress, as the result – in terms of shared institutions, shared resources, a shared space – of a movement capable of constantly reinventing what Étienne Balibar (1992) has defined as *égaliberté*, the indissoluble unity of freedom and equality.

It is not an utopian project: while it points to the necessity of inventing new institutions, new "organized networks" (Rossiter 2006), for instance, it gives us a general criterion that also allows us to value the action of traditional institutions, which can be made internal to the political subjectivation of the multitude insofar as they are able to open up and consolidate elements of commonality: "nodal points which partially fix meaning," to go back to Laclau and Mouffe, and that can become tactical junctures of articulation of the multitude. We are very close to the horizon of "radical democracy" indeed; but we interpret (and therefore keep alive) within this horizon the fundamental legacy of the communist critique of democracy insofar as we put at the center of our theoretical endeavor the material power of the multitude, as a partial subject, to *produce* the common. At the same time, while especially the strategic character of migration and practices of mobility in the compo-sition of living labor leads us to underscore the global scope of the con-temporary composition of living labor, the concept of the multitude does not end up in abstract theorizations of a new global democracy. It rather points to the possibility of "rooting" radical political projects in particular spaces, from the local to the continental level, developing in a creative way the "possibilities of geography" referred to by Anna Tsing and making concrete a new cosmopolitanism.

Freedom and equality become themselves along these lines "place holders" (Chakrabarty 2000: 70), sites of communication and translation where their very content is open to a constant transformation. While this crucial position of freedom and equality distinguishes the project of the multitude from a simple criticism of "Eurocentrism," these two concepts themselves need to be conceived of as "living in transition" and *therefore in translation*. Freedom and equality are not defined as transcendental conditions of politics, they do not preexist as "universals," to put it with Judith Butler, to "particular" social movements: the possibility itself of conflicting notions of universality must be taken into account, requiring a practice of translation that is quite different from the one implied by the traditional concept of hegemony (Butler 2000: 162–69). Freedom and equality are rather to be conceived of as Derridian *traces*, as the potential negation of domination and exploitation that is bound to be made actual by movements and struggles of subjective constitution that challenge them and open up a new field of the politically possible. The concept of the multitude tries to grasp the complexity of these movements and struggles of subjective constitution against domination and exploitation, rooting their convergence in practices of social cooperation capable of producing a new *common*.

Since the common does not preexist these movements and struggles, these practices of social cooperation, the multitude is a "non aggregate community of foreigners": that is, as Naoki Sakai has written, "a community where we relate ourselves through the attitude of the heterolingual address" (Sakai 1997: 9). Far from preexisting it, the language of a "non aggregate community of foreigners" – its *common* – only emerges from a communication that takes the foreignness of both the addresser and the addressee as its point of departure independently of their "native language." Translation is the language of a *subject in transit*. Not abiding "by the normalcy of reciprocal and transparent communication," but instead assuming "that every utterance can fail to communicate because heterogeneity is inherent in any medium, linguistic or otherwise," the heterolingual address clearly implies that "translation must be endless." It therefore challenges the borders that, through "national, ethnic, or linguistic affiliation" (Sakai 1997: 8), define commensurable communities as conditions of the "homolingual address" and its transparent ideal of translation. It disrupts the very idea of community we have inherited from modern history and thought, that continues to be a strategic site "of primitive accumulation for the construction of majoritarian subjects of domination," of "authoritative bodies" and of "forms of relation regularized according to the apparently natural boundaries of "the individual" and its corollary, the collective" (Sakai and Solomon 2006: 20–21).

Far from being limited to the strategic task of imagining new forms of transnational practice of theory in cultural and postcolonial studies, this disruption of the very idea of community that lies behind the homolingual regime of translation helps us to question any simple notion of the "We" we refer to in our political practices. But at the same time it leads to intensify the search for a new ground of commonality capable of making social life richer, more equal and free. As Meaghan Morris writes, Naoki Sakai's approach "asks what actually happens in an effort of translation, rather than beginning with a presupposed ideal or an already accepted story of what a world without need of translation – without the 'dust' created by linguistic difference and textual materiality; without folds of incommensurability and the grit of incomprehension, in short, a world without language – would or should be like" (Morris 1997: xiii-xiv). We can answer the question in a rather simple way: what happens in an effort of "heterolingual" translation is precisely that a new commonality is produced precisely while difference is produced out of incommensurability. This seems to me a good way to describe the kind of common we have in mind when talking about the multifarious social struggles that make up the multitude.

Bibliography

Althusser, L. (1982) La courant souterrain du matérialisme de la rencontre. *Écrits philosophiques et politiques*, Tome I, 553–91.

——. (2006) *Les frontieres de la démocratie*, Paris, La Découverte.

Balibar, É. and Mezzadra, S. (2006) Citizenship, War, Class. A Dialogue moderated by I. Saint-Saëns and Manuela Bojadzjiev. *New Formations*, 10–30.

Butler, J. (2000) Competing Universalities. In J. Butler, E. Laclau and S. Žižek (Ed.) *Contingency, Hegemony, Universality. Contemporary Dialogues on the Left*. London, Verso.

Chakrabarty, D. (2000) *Provincializing Europe. Postcolonial Thought and Historical Difference*. Oxford, Princeton University Press.

Davis, M. (2006) *Planet of Slums*. London, Verso.

De Angelis, M. (2007) *The Beginning of History. Value Struggles and Global Capital*. London, Pluto Press.

Ferguson, J. (2006) *Global Shadows. Africa in the Neoliberal World Order*. Durham – London, Duke University Press.

Gallic, C. (2001) *Spazi politici. L'età moderna e l'età globale*. Bologna, Il Mulino.

Guha, R. (2002) *History and the Limit of World-History*. New York, Columbia University Press.

Hali, S. (1986) On Postmodernism and Articulation. An Interview. *Journal of Communication Inquiry*, 45–60.

——. (1992) Cultural Studies and its Theoretical Legacies. In Grossberg, L. and Treichler, P. A. (Eds.) *Cultural Studies*. New York, London, Sage.

Hardt, M. and Negri, A. (2000) *Empire*. Cambridge, Mass., Harvard University Press.

——. (2004) *Multitude*, Penguin.

Harvey, D. (1989) *The Condition of Postmodernity. An Enquiry into the Origins of Cultural Change*, Oxford, Cambridge, Mass., Blackwell.

Laclau, E. and Mouffe, C. (2001) *Hegemony and Socialist Strategy. Towards a Radical Democratic Politics*, London, New York, Verso.

Marazzi, C. (2002) *Capitale & linguaggio. Dalla new economy all'economia di guerra*, Rome, DeriveApprodi.

Marx, K. (1857–58) *Grundrisse der Kritik der politischen Ökonomie*, Frankfurt a.M., Europäische Verlagsanstalt.

——. (1867) *Das Kapital. Kritik der politischen Ökonomie*, Berlin, Dietz Verlag.

Mbembe, A. (2000) At the Edge of the World. Boundaries, Territoriality, and Sovereignty in Africa. *Public Culture*, 12, 259–84.

Mezzadra, S. (2006) *Diritto di fuga, Migrazioni, cittadinanza, globalizzazione*, Verona, ombre corte.

Mezzadra, S. and Rahola, F. (2006) The Postcolonial Condition: A Few Notes on the Quality of Historical Time in the Global Present. *Postcolonial Text*. 2006 ed., Online: *https://postcolonial.org*.

Mignolo, W. (2001) La colonialidad a lo largo y a lo ancho: el hemisfero occidental en el horizonte de la modernidad. In Lander, E. (Ed.) La colonialidad del saber: eurocentrismo y ciencias socials. *Perspectivas latinoamericanas*. Buenos Aires, Clasco.

Morris, M. (1997) Foreword. In Sakai, N. (Ed.) *Translation and Subjectivity. On "Japan" and Cultural Nationalism*. Minneapolis, London, University of Minnesota Press.

Moulier Boutang, Y. (1998) *De l'esclavage au salariat. Économie historique du salariat bridé.* Paris, Presses Universitaires de France.

Neilson, B. (2004) *Free Trade in the Bermuda Triangle and Other Tales of Counter-globalization.* London, University of Minnesota Press.

Ong, A. (2006) *Neoliberalism as Exception. Mutations in Citizenship and Sovereignty.* Durham, NC, Duke University Press.

Perelman, M. (2000) *The Invention of Capitalism. Classical Political Economy and the Secret History of Primitive Accumulation.* Durham, NC, London, Duke University Press.

Read, J. (2003) *The Micro-Politics of Capital. Marx and the Prehistory of the Present.* Albany, NY, State University of New York Press.

Rigo, E. (2007) *Europa di confine. Transformazioni della cittadinanza nell'Europa allargata*, Roma, Meltemi.

Rossitier, N. (2006) *Organized Networks. Media Theory. Creative Labor. New Institutions.*, Rotterdam, NAi Publishers.

Sakai, N. (1997) *Translation and Subjectivity. On "Japan" and Cultural Nationalism*, Minneapolis and London, University of Minnesota Press.

——. (2000a) You Asians: On the Historical Role of the West and Asia Binary. *South Atlantic Quarterly*, 99, 789–817.

——. (2000b) Subject and Substratum: On Japanese Imperial Nationalism. *Cultural Studies*, 14, 462–530.

——. (2005) *Dislocation in Translation.* Sinij Divan, 7, 15.

Sakai, N. and Solomon, J. (2006) Introduction: Addressing the Multitude of Foreigners, Echoing Foucault. *Translation, Biopolitics, Colonial Discourse.* Hong Kong, Hong Kong University Press.

Sassen, S. (2006) *Territory, Authority, Rights. From Medieval to Global Assemblages.* Princeton/Oxford, Princeton University Press.

Spivak, G. C. (1999) *A Critique of Postcolonial Reason. Toward a History of the Vanishing Present.* Cambridge, Mass. London, Harvard University Press.

Steinfeld, R. J. (1991) *The Invention of Free Labor. The Employment Relation in English and American Law and Culture, 1350–1870.* Chapel Hill, London, University of North Carolina Press.

——(2001) *Coercion, Contract, and Free Labor in the Nineteenth Century.* Cambridge, New York, Cambridge University Press.

Tsing, P. (2000) The Global Situation. *Cultural Anthropology.* 15, 327–60.

Vila, P. (2000) *Crossing Borders, Reinforcing Borders: Social Categories, Metaphors, and Narrative Identities on the U.S.-Mexico Frontier.* Austin, University of Texas Press.

Virno, P. (1999) *Il ricordo del presente. Saggio sul tempo storico.* Torino, Bollati Boringhieri.

——(2004) *Grammar of the Multitude.* New York, Semiotext(e).

Walters, W. (2002) Mapping Schengenland: Denaturalizing the Border. Environment & Planning D: *Society & Space*, 20, 561–80.

Wright, S. (2002) *Storming Heaven. Class Composition and Struggle in Italian Autonomist Marxism.* London, Pluto Press.

8 Transition to a world society

Naoki Sakai's work in the context of capital-imperialism

Jon Solomon[1]

Translation, biopolitics, colonial difference: Sakai's work in context

The primary imperative of subjective formation under the post-Fordist regime of immaterial labor is, as Maurizio Lazzarato and Toni Negri observed nearly two decades ago, communication. "The [post-Fordist] subject," writes Lazzarato, "is a simple relay of codification and decodification, whose transmitted message must be 'clear and without ambiguity,' within a context of communication that has been completely normalised" (Lazzarato 2004). Subjects of communication face the especially daunting task of accounting for enormous differences and diversities throughout and across global populations. Hence, if communication is to be effective, it requires an ideology of anthropological difference according to which the normalization of diverse populations can be universally instituted. Needless to say, in the era of postcolonial governance, such normalization would encounter impossible resistance were it to proceed according to a model of uniformity that would inevitably highlight the uneven relations between center and periphery. What is needed, rather, is a strategy of normalization that accounts for and includes difference, yet organizes it according to predictable codes. Amidst the litany of various classificatory schemes that have arisen since the nineteenth century, none is more pervasive, historically persistent *and* considered to be politically-neutral than that of "culture." Culture provides communication with the crucial classificatory framework necessary both to preserve difference at a level acceptable to postcolonial governance and to ensure sufficient regularity in codification. According to this scheme, "translation" names the process of encoding/decoding required to transfer informational content between different linguistico-cultural spheres. Just as the post-Fordist subject must "communicate," the nature of "communication" itself is codified according to a grammar of pronominal identities and representational positions that codifies linguistic exchange according to an predetermined representational scheme of mutually-determined anthropological codes.

In 2006, Naoki Sakai and I co-edited an issue of the multilingual series *Traces* entitled *Translation, Biopolitics, Colonial Difference* in which we presented an argument for articulating the indeterminacy of translation as a mode of social practice to the contingent commodifications of labor-power and the nexus of knowledge that governs anthropological difference.[2] The call for papers proposed to prospective authors the idea of bringing *translation* into a politically-informed discussion about the production of social relations and humanistic knowledge in the context of anthropological difference inherited from colonialism. Central to this discussion was the notion of a *biopolitics of translation*. In a series of lectures in the late 1970s, Michel Foucault introduced and elaborated the assorted concepts of "biopolitics" and "governmentality" as tools for thinking about the way in which the processes of life – and the possibility of controlling and modifying them through the technical means – enter the sphere of power and become its chief concern. Foucault's effort has generally been understood as an innovative attempt to introduce a new ontology, beginning with the body, that would provide a way of thinking of the political subject outside the dominant tradition of modern political philosophy that frames it as a subject of law (Lazzarato 2002: 100–111). "Biopolitics" thus names a quotidian sphere of ostensibly apolitical (or depoliticized) social action and relations – what Foucault calls "the entry of life into history" – that is nevertheless invested with crucial effects for the production of social subjects. These effects, far removed from the role traditionally ascribed to politics per se inasmuch as they concern population management, nevertheless bear upon the construction of what is at stake in the formation of power relations.

We found it was not only possible but also necessary to subject the latent and pervasive Occidentalism in Foucault's work to a thorough critique while at the same time opening up possibilities for an understanding of biopolitics in a global context. The notion of a "biopolitics of translation" acquires critical importance with a view to the specifically modern phenomenon of the linguistic standardization associated with nationalization and colonial land appropriation. Ever since the concomitant birth of philology and biology, modernity has been associated with the advent of a global cartographic imaginary that places peoples with no prior "memory" of migratory contact into relation through the mediation of an imperial center. As the transition to a global form of spatial imaginary, *modernity* begins when the project of standardization is extended across all manner of social differences to encompass diverse populations in the process of national homogenization and domestic segmentation (Bidet 1999). This process must be seen, in turn, in the context of contact with other *global* populations undergoing the same process of systemic definition and structural segmentation. The *biopolitics of translation* thus names that space of exchange and accumulation in which politics appears to have been preempted by the everyday occurrence of language. Our research shows that when "translation" is understood according to a representational scheme of the epistemic subject, it names not the operation by which cultural difference is "bridged," but the pre-emptive operation through which originary difference is segmented and organized according to the various classificatory schemes of knowledge emerging out of the colonial encounter.

The modern regime of translation is a concrete form of "systemic complicity" whose primary function is population management within the purview
of imperial domination. It is a globally-applicable technique of segmentation
aimed at managing social relationships by forcing them to pass through circuits on the "systemic" level. In Sakai's work on the relation between imperial
nationalism and the maintenance of ethnic minorities, we learn that the geography of national sovereignty and civilizational difference indicates an
important kind of subjective technology or governmental technique that has,
until recently, been thoroughly naturalized by an anthropological discourse of
"culture" (Sakai 2000: 462–530). It is only today that we can begin to see how
a multiplicity of disciplinary arrangements forming an economy of translation
actually produces differentially-coded subjects, typically national/racial ones,
whose constitution is interdependent and actually complicit in a single, yet
hierarchical, state of domination. Our aim in the *Traces* volume was thus to
trace a series of genealogies within which "translation" is no longer seen as
simply an operation of transfer, relay, and equivalency, but rather assumes a
vital historical role in the constitution of the social.

Sakai's research into the position of the translator within the modern
regime of co-figured, nationalized language shows a precise parallel to the
logic of sovereignty. Just as Giorgio Agamben has shown how sovereignty is
based on the form of exception (embodied by the figure of the sovereign), the
position of the translator in the modern era has been represented in a similarly exceptional fashion. Sakai's work has turned this relationship inside out,
demonstrating that the regularity of the "national language" as a formation
in which the (hybrid) position of the translator has been deemed irrelevant is
in fact produced in a representational manner only after the practical
encounter of social difference in translation. By proposing to look at the formation of national language through the ostensibly exceptional case of
translation, Sakai has been able to show that it is indeed a systemic, or
international, technique of domination. This discovery parallels the growing
awareness of the crucial role in Capitalist expansion played by the various
forms of irregular and slave labor, rather than the regularized forms of wage
labor (Moulier Boutang 1998). In effect, translation appears to us as the
social relation from which the critique of communication and its corollary
"culture" as the reigning ideology of Capital is most directly linked to a politics of life, or again, the politics in which life becomes invested by Capital.

In the various exceptions that alternately govern labor, life and language,
we begin to grasp the way in which "the West" has established and maintained its "identity" as a specter for the last few centuries as the leading,
knowledgeable region of the globe that supposedly exports innovation
and development to other regions. Yet the very concept of the global according to which regions as such are imagined is intrinsically indebted to the
legacy of colonialism. Although the colonial encounter produced the first
truly *global* relation, "the West" identified itself as a particular and unique
region only by claiming exemptive subtraction from this relation while at

the same time undertaking unprecedented accumulation through originary expropriation.

The presentation of a biopolitics of translation requires more elaboration than can be provided here, so in the remainder of this chapter, I highlight the value of what Sakai calls "heterolingual address" in relation to a critique of the West by referencing a fault-line in the work of Giorgio Agamben. While the two thinkers' approach to language (and, indeed, sovereignty) emphasizes the epistemological and practical problems of exceptionalism, their fundamental divergence with regard to "the paradigm of the West" has crucial ramifications for politics and knowledge.

Address vs. communication

The two aspects of Sakai's understanding of translation are: 1) the distinction between separate moments of "address" and "communication"; and, 2) the exceptional position of the translator. Both of these aspects reflect concerns central to poststructuralism: the former with the "event of language" (Fynsk 1996) above and beyond the determinate meaning of any particular utterance – the fact, as yet inexplicable to science, that linguistic utterance in general is possible for human beings; the latter with the logic of the exclusion or exception.

According to Sakai, whereas "address" indicates a *social relation* (that between addresser and addressee) that is primarily practical and performative in nature, hence undetermined and open to the negotiation of meaning, "communication" names the imaginary representation of that relation in terms of a series of unities denoted by pronominal identities and informational content. Theories of communication, normative by necessity, regularly obscure the fact of address in communication. They are derived from the extra-linguistic assumption that supposedly "we" should be able to "communicate" among ourselves if "we" are a linguistic community. The institution of homolingual address (Sakai 1997: 6) is thus a form of homosociality based on a model of community abstracted from the notion of communion or fusion, what Jean-Luc Nancy calls "immanentism," (Nancy 1991: 3) among its members. The introduction of a distinction between *address* and *communication* allows us to conceive the radical exteriority of social relationships to the production of meaning. Sakai writes: "addressing does not guarantee the message's arrival at the destination. Thus, 'we' as a pronominal invocation in *address* designates a relation, which is performative in nature, independent of whether or not 'we' actually communicate the same information" (Sakai 1997: 4–5).

In itself, "address" does not communicate anything, except to indicate the presence of "communication" as a possibility to be actualized or not in the course of translation. Address is thus an initiation to potentiality: it indicates a relationship essential for signification to take place and order meaning, yet it does not signify anything in particular. Although this potentiality is inherent in any linguistic situation, it is particularly evident in translational exchange because the possibility of failure, of "not communicating," is immediately apparent to all participants. What Sakai calls "the regime of homolingual address" is the model according to which this negativity is understood as a lack of signification, rather than as an unconditioned potentiality "to not be" in the context of a positive relation. In other words, if in translational exchange I do not understand you, it is only under the influence of the homolingual address that I can *assume* the reason for this incomprehension is due to factors such as membership in representative communities. In fact, if we really were not to understand each other, there would be no way for us to check with each other to see if the problem in fact arises from any factor (such as communal membership) in particular. To equate not being "in" communication to the notion that addresser and addressee are not "in" the same social group is to confuse potentiality with representation. Being "out" of a social group concerns a question of status that can only be verified through protocols of representation. The potentiality to be "out" of communication, however, is the force of address that inheres in every instance of communication regardless of representative social status. Any instance of communication indicates a potentiality (the moment of address) as well as signifies a determinate meaning. As such, it includes two sides: one side is the actuality of the event, the fact that there is language. It both *indicates* a social relationship (language is always initially a relation between two or more people) as well as *signifies* a certain meaning. The other side is the fact that this actuality (the failure to communicate) does not present itself as the result of a power that has not been realized, but rather as the effect of a power not-to-realize. Needless to say, if it is possible to choose to communicate, it is always equally possible to try not to communicate. Can one be certain that the attribution of non-communication to "objective" factors such as communal membership is not in itself replete with unexamined institutionalized choices (such as the standardization of language into national forms) that would make trying not to communicate into a form of communication? Such certainty can only be achieved at the unacceptable price of rejecting the notion of social construction. Evidently, the effectivity of this power "to not be" does not occur simply because of presumed gaps between linguistic communities, but also because to try to communicate is to expose oneself to exteriority, to a certain exteriority that cannot be reduced to the externality of a referent to a signification (Sakai 1997: 7). The social praxis denoted in our age by the word "translation" is the linguistic situation that makes this feature most evident precisely because it contrasts with the representation of exchange between discrete spheres of *a priori* communal difference.

We can now summarize several preliminary conclusions concerning the heterolingual address: 1) it is not based on which *position* one adopts (or, most likely, the position into which one is placed), but is rather based on the potentiality thrown into relief by the exceptional position of the translator; 2) the plurality of languages in a given situation does not in itself guarantee access to the heterolingual mode of address, which still requires the recognition of and commitment to heterogeneity in all situations, even those normally thought to be "monolingual" (hence the ubiquitous rejection of Jakobson's notion of "translation proper"); 3) the ethics of heterolingual address calls for the invention of new figures that combine the common and the foreign.

What does the experience of heterolingual address tell us, then, about social relations? Significantly, Sakai characterizes it in terms of *distance*: "In our case, failure in communication means that each of us stands exposed to, but *distant* from, the other without grasping the cause for 'our' separation" (1997: 7). The heterolingual address is thus a form of ethics, in which all parties to communication remember, in view of address, the element of distance in every social relation.

"*As you now speak, that is ethics*" (Agamben 1991: 108). Such is the deceptively simple formula proposed by Agamben at the end of a work on the metaphysical implications of pronominal invocation that he calls, following Jakobson, "shifters." Agamben's ethics of enunciation is construed not in terms of *positions* but in terms of *potentiality and negativity* – precisely, the potential not to be. For the poststructuralist critic of translation, the point of interest would thus inevitably be drawn towards the ways in which such potentialities are variously organized and reorganized into modes of silence, rhetoric and logic.[3]

Does this ethics carry only a negative injunction to maintain "distance", as Sakai apparently maintains, or can it allow, even necessitate, certain forms of proximity? If the "intimate enemy" – to borrow from the title of a well-known work by Ashis Nandy – is a salient feature of postcolonial relations, violence in our postcolonial world cannot be thought without reference to intimacy. Beyond this, we will want to ask: to what extent might the economy of distance required by the ethical relation of heterolingual address be implicated in other practical social relations, such as gender, where the distinction between public and private plays an enormously important role, or again, intellectual difference, where the distinction between levels of knowledge plays a crucial role in the organization of property? Normally, the intimate is what is most consistently disqualified by public institutions devoted to the exercise of public reason, yet feminists have long shown how this distinction is related to gender inequality, while Marxists have shown that it is related to the construction of property. Although Sakai's understanding of distance in the heterolingual address is undoubtedly designed to admit difference in social relations, the implicit equivalence between distance and difference remains inconclusive: distance could easily be recuperated into republican concepts like equality, i.e., equi-distance, through the assumption of identity. Needless to say, the institution of equality, in a juridical sense, has never prevented gross inequities in the social formation. Hence, it is precisely because of these questions that Sakai's notion of heterolingual address would greatly benefit by taking heed of the call for *intimacy* issued by critics such as Gayatri Spivak:

"the requirement for intimacy," she explains, "brings a recognition of the public sphere as well" (1993: 188), especially when it concerns segmentation due to class and gender difference in a postcolonial context of translation. The emphasis Spivak places on the importance of being able "[to speak][...] of intimate matters in the language of the original" can be read as an invitation to rethink the theoretical boundaries of community – precisely the field into which gender relations intervene. Intimacy[4] could thus also be construed as a call to obviate translation by taking a "non-native" language as one's own while at the same time requiring of native speakers a comparable readiness to recognize in foreign accents and non-standard usage of all sorts a new kind of social intimacy. I propose that we call this form of public embrace of the foreigner in all social relations and institutions the "heterolingual intimacy."

Invoking the West

This introduction to the distinction between address and communication leads us to become "attentive to ... uses of the pronominal 'we' and other markers of collective invocation" (Sakai 1997: 4). Once our attention has been drawn to the link between pronominal invocation and homosocial relationships, we can find many occurrences in academic discourse as well as everyday cultural productions. One very interesting example is found in the work of Agamben – interesting precisely because his work has gone further than perhaps any other philosopher in the poststructuralist idiom to explore from a philosophical angle the problem of pronouns and linguistic referentiality to which Sakai's notion of heterolingual address draws our attention.

Agamben's writings on sovereignty and metaphysics since the 1990s have attracted considerable critical acclaim because of the theoretical and historical perspective they bring to contemporary issues related to the so-called "War on Terror" like indefinite detention and the suspension of *habeas corpus*. For Agamben, the camp is the modern paradigm of the political inasmuch as it reveals an essential crisis, or displacement, thrusting "life" into the heart of the exceptional logic upon which secular sovereignty is founded. However, as the "War on Terror" and the supposed "clash of civilizations" suggest, the stakes of this conjuncture could never be attributed to a single nation or group of nations, but always return to the problems inherited from colonialism that beset social relationships.

Curiously, even as Agamben notes that the camp as a political form of population control has its roots in the context of colonial governmentality (Agamben 1998: 166), the historical experience of the non-West is noticeably absent from his work.[5] Elided from the main narrative on the development of biopolitics, the "non-West" returns to make a second appearance in Section III of *Homo Sacer*, the "Camp as paradigm," at the end of the crucial, penultimate chapter, titled "The Camp as *Nomos*." "[T]oday's democratico-capitalist project of eliminating the poor classes through development," writes

Agamben, "not only reproduces within itself the people that is excluded but also transforms the entire population of the Third World into bare life" (1998: 180). Significantly, the fundamental paradigm of modernity – the camp – was first practiced in a colonial situation; decades later, the progression of this history threatens to overwhelm subsequently decolonized populations in a new biopolitical trap. The implicit teleology within which Agamben situates the Third World does not, however, include consideration of subjective agency. Like the return of the repressed, the "Third World" is cited in a way that amounts to little more than capitalizing upon the moral authority of its role, well-described by Gayatri Spivak in her "Can the Subaltern Speak?" as the silent witness.

Although the absence of the non-West in Agamben's historical account is remarkable, it might seem unwarranted to call into question this absence in view of the parameters delineating the object of study. After all, Agamben apparently does not mean to talk about anything *other* than the West (apart from those two instances we just cited, the non-West is otherwise never mentioned in *Homo Sacer*). His narrative begins, in the fashion proper to civilizational history, with the Greeks, developing a geneaological focus on "the tradition" specified by the proper noun, "the West." This same basic narrative structure is common, in fact, to all of his writings, including the early work, *Language and Death: The Place of Negativity* (Agamben 1991), which attracts our attention in the following sections for its treatment of the problems of pronouns and linguistic referentiality.

Doubt is unquestionably warranted, however, when a presumably spatial category, the West, gives way to a temporal one – the modern, or what Agamben also calls in *Homo Sacer*, "the 24 centuries that have gone by since [the foundation of Western politics]" (Agamben 1998: 11) – that enables the transformation of a proper noun into a universal history and grammar. When we read Agamben's early work, we learn that the oscillation from the empirical to the transcendental is an integral feature of the way pronouns have historically been conceived. In a following section, we will use the word *shift* to denote the oscillation or transformation enabled by "the West" in order to highlight its connection to Agamben's discussion of Roman Jakobson's notion of the linguistic role played by "shifters." As many have shown, the constitution of "the West" itself cannot be accomplished without reference to a specific history and a certain hierarchically-organized representation of what constitutes the relation between binary pairs such as outside and inside that typify the social – precisely the essential problem of what Agamben calls "the logic of sovereignty." Needless to say, this form of reference, like any other form, cannot be separated on the one hand from the problems of referentiality (de Man 1996: 34–50)[6] that were at the heart of poststructuralism since Derrida, nor can they be separated on the other hand from a certain discipline of translation – a key theme in Sakai's understanding of the social – that binds various different levels of externality into a single, coherent referent.

Pronominal invocation and shifters

In *Language and Death*, Agamben shows how the problem of pronominal usage constitutes a hidden matrix, running from thinkers as deeply opposed as Hegel and Heidegger, for the philosophical negativity that determines the metaphysical effects of linguistic referentiality. The attempt to find an alternative to the philosophical experience of language that rests on negativity is pursued, to no avail, through the historical experience of poetry. Thomas Carl Wall adroitly summarizes Agamben's conclusion: "neither philosophy nor poetry is able to grasp the taking-place of language" (Wall 1999: 129).

Language and Death begins by noting a curious parallel between Hegel and Heidegger, two philosophers who otherwise exhibit considerable mutual dissonance. Although we take sense-certainty for granted as the most concrete manifestation of the real, Hegel shows how the demonstrative pronoun (this), in its universal applicability, actually introduces an element of negation into what was thought to be most positive and certain. The introduction of this negativity serves as the point of departure for the crux of Hegel's philosophical system and dialectical teleology in general. In Heidegger, whose writings devoted considerable effort to disqualifying Hegelian dialectic without recourse to the reductive "leap of faith" required by positivism, negativity enters through the demonstrative pronoun "there" (or *da* in German) which forms an integral part of his non-dialectical replacement for subjectivity – *Dasein*. The demonstrative pronoun (there or this), occupying a crucial place in the systems of philosophers as deeply opposed as Hegel and Heidegger, sits at the crucial fault line between *signification* and *indication*.

Agamben asserts that the problem of indication "constitutes the original theme of philosophy" (1991: 16). This retrospective look initiates an historical narrative that traces the mutual imbrication between grammatical studies and metaphysical reflection on being and essence running from Antiquity through the Middles Ages up to the Modern, leading Agamben to conclude that the pronoun has occupied "a privileged status ... in the history of medieval and modern thought" (1991: 20). Agamben describes three "crucial" or "decisive" moments in this history: the first comes with the Aristotelian determination of first substance (*prote ousia*) through reference to demonstrative pronouns. The Aristotelian formation, however, was only implicit in the formula. A further "decisive step" was taken by Alexandrian and then Latin grammarians from the second through fifth centuries AD explicitly thematizing the connection between the pronoun and the sphere of the first substance (Agamben 191: 20). This history, binding grammar to metaphysics, culminates in the "decisive step" taken by modern linguistics to understand the distinction between "signifying" and "showing" (Agamben 1991: 23) operated by a grammatical class of words that Emile Benveniste first described as "indicators of the utterance" and which Roman Jakobson subsequently called *shifters*. Crucial to our argument, a lengthy citation is necessary:

In an essay published a year after Benveniste's study, Jakobson, taking up the French linguist's definition in part, classified pronouns among the "shifters": that is, among those special grammatical units that are contained in every *code* and that cannot be defined outside of a relation to the *message* ... [H]e defines shifter as a special class of signs reuniting the two functions: the *symbol-indices* ... As symbol-indices, they are capable of replenishing their significance in the code only through the deictic reference to a concrete instance of discourse ... The proper meaning of pronouns – as shifters and *indicators of the utterance* – is inseparable from a reference to the instance of discourse. The articulation – the shifting – that they effect is not from the nonlinguistic (tangible indication) to the linguistic, but from *langue* to *parole*. ... Pronouns and the other indicators of the utterance, before they designate real objects, indicate precisely *that language takes place.* In this way, they permit the reference to the very *event of language*, the only context in which something can be signified ... metaphysics is that experience of language that, in every speech act, grasps the disclosure of that dimension, and in all speech, experiences above all the "marvel" that language exists. Only because language permits a reference to its own instance through *shifters*, something like being and the world are open to speculation.

(Agamben 1991: 24–26)

Agamben asks what it means to *indicate* the instance of discourse. Modern linguistics leaves this question unanswered, or else implicitly resolves it, according to Agamben, in the metaphysical recuperation of immediacy – what Jakobson calls an "existential relation" between the "I of discourse" and the "I of existence" (Agamben 1991: 31–32). Presumably the I-of-existence is the one that actually is born, breathes, and dies. It is impossible, however, to reconcile this notion of existential-I distinct from linguistic-I with Benveniste's demonstration that time is merely an effect of discourse. The temporality of the "I of existence" would therefore have to be thought in conjunction with the temporality of the "I of discourse" (Agamben 1991: 35–37). Of course, the existential-I should be the one that we can most readily point to without the aid of language. Hence, modern linguistics continues to rely upon an essential distinction between *indication* and *signification* that represents, in Agamben's argument, a primary metaphysical decision. Agamben attempts to capture the stakes of this primary decision through the conceptual category of *voice*.

Since antiquity, voice came to be understood, Agamben argues after excavation, as "a pure intention to signify" (Agamben 1991: 33). In modern linguistics, the voice, the animal voice, is presupposed by the shifters that indicate the instance of discourse (Agamben 1991: 35). Yet it must be removed, says Agamben, in order for meaningful discourse to occur. This removal or elision of that indicative moment without determinate meaning is what Agamben names *Voice* (with a capital V). This is "the voice as a pure *indication* – within the structure of shifters – of the instance of discourse"

(Agamben 1991: 32). Voice (with a capital V) is no longer voice and not yet meaning, and yet without it meaning and nonsense would be indistinguishable. Agamben calls Voice the "supreme shifter" that marks the essential negativity that opens up the various foundational binary splits of metaphysics to which both philosophy and poetry – ostensibly opposing forms of expression – fall prey, albeit in conflicting ways.

This amounts to a strong presentation of the metaphysical presupposition of speaking subjects as the foundation of social ontology. A recent trend in European studies of migration and capitalist development demonstrating that the importance of "exit" or "exodus" often surpasses that of voice in the determination of the political suggests the importance of rethinking the privilege granted the latter categorization.[7] Agamben attracts our attention precisely because he is one of the few contemporary philosophers overtly committed to the importance of rethinking the metaphysical basis for the determination of human being exclusively as speaking subject.

Paradigm shift

It should be obvious by now that an affinity exists between Voice (Agamben) and address (Sakai). Just as address precedes communication but bears in itself nothing more than an indicative function naming a relation and a potentiality (Sakai), so Voice only marks the event of language (Agamben) through which all other metaphysical systems of binary opposition are initiated. The major difference between the two conceptual categories concerns not so much their conceptual content as their mode of representation, as in the sense of staging, or, indeed, signification.

Between Agamben's discovery of the "supreme shifter" and the historical narrative deployed to facilitate this discovery, an irreconcilable gap appears. The pragmatic function attributed to the proper noun "the West," which enables all manner of diverse texts in different languages and different historical contexts to be assembled into a unitary frame of pronominal reference, is nowhere placed in proximity to the theoretical attempt to wrest originary difference from the metaphysical oscillation introduced by the shifters. In the absence of any attempt to explain or problematize the unity and/or construction of "the Western metaphysical tradition," such pronominal references insert a form of distance that enables the deictic function: they point to what they refer to, as though "the West" were simply "there." Lacking an explicit definition of the term, the reader would be very tempted to assume that the definition of the West is fundamentally spatial and in that sense constitutes a form of tangible indication. If the signification of any particular word does not have to be defined and yet still has meaning, it is because usage permits us to use it to indicate a tangible reality at hand. Demonstrative pronouns like "there" perform this linguistic function. Of course, words like the West indicate directional sense only in relation to other points of reference. If we are looking in the direction of the West and hope to keep our view on a specific series of objects, it will be necessary to remain stationary. Otherwise, as soon as we turn, not only would the objects in view be different, but so would the orientation of the viewer. Likewise, it is entirely possible to imagine that what we today refer to as "the West" might not be what is referred to by that term tomorrow (nor yesterday) – not to mention the fact that even today what "we" mean by the term can vary widely depending on the point of enunciation. Hence, it should be obvious that "the West" is not *simply* a spatial entity but also a reference to social relations. As Sakai writes,

> Though it is generally believed to designate a place, the West is a name whose indexing function is evoked in order to represent *spatially* the events of the past, the present and possibly the future in chronological order. ... Thanks to this spatial mapping of a chronological order onto a cartographic plane, it used to be possible to say meaningfully that the West was *ahead* of the rest of the world.
>
> But, it is important that what obtains in this cartographic mapping of the chronologial order is the corroboration of a particular social relationship which exists – say, between the rich merchant and the peasants from the countryside, the colonizer and the native, the educated upper-class colonial official and the poor displaced 'mixed-blood' from the countryside, and the wealthy local landowner and the impoverished labouring immigrant – in the guise of spatial direction at the very site where reference to or distinction regarding either the West or the Rest is enunciated. ... The putative unity of the West is nothing but one result of this operation by which to generate an apparent taxonomic coherence where real coherence is impossible. Here, it is important to keep in mind that it is equally possible to conceive of this social dynamics *temporally*, without spatial representation".
>
> (Sakai 2005: 183)

In the context of a discussion about *Language and Death*, the question to be posed is not whether there are archives of texts bearing within them all manner of material differences as well as a high-degree of intertextual referentiality organized around shared themes and conceptual concerns. The question is rather the relation between those archives and social formation. From this perspective, which is fundamentally that of the subject of knowledge, archival texts engage and sustain a multiplicity of readings open to interpellation by whatever social formation. When those readings are uniformly funneled into an adverb-turned-proper noun, as in the case of "the West," the function of *shifters* becomes *supremely* evident. In the final analysis, "the West" in Agamben's text performs an indexical function even as it creates its own signification. The metaphysical oscillation between indication and signification, time and space, initiated by the institutionalization of the West is, in other words, much like a demonstrative pronoun masquerading as a proper one.

In his discussions of the relation between translation and philosophy, Derrida shows how the oscillation between metaphysical oppositions is generally accomplished by the deployment of metaphor. Derrida radically proposes an understanding of metaphor as nothing other than the metaphor of translation: the inevitable gain and loss of meaning that occurs in *every* linguistic exchange, even those deemed to occur "within" the same language. Derrida's explicit rejection of Roman Jakobson's exclusion of certain forms of address from "translation proper" reveals an operation essential to the use of shifters. Apparently, the brilliance of Jakobson's discovery of the shifter blinded him to its relation to translation. Yet once we abandon the exclusions in his categorization of translational practice as secondary and derivative, it becomes impossible to deny that when I say "here" and you say "there," the shifter operates in the mode of translation. Even when both words refer to exactly the same place, the difference in our respective orientations, which inevitably produces different views, suggests the gain and loss of meaning typical of any translational exchange.

Hence, it is no surprise to find that translation plays a crucial, yet wholly unthematized, role in *Language and Death*. The salient attribute of "the West" in that text is defined by a series of citations assembled from a very diverse range of texts that form a chronology of questions about grammar and metaphysics. Most, if not all, of these texts would remain unreadable for contemporary non-specialist readers without the aid of translation. Indeed, in numerous passages from Greek, Latin and Provençal texts among others, Agamben displays considerable interest in etymology and a talent for translation. Is it thus a coincidence that Agamben's illustration of the discovery of the Voice following Aristotle occurs in the translational situation, when Augustine "presents, perhaps for the first time in Western culture, the now-familiar idea of a 'dead language'"(Agamben 1991: 33)? The scene of "Western culture" actively staged by the text, which enables the apprehension of first-time events, cannot be comprehended without deploying the apparatus of translation. Beyond the thematic concerns that bind the diverse texts cited by the historical narrative, the one common thread amongst them all is translation. This commonality reveals, once again, an intention to signify apart from any determinate meaning. All the texts, regardless of what they contain, have to be translated for the living. What is "the West," thus, if not precisely one of the results – and productive sites – of translation? Once the effects of such translation are projected onto the image of a direction, the shift that occurs in moving from the West as an index of orientation to the significance of a proper noun and a subject of history is engaged.

Now we can sum up two conclusions: 1) the paradigm of "the West" deployed by *Language and Death* is nothing other than that of the shifter in its metaphysical aspect; and 2) translation is the operation that enables this shift. Although there is not a significant conceptual difference between Voice and address, the manner of *presentation* is decidedly different. While both

Voice and address ultimately require that we become attentive to metaphysical oscillations between signification and indication, address uniquely calls on us to bear in mind the practical aspect of translation as a social relation. From this perspective, address now names the thematization of the Voice in the context of translation-as-social praxis. Although the crucial inclusion of translation does not change the fundamental conceptual account of Voice, the mode of presentation itself ushers in what Derrida would call a "general economy" of Jakobsonian shifters. Within this general economy, the tandem exclusions effected by "translation proper" in one context and "the I of existence" in another are inoperative. Indeed, we are always reminded that there are innumerable ways to say "Voice," these ways must be subjected to the concrete instance of translation, and the lack of capital letters in certain systems of writing cannot be taken as the sign of *either* translatability *or* untranslatability. Within this general economy, the metaphysical function of mega-shifters like the West is more evident than ever.

Needless to say, the liberation in social and political terms from this mega-shifter will not be accomplished simply by endless metaphysical deconstruction. Yet Perry Anderson's pronouncement that "in the hollow of the pronoun lies the aporia of the programme" covers up, as Spivak deftly points out, the possibilities for new types of social relations beyond those prescribed by the desire for recognition according to the neo-colonial terms of the West and the Rest binary. "For those of us who feel," writes Spivak, "that the 'subject' has a history and that the task of the first-world subject of knowledge in our historical moment is to resist and critique 'recognition' of the Third World through 'assimilation', this specificity is crucial" (Spivak 1988: 292).

Sakai's focus on the moment of address in translation, rather than simply the discovery of Voice through the historic travails of a metaphysical tradition, ushers in a veritable *paradigm shift*, enabling the poststructuralist concern with the metaphysical effects of pronominal usage to be placed in the context of social praxis. Undoubtedly, as Spivak argues, this is not a replacement for a tool kit that includes economic, political and historical analysis, but rather a complement to the two. The nature of this tool in its subjective dimensions remains, however, to be determined.

Specific intellectuals and the social movement of knowledgeable bodies: surviving the transition to a world society

Previous critiques of Occidentalism have focused on themes such as colonial ambivalence and the reversal of established hierarchies, yet tend to leave the basic structure of anthropological difference intact inasmuch as it is linguistically-encoded in the complex and mobile relations between major and minor languages; by contrast, a project in the biopolitics of translation brings to the critique of the West both an epistemological critique of the anthropological basis of knowledge and a practical engagement with the contemporary social formation at the level of expression. Just as the Marxian critique of the commodity fetish reminded us that the fruits of labor, now reified, actually bear within them the trace of a social relation, we argue that translation can also be understood as a form of social relation requiring similar critique of elements assumed to be extraneous to the production of meaning and bearing similar creative potential. From the geneaological perspective of a biopolitics of translation, the emphasis is on not what we are but rather what we can become (Hardt and Negri 2004: 105) at the same time as we rethink the consequences of historical responsibility vis-à-vis the colonial encounter that produced a global society.

Crucial to that potentiality in the post-Fordist era is what Foucault would call the role of the "specific intellectual." Needless to say, not everybody labors and lives under conditions that would permit intervention into highly abstract structures such as "shifters" and their metaphysical presuppositions. This sort of critique must face up to its own inscription in a system of professional competency that is part of the production of social distinctions such as class. Sakai's critique of translation as a form of social production forces us to reconsider the institutional role of intellectuals and the possibilities for specific intervention. Seen from this perspective, universities of the nineteenth and twentieth centuries are nothing but institutions of paradigmatic "national translation." The normalized form of "national culture" emerges through globally-codified relations of domination, or cultural translation, typically carried out in universities. Professional (that is, "organic") intellectuals are the translators, in a sense that goes far beyond the rendering of specific texts: they are the ones who fashion the forms of expression. They not only make them fit over the functional requirements of international exchange, they also substantially embody or "wear" those forms, becoming institutionalized forms of "knowledgeable bodies" essential to concrete social production. The subtle negotiations of that fit and fashion – which constitute a certain plasticity of social bodies in general – are then called "culture." Typically, national formations of culture repress differences such as the indeterminacy of the translator and the historical repression of local ethnic, class and gender difference. By the same token, professional intellectuals are also the ones who take the operational knowledge of the international exchange society and render them into the terms of a national class system, where any resistance can again be called, in a derogatory sense, "culture" (i.e., cultural burdens, cultural idiosyncrasies, cultural atavisms, etc.).

Undoubtedly, the struggle for control over the exceptions of anthropological difference as it plays out within and between disciplines as well as within and between nationalized populations favors today the production of subjects bound by the expression of *ressentiment*. Control over the codification of this representational scheme invariably involves preemptively identifying with an exceptional position that is subsequently disavowed even while actively promoting its reproduction through disciplinary institutions. This is the contradiction we saw in Agamben, whose attentiveness to the logic of the exception does not prevent a Western exceptionalism from creeping into his work.

It is within this context that we can fruitfully expand upon Lazzarato and Negri's seminal observation that the role of the intellectual today "cannot thus be reduced to either a critical and epistemological function or to an engagement with and witness to liberation: it is on the level of *collective agency* itself that he intervenes" (Lazzarato and Negri 1991).[8] Within the biopolitics of translation, the construction of collective agency occurs each time anew in what Sakai's research has called *the mode of the heterolingual address*: in this mode, "you are always confronted, so to speak, with foreigners in your enunciation when your attitude is that of the heterolingual address. Precisely because you wish to communicate with her, him, or them, so the first, and perhaps most fundamental, determination of your addressee, is that of the one who might not comprehend your language, that is, of the foreigner" (Sakai 1997: 9).

Guided by Sakai's ethics of heterolingual address, several preliminary conclusions could be obtained: 1) the prevalence of homolingual address is not based on which position one adopts, but is rather based on the operation of bilateral shifters such as "the West"; 2) the plurality of languages in a given situation does not in itself guarantee access to the heterolingual mode of address, which still requires the commitment to heterogeneity in all situations, even those normally thought to be "monolingual" (hence the rejection of Jakobson's notion of "translation proper"); 3) the ethics of heterolingual address call for something like what Wall identifies, in reading Levinas, "as an infinite responsibility, or even an uncontrollable compulsion to be for-the-other, which can never be satisfied or used up" (Wall 1999: 77) and 4) this infinite responsibility is a response to the infinite oscillation permitted by mega-shifters such as "the West."

Sakai suggests that there is both a constraining discipline and an emancipating politics of translation for those placed between the national class-structures and the global exchange-systems organized around what is called "the West." In terms of a constraining discipline, intellectuals are called upon to translate not just content specific to other cultures but, most important, the general rules of international exchange. Even as we, in our role as translators, adapt concepts and images to the needs of the local class structure, we are also contributing to the solidification of a segmented structure analogous to class in the emerging global-State. We can resent this role as translators, and then resent the whole "verbiage" of intellectuality which we have made into our trade; this sort of posture regularly leads intellectuals to privilege either a site of "real struggle" in "the outside world" while abandoning "theory" as a site of struggle altogether, or else to retreat into esoteric, aestheticized representations incomprehensible outside of a professional caste. Rather than adopting either of these approaches, which seem to me to preserve, in spite of great differences, the exceptional role of intellectuals as mediators and distributors of the heterogeneity between world and knowledge (a role that ultimately institutionalizes the role of elites, regardless of which side one is on, by denying the relative autonomy of specific social practices), we can instead set about using the tools of the trade to work against its normalized effects. But how to go about that?

As we have seen, Naoki Sakai presents a very interesting answer, which concerns a kind of translocal, translinguistic practice, a practice which is both contextual and respectful of the "foreigner" in all of us. In the face of sophisticated discourses embedded in Western institutions, such as Agamben, what could be asked each time, as Holmes suggests to me, is: how could this material be used to overcome the causes and effects of capitalist imperialism? And if it is potentially useful, then how can it be translated against the grain of whatever class structure one is in, with its particular hierarchy of inclusions and exclusions, signified and covered up by its particular culture? And if those counter-translations have been done, then how could they in turn be exposed to heteronomous translations from elsewhere?

These questions would require us to reconsider how we typically translate and naturalize certain discourses, particularly, as we have seen in Agamben's case, by fetishizing a proper name or mega-shifter, the better to forget the real situations and processes from which they were subtracted. But the same questions also point toward a possible development of cultural dreams, organizational forms and productive techniques that could help people everywhere to survive the transition to a world society. Intellectuals are not required to perform the heroic role of architects and social engineers who provide blueprints for the whole of society – in fact, such a role amounts to little more than a self-aggrandizing hallucination; but, like every other kind of laborer, they can respond to the specific situations of their trade, develop corresponding autonomous responses, and then translate them into other situations.

These requirements and their multiple expressions can then become the basis for a vast reorganization of disciplinary divisions and subjectivities in the human sciences carried out in multiple sites across the globe. As Foucault noted, it is not because there are objects demanding study that the disciplines arise; on the contrary, it is rather only once the disciplines are in place that their corresponding objects, methods and theses arise. To achieve that transformation, we will need a social movement within the "edu-factory" that militates for specific institutional changes. Otherwise, we can be sure that the coming reorganization of the Humanities will proceed solely according to the ideological parameters of neoliberalism.

I see, in closing, in the biopolitics of translation the nascent form of social movement that corresponds most *specifically* to the globalized intellectual laborer of today – a practice of knowledge, in other words, as a social movement of "permanent translation" devoted to surviving and thriving in the transition to a world society (Ivekovic 2002: 121–45) – the multitude of foreigners we are becoming.

Bibliography

Agamben, G. (1991) *Language and Death: The Place of Negativity.* Minneapolis, University of Minnesota Press.
——. (1998) *Homo Sacer: Sovereign Power and Bare Life.* Stanford, CA, Stanford University Press.
Bidet, J. (1999) *Théorie Générale*, Paris, Presses Universitaires.
De Man, P. (1996) The Epistemology of Metaphor. *Aesthetic Ideology.* Minneapolis, University of Minnesota Press.
Fynsk, C. (1996) *Language and Relation ... That there is language.* Stanford, CA, Stanford University Press.
Grandmaison, O. L. C. (2005) *Coloniser, Exterminer: sur la guerre et l'état colonial.* Paris, Fayard.
Grau, M. (2002) Erasing "economy": Derrida and the construction of divine economies. *Cross Currents,* http://findarticles.com/p/articles/mi_m2096/is_3_52/ai_94983821.
Hardt, M. and Negri, A. (2004) *Multitude*, Penguin.
Ivekovic, R. (2002) La traduction permanente. *Transeuropéenes,* 121–45.
Lazzarato, M. (2002) *From Biopower to Biopolitics.* Pli.
——. (2004) General Intellect. *Multitudes,* http://multitudes.samizdat.net/General-intellect.html.
Lazzarato, M. and Negri, T. (1991) Travail immatériel et subjectivité. *Futur Anterieur,* Été.
Moulier Boutang, Y. (1998) *De l'esclavage au salariat. Économie historique du salariat bridé.* Paris, Presses Universitaires de France.
Mullarky, J. (2007) *Post-Continental Philosophy: An Outline.* New York, Continuum.
Nancy, J.-L. (1991) *The Inoperative Community.* Minneapolis, University of Minnesota Press.
Nelson, C. and Grossberg, L. (1988) *Marxism and the Interpretation of Culture.* Urbana, Chicago, University of Illinois.
Rao, S. (2005), Peut-on envisager l'avenir de la traduction sans plaisir ? Pour une érotique du traduire, META, vol. 50, no. 4, December 2005. http://www.erudit.org/livre/meta/2005/000222co.pdf.
Sakai, N. (1997) *Translation and Subjectivity: On "Japan" and Cultural Nationalism.* Minneapolis, London, University of Minnesota Press.
——. (1997) Return to the East, Return to the West. *Translation and Subjectivity. On "Japan" and Cultural Nationalism.* Minneapolis, London, University of Minnesota Press.
——. (2000) You Asians: On the Historical Role of the West and Asia Binary. *South Atlantic Quarterly,* 99, 789–817.
——. (2000) Subject and Substratum. *Cultural Studies,* 15, 462–530.
——. (2005) The West – A Dialogic Prescription or Proscription? *Social Identities,* 11, 183.
——. (2006) Two Negations: fear of being excluded and the logic of self-esteem. In Calichman, R. (Ed.) *Contemporary Japanese Thought.* New York, Columbia University Press.
Solomon, J. (SU, Z.). (2007) *Xianfazhiren de huisheng. Tamkang Studies of Foreign Languages and Literatures.* 9, 105–124.
——. (2009) The Proactive Echo: Ernst Cassirer's 'Myth of the State' and the Biopolitics of Global English. *Translation Studies,* 2:1, 52–70.
Spivak, G. C. (1988) Can the Subaltern Speak? *Marxism and the Interpretation of Culture.* Urbana, Chicago, University of Illinois.

——. (1993). The Politics of Translation, *Outside in the Teaching Machine*, New York, Routledge 1993, 179–200.

Wall, T. C. (1999) *Radical Passivity: Levinas, Blanchot, and Agamben*, New York, State University of New York Press.

Notes

1 Many of the ideas and expressions herein were developed in dialogue with Naoki Sakai, Brian Holmes, Richard Calichman, and Frédéric Neyrat. Footnotes alone cannot express my admiration and indebtedness. All errors are my own.

2 This three-part staging of agency in language is taken from Gayatri Spivak, "The Politics of Translation" (1993: 179–200).

3 A simple reference will have to substitute in this limited space for a detailed discussion of the promising concept of caress in translation advanced by Sathya Rao (2005).

4 An important corrective to this debilitating "oversight" in Agamben's account of the historical development of the logic of the exception can be found in Olivier Le Cour-Grandmaison's work on the French colonial experience in Algeria, which demonstrates how exceptional juridical and military techniques developed in the colonies were later used to suppress class insurrection in the metropolitan country. Any attempt to understand the "hidden matrix of the political" (Agamben) through the "logic of the exception" codified by sovereignty necessarily needs to account for the "state of exception" seen in colonial – and postcolonial – violence (Grandmaison 2005). With all the attention given to Hannah Arendt's *Origins of Totalitarianism* in Agamben's *Homo Sacer*, it is significant that Agamben draws scant consequence from the implicit significance of Arendt's essential insight in that work: The argument, convincingly laid out by Arendt, that twentieth-century European fascism must be seen as an importation of imperialist methods into the metropolitan countries of Europe implicitly suggests that the only way to really understand the "logic of the exception" in its biopolitical and historical dimensions is to privilege the historical experience of colonial violence.

5 Paul de Man's essay "The Epistemology of Metaphor" provides a useful introduction.

6 The best representative of this trend may be found in volume 19 (Winter, 2004) of the French revue, *Multitudes* (Paris: Exils).

7 English translation by Jon Solomon.

9 Total war and subjectivity

"Economic ethics" as a trajectory toward postwar

J. Victor Koschmann[1]

It is common among chroniclers of Japan's recovery from World War II to observe that the late 1940s was uniquely a time when the capacity for autonomous, creative action that is evoked by the term *shutaisei* (active subjectivity) was of central concern to intellectuals. They generally note that creative spontaneity and individuality had been suppressed during the "dark valley" of totalitarianism and war. Thus, they see it as natural that the early-postwar period should be the moment in which *shutaisei* was most fully theorized, reflected upon, and debated.[2] The problem with this periodization is simply that it ignores the prevalence of extended discussions of *shutaisei* in books and journal articles published between the mid-1930s and 1945. Wartime publications are filled with controversy over and theories of *shutaisei* and the need for it in a period of crisis.

The historiographical lapse is noted by the intellectual historian Iwasaki Minoru in a provocative essay on wartime Japanese theories of subjectivity/*shutaisei* that focuses on wartime technology theory as a major predecessor to the postwar debate. Indeed, according to Iwasaki the postwar debate was merely a "poor and emaciated repetition" of the more sophisticated and extensive wartime discussions (Iwasaki 1998: 160). The present chapter will expand on Iwasaki's study by investigating another wartime approach to the problem of *shutaisei* that was related to the discussions of technology but quite distinct from it: the debate on "economic ethics."

In tune with the purpose of this volume, it is appropriate to note briefly how much the argument of this chapter owes to Naoki Sakai's multifaceted influence over the many years of our intellectual and personal association. I did not originally intend this chapter to be an illustration or exemplar of Sakai's approach, so whatever marks it bears are there because his influence has been pervasive and often profound. That influence tends to be of a certain kind, reflecting a particular relationship to Sakai's work that is only one among many possible ones. As Meaghan Morris suggests in her foreword to Sakai's *Translation and Subjectivity,* his work has an "involving" quality and an openness that allows it to "send readings off in many directions unanticipated 'in' the text" (Morris 1997: xiii, xv). My own reading of Sakai's work is attentive primarily to its ramifications for the practice of the intellectual history of empire, especially wartime Japan in Asia and Japan–U.S. relations.

Of all the interrelated facets of Sakai's work to date, the ones that have most directly influenced this chapter are his analyses with respect to Japan and the U.S. of the universal/particular binary and especially its implications for the relationship between West and East (Sakai, Naoki 1997: Chapters 3, 4, and 5). Accordingly, the chapter attempts, among other things, to show that Japanese thinking and planning in regard to the New Order in East Asia was coeval and deeply implicated with contemporary thought in the US and Europe. That is, one could say that major dimensions of Japanese fascism were cosmopolitan in their intellectual origins and reference points. At the same time, however, this chapter seeks to take seriously the particularistic, self-orientalizing side of Japanese fascism as well, giving it more play than Sakai typically does.

Among the many processes stimulated by the Japanese invasion of China in 1937 were intense efforts among Japanese intellectuals to make their academic knowledge and insight relevant to the contemporary crisis. War demanded the massive expansion of economic production which, in turn, would require not only resources and machinery but the national mobilization of human talent and effort. It would also require that new economic controls be imposed at the national level. That is, as a result of the military crisis the state was given new salience as an economic unit, and new intensity was injected into discussions of how the national economy should be organized and what measures were needed to expand the productive forces, allocate labor power, and reproduce the means of production.

The resulting controversies were scarcely limited to price and wage controls, resource procurement, consumption limits, and other strictly economic issues. Discussion of the urgent need to mobilize human beings directed attention to questions of subjective intentionality and motivation. What sorts of appeal would be effective? Was narrow self-interest the only effective motivational mechanism? Historically aware economists and social policy experts responded by raising the issue of "economic man" (*keizaijin*) and his or her relationship to the ethics of action. The result was a debate on what came to be called "economic ethics" and, more broadly, the subjective relationship between ethics and interest. This chapter will extract from the works of several of the major participants in this wartime discussion the main outlines of the "new economic ethic" (and the "new human being" that was to be its bearer) that they proposed, while also outlining some of the various traditionalist/Japanist alternatives. The chapter will conclude with some tentative observations about the continuities and discontinuities between wartime and postwar theories of active subjectivity.

Ethics of cooperativism

In 1939 and 1940, philosopher Miki Kiyoshi and economist Ryû Shintarô, who were prominent members of the prime minister's think tank, the Shôwa

Kenkyûkai (Shôwa Research Association), teamed up to explore questions related to ethics and interest in as inclusive and systematic a manner as possible (Fletcher 1982: 180, n. 36).[3] They and other progressive intellectuals had interpreted the war with China as a world-historical event that was destined to bring about far-reaching change in East Asia; therefore, they raised questions beyond the immediate need to expand production and improve efficiency, questions related to Japan's ethical mission and the society of the future. They saw their new social model as a way of solving the problems of liberalism while also fully realizing the goals of freedom, equality, and productivity that liberalism had failed to solve. The paper that resulted from their efforts was to become part of the blueprint for Japan's New Order from 1940 on, and although the Order itself was abortive, one could argue that some of its elements were revived as part of the postwar social system.

Miki and Ryû set out to conceptualize the permanent transition from a liberal to what they called a "cooperativist" (*kyôdôshugiteki*) economic system. Rather than based on profit, this new economic system was to be devoted to the public interest and would be "ethical in essence" (Sakai 1979: 343).[4] It was to be the institutional embodiment of a "new economic ethic," defined in the following terms. First, this ethic was to be devoted primarily to the task of developing the forces of production, not in order to maximize profit, but to maximize consumption. Second, it was to be premised not on the profit calculations of "economic man" but rather on the social contribution of "occupational," or "functional man" (*shokunôteki ningen*) (Sakai 1979: 347).

Their introductory argument invokes Immanuel Kant as well as Karl Marx, providing an initial indication of the genealogy of their thought. Liberalism, they recall, had pursued human freedom, but what it produced was merely freedom for the "haves," leaving the "have-nots" in an "inhuman state of subordination." Indeed, in a deeper sense, both "haves" and "have-nots" were destined to lead an inhuman existence under capitalism because rather than autonomous personalities in control of their fate, they were equally subordinate to "the abstraction, capital":

> The so-called economic man envisioned in liberal economy is not an actual human being who is the subject of autonomous will, but rather a person consumed by purely monetary calculation. The freedom bestowed upon such an economic man is, in fact, none other than the freedom of capital accumulation. ... Thus, in a society where production and distribution are disorderly, economic life is ruled by a blind necessity that operates oblivious of all individual or communal will, and relations between people appear as relations among things. Human freedom can become actual only in a social economy which, rather than being ruled by the blind forces of market and competition, is controlled according to a consciously executed plan.

(Sakai 1979: 343–44)

The cooperativist economic ethic that Miki and Ryû devised to address this situation was governed by three basic principles: functional capacity, utility, and public interest.

By the principle of functional capacity, Miki and Ryû meant the dialectical unity in the human being between a functional dimension that was immanently social and a personal dimension that was transcendent and free. According to them, the principle of functional capacity presumed the primacy of the whole, but was not "totalistic." That is,

> In cooperativism, emphasis on individual autonomy and spontaneity are connected to an ethics of respect for personality. The meaning of being human is not exhausted in functional capacity, but also includes personal meaning. [Therefore] ... the human being is an instrument but at the same time an end in itself ... furthermore, as personalities human beings are free and, as free entities, are responsible subjects. If humans were not free it would be impossible to attach responsibility to them.
>
> (Sakai 1979: 349–50)

Although Miki and Ryû recommended a thoroughly controlled, planned economy where the whole would definitely take precedence over the parts, one can argue that they tried to conceive of that whole as a dialectical process that made substantial room for liberal conceptions of freedom and autonomy. In this light, despite its fascist overtones, their project begins to emerge as an attempt to develop (and in some ways "distort") liberal thought rather than reject it outright. It was only logical that they should seek to make a place for individual initiative, because, as they pointed out, "Unless the power of the nation's people is set in motion, economic development toward the objective of expanding production will be impossible" (Sakai 1979: 356).

By the second principle, that of utility, Miki and Ryû meant arrangements that "activate things toward their greatest effect and productivity." For example, they conclude that "the principle of utility demands that management be given superiority over ownership" (Sakai 1979: 351). The separation of capitalists, including stockholders, from managers in their system, and the devolution of power to the latter, was consistent with the shift from profit-orientation toward the maximization of productivity in the public interest. That is not to say that private ownership was to be liquidated; indeed, Miki and Ryû confirm that it should be respected. But only managers who were thoroughly professionalized, committed to central planning and the public interest, and had nothing to gain from maximizing profits could be trusted to manage large firms. Indeed, industrial and commercial firms themselves had a dual character that reflected the distinction between ownership and management: "On the one hand, the firm carries out the function of capital ownership and to that extent is animated by the pursuit of private interest; on the other, it performs a public, social function and in this dimension it contributes to the public interest. The maintenance and development of the national economy are carried out as the sum of these twin functions" (Sakai 1979: 352). The principle of utility also required that under cooperativism technology should be open and shared as a "joint possession of society" rather than monopolized and jealously guarded, as was the case in liberal capitalism (Sakai 1979: 353).

At least some of these principles, and many other measures intended to rationalize industrial operations and enhance efficiency during wartime, originated in the efforts that had begun in the 1920s to apply the American doctrines of Scientific Management pioneered by Frederic Winslow Taylor. Indeed, according to historian William Tsutsui,

> Scientific Management was more than just a tool in the hands of the Japanese wartime state. Indeed, Taylorism and the logic of efficiency which underlay it were among the intellectual building blocks of the entire wartime structure of economic and poitical control. The values of economic optimalization, technocratic neutrality, managerialism and bureaucracy which characterized modern management also suffused the "New Order" and what has been labelled "Japanese fascism".
>
> (Tsutsui 1998: 103)

The few major modifications that were entailed in this indigenization were broadly consistent with American "revised Taylorism," even though wartime proponents of the American methods were forced to make them appear "Japanese." In short, "While German science and spirituality were widely praised, it was American methods and American accomplishments that continued to define the 'state of the art' to Japanese managers" (Tsutsui 1998: 121).

The third principle, that of public interest, demanded that "all economic activity should be regulated from the standpoint of the interest of the whole economic community" (Sakai 1979: 353). Under liberal capitalism, economic activity was allowed to proceed more or less unencumbered by concerns about the general social welfare, because the so-called public interest was upheld by social welfare organizations and other non-economic operations whose ethical purpose was to ameliorate the negative effects of capitalist activity. Under cooperativism, on the other hand, economic activity itself was to be driven by both public interest and ethics, in the sense that the economy was supposed to contribute to rather than detract from fairness and equity in addition to promoting maximum productivity for everyone's benefit. As an additional measure to insure this, along with the separation of ownership and management, Miki and Ryû proposed percentage limits on profit.

The authors were well aware of the argument that since profits provided the fundamental motivation for economic activity, any limits on it would cause declines in production. However, according to them, "If selfishness represents the human desires for self-preservation and self-expansion, those desires need not be expressed as lust for profit." Desires were expressed that way because the capitalist economy was "based on free competition ... and the individual was forced to exist in an unstable environment." If the system were transformed into one oriented to the public interest, the desires for self-preservation and self-expansion would be satisfied in other ways. "The competitive spirit would no longer be linked to profit but transformed into competition for social merit" (Sakai 1979: 354).

Such thinking was not, of course, limited to Japan. In late-1930s North America, for example, the sociologist Talcott Parsons argued that in a modern economy the importance of economic self-interest as a motivator had already declined markedly among businessmen as well as professionals. He wrote, "It is seldom, even in business, that the immediate financial advantage to be derived from a particular transaction is decisive in motivation. Orientation is rather to a total comprehensive situation extending over a considerable period of time" (Parsons 1954: 43). Paralleling Miki and Ryû, Parsons also notes that "the *content* of self-interested motivation itself, the specific objects of human 'interests,' cannot, for the purposes of any broad level of generalization in social science, be treated as a constant." Institutionally-based forms of satisfaction, including self-respect, recognition, pleasure and affection, were often of crucial importance. Usually, the "content of self-interest" was organized in and by social institutions.

> It thus depends on the standards according to which recognition is accorded, on the specific lines of action to which pleasure has become attached, on what have come to be generally accepted symbols of prestige and status, what, in concrete terms, will be the *direction* taken by self-interested activity and hence what its social consequences will be. Again this applies to what are originally thought of as "economic" interests just as it does to any others.
>
> (Parsons 1954: 61–62)

It would appear, therefore, that some of Miki and Ryû's ideas were perfectly in tune with influential American thinking at the time. Of course, the contemporary German situation was always close at hand: For example, in their conclusion Miki and Ryû note the importance of the "leader principle" (*shidôsha no genri*), or "Führerprinzip" (Sakai 1979: 356).

Contending approaches

At the same time (1939–40) that Miki and Ryû were putting forward their conception of a "new" economic ethic, others of a more traditionalist, or Japanist, persuasion were busily (re)formulating and advocating renewed commitment to various versions of Japan's "old" economic ethics. Because the elaboration of Japanist approaches to economic ethics roughly paralleled the articulation of the modern, rationalist approach of the Shôwa Kenkyûkai members, it is useful to sketch in some elements of the former before moving on to other, later contributions to the rationalist approach. One Japanist scholar, who in 1940 explained his notion of economic ethics in the official magazine of the Spiritual Mobilization Movement, *Kokumin seishin sôdôin* (National Spiritual Mobilization), as well as in the intellectual journal *Risô* (Ideals), was Tokyo Imperial University economics professor Nanihata Haruo.

As summarized in the *Risô* article, Nanihata's construction of economic ethics in Japan relied fundamentally on notions of climate and culture very similar to those of Watsuji Tetsurô, combined with ideological formulations of *kokutai* (national polity, or essence) selected from the texts of early-modern National Studies (Kokugaku). Suggesting that the typical national subject was formed out of interaction between nature and history, Nanihata begins with Japan's monsoon, which favored wet-rice agriculture, and also the Japanese islands' volcanic origins, which resulted in a mountainous terrain that necessitated the investment of a great deal of labor in terracing and other forms of development, and therefore led to very stable settlement patterns. All this, in turn, supposedly contributed to the formation of a strong family/ household unit in order to provide for secure inheritance. Thus, the household (*ie*) is the primary structural element of the Japanese subject.

Nanihata argues further that at harvest time in particular, wet-rice agriculture required cooperation on a scale that transcended the household. Such cooperation necessitated strong social ties *among* households, and thus he posits the "local area" (*kyôdo*) as the second structural element.

The third element, the *kokutai*, was less the result of environment than of the nations' "unique" historical development. In Nanihata's view, the *kokutai* was a national community premised on consanguinity and spiritual unity centering on the emperor. The Japanese nation was unique in the degree to which solidarities within it were not dispersed but rather unified in response to the unmovable center provided by the emperor. An important dimension of this unity was spiritual and ethical consensus. Appealing now to Kokugaku philology, he asserts that the essence of imperial rule resided in the emperor's "knowing" (*shirasu*) through "listening to" (*kikoshimesu*) and "observing" (*misonawasu*) the people, and is thus entirely receptive and passive. It was, therefore, appropriate that Japanese nationals should respond actively by "serving" (*tsukae matsuru*) the emperor. Moreover, inasmuch as the emperor was purely passive and devoid of self-assertion, he had no private dimension or interest; the emperor was entirely "public." Thus, although the ethic of national subjects ought to consist solely in "serving" the emperor, the latter's lack of private interest and self-aggrandizement meant that the people's productive "service" benefited only themselves. There was no contradiction between public interest and self-interest; serving the emperor amounted to serving oneself, thus unifying economic "logic" with economic "ethic" (Nanihata 1940).

It is important to note that Nanihata was not opposed to moderate profit-making and favored retention of a non-liberal form of capitalism. Indeed, he fervently opposed any efforts, especially those on the part of "leftists," to

replace capitalism with any form of planned economy. He was a major critic
of the Shôwa Kenkyûkai because he considered it to be left-wing. In a 1943
discussion with Shôwa Kenkyûkai member Hozumi Shichirô, for example,
Nanihata especially criticized the tendency of major Kenkyûkai publicists to
insist that any effort to "solve" the so-called China Incident had to involve
domestic institutional reforms directed against the pursuit of profit and the
prerogatives of capital ownership in Japan. So long as Japan retained its
existing capitalist institutions, they reasoned, its military approach to China
would amount to nothing more than conventional imperialism. Indeed, in his
discussion with Hozumi, Nanihata intimated his suspicion that rather than a
means of "solving" the China war the Kenkyûkai's support for anti-capitalist
reform was actually the main goal, with the further objective of moving Japan
toward the "next historical stage" which, implicitly, would be some form of
socialism (Hozumi and Nanihata 1943: 27).[5]

Of course, as historian Yanagisawa Osamu has recently demonstrated,
wartime debates on economic ethics were much more complex than a simple
confrontation between Japanists like Nanihata and rationalists like Miki and
Ryû. Many participants in the debate can be characterized as falling some-
where between Japanism and rationalism, borrowing elements from each.
Participants also divided along other important axes that bisected the tradi-
tionalist/rationalist divide, such as that between pro- and anti-capitalism.

Economist and Keio University professor Takemura Tadao was one who
relied primarily on modern economic analysis to demonstrate the need for a
new economic ethic, but fell back on traditionalist categories when describing
the kind of ethic required. His explanation for the necessity of a new economic ethic depended upon an economic stage theory. In brief, he argued that
as liberal capitalism – in which he considers profit-seeking activity to have
played a constructive role economically as well as ethically – gradually was
transformed into monopoly capitalism – under which profit-seeking becomes
increasingly unethical and dysfunctional – the results included chronic over-
production and structural unemployment. The antidote typically offered for
such problems was one form or another of controlled economy, whose purpose was to overcome the contradictions of monopoly capitalism. However, it
would soon become clear that in a controlled economy (especially in wartime), the profit orientation of private enterprise actually impeded economic
reproduction. This made it completely logical to restrict profit-seeking and
firmly establish the priority of the public interest over private. At the same
time, the objective logic of controlled economy encouraged pooling (profit-
distribution cartels) and joint sales, which were also conducive to equalizing
profits and restraining competition. In other words, controlled economy fos-
tered a gradual transition from individual profit-seeking to an ethical focus on
the collective good – that is, a new economic ethic. Thus, the new ethic could
be said to emerge from the inner logic of controlled economy itself.

Although Takemura based his conception of a public-centered economic
ethic on modern, rational economic analysis, including the work of the

contemporary German economist Friedrich von Gottl-Ottlilienfeld, the categories he used to describe the Japanese "cooperative body" and its elements were decidedly Japanist.[6] He grounded ethicality in the "spirit of harmony" latent in the "fundamental principles of the national essence" and in the "spirit of industry" based on service in an "occupational calling" (Takemura 1940).[7]

Others advocated a broad-based "renovation" of capitalism toward some form of planning and control, but conceived of that "renovation" as a return, dialectical or otherwise, to a traditionalist ethic of public service. Like the highly-reputed Kyoto School of philosophers, several members of the economics department of Kyoto Imperial University, who included Sakuta Shôichi, Ishikawa Kôji, and Taniguchi Yoshihiko, often framed their views in relation to the popular notion of "overcoming modernity." Sakuta, for one, sought to transcend the profit motive by establishing an "imperial economy" centering on the emperor, in which business would be managed at the national level via public corporations which would also own farm land and foster a transition to cooperative agriculture (Yanagisawa 2002: 128).

As in the case of Miki, Ryû, and other renovationist modernists, Nanihata, Takemura, and others who participated in the debate from traditionalist perspectives also insisted that priority be given to the subjectivity and ethics of economic agents. They shared the perception that rather than imposing rigid forms of control it was necessary to motivate workers to contribute spontaneously and creatively to economic expansion.

In sum, the debate on economic ethics included a variety of positions: the rational renovationists such as Miki, Ryû (and Okôchi Kazuo and Otsuka Hisao, whose ideas we will discuss next) called for the overcoming of liberal capitalism and an ethic premised on intrinsic rewards for contribution to the national totality; the Japanist, or traditionalist renovationists, such as Sakuta and to a lesser extent Takemura, also opposed capitalism and liberalism but strove to replace it with a return to some form or other of "uniquely Japanese" economic ethic of service; and capitalist Japanists, such as Nanihata, staunchly opposed any effort to abolish, overcome, or renovate capitalism, which they believed to be consistent (in its non-liberal varieties) with a Japanese economic ethic premised on the extended household, traditional community, and *kokutai*. It is important to note that whether Japanist or rationalist, all the above writers shared the perception that rather than subjecting workers to rigid "command and control," it was necessary to motivate them to contribute spontaneously and creatively to economic expansion.

Ethics of production

Now, let us return to the rationalist, cosmopolitan side of the argument to sketch in the views of two scholars whose work was destined to remain influential even after the war. Okôchi Kazuo was an imperial university professor, former bureaucrat and influential specialist in social policy who was also a member of the Shôwa Kenkyûkai. In a 1942 essay, entitled "'Keizaijin' no shûen" (The end of economic man), it is unclear whether Okôchi borrowed from Peter Drucker's 1939 book of the same title, but in any case his argument is very different from Drucker's. Okôchi outlined a new form of economic *shutaisei* that would be capable of unifying ethic and interest, that is, of evoking an ethic that shared the logic of political economy. To illustrate the feasibility of such a unity, he reminds his readers of the ethical system of laissez-faire that the classical political economist Adam Smith had called attention to in his theory of *homo economicus*. According to Okôchi, rather than limiting or constraining economic behavior from outside (as, for example, a religious or political ethic might have done), the theory of the "unseen hand" had successfully merged ethics with economic interest through the mediation of productivity: economic man's unrestrained profit-maximization was itself ethical because it spurred production, and production benefited the whole society.

However, it was perhaps inevitable that faith in the "unseen hand" would eventually decline. In Japan, as well as somewhat earlier in Germany, "social problems" had eventually become too intrusive to ignore, so ethics in the form of social policy had gradually abandoned the economic realm and sought to constrain or ameliorate economic activity from outside. As Okôchi wrote, social policy was in his view still situated unproductively outside the economy, seeking merely to intervene against what were seen as the intrinsically unethical tendencies of capitalist logic. Under the New Order, therefore, it would be necessary for ethics to merge again with interest: ethics (as social policy) had to reenter the economy, not in order to constrain economic activity but to stimulate and accelerate it, and to do so without any return to the unbridled profit-seeking of *homo economicus* (Okôchi, "'Keizaijin' no shûen 1969: 414–19).[8] Indeed, Okôchi viewed Smith's economic man as a rather primitive organism that acted not rationally but "instinctually," out of lust for profit. What was necessary, he felt, was a new economic actor who would be both rational and ethical:

> The [new] subject of economic life is ... not an instinctual *homo economicus* but rather a rational human being; in other words, a person of intelligence who has the knowledge and insight necessary to grasp the objective facts of wartime economic controls, and who has an active, spontaneous desire to size up the situation and determine what kind of economic activity is required. ... In sum, if the Smith-type, instinctual *homo economicus* was led by God's "unseen hand" and was able to contribute to the material welfare of society only unconsciously, via the moment of free competition, what we have here is a rational producer, aware of his social vocation, who is subjectively conscious of the inner connection between individual economic activity and the totality of the controlled order.
>
> (Okôchi "'Keizaijin' no shûen" 1969: 421–22)

Whereas the ethic of laissez-faire had relied on the "natural" equilibrium produced by an "unseen hand" and therefore had favored an economic subject who knew only his own interests and was motivated by them, without thought for the public good, the new economic ethic was more intellectual: It emerged in parallel with central planning and therefore favored a knowledgeable subject who could internalize the standpoint of the totality, and be motivated by conscious awareness of how his effort contributed to the national economic system as a whole.

Thus, the new economic ethic must be an "ethic of responsibility," not just the interpersonal form of responsibility that operated in civil society but responsibility toward "economic society as a whole" (Okôchi "'Keizaijin' no shûen" 1969: 424). As such, it could be encapsulated in the concept of occupational functionality as a "functional ethic" that was compatible with constant expansion of the productive forces. In the standpoint of such a subject, freedom merged with central control. According to Okôchi, "the controlled economy should be embraced not as something that impinges 'from outside' but as a force that emerges 'from inside'; it needs to be seen as something constructed within people's daily economic life in response to the new need for discipline" (Okôchi "'Keizaijin' no shûen" 1969: 409).

How could such a "spontaneous" ethic of national responsibility be encouraged? Okôchi clearly felt that social policy could help to cultivate it. Social policy had to become a constituent economic element, and its primary function had to be preserving labor power. Such a function was essential because it was clear to him that private companies often found it temporarily advantageous to waste labor power, and even to use it up in a manner detrimental to the economy as a whole. He argued, therefore, that social policy had to adopt the integrative, holistic perspective of what he called "total capital" (*sôshihon*), and from that perspective to regulate private capital's treatment of labor. But more directly to the point of encouraging a new economic ethic, he argued that social policy was obligated not only to preserve labor power but to insure its qualitative improvement through training and technological upgrading. Even more important were efforts to enhance workers' autonomy, because it was "of utmost importance in the wartime configuration of social policy to secure workers' active cooperation and understanding." Okôchi was confident that if that were done, the workers' new subjectivity, expressed in the new economic ethic, would "not be converted into energy on behalf of class conflict" but would be expressed in "active cooperation 'from below'" (Okôchi "Senji shakai seisaku"1969: 26).[9]

Another rationalist participant in wartime discussions regarding the new economic ethic was the economic historian of Western Europe and Tokyo Imperial University professor Otsuka Hisao. In a 1944 essay, for example, Otsuka sought to show the importance of the work ethic in expanding production. Following the nineteenth century political economist Friedrich List, he set forth a tripartite model of the productive forces, as consisting in labor, technology (machinery), and resources. He also followed List in selecting out labor as the most important of these, because: "Labor alone is the subjectively formative element of the 'productive forces,' and without it, no matter how plentiful might be the other elements of production, they will amount to no more than objectively inert matter." The fundamental determinant of labor power, in turn, was "the historical, spiritual circumstances of the nation" that gave it sustenance ... [that is] the "spiritual capital of the nation" (*Geisteskapital der Nation*) (Otsuka "Seisanryoku to keizai rinri"1969: 325–26).[10]

For Otsuka, this "spiritual capital of the nation" was manifested most directly in the *will to work* (Otsuka "Seisanryoku to keizai rinri"1969: 327). Accordingly, the problem confronting Otsuka and, indeed, the wartime Japanese state, was: What factors determined the level of a people's "will to work"? For an answer, he turned to the question of "economic ethics" as investigated by the German social theorist Max Weber.

Otsuka reviewed Weber's contention that, rather than the mere search for profit, the crucial element in the Western European economic ethic was "secular asceticism." Otsuka did not deny that the profit motive could be an important factor under some historical conditions. However, rather than the selfish search for profit as such, what for Otsuka was most deeply connected to the will to work was an ascetic mentality – that is, a certain ethos. To illustrate, Otsuka referred to Weber's discussion of the relationship between higher wages and the will to work. Referring to the case of piece-work payment at harvest time in Germany, Weber had noted that "raising the piece-rates has often had the result that not more but less has been accomplished in the same time, because the worker reacted to the rate increase not by increasing but by decreasing the amount of his work. ... The opportunity of earning more was less attractive than that of working less" (Otsuka "Seisanryoku to keizai rinri"1969: 336). Weber's conclusion, adopted by Otsuka as well, was that workers would favor rationally-organized economic enterprise only if they had learned to consider labor as "an absolute end in itself, a calling" (Otsuka "Seisanryoku to keizai rinri" 1969: 338). Note the parallel between Weber's secularized notion of the calling and Okôchi's appeal to vocation as the basic building block of the New Order.

Of course, Otsuka also followed Weber in insisting that what was at stake was not merely an attitude, in the narrow sense, but a total way of life with a "practical structure" that "contributed to the welfare of the whole"(Otsuka "Keizai rinri no jissenteki kôzô" 1969: 308).[11] What were the characteristics of this "practical structure"? It was ascetic, organized, and methodical. That is, it consisted in "a life of good works combined into a unified system." Indeed, the typical human embodiment of this economic ethic – the Calvinist – "guarded and inspected himself in a 'systematic, organized way,' and 'trained' himself 'methodically' in the correct way of life" (Otsuka "Keizai rinri no jissenteki kôzô"1969: 313).[12]

Otsuka was not recommending that Japanese workers become Calvinists. To the contrary, he argued that the work ethic was shifting away from the profit motive toward something like what Sugimura had called a "service

ethic." That is, in Otsuka's wartime view the profit-oriented spirit of capitalism was indeed being replaced by a "new economic ethic" in which motivation stemmed not from desire for profit but rather from devotion to the sort
of institutionally-based recognition and self-respect that Talcott Parsons
found to be effective among Americans. According to Otsuka, Japanese
workers and managers alike had thoroughly internalized the perspective of
what Okôchi had called "total capital" and were clearly aware of their
"responsibility for production"; they were "directly conscious of the links
between private 'management' (and individual labor) and the 'whole' (state)
plan" (Otsuka "Saikôdô 'jihatsusei'" 1969: 341).[13] Here, indeed, was not
homo economicus but the skilled worker also idealized by Okôchi, who was "a
rational producer, aware of his social vocation, and subjectively conscious of
the inner connection between individual economic activity and the totality of
the controlled order."[14]

Paralleling the hypothetical suppositions of Okôchi and Otsuka, the labor
historian Saguchi Kazurô and others have shown that at least desultory
efforts were actually made during the war to interpellate highly-skilled workers who were able to find motivation in a self-conscious understanding of
their role in the "totality" of an imperial economy. The "Guidelines for
Establishing a New Order for Labor" (*Kinrô shintaisei kakuritsu yôkô*) of
April 1939 suggested that the ideology of the fascist Industrial Patriotic
Association (Sanpô) would be focused on *kinrôsha* – workers who dedicated
their labor to the state and therefore were all equal as productive subjects.
According to Saguchi,

> The real significance of the new work ideology lay in its premise that the
> worker is actively and purposefully engaged. As a lofty pursuit that
> 'expresses one's full personality' and has public significance as service to
> the state, "work" could not, of course, be considered drudgery, but was
> rather to be understood as "creative and "spontaneous." Inasmuch as the
> worker was "recognized as a human being" by the state on account of his
> subjective identity, he or she was also situated in relation to the produc-
> tive process as an active subject who exercised "creativity" and "auton-
> omy". ... When "work" was understood in the above sense, it could not
> be motivated by a desire for wages as compensation and, accordingly,
> could not be assimilated to a system in which wages were believed to be a
> powerful stimulus to efficiency. Insofar as the worker's "honor" was
> worthy of respect, it became necessary to see that his or her livelihood
> was stabilized. This gave rise to the notion of a stipend that would pro-
> vide for the workers' livelihood, aside from all considerations of labor
> supply. ... In juxtaposition to the ideological dimension in which the
> worker was recognized as an active subject in the productive process, this
> logic situated him or her as an entity whose service to the state had to be
> maintained via a stable livelihood.
>
> (Saguchi 1998: 272–73)

Of course, the extent of the effectiveness of such efforts should remain in doubt; yet Saguchi notes that, "The workers who chimed in with the work ideology were not merely overcome by temporary enthusiasm. They supported it because it was premised on essential elements of the ideology that governed labor relations in Japan, and because it did result in a system that, although inadequate, did give some credence to the principle of the need-based wage" (Saguchi 1998: 282).

Toward postwar

How and to what extent was the wartime preoccupation with active subjectivity continued after the war? In the context of the U.S. Occupation's postwar reforms, liberal-to-left rationalism and modernism returned to center stage, supported by a visceral reaction against the irrational obscurantism that was now associated with the wartime era. That is, from the postwar vantage, the total war system came to be viewed as monochromatically irrational and "premodern"; liberal-rationalist aspects of the New Order were conveniently forgotten. In the meantime, wartime conceptions of *shutaisei* as an institutionalized ethic of responsibility were recycled in the postwar era as part of a continuing drive toward modernization. Moreover, that drive was again manifested as a process of mobilization designed to produce a "new human being," this time in the form of the "modern man."

In the wake of the war, therefore, Okôchi Kazuo, Otsuka Hisao and many others who during the war had been rationalist proponents of the "new economic ethic" and the "new human being" were able to resume essentially the same arguments they had made during the war, except that in the postwar era their ideas came much closer to being generally accepted. Otsuka insisted in the early-postwar era on the need to "educate the people to fit the modern, democratic human type" – a "type" (subject) that would also manifest the economic ethic required to fuel economic recovery and growth. According to Otsuka,

> The people must develop an internal consciousness of respect for the human being. Rather than having it bestowed upon them in the manner of premodern natural law, they must themselves become "a free people" who, in a self-disciplined manner, will maintain a forward-looking social order and enhance the common welfare. ... Such a "free people" is itself the decisive element in the formation of modern forces of production. Indeed, it *is* those forces.
>
> (Otsuka "Kindaiteki ningen ruikei"1969: 172)[15]

Evident in such statements is a paradoxical form of continuity in which a model of institutionally-integrated "freedom" that had been proposed but not fully actualized during the war was reappropriated after defeat to become the basis of a powerful movement toward modernization, production, and "democratization." In this sense, total war catalyzed a conception of the human actor, or subject, that was already fully adaptable to national mobilization under the emerging system of "postwar democracy."

Otsuka was certainly an important participant in the postwar "debate on subjectivity," and to that extent one might be justified in following Iwasaki in figuring the postwar debate as a counterpart (whether "emaciated" or not) of wartime debates on technological and economic subjectivity. Nevertheless, Otsuka's preoccupation with expanding the "productive forces" was actually quite unusual in the postwar debate. Rather, the center of gravity among postwar theories of *shutaisei* (as opposed to the various forms of objectivist materialism arrayed against them) was solidly in the realm of politics instead of production. That is, postwar arguments tended to emphasize personal decision-making and commitment issuing in political action under conditions of uncertainty. Instead of focusing on fabricating or producing objective things, such arguments are oriented heavily toward formation, revelation and expression of the self. As we have seen, quite the opposite is the case in regard to the wartime debates on economic ethics and technology, which usually conceived of subjectivity in the context of activity directed toward formation of objective things rather than the self, in the economic rather than political milieu. In other words, we might say that arguments for *shutaisei* typical of wartime debates on technology and work were concerned principally with constructive activity in the mode of *poiesis* whereas postwar arguments gave priority to expressive action, or *praxis*.[16] If broadly valid, this would imply that the postwar debate on subjectivity is not the most promising venue in which to seek postwar continuations of wartime thought on subjectivity. Rather, the wartime legacy of constructive subjectivity might find its most compelling postwar equivalents in debates and policies concerned with labor management in the context of the zealous postwar attempts to promote productivity. Indeed, one can easily find circumstantial evidence for continuity in the mobilization of productive subjectivity.

For example, Saguchi points out that in postwar Japan, unions demanded a need-based wage on the basis that this was a necessary means of "promoting Japan's economic reconstruction," and that such demands closely resembled "the work ideology of wartime that positioned workers as subjects actively contributing to the state and defined the stabilization of their lives as means to that end" (Saguchi 1998: 283–84).

From the perspective of managers, there remained in postwar Japan a high level of concern with mobilizing and raising the satisfaction level of workers without relying entirely on monetary compensation. For example, the management organization, Keizai Dôyûkai (Japan Association of Corporate Executives) emerged in 1946 convinced of the need for cooperative relations with the labor unions that were mushrooming in the postwar period and flexibility in the face of changes in capitalism that originated in wartime. According to Tsutsui, "In positing a 'middle road' between socialism and

172   *J. Victor Koschmann*

laissez-faire capitalism based on technocratic management and comprehensive planning, the Dôyûkai model mirrored the 'New Order' dream, albeit with private-sector (rather than bureaucratic) leadership" (Tsutsui 1998: 128). Keizai Dôyûkai helped establish the Japan Productivity Center (Nihon Seisansei Honbu), which was actively promoted and supported by the U.S. embassy in Tokyo.

Among the approaches to management that the Productivity Center promoted were Human Relations management and Quality Control, both of which had roots and predecessors in the wartime period. In the 1950s, the Human Relations approach to labor management, with its emphasis on meeting the social and psychological needs of workers, was seen as conducive to the democratization of industry as well as to raising worker productivity. Meanwhile, Quality Control Circles were "designed to create an environment where employees would naturally align individual interests with corporate goals and standards." This clearly suggests that some of the central strategies for mobilizing subjectivity that were developed out of the wartime discourse on economic ethics were continued with new energy after defeat, not among leftists in the "debate on subjectivity" but among efficiency experts in corporate board rooms and among workers on the shop floor.

In regard to the mobilization of subjectivity, as in many other respects, therefore, wartime was undeniably a time, not only of particularistic celebration of what seemed to be traditional and essentially Japanese, but also of modern rationalistic thought and planning on par and resonant with contemporary thought in the U.S. and Europe. Moreover, in a number of ways, wartime contributed directly to postwar mobilization for economic growth and democratic modernization.

Bibliography

Allen, J. (1996) Fordism and Modern Industry. In Hall, S., Hubert, D. and Thompson, K. (Ed.) *Modernity: An Introduction to Modern Societies.* London, Blackwell Publishers.
Arendt, H. (1958) *The Human Condition.* Chicago, The University of Chicago Press.
Crowley, J. B. (1971) Intellectuals as Visionaries of the New Asian Order. In Morely, J. W. (Ed.) *Dilemmas of Growth in Prewar Japan.* Princeton, Princeton University Press.
Fletcher III, M. W. (1982) *The Search for a New Order: Intellectuals and Fascism in Prewar Japan,* Chapel Hill, University of North Carolina Press.
Iwasaki Minoru. (1996) Poieishisuteki meta-shutai no yokubô. In Yasushi, Y., Koschmann, J. V. and Ryuichi, N. (Ed.) *Sôryokusen to gendaika.* Tokyo, Kashiwa Shobô.
Koschmann, J. V. (1996) *Revolution and Subjectivity in Postwar Japan,* Chicago, The University of Chicago Press.
Morris, Meaghan. (1997) "Foreword." In Sakai, N., *Translations and Subjectivity: On "Japan" and Cultural Nationalism.* Minneapolis, MN: University of Minnesota Press.
Nanihata Haruo and Hozumi Shichirô (August 1943) Senryoku to kokumin soshiki: kokumin soshiki to keiei no kakushin wo chûshin to shite. *Kagakushugi kôgyô* 7, 26.

Nanihata Haruo. (October 1940) Nihon Keizai no rinri. *Risô*, 5–22.

Okôchi Kazuo. (1969) 'Keizaijin' no shûen: atarashii keizai rinri no tame ni. *Okôchi Kazuo chosakushû 3* Tokyo, Seirin Shoin Shinsha.

——. (1969) Senji shakai seisaku no kihon mondai. *Okôchi Kazuo chosakushû 4* Tokyo, Seirin Shoin Shinsha.

——. (July 1939) Senjji shakai no kihon mondai. *Keizaigaku ronsô 9*.

——. (June 1942) 'Keizaijin' no shûen: atarashii keizai rinri no tame ni. *Chûô kôron*.

——. (1942) Keizai rinri no jissenteki kôzô: Makkusu Uêba no mondai teiki ni kanren shite. *Tôsei keizai 5*.

——. (1944) Seisanryoku to keizai rinri. *Tôsei keizai 8*.

——. (1969) Seisanryoku to keizai rinri. *Otsuka Hisao chosakushû 8*. Tokyo, Iwanami Shoten.

——. (1969) Keizai rinri no jissenteki kôzô: Makkusu Uêba no mondai teiki ni kanren shite. *Otsuka Hisao chosakushû 8*. Tokyo, Iwanami Shoten.

——. (1969) Saikôdo 'jihatsusei' no hatsuyô: keizai rinri to shite no seisan sekinin ni tsuite. *Otsuka Hisao chosakushû 8* Tokyo, Iwanami Shoten.

——. (1969) Kindaiteki ningen ruikei no sôshutsu: seijiteki shutai no minshûteki kiban no mondai. *Otsuka Hisao chosakushû 8* Tokyo, Iwanami Shoten.

——. (April 21, 1946) Kindaiteki ningen ruikei no sôshutsu: seijiteki shutai no minshûteki kiban no mondai. *Daigaku shinbun*.

——. (July 11, 1944) Saikôdo 'jihatsusei' no hatsuyô: keizai rinri to shite no seisan sekinin ni tsuite. *Daigaku shinbun*.

Parsons, T. (1954) The Professions and Social Structure. *Essays in Sociological Theory*. 2nd ed. Glencoe, IL, The Free Press.

Saguchi Kazurô. (1998) The Historical Significance of the Industrial Patriotic Association: Labor Relations in the Total-War State. In Yamanouchi, Y., J. V. K., and N. Ryûichi (Ed.) *Total War and Modernization*. Ithaca, Cornell East Asia Series 100.

Sakai, Naoki (1997) *Translation and Subjectivity: On "Japan" and Cultural Nationalism*, Minneapolis, MN: University of Minnesota Press.

Sakai Saburô (1979) *Shôwa kenkyûkai: aru chishikijin shûdan no kiseki*. Tokyo, TBS Buritanika.

Sugiharo Shirô and Chô Yukio (Ed.) (1979) *Nihon keizai shisôshi tokuhon*. Tokyo, Tôyô Keizai Shinposha.

Takemura Tadao. (October 1940) Tôsei keizai no rinrisei. *Risô*, 23–38.

Tsutsui, W. (1998) *Manufacturing Ideology: Scientific Management in Twentieth-Century Japan*, Princeton, Princeton University Press.

Yanagisawa Osamu. (February 2002) Senjiki Nihon ni okeru keizai rinri no mondai I: Otsuka Hisao-Okôchi Kazuo no shisôshi, gakusetsushi kenkyû no haikei. *Shisô*, 934.

——. (April 2002) Senjiki Nihon ni okeru keizai rinri no mondai II: Otsuka Hisao, Okôchi Kazuo no shisôshi, gakusetsushi kenkyû no haikei. *Shisô*, 936.

Notes

1 Thanks to the University of Tokyo Press for permission to use portions of this essay previously published in Japanese in "Shutaisei to dôin," *Sengo to iu chisei-gaku*, edited by Nishikawa Yûko (Tokyo: Tokyo Daigaku Shuppankai, 2006), pp. 43–68. The author would also like to thank Ms. Akiko Ishii for helping with the research for this chapter.

2 A view of the early-postwar period as uniquely the "era of *shutaisei*" is implicit in J. Victor Koschmann (Koschmann 1996).

3 See also Saburô Sakai and James B. Crowley (Sakai 1979; Crowley 1971).

4 In Sakai citations, the quotes are in "Kyôdôshugi no keizai rinri" unless otherwise noted.

5 The dialogue is discussed by Yanagisawa Osamu (Yanagisawa 2002: 90–91).

6 Friedrich von Gottl-Ottlilienfeld (1868–1958) wrote such works as *Volk, Staat, Wirtschaft und Recht* (1939) and *Wesen und Grundbegriffe der Wirtschaft* (1942), both of which were translated into Japanese.

7 Discussed by Yanagisawa in *Shisô* 936 (Yanagisawa 2002: 129–30).

8 This is the reprinted version that appears in *Okôchi Kazuo chosakushû 3*; for the original see (Okôchi 1942).

9 This is the reprinted version in *Okôchi Kazuo chosakushû 4*. For the original see (Okôchi 1939).

10 Reprinting of "Seisanryoku to keizai rinri" appearing in *Otsuka Hisao chosakushû 8*. For the original printing see (Otsuka 1944).

11 This reprinted version of "Keizai rinri no jissenteki kôzô: Makkusu Uêba no mondai teiki ni kanren shite"appears in *Otsuka Hisao chosakushû 8*. For the original see (Otsuka 1942).

12 Ibid.

13 This reprinted version of "Saikôdo 'jihatsusei' no hatsuyô: keizai rinri to shite no seisan sekinin ni tsuite," appears in *Otsuka Hisao chosakushû 8*. For the original see (Otsuka 1944).

14 For more on Otsuka Hisao's thought concerning *shutaisei* in wartime and postwar, see J. Victor Koschmann (Koschmann 1996: 149–70).

15 This version of "Kindaiteki ningen ruikei no sôshutsu: seijiteki shutai no minshû-teki kiban no mondai," is reprinted in *Otsuka Hisao chosakushû 8*. For the original see (Otsuka 1946).

16 In making this distinction I am employing *poiesis* and *praxis* in much the same way as Hannah Arendt (Arendt 1958).

Part III
The modern West and its outside

10 The Western relation

The politics of humanism

Frédéric Neyrat
Translated by Flannery Wilson, Maxime Blanchard and John Namjun Kim

Un humanisme bien ordonné ne commence pas par soi-même. En isolant l'homme du reste de la création, l'humanisme occidental l'a privé d'un glacis protecteur.

(C. Lévi-Strauss)

The separation of spheres ... is an act of complicity.

(E. W. Said)

The West thinks itself to be ubiquitous.

(N. Sakai)

Directly to the West ... [1]

To critique the West is to enter a trap. The trap of its identification. To identify a difference specific to the West is to participate unintentionally in its self-definition, its self-affirmation as an *exception, similar to nothing else.* One resolution seems to emerge: to escape from this trap, it might suffice to refuse the possibility of an identification with the West and to maintain that there is no "essence" of the West. This critical gesture risks masking the real effects of *naming the West as an exception,* and hence participating in the *maintenance* of its *scheme of exploitation and destruction,* and its perpetuation in a form that might be rendered literally imperceptible. Dilemma, puzzle, double bind ... The identification and non-identification of the West amount to the same thing. Is there a way out of this trap?

In shifting the focus from identification of one specific trait to that of a *relation,* we can consider how the relation constructs itself over time, and how it might henceforth be qualified as specifically Western. Its fundamental characteristic is that it exhaustively searches for all possible means to deny the very existence of this relation, the existence of its constituent Two, to the advantage of the production of a *relation of exception.* The Western production of the relation as non-relation obeys the following logic: *first,* deny its existence, *second*, take action so that the denial rings true. This takes the form of extermination, genocide, or the assignment of identities without a future, which is the soft variant characteristic of our "democratic" societies. Without a doubt, 1492 can be figured as the primitive scene of the modern West, as the epoch when the Western relation deteriorated. The expulsion of the Jews from Spain, then the Native American genocide.[2] Each time, there was a denial not of an other but of a *similar other* – not exactly the Same, not exactly the Other. There is something mad in all this, a Western madness.

But the madness is not without coherence. This is the source of the problem: the Western relation solidly links an anthropological project to a political project by way of a cultural project. Hence the following is devoted successively to Claude Lévi-Strauss, Edward W. Said and Naoki Sakai. For the political sphere is not a dimension that is closed upon itself, as a certain Modernity would have us believe, neither is it a "theater of shadows" nor an autonomous will. The political sphere is articulated as an anthropo-technique, from technologies that function to make space between the Self and the non-Self, sovereign Subjects and the Subjugated, etc. There is certainly, as Naoki Sakai argues, a "humanist" scheme that works at a deeper level than the "national" sphere. An anthropo-technical humanism that results in what Naoki Sakai calls a "bi-polar configuration" – but a denied configuration.

This raises a definitive question, or rather a worry: if the Western relation is so bleak, the roots of evil so deep, how can one hope for the least amount of change? The least amount of remedy? Is it necessary to change civilization?

The structure of exception (C. Lévi-Strauss)

The Western relation is first of all a reversed relation. That is what Claude Lévi-Strauss noted in 1963 when asked to reflect on the means of exporting industrialization from developed countries to countries "on the path to development." The *will to exportation* serves only to reverse the origin of Western industrialization, its moment of "primitive accumulation," which is nothing more than an *original expropriation* – this is the overwhelming lesson of *Capital* (Vol. I, Ch. XXVI). For Marx and Engels, writes Lévi-Strauss, "industrialization is a function and an indirect result of the condition of so-called 'primitive' societies or, more precisely, of the historical relation between them and the West" (Lévi-Strauss 2003: 367–68). This historical relation is the relation of exploitation, the original expropriation that starts the machine of surplus value – in a word, the colonization that is, to return to Lévi-Strauss after Marx and Engels, "historically and logically anterior to capitalism" (Lévi-Strauss 2003: 367–68). It is not *development,* therefore, that is the specific trait of "Western civilization," but *exploitation*. This is the absolute reversal of the originally proposed perspective, the one that considered the movement of exportation from "developed" countries towards "under-developed" countries. The second phenomenon: "development" rests on the first phenomenon, the "destruction" of the colonized countries. This is the thesis that Fanon brought to its logical conclusion: "Europe is literally the creation of the third-world" (Fanon 2002: 99). To lift the denial that burdens this first phenomenon is to affirm, as Lévi-Strauss argues in a less political manner than Fanon's, the "complementary relation" that exists between "so-called underdeveloped societies" and "mechanical civilization," a term that Lévi-Strauss uses as a substitute for the West. It is still to be determined how these mechanics are linked to this denial of the "complementary" relations, this primitive reversal of the relationship that might be determined to be one of the traits of the West – its *paranoid trait.*

Claude Lévi-Strauss uses the image of the virus as the figure of the paranoid machine of the West. Even prior to reaching out to populations that have remained foreign to it, the West seems capable of destruction "in anticipation," "at a distance" because its "pathogenic germs" travel faster than its men and machines (Lindqvist 2007: 76).[3] Western contact is preceded by its viral double that anticipates expropriation – the devastation "is felt several years, and at times several decades, before contact itself is made," adds Lévi-Strauss. This then signals the destructive adoption of a new technology by the culture and tradition of a people, one that will depend on this technical contribution "by means of wars, marriages, commercial exchange" (Lévi-Strauss 2003: 370). The West – or the "destruction at a distance" that undeniably takes place even *before arriving.* And if the place is not obvious upon arrival, *one will act as if it is*, one will declare the territory free of owners, *"terra nullius."* Like a type of *negative hallucination* that is elevated to the scale of civilization. But what's the origin of this viral aspect, this propensity for negative hallucination?

Without any doubt, it is from the denial of otherness. Yet it is an active, powerful denial, reduced by the forces brought about by the alliance of Capital and Techno-science – the Western relation is constituted of many threads: it is certainly not an "essence," but a bad encounter among an economy, technique, and cultural formation. After all, the best way to make sure that a land is *truly* without owners is to exterminate every last one of them. In this sense, the declaration "terra nullius" will not have been – a terrifying future perfect – but an anticipation of perception. The negative hallucination will have preceded its reality, as if it entailed a visual performative. 1) There are no Native Americans here; 2) exterminate them. In other words, in order to ensure that there are none *similar, no similar other,* the best course of action is to liquidate them all by transforming them into the Same, just like Mr. Smith in *The Matrix,* who transforms everyone else into Mr. Smith. This is precisely the very effect of a virus that, reducible to a single "genetic formula," injects itself into other organisms and, in this way, forces them to "betray their formula in order to obey its own, and thus to manufacture other identical beings" (Lévi-Strauss 2003: 332). The West devours the similar other and transforms it into the same. In a certain sense this analysis is still not quite formulated, because it assumes an *a priori* recognition of the other, yet the other-as-similar-other is denied by the paranoid reversal. There really is no other here, but a formless matter to which it will be necessary to give the status – the form – of the West.

In effect, *there would not be a Western virus if there were not a process of making an exception.* This is the ultimate secret of the West. This explains the paranoid reversal, the negative hallucination and the viral formula. If Lévi-Strauss used the term virus, it was because the "reality" of all this is "almost of an intellectual order." Lévi-Strauss credits Descartes for his knowledge of the "originality" of our civilization, which consists "essentially in a method whose intellectual nature deems it improper to generate flesh and blood from other civilizations, yet that can impose its own formula on these civilizations and force them to become just like itself." The post-Cartesian West took itself as an exception by a process of dematerialization and intellectualization formed *against* flesh, blood, the body (nature). Such are the "extreme mani-festations of this great march understood as humanist, which claimed to constitute man in a separate kingdom." By now the West has become "a kind of imprisonment that man inflicts on himself daily at the heart of his own humanity," neither more nor less than an "closed world" (Lévi-Strauss 2003: 330). The secret of the West is its self-expropriation outside of nature, the "segregation of man from the natural environment." The effect of the "humanism" denounced by Claude Lévi-Strauss is the "separation of man from other forms of life" (Lévi-Strauss 2003: 334). This is the *humanist exception* that, in removing the Western man from the heart of immaterial space, *allows him never to have to encounter the similar other* (Todorov 1991).[4]

Culture as "protective enclosure" (E.W. Said)

Edward Said helps us to understand this immaterial space as culture. For, it is culture that allows the West to operate its movement of originary expropria-tion (colonization) while at the same time situating itself, elsewhere, directly in the West, in a sphere that is absolutely separated from these base tactics of gunpowder and blood, death and flesh. What is asked of this culture is *not to feel anything at all anymore.* Said defines it as a "protective enclosure," requiring that all political ideas are left outside before entering within (Said 1994: xiv). Of course, European culture doesn't cause imperialism – but it does "enable" it, "encourage" it, "assure" it (Said 1994: 80). Culture doesn't take the sea, but it does "little" to "stand in the way of the accelerating imperial process," it does not stop it (Said 1994: 82). And this indicates the means, from afar, overhead, elsewhere – "culture is in advance of politics, military history, or economic process" (Said 1994: 200). Conrad's novel *The Heart of Darkness* is not just a work of literature; it participates in the fight for the representation of Africa and its consequences, its settlement, and decolonization, because for certain Europeans this novel was their only experience of Africa. This *advance* of culture over politics is not without link to the viral-quality that Lévi-Strauss describes. In fact, imperialism means "thinking about, settling on, controlling" a territory "that is distant, that is lived on and owned by others" (Said 1994: 7): split off from politics, culture installs itself at a *real distance,* and it prepares, anticipates, *the installation of imperialism at a distance.*

The sole means of destroying the Western status of exception consists in placing culture as a space of indemnification and imperialism as an agent of destruction into a relation. In ontological terms, it will be a matter of relating the unscathed and the destructible. In political terms, it means placing the *formation of cultural knowledge* and the *formation of imperialist power* in contact with one another. Because "the history of fields like comparative literature, English studies, cultural analysis, anthropology can be seen as affiliated with empire," writes Said, "Western cultural forms can be taken out of the autonomous enclosures in which they have been protected, and placed instead into the dynamic global environment created by imperialism, itself revised as an ongoing contest between north and south, metropolis and periphery, white and native. We may thus consider imperialism as a process occurring as part of the metropolitan culture, which at times acknowledges, at other times obscures the sustained business of the empire itself" (Said 1994: 50–51). On the other hand, the best way to deny the existence of this "ongoing contest" is to *separate the spheres of existence* in accordance with the falsely neutral humanist gesture masking real struggles. Consequently, we can thus formulate the thesis defended in *Culture and Imperialism*: a relation exists between the division of the spheres of existence and of identities, and the division of culture and of politics; a relation exists between this double layer of rupture, vertical (culture/politics), and horizontal (between identities).

For a divided culture separates out identity. And the West excels at this type of absolute separation between culture and spheres of existence – races, nations, "Englishness," "Orientalism," "Asian particularity," an individual with a "Japanese" or ... "Western" allure. This is what has defined us since the seventeenth century "at least," writes Said, well before the imperialist expansion, the "essence of experience in the West," "all these attest in my opinion testify to an ideology whose cultural correlatives well precede the actual accumulation of imperial territories world-wide" (Said 1994: 58). Among the ideas that were able to promote imperial domination, Said insists on the "fundamental ontological distinction: West and the rest of the world," to which it will be necessary to attach the "denial of coevalness in time" (Johannes Fabian) and the possibility of a "radical discontinuity in terms of human space" (Said 1994: 108). It is on this basis that ethnography of the "primitive," the "savage," the "degenerate," the "natural" and the "unnatural" develops, notions that we will return to later. Certainly, "All cultures tend to make representations of foreign cultures the better to master or in some way control them. Yet not all cultures make representations of foreign cultures *and* in fact master or control them. This is the distinction, I believe, of modern Western cultures" (Said 1994: 100). The pursuit of the exception indemnifying – trying to protect absolutely – a civilization is without doubt not unique to the West, but the West pushes it to a technological extreme: the "mechanical civilization" of which Lévi-Strauss speaks is the industrialization of an indemnity that is a purveyor of death.

Therefore, if one must start by reintroducing culture into the world in a movement created by imperialism, one should notice – the second divide to be destroyed – at what point reality is made of overlaps and interdependence. For identitarian essence does not exist; rather there is always a "formation of cultural identities" in "counterpoints" – no identity exists in isolation (Said 1994: 52). And what defines Western specificity is the refusal of this formation in counterpoints. This has become unquestionable because of imperialism itself, and this is certainly why it must be turned against itself. "Colonial fracture" is not an abyss, but a sharing that obliges thinking together "the experiences of domination and being dominated," about imperial domination and resistance "as a dual process evolving toward decolonization, and then independence" (Said 1994: 259), a double helix structure (the D.N. A. of the contemporary world). The post-imperial world is a world in counterpuntal ensemble denying itself the historical possibility of an identity at full stop, an isolated identity such as Occidentalism or nativism.[5] It therefore does not involve liquidating identities, but identifying their gaps: not closed, not withdrawn into a menial culture of shields or tanks, identity finds itself to be, according to Said's splendid formula: "not exhaustive" (Said 1994: 290).

Opening, relation, insufficiency: it is not an accident that Said uses the term "ecology" on several occasions to define his thought.[6] For a well-thought out ecology promotes the Relation against the divisions and processes of lethal indemnification, or to reuse Lévi-Strauss's term mentioned earlier, against the "closed world" of culture.

The "bipolar configuration" (N. Sakai)

We have identified a double level of rupture, between culture and politics on the one hand, and between identities on the other. The concept of culture is nevertheless problematic because the division affects not only the relation culture/politics, but culture itself, the whole field of knowledge as well as the subjects *of* this knowledge – understood on the one hand as an objective genitive (knowledge that produces certain subjects), and on the other hand as a subjective genitive (knowledge that produces other "subjects"). What Naoki Sakai helps us to understand is the fundamental asymmetry that structures this strange *subjective-discursive double formation* constituting "the-West-and-the-Rest."

Let us call one of the two poles of this double formation "Imaginary People of the West" (I.P.W.). What Naoki Sakai's analysis helps us to understand[7] is that the I.P.W. has a strange relation to knowledge in which it thinks of itself as excepted. The I.P.W. would be the effect of a kind of Subjective Event discharging all possible knowledge: in effect, it does not consider itself to be an *object* of study at all, an object of knowledge, but instead *the set of subjects that produce the conditions of analysis for this knowledge.* Considered out of reach from all inquiries, from all real investigations, these conditions of analysis will thus be separated from any possible – and as a result they can be applied to any possible object because they are *assumed separate*. Sakai calls these abstract conditions "theory" *or* philosophy. As a matter of course, the I.P.W. can become an object of knowledge, but an object that is necessarily *second*: not something that is natural, but a reality that has been modified by the practices that knowledge has rendered possible. For the I.P.W. is not defined by any natural attribute, or even cultural if what is understood by that is some sort of reified tradition, pre-established knowledge, etc. No, the I.P.W. is defined precisely by its ability to tear itself from any innate determination, any "ethnic" definition. The conditions of analysis can be endlessly modified by self-reflexivity as long as the I.P.W. is considered a self-reflexive subject – as a subject for which self-reflexivity provides the foundation. That is to say, a non-foundation, a foundation produced by a foundation of non-foundation, pure contingency freed from all necessity.

This corresponds to a *humanist* definition of man, if one considers humanism – after and according to Heidegger – in "metaphysical" terms, to view man as a being who is nothing other than what he decides to become, a being that "is not born man, but becomes it" (Erasmus), a being "without qualities," without a real face who is able to "freely change its form" (Pico della Mirandola),[8] a "chameleon" as Aristotle had already claimed – on this point moreover, it seems that the origins of humanist production extend beyond the "locus of modernity" (Sakai 2001: 73) back to the Greek establishment of metaphysics, and perhaps even before that. This, then, allows us to understand Naoki Sakai's formulation: "'theory' is presumably the essence of Western humanity" (Sakai 2001: 74). The natural attribute, ethnicity, the primary object of this knowledge, is for others all that is not a part of the I.P.W. but defined as the "suppliers" of this knowledge. They are certainly humans, *they can be compared* with the inhabitants of the West, but – indeed – but only by comparison: they are certainly humans, but not men, Naoki Sakai tells us, if Man-writ-large is the result of the humanist construction as previously described. Because they are also humans, we can determine from case to case, from particularity to particularity, from ethnicity to ethnicity, what they all have in common, namely *human nature in general*. This *generality*, taken from the depths of human empirical material, is therefore radically distinct from the supposed *universal* definition of Man as a subjectivity-wanting-to-be-itself.

It is within this radical distinction between passive and active, object and subject, *anthropos* and *humanitas*, generality and universality, sciences of man and theory/philosophy that the difference between "the West and the rest" lies. *As if by accident*, the result is that the most pointed partitions are superimposed on to the supposed territorial partition between the West and the rest, which is superimposed on the partition between center(s) and peripheries, which is superimposed on the partition between metropole(s) and colonized countries. Henceforth, we understand indeed what is really at issue in a *supposed* territorial partition. It is, in a very real sense, supposed by the production and shaping of knowledge: geographical names, aside from their function, have at least the effect of foreclosing all comprehensive access to this production. Yet nothing precludes thoroughly Westernized populations from residing at the heart of territories thought exterior to the West, writes Naoki Sakai (Sakai 2001: 76). And nothing precludes the opposite as well: the inhabitants of the *banlieues* in the West considered as objects of knowledge. The "riots" of November 2005 in France were a perfect example of this: some intellectuals deny that there was any "political" relevance in these riots, any possibility of revolt, thus lowering the inhabitants to the position of *silent objects* suffering from the "retreat" of politics ... the West is therefore not a territory, but a conceptual "place" from which its difference with the outside is produced, the "place where the very opposition between the terms occurs" (Sakai 2001: 79), the condition of the possibility for an *epistemic schematization* leading to what Naoki Sakai calls the "bi-polar co-figuration." This explains the "oxymoronic" character of the West. It is at once a particular locality in an obvious sense, yet it simultaneously resides everywhere. Except that this *potential omnipresence* will be retraced wherever it can lodge a partition between what it represents, Humanity, and that from which it distinguishes itself, *analogous humans.* This analysis is crucial for understanding the origin of a type of racism that is likely to arise and take place nowadays, so long as those beings who suffer wrongs are considered non-humans (un-humans) or less than humans: *it is sufficient to consider them non-Men.*

It is thus impossible to reduce the West to Europe, or to the U.S.A.: "in principle, every point on the earth could have its own west" (Sakai 2001: 79). We can say something along the lines of: there is a West "whenever a difference between the West-and-the-Rest is invoked" (Sakai 2001: 83). And the West as signifier will have the function of *making spatial what is special,* of *denying specialization in favor of spatialization.* But it will be a spatialization that is "configured" in a bi-polar way. Yet this division needs to be seen as a true obligation that is both political and ontological, an obligation that works to "disavow the dissolution which may well be brought about by globalization" (Sakai 2001: 88). A dissolution that promises the possibility of moving beyond imperial divisions.

From "national humanism" ...

To summarize: the universality that produces the West is the result of an operation on knowledge, which involves separating knowledge from its evil double, generality. Indeed, a simple subtraction of the universal from the sense data of "ethnos" or "culture" would be too brazen, and would establish itself too quickly and too clearly as a subterfuge. Therefore the mediation of generality is needed, that is to say, a crude beginning operation of extraction. And it is at the height of generality, far from the ground, that the parthenogenesis of the universal is executed, which is not only a denied particularity but also a split generality. The universal is not just an overhanging point, but also a lateral point (side-hanging ...).

On this basis, it is possible to understand what Naoki Sakai calls the "complicity" between "universalism (more specifically it should be called generalism) and particularism" (Sakai 2001: 86). Because there is no "anti-nomy" between "universalism" and "particularism," the one "reinforces" the other (Sakai 1997: 157). Naoki Sakai illustrates this complicity through an analysis of post-war Japanese nationalism that, far from opposing American hegemony – the occupation – participated in it: in distancing itself from its close neighbors (the "neighboring countries" of East and Southeast Asia) this nationalism did nothing in fact to stop Japan from accepting the "scenario of pax americana" (Sakai 2003: 34–43). The national illusion, which is only one major example of the identitarian illusion, entails thinking of oneself as pure ipseity, an origin that no Other will have chipped. We can thus study the imaginary at work in these processes of identification, using the term the Imaginary in its Lacanian sense: the production of supposedly "equal" sub-jects, those that are identified by their "ethnos," their languages, their land of "origin," by the magic operation of national belonging, is based on forgetting the fiction of assimilation, of *mytologema*, to speak in the Platonic language of *Laws*. Thus, for those who are from Japan, the Emperor is the "symbol of Japanese unity," to echo the terms of the constitution as composed by the American government in 1947 after the end of the war. The Emperor is a "symbol" that has been emptied (of all responsibility during the war just as during the colonial process) for the purpose of providing a body for national *plenitude*. What this means is the following: *the process of indemnification* that we have seen in the work of Lévi-Strauss and Said is *an important part of national formation.* For us, the complicity of which Naoki Sakai speaks, is an *ontological complicity.* This allows us to explain, as Sakai does, how cer-tain refusals of Western universality can at times mask, when not carried out in the open, a Universal Will,[9] a term that we can clearly link to Nietzschean Will to Power (a link that is more than a simple formality).

"Cultural specificity" does not therefore guarantee that a country will be able to preserve itself (remove itself, protect itself) from a force, from a dominant State and/or an imperialist system. Even worse, Naoki Sakai tells us: "complicity" maintains the "separation" inherent in the schema of "bipolar co-figuration," in which an "imperial super-state" rules a Great Divide of the World with the help of its "suppliers," to reinvoke this term cited earlier, and with the help of its national *furnishers* on the peripheries: supplies in the form of men, in that of raw materials, in that of global sur-veillance, in that of the struggle against international terrorism, in that of controls over the "transnational flow of immigration," in that of military force if necessary. It seems that this analysis can be fully superimposed onto the European framework: *"national humanism"* has the intrinsic capacity to replicate itself almost everywhere. National humanism says that "a human being is first of all a member of the nation-state; and judicially a non-national cannot be treated as a human being" (Sakai 2006: 187). Etienne Balibar was able to show a true "European apartheid" in action, the response of the European states when faced with their own political impotence: incapable of (wanting to) regulate financial flows, European States will often attempt to regulate population flows by a veritable "*logic of the camp*" (Balibar 2002: 112–13). This apartheid was instituted as such by the Maastricht treaty (1992) *which attributes European citizenship only to nationals of member countries.* These are signs of a reactionary policy, which, due to its inability to oppose the trans-nationalization of capital, *nationalizes itself politically*—so that nearly 8 percent of the European population is of foreign origin.

... to republican humanism

Now in terms of a specifically French framework, the massive existence of *republican humanism* revealed itself alongside several events that arose to contest its legitimacy: 1) the attempt, finally repealed, to recognize on February 23rd 2005 the existence of "positive aspects of colonization;" 2) the movement by the "Natives of the Republic,"[10] denouncing the existence of any extension of the colonial scheme *in effect*, in a new form but denied beyond its supposed vanishing on the current "metropolitan" territory; 3) the publication of books and dossiers dedicated to the post-colonial question that remains, with a few exceptions,[11] still occulted to this day; 4) the "revolts" in the French projects in November 2005 (Moulier-Boutang 2005). Republican humanism will always consist of strictly separating the egalitarian republican project from what could appear to be a clear surrender on its part and the initial reality of colonialism from a certain post-colonialism that might still effect the current populations on French territory. Faced with obvious defeat, republicanism will demand more than republican equality, not seeing that the strengthening of its scheme will only reinforce the present difficulties. One should thus say to republicans what Deluze and Guattari said to psychoanalysts: in wishing to oedipanize the individuals for whom a procedure has failed, you do nothing but add failure to failure! For the republican scheme fundamentally rests on a *negative hallucination*, whose logic we've explained above, through which the Anglo-Saxon term "color blindness" becomes understandable. This negative hallucination states: in the Republic, there is no particularity, no skin color, only individuals who are considered to be equals to one another as long as – as long as what exactly? If we say as long as they are citizens, we limit equality to the status of the national-citizen, and we therefore confirm Sakai's analysis dedicated to the "identification of Humanity in general with Stateness" (Sakai 2006) and also the "European apartheid" that Etienne Balibar analyzes and denounces. It is, in a certain way, absolutely true: universality, which we have just come face to face with as it forces itself into open space, as it departs with difficulty from its *general matrix*, finds a place to bloom in the nation-state, in this case the *French* Republic, this particularity. But the republican universalist will always tell you: "let us admit that there is a particularity; the difficulty is extracting oneself from it, shrinking away from it, breaking free from it. The republican position is a welcome place for the individual who has been torn away from his ethnos, his family. Would you prefer instead the natural decline of the family, the links to blood and soil?" This is the discourse that drives the subjective-discursive double formation analyzed by Naoki Sakai, arising from within the Republic.

Yet the negative hallucination, as always, has its counterpart. It does not inevitably disappear because of destruction, direct physical violence, but at times because of a sort of second identification, an *ethnic construction to the second degree*. The sociologist Nacira Guénif-Souilamas speaks in a similar way about the technique of "assigning difference" which consists of "constructing" a "sexed and ethnicized nature" for "a specific type" of French people: the descendants of North-African immigrants (Guénif-Souilamas 2006). This designation works as a structure with four dead-ends – a "combinatorial that is always oppositional": the "veiled girl" and the "Arab boy" on the one hand, the "*beurette*" (second generation girl of North African descent) and the "lay Muslim" on the other. The first two do not possess the status of subjects, but of objects: the "veiled girl" is "acted" by the veil, and behind the veil by " 'bearded' men following behind her, a shadow brought on by the Islamic menace" – "thus, the veil metaphorically designates men who impose it on their daughters, and *this can therefore not be thought of in any way as a subjective choice* [underlined]" (Guénif-Souilamas 2006: 114–15). As for the "Arab boy," he is affected by his "body," his destructive and sexual drives, a true "wild-child" – a word that was used by the French Interior Ministry (Guénif-Souilamas 2006: 118–20) ... On the other side, we have what might be called "quasi-subjects," like-subjects who resemble *analogous humans* as they are described above: the "beurette" as a "colored French girl," and the "lay Muslim" as a "Frenchman on reserve," wandering in a limbo that ranges between Arab and unconditionally-French. They are subjects in waiting, at the end of the day, always "more objects than subjects of their existence" (Guénif-Souilamas 2006: 128). This is to say that *they will never become* French Subjects, not really, as long as the Republic treats a portion of its members as natives, that is to say delinquents or would-be terrorists. To each his own Korean.[12]

Thus we can see the logic that puts humanism to work under the guise of the Republic: 1) humanism declares that, in the Republic, there are no distinctions, and that we are all equal – the negative hallucination; 2) however, it fabricates second-hand differences through which it is able to measure *fundamental* inadequacy using the republican citizen model. When we can no longer exterminate,[13] we regulate.

Dislocation, relocation

The West, Naoki Sakai tells us, cannot be defined in terms of a fixed geographic entity, the "assumed unity" (Sakai 2001: 72) of the West has other means. Neither can the need for a definition in terms of *geographic containment* be replaced by an identification with *content* (traditions, religions). It is equally impossible to maintain, for example, that the West alone is capitalist or consumerist (Sakai 2001: 81–82), and we must define it differently, as West-and-the-rest, a bipolar configuration; as we have seen we must determine its *relation*.

This relation is overwhelming. With Lévi-Strauss, we defined the West as a sort of paranoid virus with a destructive tendency … the error, though, would be to believe that this is an excessive definition. It is instead only partial, and this point is fundamental. In fact, what Lévi-Strauss does not see is that the West does not just produce the Same, it also produces differences (cultural, sexual, ethnic) that are not given, but rather are constructed. *It produces a differentiation without which there could not be the Same.* In this regard, Lévi-Strauss' excellent analysis is also and still, partially, a modality of self-explanation that the West does with itself. And it is in politicizing the *relation* that Said attempts to liberate us from the trap: this is not only about putting the Western relation back on its feet, about reversing the reversal; this is truly about showing how independence, rotating in a spiral with imperial power, needs to forge its own path of escape without allowing European nationalism to repeat itself.

But the theoretical trap that we described at the beginning of our discussion seems to expand with the phenomenon of *globalization* of the world. This phenomenon seems, in fact, to have rendered null and void the hypothesis that the West is a geographic location. Though at this point we should distinguish between two phenomena: on the one hand, the original "dislocation" of the West that, as we have seen, clings to its bipolar configuration, to its *relation*, and hence has the capacity to territorialize anywhere; and on the other hand, the potential de-localization of the West as it is affected by globalization. However, the latter could have the effect of reinforcing the imperial "ubiquity" of the West. On this point, Naoki Sakai is very clear: despite globalization, "we cannot conclude that the West will cease to be distinctive from the Rest," the fragmentation of the West linked to globalization is not going to lead to its disappearance: deconstruction in action does not directly lead to "transcultural dissemination."

Yet it is moreover very certain that the only possible remedy to Western madness is – at first – the following: "re-articulate the very distinction between the West-and-the-Rest in such a way as to allow us to see the traces of the West as well as of the non-West in all of us" (Sakai 2001: 90). The problem is that globalization leads to the dissemination … of the Western relation itself, made even stronger because it is integrated into the development of eco-technology as funded by Capital. This very clearly signifies that one cannot simply *discover* the existence of "traces" of the West or of the non-West: as Deleuze and Guattari maintain, the "plane of immanence", that which materially refuses divisions and places of exceptional indemnity, must be *constructed*. The practice of translation, the *horizontal translation* that constitutes one of the fundamental points in Naoki Sakai's thought, is a device to be privileged in this construction.

It seems however that the remedy has to be stronger: the construction of this Global Plane of Immanence against the Imaginary People of the West will also need to be executed on a more "vertical" plane – not on an elevated one, close to transcendence, but close to the bottom, what lies beneath our feet, accompanying our steps. National humanism and republican humanism are also the rejects of a trans-historical humanism involving the relation of the human being with that which is not only non-Western, but also non-human. And it is here that Claude Lévi-Strauss unflinchingly awaits us with his anti-humanism, his very special kind of "deep ecology". If we want to rid ourselves of Western madness, not only do we need to depart from the political form of the Nation-State, but we also need to change the disastrous modalities of Western anthropo-technology.

Bibliography

Alizart, M. (2006) L'Anti-Humanisme. *Fresh théorie II*. Paris, Léo Scheer.

Balibar, É. (2002) *Droit de cité*, Paris, P.U.F. Quadrige.

Bancel, N., Blanchard, P. and Vergès, F. (2003) *La république coloniale*, Paris, Albine Michel.

Blanchard, P., Bancel, N. and Lemaire, S. (2005) *La fracture coloniale*, Paris, La Découverte.

Fanon, F. (2002) *Les damnés de la terre*, Paris, La Découverte Poche.

Guenif-Souilamas, N. (2006) La Française voilee, la beurette, le garçon arabe et le musulman laïc. Les figures assignées du racisme vertueux. *La république mise à nu par son immigration*. Paris, La Farbrique.

Levi-Strauss, C. (2003) *Anthropologie structurale*, Paris, Agora Plon.

Lindqvist, S. (2007) *Exterminez toutes ces brutes!*, Paris, Les Arènes.

Moulier-Boutang, Y. (2005) *La révolte des banlieues ou les habits nus de la République*, Paris, Editions Amsterdam.

Neyrat, F. (*2008a*) *Biopolitique des catastrophes*, Paris Editions MF.

——(*2008b*) Civilisation as crash test. *Caderno Sesc Videobrasil. Vol. 4*.

——(*2008c*) Empêcher d'exister. Une hypothèse cosmopolitique négative. *Rue Descartes n°62 : Terreur, terrorisme, état et sociétés*.

Said, E. W. (1994) *Culture and Imperialism*. New York, Vintage.

Sakai, N. (1997) *Translation and Subjectivity. On "Japan" and Cultural Nationalism*, Minneapolis, London, University of Minnesota Press.

——(2003) Nationalisme japonais de l'Après-guerre – complicité entre Etat périphérique et super-Etat. *Mulititudes*, 34–43.

——(2005) The West – A Dialogic Prescription or Proscription? *Social Identities*, 11, 183.

——(2006) Two Negations: Fear of Being Excluded and the Logic of Self-Esteem. In Calichman, R. (Ed.) *Contemporary Japanese Thought*. New York, Columbia University Press.

Sakai, N. and Hanawa, Y. (2001) Dislocation of the West and the Status of the Humanities. *Traces: 1. 'Spectre of the West'*. Ithaca, NY, Traces, Inc.

Todorov, T. (1991) *La conquête de l'Amerérique – la question de l'autre*, Paris, Points-Essais Seuil.

Notes

1 This pertains to a French expression, of the popular type, that means to not be in one's natural state, and therefore to appear as "elsewhere," totally detached from any relationship to the context; not to have one's feet on the ground.

2 The expulsion of the Jews from Spain follows the Alhambra Decree issued on March 31st 1492 by the Catholic royals Isabelle de Castille and Ferdinand d'Aragon, after their triumph against the Moors and the fall of Grenada (the surrender of Boadil). The expulsion of the Muslims and the "false" converts (the Moriscos for the Muslims, the Marranos for the Jews) would come ten years later. It was in the midst of the euphoria of this victory against the supposed Others that Columbus' plan was accepted, a project that, we must remember, might have been judged completely crazy: to reach Asia with its spices through the Atlantic Ocean.

3 Sven Lindqvist describes "art that kills at a distance" as a "European specialty": to kill without contact is to kill without danger (Lindqvist 2007: 76).

4 We must insist on a point that cannot be stated here : the "question" is perhaps not so much about the other as it is about the other similar.

5 "To accept nativism" adds Said, "is to accept the consequences of imperialism, the racial, religious and political divisions imposed by imperialism itself. To leave the historical world for the metaphysics of essences like négritude, Irishness, Islam or Catholicism is to abandon history for essentializations that have the power to turn human beings against each other" (Said 1994: 228–29).

6 Said speaks of an "ecology of literature" (1994: 318), and he strongly associates the question of ecology with that of democracy (330).

7 We should especially rely on the text entitled "The Dislocation of the West and the Status of the Humanities" (Sakai 2001). And for more on the same theme see also Sakai 2005: 177–95.

8 On this point allow us to refer to our study "Anti-Humanism" (Alizart 2006: 387–401).

9 We return here to the fifth chapter of *Translation and Subjectivity*, "Modernity and its Critique: The Problem of Universalism and Particularism," in which Naoki Sakai criticizes the discourse of two young Japanese philosophers, Kôyama Iwao and Kôsaka Masaaki: "What annoyed them in monistic history is not the fact that, in that Eurocentric arrangement of the world, the putative unity of the Japanese happened to be excluded from the center. They wanted to change the world so that the Japanese would occupy the position of the center and of the subject that determines other particularities in its own universal terms" (170). In reference to a popular comic strip in France (Iznogoud), one might say that what is at issue here is "Calife instead of Calife".

10 See their website: http://www.indigenes-republique.org/.

11 Cf. the Editions d'Amsterdam publications, *La fracture coloniale* (P. Blanchard, N. Bancel and S. Lemaire 2005). See also *La république coloniale* (N. Bancel, P. Blanchard and F. Vergès, 2003), the journal *Multitudes – n°26* which is dedicated to these questions, as well as the issue *Labyrinthe n°24; Faut-il être postcolonial?"*, (Paris, Maisonneuve and Larose, 2006).

12 We can thus find a parallel between Japan and France, Koreans and the descendants of North African immigrants. For the question of subjectivity see Sakai 1997: 44, 47. On the really subjective aspect of this question see "Two Negations" (Sakai 2006): it was asked of the Koreans to be loyal subjects of the Great Japanese Nation, while simultaneously being condemned to the fate of never being *truly* Japanese – except when one dies, sacrifices oneself. A double bind. From this arises Sakai's specific thesis: it is not enough to simply denounce imperial nationalism, as all nationalistic imperialism, under the pretext that this would be necessary for nationalism's egalitarian promise, and that this would be the height of its

commitments and ideals; we must also show the effects of the dubious methods of thanatopolitics: insomuch as nationalist ideology demands identification it renders impossible at the same time (double bind), the only possible subjective path that it offers at times, in its hard version, is sacrifice (let's call it suicide …).

13 Directly exterminating all at least – for this continues even today, with AIDS in Africa for example. And without a doubt in a more profound way with all the *people-in-excess* who suffer the effects of climate change. To this we must add the planned extermination of numerous animal species, which are considered to be less-than-nothing by humanist "theory." About these points, cf. my *Biopolitique des catastrophes* (Neyrat 2008a), and these essays: "Civilisation as crash test" (*Caderno Sesc Videobrasil. Vol.4.*, 2008b), "Empêcher d'exister. Une hypothèse cosmopolitique négative" (*Rue Descartes n°62 : Terreur, terrorisme, état et sociétés*, 2008c).

11 Modernization, modernity, and tradition

Sociological theory's promissory notes

Andreas Langenohl

Introduction: the substitution of modernity for modernization

The notion of modernization has become problematic. It is dismissed as an instance of macro-sociology's tendency to overgeneralize, or even universalize, a model of historical development that has appeared in the context of the European colonization of those regions which were then referred to as the non-West. At the same time, though, the notion displays a remarkable resistance against its dismissal precisely because it has been part and parcel of the processes that it pretended merely to describe. It is as if, in the current shift from modernization to modernity characterizing the discourse of contemporary macro-sociology, the term "modernization" still haunts its proclaimed alternative, that of modernity. Thus, Thomas Lamarre writes,

> A number of questions arise, however, about the relation between modernity and modernization. There have been efforts to separate modernity (as cultural modernity) from modernization (as societal modernization). Arguments for the complete autonomy of modernity from modernization remain unconvincing because some degree of complicity is always in evidence. Nevertheless, modernity and modernization are not the same thing. The question is, how does modernity – first and foremost a temporal marker – relate to modernization, that is, to totalizing forces or processes? (2004: 3)

It is now a truism that sociological depictions of modernization have been instrumental in bringing about some of the totalizing processes to which Lamarre alludes. Still, it is of interest to see how the discipline has reacted to these critiques. The most outspoken approach in current macro-sociology, in regard to the incorporation of those critiques into its research agenda, is the so-called Multiple Modernities paradigm (hereafter MM; cf. Eisenstadt *et al.* 2002; Eisenstadt 2002; Sachsenmaier 2002; and Kocka 2002). This paradigm – and also affiliated approaches which differ in detail – abandons the notion of modernization and instead speaks of modernity in the plural. Its basic argument is that historically and culturally specific ways, which are called "traditions," "cultural programs," or "culture," of entering modernity, understood as a set of globally diffused structural and procedural moments which originated in the historical West, have been constitutive for the formation of specific modernities. Thereby processes of transmission and imposition from the European metropolises to other world regions are appropriated and transmogrified in culturally and historically particular ways.

The MM paradigm differs from the classical stage of modernization theory in three important ways. First, as the summary term already indicates, it conceives of modernity as a plural phenomenon, which means that in the modern world there are a number of different modes of being modern. There are different opinions as to how this plural constellation still allows speaking of modernity as such; still, the core characteristic that, according to most contributors to the debate, characterizes modernity and therefore underlies all modernities is a high degree of societal differentiation, that is, the crystallization of institutional arrangements around a number of key processes in society (Eisenstadt 2002: 28). In view of the fact that differentiation is a descriptive, not an explanatory category, this theoretical common denominator in the MM approach permits maintaining a notion of modernity while at the same time appreciating the causal complexity and plurality of the historical processes that led to specific modernities.

Second, the MM approach takes into account that culture, and especially religious traditions, matter in trajectories that led to different modernities. In fact, culture and religious tradition serve as explanatory categories that are held to give an understanding of why there are different modernities, and what the factors that impacted upon their crystallization were (Knöbl 2007: 81–86).

Third, the MM approach departs from the methodological nationalism of earlier modernization theory in that it identifies not (national) societies, but "civilizations" as the conceptual frame for explaining the emergence of different modernities. The most fully elaborated conception of this frame is found in the work of Shmuel Eisenstadt, who introduced Karl Jaspers's term "axial age" into modernization theory. This introduction signals a turn toward the historical-cultural foundations of what Eisenstadt came to call "civilizations." According to Eisenstadt, axial age(s) refer to periods, "from 500 B.C. to the first century of the Christian era, or even to the rise of Islam" (Eisenstadt 1996: 13), of the formation of sustaining cultural symbols and belief-systems and their crystallization in societal institutions crosscutting the structural differentiation in society and transcending its spatio-social boundaries.

To sum up, the MM paradigm, which can be seen as the most important trend in current macro-sociology, highlights the fundamental plurality of the modern condition and ascribes it to cultural and religious traditions that exceed the methodological frame of the nation-state by virtue of their historical depth and their geographical extension. Given this focus on modernity as a contemporary and plural phenomenon, what, then, has become of "modernization"? In stressing the enduring, if transformed, role of traditions in different modernities, the MM paradigm returns modernization processes to history and historiography. What distinguishes the different modernities from each other is, according to this strategy, a phenomenon that seemingly resists modernization-theoretical explanations. Having modernity proclaimed as a common, if plural, condition, the trajectories that led to it – the different "traditions" – can only be approached in a historiographical fashion. Hence the inclination of the MM paradigm toward historical investigations about other parts of the world; hence its interest in "comparative historical sociology," "world history," and related historicizing approaches (cf. Knöbl 2007, Spohn forthcoming).

On the one hand, a historicization of processes which were once grandly termed rationalization, differentiation, individualization, or domestication (cf. Loo and Reijen 1992) can be appreciated as a self-critical answer to the critiques issued against modernization theory. In this endeavor, the MM approach stays true to the idiom of modernization in that it moves a core category of this idiom into its center: that of tradition. On the other hand, though, it seems that this notion of tradition is itself used in a fairly traditional way in that it denotes cultural patterns of orientation which are handed down from the past to the present, albeit maybe in a transformed shape. In this use, "tradition" serves as an historically explicatory category and at the same time as an alibi permitting macro-sociology to withdraw from the unavoidable question of the, in Lamarre's words, "totalizing forces and processes" (Lamarre 2004: 3) of modernization which are the flip side of modernity in the plural.

Björn Wittrock (2000) characterizes modernity as a cultural order that issues "promissory notes" to its members. The latter term makes reference to the cultural dimension of modernity insofar as modernity hosts a variety of promises and projects (like gains in personal autonomy, a decent life, justice, etc.) which can never be completely obtained but survive as regulative idea(l)s. Modernity constantly renews itself by virtue of the gap that opens up between visions of a good life that characterize modernity and the impossibility to completely bring them into existence (cf. also Wagner 2001). Those visions therefore serve as a legitimation of modernity as long as it is viewed as an incomplete, as opposed to failed, project. It seems now that modernization theory, and so the MM paradigm, also signed such promissory notes in that they have promised to make sense of the very "totalizing processes" that made their appearance as a theoretical discourse possible. In fact, this has been sociology's self-legitimization since Auguste Comte: explaining the macro-societal processes that made this science possible. However, much of the work being done within the MM paradigm denies its signature on the promissory note of theorizing how modernities have been brought about through "totalizing processes and forces." Concomitantly it is especially the notion of "tradition" that allows for such denial, as it substitutes the (now discredited) promise of earlier modernization theory to explain social change in general terms with close descriptions of why those changes were never that general as was once assumed. Sociological theory, as it were, passes on its promissory notes to cultural history, and it does so using the term "tradition" in a traditional way.

This escape to historiography is problematic for a more fundamental reason, as it fashions the underlying assumption that there are *contemporaneous* multiple modernities or, to put it differently, that it is *now* that modernity is plural. Evidently the MM paradigm is aimed at inter-civilizational comparisons, for instance, when it comes to the question of why "capitalism" or "the state" have fanned out into varying institutional crystallizations. But what underlies such adherence to plurality and historical contingence is the assumption that the current varieties of modernity are contemporaneous. And what in turn is effaced by this tacit assumption is that the concept of contemporaneity is itself a product not of modernity, but of a very narrow understanding of it. In an expression that Benedict Anderson (1985: 31; cf. also Anderson 1998: 34) borrowed from Walter Benjamin, this is an understanding of "homogeneous, empty time" which, according to Anderson, spread throughout the world with the West's implementation of the nation-state as the ultimate macro-political form and print capitalism as the cultural vehicle of such implementation. Harry Harootunian (2004) has argued that it is capitalism, and its fetishization of the commodity form, that has forced highly variegated temporalities into a single time horizon, namely, that of labor time. Whatever stake one takes in the debate, whether it be print capitalism or the commodity form as such that forcibly synchronized divergent temporalities, the consequences for the MM paradigm are evident: the approach of multiple contemporaneous modernities implicitly rests upon violently universalizing macro-processes that it cannot account for because it has abandoned the very idea of such processes. In other words, the concept of contemporaneity is an instance for the totalizing force of modernization from which the MM paradigm tries to escape in arguing that there is no modernization but only modernity in the plural, effected by different "traditions."

What will be attempted in the present chapter is a revisiting of the notion of "tradition" in a way distinct from its use in the MM paradigm. This attempt is guided by a notion of tradition that vouches for the validity of a processual understanding of rationalization as the central feature of modernization, with rationalization reinstalled as the "totalizing," though by no means homogenizing, "force" characterizing modernization. In other words, I will attempt to rescue an understanding of modernization by revisiting the notion of tradition, and thus face the impossibility, and yet inescapability, of theorizing modernization.

Tradition as rationalization

Tradition is the term most commonly used in the MM paradigm to explain the different trajectories and persistence of culturally specific features in the varieties of modernity. That is, tradition is made an element of modernity. If one sociologically theorizes the notion of tradition in this use (which has so far not been done in the MM paradigm), one begins to see that tradition refers not to a cultural substance but to a mode of handing over that substance – that is, it refers to a *process*. This, in turn, has implications for the relation between tradition and modernity.

The noun "tradition" derives from the past tense passive participle *traditus/-a/-um* of the Latin verb *tradere*, "to hand over." This etymological trace of the verb in the noun already casts doubt on the usual meaning of "tradition" in most theorization about modernization or modernity which employs it in order to denote a certain *cultural substance*. As it is certainly Max Weber who has the most differentiated and nuanced use of "tradition" and who employs the term, *inter alia*, in its processual sense,[1] I will start my discussion of the notion of tradition with his work, arguing that it is possible to rescue from it a processual understanding of tradition.

In most interpretations of Weber's oeuvre, "tradition" does not function as a prominent category. This has to do with the fact that most readings of Weber focus on rationalization as opposed to tradition, which Weber allegedly identified with the non-Western world religions. However, this mainstream reading effaces a fundamental quality of Weber's discussion of religious systems in India and China, namely that he deliberately makes a connection between tradition as a way of handing down cultural patterns and their consequential *rationalization*. Weber introduces "tradition" in this sense in order to explain why, unlike Protestantism, certain other cultural-religious stocks did not work the societal structures toward change. It is not necessary here to reconstruct in detail Weber's arguments. Suffice it to recall that he identifies both in India and China cultural-religious constellations that resulted in an affirmative stance toward the worldly order and in modes of life-conduct not aimed at worldly change (Weber 1991 [1920]; Weber 1998 [1921]). These developments of religious systems of thought were, according to Weber, conditioned by the sustaining consolidation of priest-intellectuals at the top of the social order and their distinction from the populace (Weber 1991 [1920]: 193–208; Weber 1998 [1921]: 99; cf. also Kalberg 2001: 173–75). In other words, religious tradition could become subject to cultural rationalization *without* spilling over into societal rationalization, in the sense of the establishment of instrumental patterns of action toward the world. What is more, tradition was culturally rationalized precisely *because* the spiritual and bureaucratic elites had an interest in securing the hierarchy of the social order through a distinction of their sophisticated cultural references from that of the populace. The semantic rationalization of traditions and their systematization thus impact the social-structural stability or changeability of societal structures (cf. Langenohl 2007: 41–50).

This brief reference to Weber's work on non-Western religious systems suggests that the "traditional" stability of societies is not due to the paralyzing power of tradition to freeze societal dynamics by virtue of its sheer cultural gravity, but is the result of the rationalization processes of tradition itself. In this interpretation, the power of tradition does not stem from its impenetrableness and taken-for-grantedness[2] but, on the contrary, from the rationalizations and refinements it allows for, and from the critiques it invites. In this sense, traditions, if understood as processes of semantic structuring, differentiation and refinement as a consequence of critique, foreshadow the advent of that what modernization theory used to reserve for modernity, namely *rationalization*.

This leads to the central argument of this chapter: traditions, if understood in a processual sense as in the Latin verb *tradere, are* the cultural substrate of modernity. Tradition, as it were, anticipates that which is only later called "rationalization" through a resemblance in the structure of the processes involved. Consequently, if tradition anticipated the mechanism of rationalization and in that sense has always been modern, then it is also true that modernity rests upon processes that have always been anchored in tradition. This argument, in its turn, has an implication worth further elaboration: If it is true that modernity has always been based upon the dynamics of tradition and its drive toward rationalization and systematization, this implies that traditions and their dynamics separate themselves from pre-traditional social and cultural orders in much the same way as modernity's separation from "the traditional" is usually conceived. If modernity has always been entangled in traditions, traditions always have been modern in regard to the social and cultural orders that preceded them.

This can be demonstrated through a brief reading of Durkheim's sociology of religion, more specifically, of his characterizations of pre-traditional – that is, preliterate – societies. Durkheim's work, which is based on a secondary analysis of ethnographic investigations about religious practices among the Arunta and the Warramunga in Australia (Durkheim 1967 [1912]), is at its heart an attempt to trace back (as some say "reduce," cf. Latour 2000) religion to society; that is, to identify religion as a functional arrangement that integrates society through conveying understandings of the world in which people live. The circumstance that it is preliterate societies to which Durkheim turns his attention is methodologically important insofar as his conception of *faits sociaux* locates them heuristically in societies characterized by "mechanical solidarity," that is, in societies which have not (yet) been entangled in the modernization process of differentiation, or, in Durkheim's own expression, "la division du travail social" (Durkheim 1893). For the present purposes, the important aspect is that, on close observation, although Durkheim identifies pre-modern societies as his focus of investigation, he in actuality does not operate *at all* with a notion of tradition. To be sure, he does make reference to tradition as "une morale et une cosmologie en même temps qu'une histoire" (1967 [1912]: 536). But if one subscribes to the (itself traditional) view that a minimal definition of tradition would have to implicate an understanding that traditional claims to validity operate through some representation of the past *as* past, then one realizes that, for Durkheim, references to the past as a distinctive mode of claiming traditional validity are functionally substitutable by other representations. Such is the case, for instance, with scenic performances among the illiterate which, according to Durkheim, do not so much *re*-present as they *present* and *enact* the past. In other words, the past does not yet function as a distinct source of legitimation. Consequently, it cannot be made subject to the rationalization processes outlined in the above discussion of Weber.

The rupture between what modernization theory used to term "traditionality" and "modernity" does, in actuality, not seem to have occurred between pre-modern and modern societies, but between preliterate and literate ones, namely with the advent of the possibility to rationalize, systematize and criticize that which could only then be called "tradition." It is startling to see how modernization theory – and for that matter, the MM approach too – has so far managed to circumvent abounding evidence from anthropology, cultural history, and indeed modernization research itself, that the real rupture in *cultural* terms did not take place on the threshold of European "modernity" but much earlier and in many other places.[3] I will only refer here to some prominent evidences articulated in anthropology and cultural history.

In cultural anthropology, the investigations of Jack Goody (1996, 2000) among the LoDagaa of West Africa have supported the argument that the notion of "tradition" as a mode of cultural handing-over should be reserved for literate societies. In his ethnographies, Goody found much counterevidence to the stereotype that the members of non-literate societies dispose of an unusual ability to memorize verbatim epic narratives, thus compensating for the lack of the medium of writing. Quite on the contrary, Goody establishes that non-literate societies, although they do dispose of a ritual calendar and engage in ritual performances on a continuous and repetitive basis, do not reproduce the texts word by word but rather actively reconstruct them during the performances in a dialogue between performers and public, the consequence being that the "texts" are constantly being reinvented and modified to a considerable degree. Consequently, the version being produced in ritual cannot become subject to criticism, rationalization or systematization: "[T]here can be no orthodoxy without a 'fixed text' of some kind or other, often arbitrary" (Goody 2000: 45). By way of extension, one may argue that there cannot be any heterodoxy without orthodoxy, just as orthodoxy's positive condition is heterodoxy. In all these respects, non-literate societies differ fundamentally from literate ones, where the "text," as soon as it is fixed in an enduring medium, can become the object of differing references and interpretations, of heterodoxy and criticism. In the light of the above elaboration of Weber's use of tradition, it now becomes evident that it is only the written text that can serve as the starting point of a tradition precisely because it can be made subject to interpretation, rationalization, and criticism. Tradition and its criticism are of the same origin; hence, tradition is inseparable from rationalization.

In cultural history, Jan Assmann's (1992) eminently influential writings about cultural memory lend additional evidence to this argument. The very term "cultural memory" (*kulturelles Gedächtnis*) presupposes that tradition, as the product and motor of such memory, relies on material externalizations that supplement "communicative memory" (*kommunikatives Gedächtnis*). This becomes evident from Assmann's delimitation of cultural memory from communicative memory. According to him, these two modes of memory differ, among other things, in regard to their reach into the past. The scope of communicative memory, which is made up by face-to-face interactions between witnesses of the times in a given society or culture, is limited to more or less four generations, because after that point no one remains whose memory would reach back farther. Cultural memory, in its turn, starts precisely at the point where communicative memory ends: it consists of texts (in the broad sense of the word) about a past that no one can remember. Now, where does "tradition" come in here? According to Assmann, preliterate societies, which have no means to exteriorize the semantic content of a given cultural memory, render tradition not as history but as foundational myth: They always keep the same distance from their past because their mythical (as opposed to historical) past begins right where communicative memory reaches its generational limit. By contrast, literate societies and cultures produce an exteriorized cultural memory which is constantly being added to. One of Assmann's most impressive examples is the Egyptian lists of pharaohs that form a tradition which is permanently extended. These examples from cultural anthropology and cultural history lend further evidence to the general argument of this chapter that "tradition" is already an incarnation of modernity vis-à-vis its predecessors.

If one accepts the argument that tradition is always implicated in modernity, this raises doubts about the value of the notion of modernity. What, actually, is modern about contemporary societies when their cultural processes have long been prepared in tradition? My answer is a sociological one: what distinguishes modern societies from others is that the dynamic of tradition, which constitutes itself only by being challenged and critiqued, is *socially extended* from intellectual (elite) discourse to all societal fields. The "societal rationalization" characterizing modernity "proper" is thus a radicalization and societal generalization of the cultural dynamics of tradition, namely, the reproduction and the modification of itself through the processing of heterodoxy and criticism. In a world in which criticisms of tradition and their consecutive rationalization, reflexivization and self-commentary have been generalized, and which in *this* sense can be considered modern, the maintenance of what Talcott Parsons (Parsons *et al.* 1950: 20–22), in a rather static expression, termed "cultural patterns" takes on an utterly dynamic shape. Modern societies do not rely on any kind of storage memory but, on the contrary, a constant exposure of cultural patterns to criticism. In this light, modern societies can be regarded as fundamentally auto-critical.

The interlinking of tradition and modernity is not due to a historical heritage through which a certain traditional substance is passed down the generational chain, but due to one and the same cultural-processual structure in which meaning claims are retroactively constituted through being exposed to criticism, defended, and modified. What is really new about modernity, therefore, is not the processual structures of its cultural mechanisms but the degree to which they are spread over all sectors of society. I shall now return to the question guiding this chapter: is there a way of understanding historicity and temporality in the modern condition that does neither denies nor universalizes the violent synchronizations that modernization brought about? While older West-centric modernization theory saw the beginning of modernity at some point in time between the fifteenth and the eighteenth century, depending on the aspects that were respectively highlighted ("secularization", "instrumental rationality", "social division of labor"/differentiation", "industrialization", among others), the MM paradigm tends to shift modernity's traces further back into the past, namely to the so-called "Axial Age civilization." At the same time, it incorporates the notion of tradition into its concept of contemporaneous modernities. All these historical foundationalisms, though, become utterly problematic if one takes seriously the idea that modernity has always been present in tradition and the process of its retroactive constitution through critique and semantic rationalization, and that today's modernities are nothing other than a social diffusion of that process of retroactive sensemaking throughout society.

This approach reinserts a generalizing component into the culturalist denial of the notion of modernization characterizing the MM paradigm, and thus rescues "modernization" for macro-sociology. The MM critique of the general modernization model has to speak of modernity because it cannot any more speak of modernization, thus abandoning any claim to capture the generality and totality of the processes that led into modernities. In contrast to this, I argue that a generalizable trace of modernization processes resides in a moment of fundamental discontinuity between traditions and "systemic" imperatives and their validity and saliency which spells itself out in tradition's propensity to be subjected to criticism. This trace, under conditions of "modernity" (as opposed to "traditionality"), is extended from intellectual (elite) discourse to all societal fields, and *this* is what characterizes the process of modernization. The "societal rationalization" characterizing modernity "proper" is thus not to be conceived of as an a-cultural decoupling of systemic imperatives from their cultural-historical motivations but as a radicalization and societal generalization of the cultural dynamics of tradition – namely, the reproduction and modification of itself through the processing of heterodoxy and criticism.

The suggested argument has consequences for the understanding of the historicity of modernity, to which I shall turn in the next sections. At this stage, though, I should say that that argument makes it difficult, and at the same time unavoidable (cf. Wagner 2001), to talk about identity and the self in modernity. On the one hand, in modernity each allegedly self-same posi-tionality – that is, every identity – can be challenged. On the other hand, such critique is always prone to constitute positionalities that, in turn, can be easily mistaken as being self-same. The "trap set up by modernity" (Sakai 1997: 176) annihilates identity but leaves the annihilator all too often with the fic-tion of being self-identical. Modernity's modernization, that is, its "totalizing forces and processes" (Lamarre 2004: 3) which have manifested themselves in relations of domination extended from the West to its self-consolidating other, the non-West, bring about an unsurpassable separation, and still unavoidable interrelation, between positionality and identity.

The historicity of modernization

As becomes evident from this view on the traditions, the cultures, and more generally the pasts of contemporary societies, the elaborations proposed here abandon any notion of historical linearity that used to come along with modernization-theoretical terms designed to capture macro-processes on a societal scale, like, for instance, differentiation, rationalization, or individua-lization (cf. Loo and Reijen 1992). Although contemporary macro-sociology has become well aware of the impossibility of talking about modernity in such over-generalizing descriptive strokes, it still sticks to the notion of historical linearity. In this respect the MM paradigm lines up with recent suggestions to cope with historical specificity and contingency through a return to history and historiography. Over the last years "new historical macrosociology," having formed in the US and since expanded, has turned its eye back on the past and on historiographical methods of dealing with it, especially in the historical subfield of "world history" (Knöbl 2007: 10; cf. also the overview in Spohn forthcoming). Such attempts at historicization are difficult to criticize because historicization is mostly held to be a desirable thing in itself. Still, in the light of the above developed argument – that modernity cannot rid itself of totalizing processes which are obscured by the notion of modernity but survive, if in a denied shape, in the denounced category of modernization – it must be asked whether such turning back to historical linearity and specificity does not occlude that fundamental characteristic of modernity and indeed is complicit in the strategy to de-represent totality.

What is at stake, therefore, is one of the core elements in macro-sociology's self-concept: namely, that its accounts move on a higher level of generality than historical accounts do. To be sure, this claim has triggered much criti-cism not only in history but also in literary and cultural studies, especially in post-structuralist and postcolonial approaches: the concerns were that mod-ernization theory all too nonchalantly ignores the specificity and situatedness of historical processes, and that it forces one dominant process model derived from representations of "the" European development onto other social, cul-tural, and historical constellations and their respective representations. Yet, while these reproaches hold true for the "classical" stage of Parsonsian modernization theory and surely helped overcome it, they cannot be that easily applied to the far more self-restricted use of the modernization "paradigm" in *early* sociology. If one, for instance, considers Weber's famous notion of the "universal-historical" (*universalgeschichtliche*, Weber 1988 [1920]: 1) significance that he attributed to modernization processes in Europe, it is clear that for Weber this significance did not at all reside in an allegedly universalized model of history that modernization processes in Europe would articulate, but in the spectacular *exceptionality* of developments in Europe if compared to such in other areas (cf. Weiß 1989: 15). The "universal-historical significance" of European modernization – postcolonial criticism has made this point very clear – consisted in its role in changing the order of world-wide intercultural and intersocietal comparisons in the direction of a hierarchization and homogenization of the units compared (Sakai and Solomon 2006: 23 and Chow 2006: 71–91). While this point, and the criticisms of Western modernity it implicates, was not accessible to Weber, it is still fully in line with his basic methodological argument: that the generality of modernization-theoretical descriptions is not derived from their homogenizing or "universalizing" force but from their capacity to identify historically situated and contingent currents as moments in a broader context of societal and cultural change. It is therefore my conviction that macro-sociology's claim to generality, while it has been often decried as contributing to the violent constitution of Western modernity in the non-West, can be rescued for a critique of that very totalizing process.

Given this precaution against an all too eager turn toward historiography, the question of *how to conceptualize historical depth sociologically* poses itself even more virulently. For sociology must come to terms with the historical dimensions of the patterned modernities and modernization processes that remain at the core of its agenda. This is especially true for an approach that, as the present one does, reintroduces the notion of tradition into the theorization of modernization.

Auto-criticism, the constitution of historical depth, and reflexive contingency

The recurring argument of this chapter has been that tradition is constituted through criticism and, in this respect, can be regarded as an ever preliminary moment in rationalization. Thus, the past is constructed, but not only as a chain of events, as constructionist models of history would have it (cf. Hobsbawm and Ranger 1983), but also as a space of "past possibilities" (cf. Motzkin 2008). This argument obviously refers itself to theorizing in literary theory but also philosophy of history, which holds that the past is not so much symbolically relevant as the causal predecessor of the present but as a reservoir of opportunities not realized, paths not trodden, and projects not coming into being.[4] The tacit question behind the criticism/constitution of tradition, which confronts one reading of tradition with others referring to the conceptual potential of the respective tradition, is this: what *could* have happened if it hadn't happened as it did? In this tacit question lies the decency of many criticisms and protests in today's societies, irrespective of their being denounced as nay-saying movements on the grounds that they do not come up with viable alternatives: in rejecting realist options as "perverse alternatives" (to use Dahrendorf's expression), they allude to a past as a space of future possibilities that could have turned out to be other than the *present* present.

If traditions constitute themselves in criticism, then each attempt to "invent" a tradition is from the very start utterly contested, because it of necessity creates the above mentioned space of past possibilities. That is, it brings into existence not only a plurality of narratives about the past but a past that contained a plurality of possible futures.[5] The process of modernization, understood as the societal generalization of an retroactive move through which traditions are constituted through criticism, thus makes reference to a dimension of historical depth that is open to post-positivist sociologization beyond the notion of the "construction of history" or the "invention of tradition." For what is being constructed in the criticism/constitution of tradition is not a history but a multiplicity of possible trajectories. Modernization is usually thought of as a particular type of social change that results in the irreversibility of its consequences. To this historical, and tacitly teleological, view one must add the self-referential process that is under discussion here, namely that modernization – understood as the societal generalization of the constitution of traditions through their criticism – carries and promotes orders of signification whose cultural coherence depends on their being constantly exposed to radical challenges coming from different interpretations of the possibilities of their pasts.

What results is a radical *contingency of the present* that becomes the organizing principle of modern societies and is made possible by multiple references to the past. The most compelling indication for this is that *memory*, and not history (cf. Motzkin 2008), becomes the source of political contestation and the construction and criticism of traditions in modern societies. Whereas in "premodern" societal-cultural orders the criticism of tradition could be encapsulated in intellectual discourse, which tended toward a universalizing and homogenizing view on the past, in today's societies historical-authoritative views on the past can be easily contested by particular views coming from memories which have a potential to be generalized – not universalized – on their own. Ironically, the institutional crystallization of a universalistic and homogenizing mode of representing history – the European discipline of historiography and the birth of national histories in the nineteenth century – took place at a time when the subversion of such universalizing representation through particular memory practices was already in full swing: "national histories" already bore the contradiction between the ambition to represent history universalistically and the self-cancellation of that project by the plurality and "seriality" of their sheer emergence (cf. Anderson 1998: 30–35). Seen from this angle, national historiographies were not a cultural project smoothly and functionally inserted into "modern" – read: national – modes of societal integration but articulated, from their very start, the gap that opened up between attempts at grasping and defining the past and counter-strategies aimed at rendering this attempt problematic. The rise of memory in the twentieth century rests on a generalization of this contestability of historical interpretations of the past that stems precisely, and reflexively, from the particularity of memory. Thus one might take up Naoki Sakai's contention that "[h]istoriography can be historical only through self-decentring and self-criticism, only if the tension between the present and the past is maintained and utilized to the fullest extent so as to ensure the possibility of defamiliarizing a given discourse" (Sakai 1991: 12), and argue that history is to be seen from the viewpoint of memory, not of History. The particular views on the past that memory entails keep open the general space of past possibilities: that it was not, but could have been, otherwise, and that it is precisely this "otherwise" that lends the present its significance.

The structure of historical depth in processes of modernization can thus be conceived of as follows. Modernizing societies do not move forward in history from past to present and future, but constantly negotiate where they could have possibly arrived. Macro-sociology, insofar as it contributes to these historical "reconstructions," is itself part of this retroactive movement of meaning, because it constructs past possibilities precisely by virtue of its grand comparative project of "multiple modernities." In this sense, it is an academic "comparative practice" (Chow 2006) next to others like comparative literature, area studies, and cultural studies, and works as a cultural agent of modernization, it despite all the plurality of those "modernities," converges on one feature: to open the past for all sectors of society, and not just for elite communication, and thus to force the radical contingency that characterizes modern societies into reflexivity. The question, then, "when did modernity start," inevitably transforms itself into the *political* question "where is it being barred?" Put differently: where are processes of critiquing and criticizing dominant claims on the past inhibited?

Conclusion: toward a modernization theory of circularity, self-referentiality and historical meaning in modernization processes

In his influential 1979 monograph on *Arbeit am Mythos,* Hans Blumenberg suggested a view on tradition and cultural memory that I would like to take as a point of departure for suggesting that macro-sociology supplement its linear model of societal development with a self-referential one, that is, with a model that allows accounting for the retroactive constitution of tradition through criticism. Blumenberg, who delineates his notion of the myth from essentialist readings that connect the substance of myths to certain historico-spatial civilizations, identifies myth as that which gives access to a substance it is deemed to have contained all along in subsequent stages of "working the myth," that is, of probing its potential to transfigure the structure of its elements. From this point of view, to transfigure the myth means to configure it in the first place. Connecting to Hans-Robert Jauß's (1977) work on the alterity and modernity of medieval literature, Blumenberg exemplarily shows how the Prometheus myth has been transfigured and reactualized in a chain of perceptions in which each perception continued the myth through inferring characteristics of it that were absent in earlier perceptions, while at the same time "forgetting" nuances of those earlier readings. Myth is that symbolic structure which always promises to uncover its full meaning through a reception of earlier readings of it and through a delimitation from them. In other words, the continuity of the mythical configuration is guaranteed precisely through its constant and potentially endless transfiguration in the perception.

Blumenberg's elaborations touch upon issues that have been recurrent throughout this chapter.[6] They advocate a retroactive and self-referential, instead of linear, understanding of the constitution of meaning in which the present is constituted not as a result of the past but as an ever renewed transfiguration, deeming itself an unveiling of a symbolic structure which allegedly has been there "all along." Each new reading of myth, in criticizing older readings and laying claim to uncovering its "real" meaning, revisits the origin of the myth as a space of possibilities that were not actualized. In this sense, the past is not an "origin" that causes a linear series of events but a cluster of different possible readings which are characterized by a fundamental undecidability.[7] The past is constantly returned to as a space whose potentialities preserve their salience.

Drawing upon Foucault's theory of literature, Rey Chow has argued that modernity is self-referential insofar as it is characterized by self-reflexive attempts "undertaken to bring to light the conscious and unconscious assumptions behind each and every utterance" (Chow 2006: 9).What, therefore, is distinctive about modernity is not the reflection upon the conditionality of utterances as such, as this mechanism is constitutive of tradition. What is novel, instead, is what Chow refers to as the "each and every," that is, the radical dissemination and diffusion of the processual structure of tradition throughout the whole of society.

It would be unfair to say that sociology has been completely unfamiliar to the self-referentiality in the constitution of social meaning. Separate from early related formulations in ethnomethodology (cf. Mehan and Wood 1975 for a summary), it was especially over the last two decades that several crucial works have been published that point out the self-referential structure of social meaning: people orient their action along presuppositions whose salience, plausibility and truth is only constituted as a result of those very actions (Knorr Cetina 1994; Pels 2002 and Pels *et al.* 2002). Social meaning, to use the most commonly known expression, operates like a self-fulfilling prophesy: the fiction that there are norms, values and information (in other words, society) that would guide individuals through the world becomes true only due to those individuals acting as if it were true.

Macro-sociology, however, has so far refused to take this self-referentiality into account. This might have to do with the circumstance that the majority of studies promoting circularity (exceptions worth a discussion being works on the "social imaginaries," cf. Taylor 2002; Lee and LiPuma 2002; Gaonkar 2002; and Gaonkar and Povinelli 2003) do not insert themselves into a modernization-theoretical background but rather put forth their arguments as contributions to general sociological theory. What would it mean, then, for research on modernization to take seriously the self-referentiality of meaning constitution?

It goes without saying that the understanding of modernization suggested in this chapter lends itself to the reconstruction of critical discourses and debates, because it is in discourses where it can exemplarily be shown how traditions are constituted only in their criticism. For instance, one might interpret the emergence and stabilization of the academic and intellectual discourse about postcoloniality as a retroactive positing of Eurocentric traditions which problematically underlie, and are made visible in, contemporary subjectifications in postcolonial societal, political, and cultural contexts.[8] These traditions are neither addressed as foundational narratives nor as an Other from which to delineate oneself, but as a constant source for questioning present proclamations about political agency and cultural autonomy. Concomitantly it is especially poststructuralism that postcolonial discourse is related to, though not in the sense that it is "influenced" by poststructuralist thought. Rather postcolonial intellectual discourse constitutes itself through a (re-)visiting of the interpretive possibilities that poststructuralism as a discourse of European origin has *not* actualized in its European context: it adopts its methodology and at the same time criticizes the historical context in which it has been developed and which precluded certain uses of it so far. In other words, the discourse of postcoloniality constitutes itself through a critique of poststructuralism as a "Eurocentric" tradition whose traditional Eurocentricity, as a relational phenomenon, comes into existence and is made palpable only through the act of critiquing.

Due to a lack of space I cannot explore further examples of how a self-referential model of meaning constitution in modernization processes might refract our understanding of such processes and their effects on several levels of society. What I want to stress toward the end of this chapter is that the approach toward modernization advocated here does not view different social phenomena at various levels of analysis as inserted within modernization processes or as their symptoms, but as active agents in a process which might be called the cultural self-constitution of modernity in modernization processes. This self-constitution follows a circular pattern, as the difference through which modernity distinguishes itself from what was before – tradition – is an effect of a revisiting/construction of tradition (in the sense of past possibilities) which comes alive as possibilities for the present and future only through the practices of criticizing and negating them.

Thomas Lamarre (2004), following Johannes Fabian's seminal work *Time and the Other* (1983), emphasizes the complicity of popular as well as academic understandings of modernization in the construction of the self-consolidating Other of Modernity-read-West. According to Fabian, the discipline of anthropology constituted itself, and the order of knowledge that made it possible, by way of inserting a time lag between the "traditional" societies its protagonists researched and the "modern" ones to which they belonged. So-called traditional societies thus vouched for the superiority, and thus legitimization, of anthropology as a modern science. Lamarre finds this figure of domination also in understandings of modernization elaborated since the heyday of Western anthropology: what brought traditional societies into symbolic existence and at the same time kept them at bay was the assumption that they eventually might "take off" and close up to the historically pioneering societies of the historical West. Macro-sociology's notorious, and sometimes deliberate, self-inscription into this project of domination cannot be undone through a simple dismissal of the notion of modernization and a return to a traditional notion of tradition; for was it not that notion that served the construction of the self-consolidating Other of modernization in the first place?

Macro-sociology cannot shake off its complicity in the totalizing processes that have brought about modernity simply by avoiding any notion of modernization or rationalization. Its silence about modernization and talk about modernities will not undo the violent totality of modernity. Instead of seeking refuge to a naïve pluralism, macro-sociology ought to revisit its own foundational moment and constitutive fictions. It ought to reconsider itself as part in the societal and cultural processes that were its positive conditions – and these were the emergence of totalizing orders of comparison erected upon a linear and teleological perspective on the past. Indeed, the discipline ought to remember the promissory notes it signed. The alternative proposed here – an understanding of tradition as a constant source of irritation and self-subversion that signifies a space of possibilities not actualized in modernization processes – might serve as a reminder.

Bibliography

Abu-Lughod, J. (1989), *Before European Hegemony: the World System A.D. 1250–1350.* Oxford University Press, Oxford/New York.

Adorno, T. W. (1973), *Negative Dialektik.* Suhrkamp, Frankfurt A.M.

Anderson, B. (1985), *Imagined Communities: Reflections on the Origin and Spread of Nationalism.* Verso, London.

——. (1998), *The Spectre of Comparisons: Nationalism, Southeast Asia, and the World.* Verso, London/New York.

Arnason, J. P. (2006), Contested Divergence: Rethinking the "Rise of the West," In Assmann, J. (1992), *Das kulturelle Gedächtnis. Schrift, Erinnerung und politische Identität in frühen Hochkulturen.* Beck, München.

Bhabha, H. (1990), DissemiNation: Time, Narrative, and the Margins of the Modern Nation. *Nation and Narration*, 291–322.

Blumenberg, H. (1979), *Arbeit am Mythos*. Suhrkamp, Frankfurt a.M.

Chow, R. (2006), *The Age of the World Target: Self-Referentiality in War, Theory, and Comparative Work*. Duke University Press, Durham/London.

Delanty, G. (Ed.) (2006), *Europe and Asia Beyond East and West*. Routledge, London/ New York, 77–91.

Derrida, J. (1988), *Limited Inc*. Evanston, Il, Northwestern University Press.

Durkheim, É. (1983), *De la division du travail social. Étude sur l'organisation des sociétés supérieures*. Alcan, Paris.

——. (1967 [1912]), *Les formes élémentaires de la vie religieuse. Le système totémique en Australie*. Les Presses universitaires de France, Paris.

Eisenstadt, S. N. (1996), *Japanese Civilization: A Comparative View*. University of Chicago Press, Chicago.

——. (2002), Some Observations on Multiple Modernities. In Eisenstadt, S., Sachsenmaier, D. and Riedel, J. (Eds.): *Reflections on Multiple Modernities: European, Chinese and Other Interpretations*, 27–41.

Eisenstadt, S. N., Riedel, J. and Sachsenmaier, D. (2002), The Context of the Multiple Modernities Paradigm. In Eisenstadt, S. N., Riedel, J. and Sachsenmaier, *Reflections on Multiple Modernities: European, Chinese and Other Interpretations*, 1–23.

Fabian, J. (1983), *Time and the Other: How Anthropology Makes Its object*. Columbia University Press, New York.

Gaonkar, D. P. (2002), Toward New Imaginaries. An Introduction. *Public Culture*, vol. 14, no. 1, 1–19.

Gaonkar, D. P. and Povinelli, E. A. (2003), Technologies of Public Forms: Circulation, Transfiguration, Recognition, *Public Culture*, vol. 15, no. 3, 385–97.

Giddens, A. (1994), Living in a Post-traditional Society. In Giddens, A., Beck, U. and Lash S., *Reflexive Modernization: Politics, Tradition and Aesthetics in the Modern Social Order*, 56–109.

Goody, J. (1996), Cognitive Contradictions and Universals: Creation and Evolution in Oral Cultures, *European Journal of Social Anthropology*, vol. 4, 1–16.

——. (2000), *The Power of the Written Tradition*, Smithsonian Institution, Washington/ London.

Harootunian, H. (2004), Ghostly Comparisons. In Lamarre, T. and Kang N. H. (Eds.), *Impacts of Modernities* (Traces: A Multilingual Series of Cultural Theory and Translation, vol. 3), 39–52.

Hobsbawm, E. and Ranger, T. (Eds.) (1983), *The Invention of Tradition*, Cambridge University Press, Cambridge/New York/Oakleigh.

Jauß, H. R. (1977), *Alterität und Modernität der mittelalterliche Literatur: Gesammelte Aufsätze 1956 – 1976*, Fink, München.

Kalberg, S. (2001), *Einführung in die historisch-vergleichende Soziologie Max Webers*, Westdeutscher Verlag, Opladen.

Knöbl, W. (2007), *Die Kontingenz der Moderne. Wege in Europa, Asien und Amerika*. Campus, Frankfurt A.M./New York.

Knorr Cetina, K. (1994), Primitive Classification and Postmodernity: Towards a Sociologal Notion of Fiction, *Theory, Culture and Society*, vol. 11, no. 3, 1–22.

Kocka, J. (2002) Multiple Modernities and Negotiated Universals. In SachsenMaier et al. (Eds.), *Reflections on Multiple Modernities: European, Chinese and Other Interpretations*, 119–28.

Lamarre, T. (2004), Introduction: Impacts of Modernities. In Lamarre, T. and Kang N. H. (Eds.), *Impacts of Modernities* (Traces: A Multilingual Series of Cultural Theory and Translation, vol. 3), 1–35.

Langenohl, A. (2007), *Tradition und Gesellschaftskritik. Eine Rekonstruktion der Modernisierungstheorie.* Campus, Frankfurt a.M./New York.

Latour, B. (2000), When Things Strike Back: A Possible Contribution of 'Science Studies' to the Social Sciences, *British Journal of Sociology*, vol. 51, no. 1, 107–23.

Lee, B. and Lipuma, E. (2002), Cultures of Circulation: The Imaginations of Modernity, *Public Culture*, vol. 14, no. 1, 191–213.

Loo, H. v. D. and Reijen, W. v. (1992), *Modernisierung: Projekt und Paradox.* DTV, München.

Mehan, H. and Wood, H. (1975), *The Reality of Ethnomethodology.* Wiley-Interscience, New York/London/Sydney/Toronto.

Motzkin, G. (2008), Forgetting Past Possibilities: The History That Never Happened, Presentation at the Conference *Zum Verständnis von Politik und Religion in Politischer Philosophie, liberaler Moderne und Politischer Theologie*, February 4–6, Collaborative Research Center "Cultures of Memory," Justus-Liebig-Universität Gießen.

Parsons, T., *et al.* (1950), The General Theory of Action. In Parsons, T. and Shils, E. A. (Eds.), *Toward a General Theory of Action: Theoretical Foundations for the Social Sciences*, Harper & Row, New York, 3–29.

Pels, D. (2002), Everyday Essentialism: Social Inertia and the 'Münchhausen Effect,' *Theory, Culture and Society*, vol. 19, no. 5/6, 69–89.

Pels, D., Hetherington, K. and Vandenberghe, F. (2002), The Status of the Object: Performances, Mediations, and Techniques, *Theory, Culture and Society*, vol. 19, no. 5/6, 1–21.

Sachesenmaier, D. (2002), Multiple Modernities – The Concept and Its Potential. In Sachsenmaier, D., Eisenstadt, S. N. and Riedel, J. (Eds.), *Reflections on Multiple Modernities: European, Chinese and Other Interpretations*, 42–67.

Sakai, N. (1991), *Voices of the Past: The Status of Language in Eighteenth-Century Japanese Discourse.* Cornell University Press, Ithaca/London.

——. 1997, *Translation and Subjectivity. On "Japan" and Cultural Nationalism.* University of Minnesota Press, Minneapolis/London.

Sakai, N. and Solomon, J. (2006), Introduction: Addressing the Multitude of Foreigners, Echoing Foucault. In Sakai, N. and Solomon, J. (Eds.), *Translation, Biopolitics, Colonial Difference.* Hong Kong University Press, Hong Kong, 1–35.

Spivak, G. C. (2008), *Other Asias.* Blackwell, Boston.

Spohn, W. (forthcoming). Historical and Comparative Sociology in a Globalizing World. In Šubrt, J. (Ed.), *Historical Sociology.* Prague.

Taylor, C. (2002), Modern Social Imaginaries. *Public Culture*, vol. 14, no. 1, 91–124.

Wagner, P. (2001), *Theorizing Modernity: Inescapability and Attainability in Social Theory.* Sage, London/Thousand Oaks/Delhi.

Weber, M. (1980 [1972]), *Wirtschaft und Gesellschaft. Grundriß der verstehenden Soziologie.* Mohr/Siebeck, Tübingen.

——. (1988 [1920]), Vorbemerkung, *Gesammelte Aufsätze zur Religionssoziologie.* vol I, 1–16.

——. (1991 [1920]), *Die Wirtschaftsethik der Weltreligionen. Konfuzianismus und Taoismus.* MWS I/19, Mohr/Siebeck, Tübingen.

——. (1998 [1921]), *Die Wirtschaftsethik der Weltreligionen: Hinduismus und Buddhismus.* MWS I/20, Mohr/Siebeck, Tübingen.

Weiß, J. (1989), Zur Einführung. In Weiß, J. (Ed.), *Max Weber heute. Erträge und Probleme der Forschung*, 7–28.

Wittrock, B. (2000), Modernity: One, Two or Many? European Origins and Modernity as a Global Condition. In *Multiple Modernities* (Daedalus: Journal of the American Academy of Arts and Sciences, vol. 129), 31–60.

Zamora, J. A. (1997), Erlösung unter Bilderverbot. Zu Th. W. Adornos Idee der Versöhnung nach Auschwitz. In Rainer, M. J. and Janssen, H. G. (Eds.), *Bilderverbot. Jahrbuch Politische Theologie*, vol. 2, 121–41.

Notes

1 Noteworthy in this regard are also the theorists of "reflexive modernization" (cf. Giddens 1994) who understand tradition as a certain way of promoting and defending social meaning.

2 This reading can also rely on Weber's characterization of socio-cultural traditions at work in the stabilization of traditional rule. According to Weber, the subjects of such rule refer to tradition *in their own interest*, for instance in order to prevent a traditional ruler from excessively exploiting them (Weber 1980 [1972]: 130, 133). In a *normative* sense, then, such traditions are indeed being "taken for granted," that is, they are being referred to by the subjects as indubitable criteria of legitimate rule, but this does not at all imply that they are also *cognitively* "taken for granted."

3 See Abu-Lughod 1989 for a seminal example of work that historically contextualizes and relativizes the claim that European modernity caused an unprecedented wave of technical innovation and economic growth (cf. also Arnason 2006 and Knöbl 2007: 112–66).

4 Cf. Adorno 1973: 13, 228 and Zamora 1997. For a summary of recent related statements in "post-European" literary studies see Chow 2006: 71–91. For the postcolonial context, Gayatri Spivak has suggested that one way of probing the past's bygone possibilities (which she, following Melanie Klein, calls "mourning") "may be the introduction of subaltern children to a literacy that carries the remote possibility of bearing witness to the intolerable burden of a history whose explanations have not, so far, involved them" (Spivak 2008: 145).

5 Cf. also Bhabha's (1990) notion that the alleged timelessness of the nation is at odds with the factual differentiations that cross it out.

6 This pertains to, for instance, the questioning of the rupture between "premodern" and "modern" societies that is regularly claimed by modernization theory. Blumenberg's work shows that it is, first and foremost, the continuity of traditions that constantly emerges from their transfigurations and criticisms of earlier readings, and that it is writing that has made possible this mode of working the myth insofar as it has made accessible earlier readings of it.

7 This reference to Derrida (1988: 116), which cannot be explored further here, highlights the political-ethical aspect of references to the past, stressing the reflexive nature of the scientific undecidability in interpretations of the past which is characteristic for contemporary societies. Precisely because history has lost its exclusive hold on the social imaginary, the past can turn into a rhetoric device that denies any final interpretation and thus lends itself for negotiating political options.

8 Cf. Langenohl 2007 for a reconstruction of debates in postcolonial theory (116–249) and in democratic criticism in post-Soviet Russia (250–367).

12 Theologico-political militancy in Ignacio de Loyola's *Ejercicios espirituales*

Alberto Moreiras

In his discussion of Maruyama Masao's *Thought and Behaviour in Modern Japanese Politics* (1969), Naoki Sakai presents an alternative that would account for the modern difference, or the difference of modernity. In Sakai's rendering, Maruyama opposes a premodern "missionary-style universalism" to the modern and largely European notion of nationalism that organized the later prevalent interstate system on a juridical basis of political equality:

> Nationalism, the guiding principle for the modern nation-state, and its essential moment, the concept of "sovereignty," are based on the premise that sovereign nation-states coexist on the same plane as equals, even if they might on occasion endorse the state's unconditional adventurism: by no means are they compatible with the centrism of the civilized center versus the savage periphery, which would never admit the true center of the world but for itself.
>
> (Maruyama, quoted by Sakai (1997: 69))

The premodern position would be the position of "theological universalism, according to which the world is constituted as emanating from a single center. ... Such a theological universalism has been upheld by missionaries and colonizers, and has served to reinforce the faith in the universality of Western civilization and to justify and empower colonialism (and post-colonialism) ever since 'the Conquest of America.' It is a universalism of self-indulgence that lacks a sense of the primordial split between 'the self' and 'the other'" (Sakai 1997: 69). What I find interesting here is the notion that a certain theological universalism, in spite of its apparent obsolescence after an alternative ideology developed, could still organize – and precisely all the way through modernity – the colonial and even postcolonial regimes. To all appearances, some states' occasional unconstrained adventurism would fall back on the theological-universalist regime to launch their expansionist projects into "the savage periphery." As a consequence, the modern schema ("nation-states coexist on the same plane as equals") was still compatible with "colonialist universality" (Sakai 1997: 69).

This is important for Sakai to the extent that it enables him to present his notion of "cofiguration." We must interpret cofiguration as a remnant – a sort of internalized residue of theological universalism on the side of the non-West as well as on the side of the West. Cofiguration is only possible on the basis of the end of the ostensible dominance of theological universalism. Given the juridical basis for a system of equality between nation-states, cofiguration arises as the ideological mechanism by means of which my nation-state depends on yours to the same extent that yours depends on mine: the consolidation of the interstate system in Europe, and its effects elsewhere, depend on a parallel system of transferential identity. In the case of Japan, Sakai shows how Japanese identity necessitated and upheld the alternative constitution of a Western identity, just as Western identity could only be posited in a relational sense vis-á-vis other parts of the world. And the consequence is:

> The schema of the coexistence among nation-states serves to conceal the complicity of the West and Japan in the transferential formation of respective identities; because of this complicity, the obsession with the West warrants self-referentiality for the Japanese. An uncritical endorsement of such a schema prevents us from detecting the hidden alliance of the narcissisms of the West and of Japan. It conceals the working of the regimes in which a paranoiac impulse to identify with the West, and another with Japan, are simultaneously reproduced and mutually reinforced by one another.
>
> (Sakai 1997: 71)

Colonialist universality survives, therefore, in the narcissistic-paranoiac regimes of cultural identity, which are therefore unrecognized surviving avatars of Western political theology. A logical conclusion of this argument would state that Western political theology is therefore not only premodern but also archi-modern, as it has managed to survive its presumptive obsolescence and remains radically active today through the very system of cultural identity functional to present-day globalization. This chapter seeks to delve into the genealogical foundations of the theological-universalist regime of the first modernity through a particular look at some aspects of Jesuit thought.

For religious consciousness in general, every act of tolerance and respect for alien ideas is fissured by an awareness of unconditional, transcendent truth. Relativism does not belong to religion, or belongs to it in a subordinate, derivative manner. For religious consciousness, relativism finds its limit in the need for service and fidelity to an unquestionable truth that may require further scrutiny but that, in itself, accepts no probabilities. The believer knows that neither he nor she, but God is the origin of truth and that truth is univocal. The novelty of Jesuit practice was to admit innumerable mediations regarding the ethico-political determination of truth, as reflected in the notion of *composición de lugar*, which translates as "situational consciousness." The place, the situation, is the instance of the decision. And every situation that calls for a practical decision is the region for the embodiment of a truth that remains unique even though it may be subject to different or even innumerable manifestations. This is what the old joke about the Jesuit and the Muslim conveys. The Jesuit says: "We both worship the same God – you in your way, and I in His" (Eagleton 2005: 19).[1] The tolerant or mundane Jesuit may be inclined to accept that the other, whether Muslim or Protestant, idolatrous or non-confessional, does everything in his or her power to be faithful to some idea of transcendent truth or even just adequate behavior, but that is never enough: the unfortunate condition of pre-Catholicity is unredeemable. However, while never enough, it is quite often good enough for practical purposes, which means: better than so many alternatives. This is the condition of political or secular practice for a Jesuit among non-Catholics. The Jesuit is a political being to an extent that members of older Catholic orders could not aspire to be. If other Catholic orders, especially in the early modern period, were fundamentalist, the Jesuit is anything but a fundamentalist, but he still comes from a fundamentalist core.

Take the situation that evolved in the first decades of the seventeenth century in Paraguay, narrated by Del Techo in *Historia provinciae paraquariae* (1673). Following Philip Caraman's account, one of the main problems not only for the proper administration but for the very establishment of the South American reductions was the endemic polygamy, both simultaneous and serial, that was a characteristic of the *modus vivendi* of the Guaraní tribal chiefs. Naturally the Jesuit-organized reductions could not permit polygamy. The efforts of the Jesuit Fathers to determine in every case who had been such and such a *cacique*'s first wife in order to proceed to a proper sacramental recognition of that union, which excluded the legality of every other conjugal union, were frequently in vain, when they did not run into impossible conflicts (for instance, when the "first wife" of a given cacique had been previously married to some other living member of the tribe). A proper adjudication was, however, necessary, as the entire structure of life in the Reductions was based upon the cacique's authority. Provided a cacique understood and accepted that only one legal wife was possible, if the cacique did not like the Jesuits' decision in terms of who was to be the one, he would not bring his people from the jungle, which meant that he would not put his people under Jesuit supervision. Caraman says: "A harsh decision based on European law, not on the realities of Guaraní tribal life, would have made substantial progress impossible" (Caraman 1975: 41–42). Confronted with many versions of this problem, Cardinal de Lugo decided to raise a petition to Pope Urban VIII asking for permission so that the Provincial Father could dissolve every pre-baptism marriage of the Guaraní caciques, "leaving them free to marry again for the first time" (Caraman 1975: 42). Urban VIII, himself formed by the Jesuits, and notorious for his quick temper, became annoyed with the consultation, arguing that the decision for dispensation had to be made in every case by the local Fathers. The Pope in effect refused to answer, on the grounds that only the local Fathers could determine whether there was a probable opinion to be given on the convenience of declaring the marriage null and void. The Pope's refusal to decide was still a papal act, a papal decision, and from then on the Jesuits had effective permission to act, not necessarily as they wished, but as the translational situation, in a context of an endemic conflict of languages and ideological practices, dictated. Situational consciousness is no doubt one of the most powerful tools for practical or political action in Catholic modernity, and it does embody to a certain significant extent the notion of heterolingual address that Sakai offers as his own solution to the problem of unrecognized colonialist universality, about which more below. The question remains as to whether Jesuit situational consciousness is in fact modern enough. Everything rests on the principle of sovereign decision, as we will see.[2]

In *Política del cielo* Antonio Rivera, who places himself in the mainstream of political tradition, thinks that Jesuit modernity is only partially, if not in fact, a contradiction in terms. For Rivera Absolutism or Calvinist Republicanism would emerge as the only properly modern options, and the Jesuit doctrine of indirect political censorship was only a half-way attempt to grant the Company a certain degree of autonomy. The doctrine of indirect political censorship basically means that the Jesuits were opposed to the finality of political authority on the grounds of their allegiance to another sphere of social action (Rivera 1999: 94). Obedience to the Pope was overriding. For Rivera, consistent with traditional considerations, the role that the Jesuits accorded to ecclesiastical power, and specifically to the Pope, constitutes an "insurmountable burden" in the path towards modernity (Rivera 1999: 94). The Pope, as the head of the Church, is the only real instance of worldly sovereignty. Any other political power can or should only admit its own heteronomy vis-á-vis the Pope. To the extent that the source of the Pope's authority is ecclesiastical and not political, there can be no properly political sovereignty. Sovereignty, that is, real sovereignty, for the Jesuits, is always already transpolitical. Now, if modernity, as tradition has it, and as Sakai confirms in his reading of Maruyama Masao, depends on the radical presumption of the autonomy of the political (which is a precondition for the juridical organization of the European interstate system), and if the Jesuits were never able to establish the latter doctrinally, then the Jesuits can be many things, but they can never be properly modern. Is this really so? What if the Jesuits kept the secret of the archi-modern political theology that remains active today, even if in a fallen version, in the narcissistic-paranoiac regime of cultural identity and therefore cultural translation?

Earlier in his book, Rivera had seemed to hesitate in his argument against the modernity of the Jesuits when he stated that "the ultimate goal [of Jesuit theory about temporal or civil power, and especially that of Mariana and Suárez] was ... to legitimize the interference of moral or religious authority in the public sphere. This heteronomous political discourse of the Company could also be taken to be a sign of modernity, since the *letterati*, the Masons, the Enlightenment critics, in spite of their deep differences with Jesuitism, would follow in their struggle against the absolute power of the monarchs a very similar indirect strategy" (Rivera 1999: 65–66). Indeed. Rivera refers to the fact that, for Enlightenment thought in general, the public sphere must be morally regulated. We need go no further than Immanuel Kant's *Perpetual Peace*, where Kant succinctly establishes the difference between the "moral politician" and the "political moralist." The former is "someone who conceives of the principles of political expediency in such a way that they can coexist with morality" and the latter "one who fashions his morality to suit his own advantage as a statesman" (Kant 2004: 118). For Kant, the moralists and the moralizers are those who "resort to despicable tricks, for they are only out to exploit the people (and if possible the whole world) by influencing the current ruling power in such a way as to ensure their own private advantage" (Kant 2004: 119). The moral politician, like the ethical individual, relates to politics in a non-opportunistic way, in fact, in a way that might force them to postpone their own advantage given not just ethical duty, but the simple legality of the situation where they find themselves: "there can be no half measures here; it is no use devising hybrid solutions such as a pragmatically conditioned right halfway between right and utility. For all politics must bend the knee before right, although politics may hope in return to arrive, however slowly, at a stage of lasting brilliance" (Kant 2004: 125). The lasting brilliance of politics depends, of course, on its conformity to right: "A true system of politics cannot therefore take a single step without first paying tribute to morality. And although politics in itself is a difficult art, no art is required to combine it with morality. For as soon as the two come into conflict, morality can cut through the knot which politics cannot untie" (Kant 2004: 125).

A "true system of politics," that is, the truth of the political, depends on its conformity to extrapolitical right. Enlightenment philosophers do not place ecclesiastical power in the position of arbiter of morality in the public sphere. For that role, rightly or wrongly, they choose reason, that is, practical reason, and the mandates of ethical law. Or at least Kant does. If the Enlightenment limits the autonomy of the political by making it subservient, in any "true system," to universal ethical law, then the Enlightenment doctrinally establishes the heteronomy of the political – there is a limit or a condition to the political, and only the interiorization of such a limit reaches the truth of politics. If, for the Jesuits, religious reason is the only possibility of true political heteronomy; in other words, if the truth of the Jesuit political is given in its accordance to papal authority, that is, to Catholic truth, then has the historiography of modernity been too quick to exclude from its presuppositions this internal limit to the autonomy of the political? Or is the Enlightenment anti-modern to the extent that it recognizes, as the Jesuits did, that the political is never in the last instance properly autonomous, or autonomous *in truth*? I suppose everything depends on whether one believes that the Pope is a true interpreter of moral law in practical-political terms.

Or, beyond that, perhaps everything depends on the status we might still be willing to give to the very notion of a universal moral law. What if there is no such thing as a moral law as the very condition of political freedom? We have a choice then: either we choose a Pope (or, beyond the Pope, an event whose consequences institute the need for a normative administration) that can interpret truth for us, or we do without it. Both options have consequences.

Jesuit thought fundamentally developed in a climate of religious war and crusade that would have already significantly marked the life of the Company's founder, Ignacio de Loyola. Ignacio's commitment to the political in the cause of the expansion of his own faith was beyond question. He took great interest from early in life in military campaigns related to the defense or propagation of Catholic faith. Ignacio's letters from 1552 to the Viceroy of Sicily Juan de Vega about the need to organize a strong fleet for the defense of Naples, of the Spanish and Italian shoreline, and for the recapture of the Greek islands from the Turks were taken seriously by military authorities in the preparation of the campaigns that would result in the battle of Lepanto, as Caraman says. From 1546 on Ignacio developed an intense correspondence with King John III of Portugal about the need to bring the schism with the Church of Ethiopia to an end. In the last year of his life, Ignacio volunteered for the Ethiopian mission, although his frailty and ill health would end up making it impossible for him to go. But, Caraman says, "the instructions Ignatius drew for Ethiopia form a charter of missionary method which was adapted with striking success by a later generation of Jesuits in China, Japan, Paraguay, and India, and remains today one of the most enlightened missionary documents of any age" (Caraman 1990: 179).

If time, for Fathers Ricci, Francis Xavier, Anchieta, and so many others in the first fifty years in the life of the Society of Jesus, was consumed in essentially political labors, of course the goal of those political labors was the establishment of total religious domination – hence world colonialism. We could call that mixture of political autonomy and heteronomy in the Jesuit conception *relational autonomy*. Situational consciousness emerges as the true key to evaluate Jesuit relational autonomy at both the doctrinal and the practical level. For instance, the very detailed instructions Ignacio sent the Patriarch of Ethiopia, Nunes Barretto, include, abysmally, the instruction not to follow instructions. Ignacio "made it clear that the Patriarch was not to consider himself bound by anything [Ignacio] had written but was to be free to deal with every situation as he judged best" (Caraman 1990: 180). One could say that this extraordinary chiasmus, i.e., "I order you not to feel bound by my orders," is in fact the rift in the fabric of the Jesuit conception of a properly religious politics, and it opens the catastrophe of political moralism. Or one can alternatively consider it the very essence of the relational autonomy of the political; that is, the only way in which any abstract law, whether the categorical imperative or papal mandates, can be accommodated in practical terms to the demands of the situation, not for the sake of moralist advantage, but rather for the sake of a better and more faithful fulfillment of the truth. Whatever the case, relational autonomy constitutes, in my opinion, the core of Jesuit modernity, and perhaps, in different forms, of every other modernity, including our own archimodernity. One wonders what Machiavelli would have thought of it, provided, of course, that it was not Machiavelli's dominant thought.

This notion of relational autonomy sends us back to the problem raised by Antonio Rivera: is the autonomy of the political an essential, or even the essential mark of modernity? Fredric Jameson has noted of contemporary critical discourse on the political that it ends up devolving "into ethical, theological, and civic republican motifs … For the Left, the present conceivability of any strategic orientation to state power has arguably imparted an abstract character to its various affirmations of 'the political' as an agenda in its own right." If we are to engage today "the problematic status of the semantics of decision, commitment, and denunciation," and address "the question of what constitutes the specifically political dimension … and whether this can be distinguished from mere partisan ideology" (Jameson), we must come to terms, I believe, with Jesuit relational autonomy. This is, incidentally, the question that Naoki Sakai's *Translation and Subjectivity* leaves with me.

Could any possible primacy of politics over history (including economic history) be considered absolute or relative? If relative, then politics would still be subordinate to history in the last instance. If absolute, then politics would be the norm of action. But an absolutely primary politics would have to rely on the total immanence of its own conditions, and would in fact be normless. A politics without a norm, that is, a politics that would itself be the normative standard, without recourse to alterity or to a heterogeneous grounding, can only be a politics of force. As such, it would have become an ontology (as in the Nietzschean case).

The alternative to an ontology of force (which would in itself create a paradox: would politics then reach full autonomy to the very extent that politics becomes ontology, and thus something other than itself?) is to think that a norm for politics can be found outside history, outside all force, including of course the ideological dissimulation of force. That norm, which for religious consciousness is self-evident and appears as transcendent truth, could take the form of a normative affect, such as what Alain Badiou has called the "communist invariant" or what Jacques Derrida calls the undeconstructible claim of the call for justice. It removes the claim of autonomy for the political. If every politics depends for its very grounding on a normative affect other than force, including the force of history, then perhaps it would be necessary to conclude that every possible understanding of the political as a primary motivator for human action would have to come under Kant's political moralism, would have to be automatically partisan. Partisan affect is not exclusively an affect of force, although force is secondarily or derivatively that which a partisan affect must try to obtain. The only possible non-partisan understanding of the political may be the understanding that politics is always already partisan. But, if politics always depends upon a prior partisan affect, then politics, whether classically understood or understood from the perspective of modernity, is not autonomous, because it must follow determinations not of its own making. Relational autonomy is only another way of saying relational heteronomy.

Where does Ignacio de Loyola find the foundations of his partisanship as a soldier of Christ, and of the Pope? In a general sense, the answer is obvious: in his Catholic faith, understood as faith in the universally redemptive character of the figure of Christ as embodied in the Church. Derivatively, of course, also in the civil powers willing to exercise their force of domination in order to promote the missionary character of the Church. At its limit, tendentially, the universalization of the Church would break through the oppressive hierarchical character of the so-called perfect community, because it would accomplish the non-fissured unity of the universal political body as mystical body of Christ: the communion of the saints. The doctrine of the communion of the saints is, in my opinion, the only possible referent for modern democratic theory, particularly if we understand democracy, following María Zambrano's 1958 formulation, as the move towards the abandonment of the sacrificial structuration of history (Zambrano 1988: 42).

Ignacio de Loyola's *Ejercicios espirituales* gives us some clues to understand this march towards the mystical body of a perfect universal community. It is a march based on theologico-political militancy, or partisanship. Nothing is clearer than the section of the *Ejercicios* known as "meditation on the two banners." Its basic tropology is founded on the analogy in political theology that Loyola gives us in the "Second Week" of the *Ejercicios* entitled "The Calling of the Temporal King Helps Us Contemplate the Life of the Eternal King" (Loyola 1997: 245). Part of the *composición de lugar*, or of the coming to situational consciousness of this "exercise" is "to put in front of me a human king, chosen by God Our Lord, whom all the princes and all Christian men revere and obey." Taking its point of departure in this temporal analogy of the spiritual reality of the sovereign presence of God in the world, the exercise says it is necessary "to look at how this king speaks to all of his subjects, saying: My will is to conquer all the land of the unfaithful; therefore, whoever would want to come with me must be satisfied to eat as I do, and to drink and dress as I do, etc.; in the same way he must work with me during the day and watch during the night, etc.; so that he can have his part in my victory as he has had it in my labors" (Loyola 1997: 246).

Loyola presents Christian life as militancy in an enterprise of conquest whose goal is victory and whose final reward is the possession of the conquered goods. The evidence for this kind of understanding is so strong that, Loyola says, "anyone with judgment and reason will offer all of his person to the task" (Loyola 1997: 247). Thus militancy is nothing but total militancy. The life of the Christian must be an infinite effort of militancy at the service of the eternal king and his goals.

Incidentally, this is the only way to understand the meaning of the foundational comparison or original parallelism in the *Ejercicios*, which is the notion that a spiritual exercise is the psychic transposition of bodily exercise (for the purposes of military training). In the first page of the text we read: "Because in the same way that strolling, walking, or running are bodily exercises, every way of preparing and disposing the soul to cleanse it of every disordered affection, and, after cleansing, every way of seeking and finding the divine will in the disposition of life for the health of the soul, is called a spiritual exercise" (Loyola 1997: 221). This parallel would make no sense if we thought that the justification for bodily exercise is merely the care of the self. If the spiritual implies distance, as Loyola says, from every kind of "self-love, willing, and interest," that is, distance from every pretension of subjective autonomy, in the same way bodily exercise does not aim at taking biopolitical care of the health of the body, but rather at making the body into an adequate instrument for its heteronomous function, which is its true function, namely, to serve temporally (Loyola 1997: 264).

The "meditation on the two banners" tropologically opposes the banner of Christ, "supreme captain and our lord," and the banner of Lucifer, "mortal enemy of our human nature," and demands "to imagine that the leader of all the enemies settles in the great field of Babylon, as in a great chair of fire and smoke, in a horrible and fearful figure ... [and] to consider how he calls innumerable demons and how he distributes them in such and such a city, and sends others to other cities, and thus throughout the world, not forgetting any provinces, places, states, or particular persons" (Loyola 1997: 253; 254). Against the banner of Lucifer, the banner of Christ, which opposes poverty, holds contempt for worldly honor, and espouses humility to Lucifer's riches, presumption, and arrogance. The soldier of Christ – and, from a Jesuit perspective, not just every soldier needed to be primarily a soldier of Christ, but every person ought to assume his or her Christian militancy as *total* militancy – attempts a conquest whose goal is the inner cathexis of the world towards spiritual and antiworldly values. Friends and enemies are opposed as Jerusalem is opposed to Babylon in an infinite game of deterritorialization. Jerusalem territorializes itself seeking the thorough deterritorialization of Babylon, in the same way that Babylon territorializes itself through the deterritorialization of Jerusalem. The final result, as conquest, is the appropriation of the goods, the appropriation of the earth. Total militancy, we should make no mistake, is political militancy for the conquest and appropriation of the earth. But political moralism in the Kantian sense is opposed to the extent that the Catholic can only proceed to an appropriation of the earth from humility, contempt for worldly honors, and radical poverty. Hence it is essential that the meditation on the two banners be followed by a supplement in the story of the ten thousand ducats. The question Loyola raises and deals with is how must Jerusalem own temporal riches and at the same time, in and through the process of world conquest, elude the temptation of total accumulation, or of a secret Babylonian reterritorialization.

The answer is of course relational autonomy. A poor appropriation of the world, or an appropriation of the world under the banner of poverty, of contempt for worldly honors, and of humility is only possible at the service of the greater glory of God, possessing for the service of God, so that the final victory, that is, the ultimate territorialization of the world by Jerusalem or by the Christian armies can also be an embrace of God as service to God. Radical colonialism thus hides within itself, as its most proper truth, a radical anticolonial project. If total militancy is total service, then the soldier of Christ finds his or her ultimate projection in a sort of dispossessing possession which is integration into the mystical body of God as deterritorialized, immaterial body, for its greater glory, in the name of the perfect community. Is this an anticipation of totalitarian catastrophe, or is it the epitome of a modern formulation of universal civilizational expansion by political means? It is both. It is as such impure. The notion of relational autonomy would not fool anyone. And neither would relational heteronomy.

Jesuit thought, understood as a militant project for the absolute territorialization of Jerusalem, necessarily incorporates, through situational consciousness, the subordination of its project of sanctity to its needs as priesthood, and simultaneously, the subordination of its priestly needs to the imperative of sanctity. This need for a double subordination remains today as the true political horizon, the very condition of a moral politics, which can only ever be a moral politics in the last instance ... or not. Antonio Rivera said that the modernity of Jesuit thought, as "the most modern Catholic thought," leads "straight to the modern professional army, the bureaucrat, the worker" (Rivera 1999: 16). This is so because the Jesuit, like its secular counterparts, lives in the very fissure between priesthood and sanctity. Religious consciousness can absorb the fissure. It refers it to a regulative transcendent truth from which situational consciousness can only derive. But the fissure remains intolerable to non-religious consciousness – no less so than the very alternative between priesthood and sanctity.

Where does that leave us (assuming that we refuse to choose between priesthood and sanctity)? For Naoki Sakai, the response to the schema of cofiguration that organizes every possible contradiction or indeed the very founding aporia of postcolonial thought (its speculative or mimetic limit, such that postcolonial thought has never yet been anything but a specular inversion of theological universalism) must be sought in a patient critique of the regime of homolingual translation in favor of its opposite, the "heterolingual address" (Sakai 1997: 4): "Only where it is impossible to assume that one should automatically be able to say what one oneself means and an other able to incept what one wants to say – that is, only where an enunciation and its inception are, respectively, a translation and a countertranslation – can we claim to participate in a nonaggregate community where what I want to call the heterolingual address is the rule, where it is imperative to evade the homolingual address" (Sakai 1997: 7). Cofiguration, that is, the mimetic regime of global dominance that is premised on the surreptitious presence of theological universalism underneath the veneer of interstate or internation equality, is a direct consequence of the homolingual regime of translation, or perhaps viceversa: in any case, they mutually implicate each other, on the basis of transferential identity. As Sakai says, "there should be many different ways to apprehend translation in which the subjectivity of a community does not necessarily constitute itself in terms of language unity or the homogeneous sphere of ethnic or national culture" (15). The heterolingual address is Sakai's recommendation for the formation of a democratic or non-oppressive translation regime, a nonaggregate community of belonging no longer recognizable in the exclusionary terms that have organized modernity as a game of friends and enemies, as the contest between Jerusalem and Babylon. And it seems true that the heterolingual address is no longer part or consequence of theological universalism, insofar as it represents its radical critique.

But does the heterolingual address rid itself of relational autonomy? Can it vanquish the Jesuit presupposition of a regime of transcendental authority? From the perspective that Alain Badiou has recently named "democratic materialism" (Badiou 2009: 1–9), where no truths come to affect the free play of languages and bodies, it is still possible to raise the difficult and perhaps destructive question concerning the still mimetic quality of every critique. If the heterolingual address is cofigured by homolingual translation, then the heterolingual address occupies the very site of theologico-political truth. A Babelic god, the god of the nonaggregate community, is still a subordinator of political life, and, furthermore, may not be efficient as such.

Bibliography

Badiou, A. (2009). *Logics of Worlds. Being and Event, 2*. Alberto Toscano transl. London, Continuum.

Caraman, P. (1975) *The Lost Paradise: An Account of Jesuits in Paraguay 1607–1768*. London, Sidgwick and Jackson.

——. (1990) *Ignatius Loyola: A Biography of the Founder of the Jesuits*. San Francisco, Harper and Row.

Eagleton, T. (2005) Spiritual Rock Star. *London Review of Books*.

Jameson, F. Thinking Politically. http://www.duke.edu/literature/institute/thinkingpolitically. htm

Kant, I. (2004) Perpetual Peace: A Philosophical Sketch. In Reiss, H. (Ed.) *Political Writings*. Cambridge, Cambridge University Press.

Loyola, I. D. (1997) *Ejercicios espirituales: in obras*. Madrid, Biblioteca de Autores Cristianos.

Rivera, A. (1999) *La política del cielo: clericalismo jesuita y estado moderno*. Hildesheim, Georg Olms Verlag.

Sakai, N. (1997) *Translation and Subjectivity*. Minneapolis, University of Minnesota Press.

Zambrano, M. (1988) *Persona y democracia: la historia sacrificial*. Barcelona, Anthropos.

Notes

1 Eagleton attributes the sentence to a Catholic in general, but I think it is better applied to the Jesuit in particular.
2 Of course the other great Jesuit joke about sovereign decision as always already sanctioned by papal authority is the following, which I owe to Karmele Troyas: "The Dominicans and the Jesuits were disputing about whether it was possible to smoke while praying, so they decided to ask the Vatican. The Dominicans asked: 'His Holiness, can we smoke as we pray?' His Holiness immediately said: 'No, idiots! To pray is too serious a thing, and it does not allow for mundane activities at the same time.' But the Jesuits asked: 'His Holiness, may we pray as we smoke?' And the Pope answered: 'Of course! Any moment is good to pray.'"

Interview with Naoki Sakai

Conducted by Richard F. Calichman and
John Namjun Kim

JK: One of the foremost aspects of your work is your critique of area studies. In one sense, the critique of area studies could be thought of as a strictly negative, epistemic project, that is, a negation of a certain historically and politically specific form of organizing knowledge around cartographic "areas." Strictly as a negative project, the critique of area studies does not seem to go beyond the destruction of the category "area." However, in another sense, your critique of area studies goes beyond the mere destruction of a category in that it is propelled by a fundamentally ethical impetus. One might say that your project is analogous to the Foucauldian critique of knowledge production around the body except that the "body" in question is not the human body, but the "body" of a cultural "area." Could you elaborate on the ethical dimension of your critique of area studies? What is the status of area studies in what is sometimes called a post-cartographic world?

NS: It is probably no longer necessary to have that kind of knowledge, or to organize knowledge on the basis of "area" because our relations to the areas have changed drastically. But before talking about the present state of area studies, I think we should pay attention to the history of the fields of Japan studies. One thing that is very important about the constitution of the discipline of Japan studies is, that, essentially, it assumes the presence of non-Japanese scholars. Like any national history or national literature, the field of Japanese studies is constituted essentially as a comparative field. Without comparatist investment, Japan as a domain of knowledge cannot be posited as distinct from other such domains. But in the case of Japan studies as area studies, it doubly assumes the viewpoint of non-Japanese scholars. The difference is that the national literature or national history in Japan is supposedly conducted by native scholars of Japan. Accordingly it is usually not called Japan studies. Japan studies can exist precisely because it is done by non-Japanese scholars. Yet there has been a separation among the students of Japanese studies. People don't pay attention to this. In the late or mid-nineteenth century, Anglo-American scholars began to study Japan systematically. People like Ernest Satow, William Aston and Basil Chamberlain established Japanese studies, and this affected similar studies in Germany and France and so forth. But there is also a very long and important tradition of Japanese studies by Chinese, Koreans, Indians, and Vietnamese scholars. Japan in the late nineteenth century was important. Hence an amazing number of scholars in China, for instance, studied the Japanese language. Until then, only a few outside Japan had paid attention to the Japan language. This was a very important source of Japanese studies, but little attention is paid to this disparity within Japan studies today. So there has been a complete separation between, Anglo-American Japanese studies and then Japanese studies conducted by Indians, Chinese and Vietnamese, Koreans, and so forth. So and their attitudes were, again, quite different. Basil Chamberlain and Ernest Satow were both, really, affiliated with the most powerful imperial power at that time. These early British Japanologists were very much involved in the racial theories of the period. Not only Japanese studies, but Chinese studies as well were hotbeds of racial theories at that time. Though it was not called area studies at that time – area studies was a post Second World War formation – it was already present. So it's very different from the kind of Japanese Studies you can find among the Chinese and Indians and Vietnamese.

JK: You are pointing out that the production of knowledge was organized around the principle of the nation as intimately tied to racialist theories of the late nineteenth and early twentieth centuries on a global scale.

NS: That is right. But because racialist theory was an important issue; because it is not only a matter for Japan but also for the United States because, in the 1920s, there were quite a few African-American intellectuals who were very interested in Japan as Marc Gallicchio taught us. Some among African-Americans were interested in Japan in the 1920s and 1930s precisely because their line of interest was closer to the Chinese, Indian and Turkish interest in Japan. This is to say there was an amazing disparity within the United States. Two visions of Japan coexisted. The best example is W.E.B. Dubois, who, even in the 1930s, believed that Japan was the leader of the colored people. He supported Japan throughout the 1920s, from the Paris Peace Conference until Japan's attack on Pearl Harbor. According to Gallicchio, even immediately after Pearl Harbor, you find an amazing number of black organizations that refused to cooperate with the federal government. Hence, there was widespread fear among white elites that Communists and the Japanese would penetrate American society and create social conflict. Of course it's in this context that Franklin Roosevelt and Henry Stimson, the Secretary of War, would organize concentration camps for U.S. citizens of Japanese ancestry there's a historical ground for it; under this political climate many Japanese Americans returned to Japan. In one of my books I discussed Edwin Reischauer's 1942 memorandum to the Department of War – Takashi Fujitani discovered the document in the U. S. National Archive and analyzed it. The latter half of this memorandum is all about racial problems within the United States. Reischauer warned the Department of War if the U.S. did not do something about the influence of Japan in East Asia, ideologically the United States will be defeated by Japan. Reischauer implied that, in the 1930s, in terms of knowledge production – or, in the phrase American intellectuals used during the Second World War, ideological warfare – Japan was imagined by American policy makers to occupy the position of universalism against America, though it was supposed to occupy the position of particularism. One of the missions of area studies, which was established during and after the war, was to disavow this crisis of ideological warfare for the United States and create the myth that the United States had constantly occupied the position of universalism. Reischauer's discussion is very clear. He suggested that if we did not win the ideological war, the Chinese, for instance, might be persuaded by the Japanese. That is exactly the line W.E.B. Du Bois used. That is to say, he took the side of Japan in the Sino-Japanese War by saying that the Chinese didn't understand the mission of Japan, because the Japanese were trying to liberate all the colored people of the world from white imperialism.

JK: W.E.B. Du Bois is interesting because he was also an admirer of German thought. He studied in Germany with very important sociologists who were also incredibly critical of the formation of knowledge within Germany; and yet, at the same time, he was also a Hegelian.

NS: Well, of course. Surprisingly enough he had much intellectual ground in common with Japanese intellectuals. He was, however, intellectually defeated when Japan allied itself with Germany and Italy because he strongly opposed Nazism and Mussolini's regime, particularly Mussolini's occupation of Ethiopia. It was a direct offense to his pan-Africanism. So he expected that Japan would interfere and go to war against Italy. Instead Japan joined Italy. So his stance was completely undermined by Japanese policies. But until then, he continued to argue that Japan carried that mission, and he received widespread support for this stance from other African-American intellectuals.

RC: This vision of Japan as somehow representative of resistance against white racism seems to have begun after Japan's victory in the Russo-Japanese War.

NS: Exactly. Or even earlier, in the Sino-Japanese War. That's what Valéry noted. The Spanish War and the Sino-Japanese War really created a sense of Europe precisely because two superpowers suddenly emerged on the horizon of world history, that is, Japan and the United States.

RC: But from Valéry's perspective, the American victory against Spain was seen as negative in the sense that war represented a victory of the non-European over the European on the basis of European technology. Nevertheless, from a racial perspective, it represented a victory on the part of whites over southern Europeans. So Valéry could have felt supportive of the U.S.'s victory over Spain in that particular sense. Here we see opening up an inconsistency between the notion of Europe and that of whiteness. In contrast, Japan's victory over China in the Sino-Japanese War had a very different dynamic. Here there is no whiteness to speak of and, if there is a European replacement or substitution, it's that Japan's victory was due in part to its incorporation of European technology. So in that sense the two wars are very different because the racial perspective does not enter into the Sino-Japanese War in the same way that it would have in the U.S. war against Spain.

NS: Yes and no. Let me talk about this problem from the Japanese perspective. What is interesting is that in the 1930s the Japanese government actually accepted an offer from South Africa: the South African government decided to treat the Japanese as white. This is before apartheid was officially introduced and enforced in South Africa. I'm not sure what their definition of white was. And historically, of course – even in the history of Europe and the United States – the category of whiteness itself has never been stable. It is well known that the Irish, the Jews and people of other ethnicities who pass as white today were not really white at one stage or another. Secondly, South African decision was not totally irrelevant to the formation of postwar area studies. In fact, John Dulles, the Secretary of State under Eisenhower, constantly used the rhetoric of whiteness. And he was not off the mark I think. I wrote on this in Japanese but I should write on it in English as well. Michael Schaller, a historian of East Asian diplomacy, actually checked the documents that are preserved in the archives of the Dulles Collection in which that memorandum is kept. Dulles said that one of the most effective ways to deal with the Japanese government was to use the card of whiteness, particularly when Dulles forced the Japanese government to sign the San Francisco Treaty in 1950. He was recorded as arguing in his private notes that the United States should use the racial card to say to the Japanese officials that the Japanese were white but the Chinese were not, or that the Russians were not white while the Japanese were. That kind of rhetoric must have been extremely effective with the Japanese. In this sense, there is a certain kind of racial complex among the Japanese policy makers. Of course, generally speaking, it is expected that races were organized coherently on a global scale. Nonetheless, racial classification always contains ambiguity and it is very difficult to position Japan within that racial hierarchy because the Japanese tend to have an extremely strong desire to be recognized as white.

RC: Implicitly, in Valéry's anxiety about the spread of European technology to the non-European, which the non-European could then possibly use against Europe itself, the same anxiety could be seen in terms of race. Meaning that whiteness, which Valéry associated with the European, could spread beyond the borders of Europe such that the non-white could potentially be seen as white once they have successfully incorporated European technology. Obviously, one effect of that would be that the distinction between the European and non-European, or the West and non-West or white versus non-white, would become invalid.

NS: There are two very interesting texts by Valéry. One is related to the crisis of European spirit, in which he used the trope of wine to express Europe: when wine is dropped into water, redness spreads just like blood. Basically this refers basically to a question of trophodynamics, that is, something is concentrated but once it is spread you cannot reverse the process. Another is a very interesting text on Hokusai. When he was young, Valéry encountered Hokusai's works for the first time, and they reminded him of his native town, Sète, where he used to swim in the Mediterranean Sea as a young boy. He recalled the blood of tuna since the fishing boats came into port and dumped the tuna that the fisherman had caught. An amazing amount of blood spread on the Mediterranean. He talked about that image in relation to Hokusai and the tremendous impact of Hokusai's prints. On that score, I am not sure whether or not Valéry identified himself with Northern Europe immediately. The Mediterranean Sea was something very important for him. But yes, there was clear anxiety there, even though he was known as a secular philosopher-poet and was rather hostile to religious authority. His essay on Blase Pascal is telling; it shows his intense dislike of religious obedience, but the essay itself is ambivalent. The other concerns the spreading of wine, which has clear connotations of race. In exactly the same way, technology spreads and therefore there is no way to reverse the process. This leads to a number of important topics.

RC: It's interesting because another tension in Valéry's thought was that, on the one hand, he was very sensitive to the movement of universalization. For him, universality was not something in which universals were simply given; rather they existed, precisely, as a movement from singularity to universalization. On the other hand, however, he believed that these movements had sources. So, for example, the spread of technology had as its source Europe because Europe was the home of technology.

NS: But only insofar as the source can constantly reinvent itself. In fact, Takeuchi Yoshimi in his discussion of modernity showed that, as a young intellectual, he learned much from Valéry. I think that his discussion of modernity repeats what he learned from Valéry. That is, only insofar as the source can constantly regenerate itself can it in effect remain itself. This is exactly the same move that Husserl made in his notion of the European crisis. For him, Europe had lost the necessary rigor to constantly repeat its origin. Positivism, for him, was the source of that decline. That is exactly the kind of teleology that one finds in the interwar period. This is to say, the question of maintaining European integrity involved not simply preserving Europe's heritage or tradition; rather it was the constant movement of destroying itself and thereby regenerating.

RC: That shows a certain politically interested conflation in the notion of Europe and the notion of universality because the movement of universalization is, in Valéry, coincident with the universalizing movement of Europeanization. So with the spread of technology, Europe destroys itself and reinvents itself. Europe never disappears, it just displaces itself. And in that sense, Naoki, I think you're right that Takeuchi is very sensitive to that movement, particularly when he talks about the spread of modernity and the West.

NS: I would like to point out that the ideological warfare, referred to by Reischauer was fought over the perception of political legitimacy in the Pacific theater. After the Second World War area studies managed to establish a perception of the international situation that would become commonsensical after the Pacific War – that is, America has always represented the moment of universality while East, Japan in particular, Asia has always represented the moment of particularity. As a matter of fact, in the early phases of the war in the Pacific, it was the reverse. This is why many U. S. policy experts, including Reischauer felt extremely insecure. They thought that, the United States was clearly losing the ideological war So Reischauer was so much concerned about the repercussions in East Asia of the American treatment of Asian Americans within the United States.. In this sense, the postwar field of Japan Studies was expanded and reconstituted as a form of area studies. One must note two moments here. One is very obvious: as the victor in World War II, the United States had control over not only Europe but also East Asia, and in this respect it was absolutely necessary to reconstitute colonial civil engineering. Nevertheless the United States deliberately avoided the rhetoric of colonialism. It really tried to create a new legitimacy against the French and British, and of course the Japanese, colonialisms. But when you look at the historical transition, inevitably there was continuity between the Greater East Asian Co-Prosperity Sphere and the US Collective Security system in East Asia. Basically, the United States inherited the Japanese colonial system, including its knowledge production. For instance, Japan at that time monopolized the sociological and anthropological knowledge of China, East Asia and Southeast Asia. That was one reason why some specialists were pardoned immediately after the war, and some of them enjoyed even diplomatic prestige so that they could come to the United States without visas. That became a scandal with the pardoning of all the members of Unit 731, who the Japanese Biological and Chemical Warfare Research Institute in Manchuria – sometimes called the Ishii Kikan after the program's leader, General Ishii Shirō – then enjoyed immunity from war crime prosecution. They received diplomatic immunity and so could bring in all relevant documents and samples into the United States.

RC: And that was done in order for the American military technicians to better" prior to "understand those biological experiments."

NS: That's right. That was one of the reasons why in 2001, immediately after 9/11, you might recall, there was an anthrax scare in the State Department. They checked the existing DNA and discovered all of the cultures came from Unit 731. In other words, the U. S. germ warfare research inherited much from wartime Japanese biological and chemical warfare research.

RC: Of course the same thing took place with the Nazi scientists.

NS: Exactly, the case of rocket technology is well known.

JK: It seems that we're approaching the question of modernity and humanism, of how humanism, in fact, produces and enforces the imperative to study things such as biological weapons. It produces the imperative of cleansing the body politic of all those impurities, as could be seen in German National Socialism. And humanism also creates the imperative to create hierarchies of the human. I was wondering if you could speak to that.

NS: It is related to the current issue of comfort women. This issue has often been approached from an unmediatedly moral perspective, but when you think about the degree of sophistication and the systematic nature of the comfort station system, it was clearly a product of population management and biopolitics. It was to maintain the welfare of the Japanese soldiers, in China first and then in places like the Philippines, Okinawa, Indonesia, and Thailand. This was done partly because there were all sorts of problems in the 1930s. As a result of long warfare in China, the Japanese army produced an increasing number of mentally disturbed soldiers. It's precisely that period when specialized mental hospitals were created in Japan. When I was a child, people used to call somebody with a psychopathological disorder *Matsuzawa byōin*. It's simply the name of a hospital, but actually it referred not to a hospital but to the insane who were kept there. I didn't know why people used that expression. But it was name for one mental institute for soldiers retiring from China, which was a secret. The Japanese government could not publicize it because it would have revealed the whole failure of Japan's policies in China. Therefore, commoners used it as an index to refer to someone who was insane, although publicly that could not be acknowledged. I only learned about the origin of Matsuzawa Hospital five or six years ago.

Precisely for the purpose of population management, in fact, a racial hierarchy was established within the comfort stations. Those women who have spoken about their experiences as comfort women are from the colonized, annexed territories. So far, no Japanese comfort women have come forward. It might be very difficult for them to do so, but nonetheless there is no officially recorded testimony by Japanese comfort women. Probably the number of Japanese comfort women was very small. The majority were Chinese, Korean, then Filipinos and Indonesian, Thai and so forth. One might note some resonances with the rhetoric of universal liberation. Officially, the Japanese government tried to endorse the idea of universal humanity. But in that policy it created a hierarchical formation.

JK: So for a Japanese woman to come out as a former comfort woman would be to ally herself with what is non-human or subhuman.

NS: Yes, that would be one of the implications. And then the human and subhuman differentiation somewhat shifts to indicate Japanese/non Japanese. I think the same logic works within Valéry and Husserl. As you know, Husserl was very explicit about that racial hierarchy. I'm interested in Kyoto School philosophy partly for that reason, since this philosophy is hardly different from European universalistic transcendental philosophy of that period. Because of that historical context, Japanese thinkers like Tanabe Hajime and Miki Kiyoshi were not just writing for a Japanese audience but for a global audience.

RC: Regarding the question of universality in your work, you refer at times to Kant's notion of the universal. When you discuss universalism, then, do you see it in strictly Kantian terms or otherwise? Because it seems to me that part of your critique of universalism, at least as it is understood by the Kyoto School, is really a critique of Hegelian universalism in which there is a link between particularism and universalism, and everything hinges on the status of mediation. That is one question, but another, related question concerns the derivative universal-particular relationship vis-à-vis the more original relationship between singularity and generality or universality. How would your conception of universality distinguish itself from the Kyoto school's conception of a derivative or relatively false notion of ontological universality in relation to a more originary universality grounded in *mu*, or nothingness?

NS: Let me first summarize the position of the Kyoto School by focusing, for the sake of simplicity, on three thinkers: Nishida Kitarō, Tanabe Hajime, and Miki Kiyoshi. All of them use the term "dialectic" from the late 1920s onward; it is a clear move away from Heidegger, for instance, for Miki and Tanabe. Nishida, for his part, never used a term like dialectic until the late 1920s, but used it often in the 1930s. One implication is that they recognized the importance of Hegel, perhaps in reaction to Marxism. That element is very clear. They had to deal with Marxism: not the Marxism of the Comintern but basically that introduced by Fukumoto Kazuo and others, a Lukácsian Marxism. So, in a sense, it was a response to the dominant position occupied by Marxism in the Japanese intellectual world, but at the same time there is a certain move towards a synthesis of Kant and Hegel. As Nishida pointed out, Hegel doesn't clearly differentiate generality and universality, so that kind of formation had to be articulated. Nishida started that move, which was then followed by Tanabe and Miki: they all tried to redefine universality in new ways. And that is the whole question of, to use Nishida's term, "continuity and discontinuity." This question of discontinuity became central. Tanabe pointed out that it is precisely the type of problem that didn't exist in Hegel because it has been very closely related to the development of mathematics and physics since the nineteenth century. Miki was not particularly strong in math, but Nishida and Tanabe were both very involved in it – a bit like Bergson or Husserl. They followed the development of modern mathematics in which the question of discontinuity became central, as this term was in a sense introduced in order to deal with the question of incommensurability and incomprehensibility. It is not a question of something being there and one must create continuity with it; rather it involves nonsense and how to overcome it in philosophy. That's why Deleuze, for instance, dealt with this question in *The Logic of Sense*. Also, these thinkers wanted to deal with the question of praxis. So universality is, in a sense, a question of praxis, but not only in terms of the Kantian notion of the *universalis*. Therefore, Tanabe appeals to Kant, not to the first critique but to the third, the whole question of reflective judgment. Reflective judgment is, basically, the discovery of universality through doing something, because it's related to the question of taste, of judgment. You sense something, yet you do not know it. Only when you actually achieve certain evaluations can you retrospectively discover your certainty. Therefore it is not of constitutive judgment, but rather of reflective judgment. In fact, universality comes when you create rupture and only when there is deadlock or nonsense, because you encounter two systems of norms and there is no way to reconcile them. One then discovers a system that is neither this nor that system; this is to say, universality comes into being for them when you create an axiomatic revolution.

RC: You often mention that the presence of Buddhism in Kyoto School texts has been very much overemphasized in the secondary scholarship. Obviously, there are political reasons why this is so.

NS: I am not saying that the Kyoto School philosophers didn't refer to Buddhist texts, names or terms. In non-philosophical essays Nishida talked about Buddhist texts, but in philosophical essays he deferred from referring to these texts. At that level, I do not think the mention of Buddhism really matters. For instance, both Miki and Tanabe refer to Shinran, the thirteenth-century founder of Pure Land Shin Buddhism, but these references are not so different from those to Augustine, Thomas Aquinas or sometimes even Kierkegaard. That is to say, they were not particularly concerned about the school orthodoxy of Shin Buddhism that is a huge organization in Japan, and I do not think they wanted to get involved in the politics of religious sects, even though they unwittingly did. Instead, again, this involves the problem of universalism in the Kyoto School, for these thinkers tried to rescue a kind of philosophical argumentation they found buried within Buddhist texts. Therefore they do not care about mixing Buddhist ideas with Christian theology or contemporary European philosophy. If we try to understand the validity of such a philosophical approach, we really have to follow their mixing; we have to take into account that authors like Miki and Tanabe were not particularly interested in recovering a certain kind of authenticity of original Buddhist argumentation of, say, the thirteenth century or earlier. That's basically my point.

In addition, we have to be aware of the historical meaning of modernity. One of the characteristics of the so-called "non-Western" world, or rather of the "modern" disciplines (particularly the humanities) practiced in the "non-Western" world, is that the term "West" was widely used to connote "modern." So if students wanted to study "modern" philosophy, they had to register in so-called "Western philosophy." Hence the Kyoto School is basically constituted in "Western philosophy." It is absolutely necessary to read these texts as "Western philosophy" even though the school was located in Japan. Of course, the major figures of the Kyoto School were extremely suspicious of the term "West" itself. Yet at least as a name for an academic discipline, they accepted the term "Western philosophy." Hence the insistence by people like Nishida that, at least in the early twentieth century, authentic philosophical argument has to be grounded in "Western philosophy." If one wants to study something like Buddhist tradition according to the protocols of modern scholarship, you have to first deal with the question of why modernity was immediately presented as "Western modernity." That's one of the reasons why emphasizing Buddhist tradition or Confucian tradition or even Shinto tradition in Japanese philosophy is simply ridiculous. Just as you don't need to be Christian in order to read Western philosophy, so you don't need to be Buddhist or Confucian to read Western philosophy in Japan.

RC: So why has there been such emphasis in Kyoto School scholarship on establishing the relationship between Buddhism and Kyoto School philosophy?

NS: This is a question very closely related to the constitution of the field of Japan studies or, in a sense, the field of Asian studies. As I mentioned, there was an ideological battle going on during the war. Two moments can be noted in the postwar constitution of area studies. One is, as I stated, colonial civil engineering. The second moment, which has been overlooked for a long time, is the ideological justification of the American presence in East Asia. Here the most widely used scheme is "the West and the Rest" format. This is to say, knowledge production has to be divided in two as if no relationship existed between them in order to conceal, as I mentioned, the continuity between the Greater East Asia Co-Prosperity sphere with the U.S. collective security system. Thus what is presented as the object of area studies is a completely different civilization or tradition dealing with an exotic tradition. The fact that both employ exactly the sort of same military technology, the same kind of colonial management, the same kind of social scientific knowledge to rule these areas, is totally disavowed. One characteristic of the formation of area studies is the presence of anti-anti-racism, because Japanese imperialism was able to use anti-racist rhetoric. This aspect has been completely overlooked. As a result, it is extremely difficult to synthesize Asian studies and Asian-American studies in the United States today. Asian-American studies has always maintained that if you want to talk about the United States you have to talk about racism, as this is a fact of American history. But, to my knowledge, very few people in Asian studies actually deal with the question of racism. There seems to be an assumed division of academic labor. I just mentioned Marc Gallicchio, who writes about the African-American encounter with Asia. It is an important breakthrough. In fact, when you trace retrace transpacific encounters historically, you can find amazing interactions: Japanese journalists talking with African Americans in New York City in the 1900s in order to gain support and get funding for the Russo-Japanese War; Japanese diplomats traveling around the United States and soliciting African American communities, and so forth. In fact, there is a long history of this, yet such interaction has been suppressed precisely because of the postwar formation of area studies, whose organizing principles coincided with Cold War policies. I think that this kind of academic division of labor is now beginning to collapse.

JK: It seems like this is a really good place to come back to the question raised earlier, the question of aesthetics in Kant. I am quite interested in a possible link to what Paul de Man called aesthetic ideology, specifically what you mentioned about the retroactive character of aesthetic judgments, or reflective judgments, as that retroactive character presents itself as if it were not retroactive in an aesthetic moment. In other words, race, the whole notion of a race, is an aesthetic concept.

NS: In fact, that is one of the reasons why I became interested in Tanabe's *Logic of Species*. Its starting point is a very careful reading of the third critique, particularly a number of texts by Kant discuss race. That's the beginning. Kant today is regarded as one of the founding thinkers of modern racism precisely because of his explanations of this notion, which were probably some of the first in the history of the term "race." In fact, that was also the starting point for Tanabe. Of course, he do not criticize the implicit racism in Kant. Instead, Tanabe struggled with how to deal with the question of aesthetic judgment, out of which he gradually constructed a logic of the nation. So, in a sense, yes, there's a very ambivalent relationship between Tanabe and Kant. For Tanabe, the nation is not a stable entity at all; it is not immutable. In the 1930s Tanabe and such sociologists as Takada Yasuma really tried to develop both an anti-racist rhetoric and the whole political dynamic of ethnicity, for ethnicity could be politically manipulated in order to, in a sense, consolidate the idea of an East Asian community. They wanted to create a new ethnicity that would match the reality of an East Asian community. They would say that the Japanese were previously confined to Japan proper, but now have to create a Japanese nation that encompasses much more different racial – or should I say, cultural and political – diversity. In that sense, as I once argued, despite entirely different institutional conditions and economic, political, and social histories between North America and East Asia, these thinkers were very much involved in the idea of the United States of East Asia.

JK: I think what Kant and Tanabe were struggling with was the problem of substitutability in the relation of the universal and the particular. Namely, the problem of aesthetics and race is that they look like fixed positions, and Tanabe focuses in *The Logic of Species* on the movement that permits the various positions and that circulation or flux.

NS: That is what Tanabe called the individual – but individual in the sense that it's not an individuum at all. Rather the individual is a logical contradiction, something which cannot be conceptualized. Hence the question of singularity comes in. The individual is the site where contradiction cannot be conceptualized in terms of an existing system of concept. That brings us again to the whole question of aesthetic judgment.

RC: In terms of the relationship between singularity and universality, one can say that the singular, unlike the individual or particular, always gives itself to substitutability. A double movement takes place: on the one hand, the singular always resists the movement of generalization, it's always outside of that system; on the other hand, however, the process of substitutability is inherent to the singular object or thing itself – meaning that the process of substitution does not supervene upon the thing but rather occurs by virtue of the thing's own self-betrayal. I wonder how that would speak to Tanabe's formulation.

NS: Tanabe called it a logical praxis. He wanted to explore that process of substitution. He always emphasized that it's a double movement. On the one hand, it's a substitution of the specific or *species and species*, but it can also be the creation of something that has not existed, whose direction he called the universal or genus. But here he connects this whole rhetoric to theology. That's why, for him, the genus is the City of God. It is a kind of universality that hasn't existed. Hence, he'll repeatedly say that the individual confronts that moment of singularity, and through death – meaning sacrifice and resurrection, to use his own terms – the individual tries to achieve the City of God. According to Tanabe, this is precisely the logical species that is, species is the form that constantly pulls down the individual's aspirations towards universality because of the presence of reality, institutional reality. There is always a contradiction between an existing social formation and what he called the individual, which itself basically exists in contradiction. Therefore, there is always antagonism between social formations and the individual, and this in fact generates the aspiration towards universality. It is this movement itself that provided justification for the Japanese state.

RC: And death, the sacrifice?

NS: Sacrifice for the state.

RC: You mean the merging of the individual into the totality.

NS: That's right. But, the merging of the individual tranforms the totality, nonetheless.

RC: But that would be very different from what I was trying to describe as the movement from singularity to universality.

NS: Substitutability.

RC: Maybe not substitutability so much as, for example, what Derrida calls dissemination. This dissemination is, in my reading, precisely the movement in which the singular betrays or negates itself in its dispersion into a universal or general space. But that is very different from what you described, which is a much more typical Hegelian model of the relation between the part and the whole, in which the part must submerge itself in order for the whole to be fully itself.

NS: Yes, the perspectives are very different because Derrida would never pretend that one could start from singularity because singularity is indeterminate, it cannot be conceptualized. But in Tanabe's case, something like the individual is, from the outset, somewhat a given. Through dialectic movement, he tries to elucidate the term "individual." From the outset, he starts within the movement of the dialectic. Hence he called his logic the logic of absolute mediation.

RC: Do you ever find that moment in Tanabe in which there is a resistance of the singularity of the *ko* [individual] vis-à-vis the *ko* understood as part or individual?

NS: So far I have not. But, I expect to find it since he pursued the question of poetics and the aleatory. I find it difficult to accept Tanabe here, as he's totally blind to, for instance, a critique like Nietzsche's. He never fully understood, in a sense, that kind of critique, which was based upon the question of textuality. He was never sensitive to that.

JK: That's interesting because it seems that, in much of what Tanabe is trying to do in *The Logic of Species*, he's struggling with a question that people in literary studies are especially attuned to, that is, the tension between the clear lines of thought that are established in understanding – so-called "understanding" – and the interruption and disruption, the rupture that is introduced in understanding through irony. In other words, he seems to have described the logical tensions, or has given a degree of political weight to, the opposition between irony and understanding, or, in contemporary terms, perhaps, between deconstruction and hermeneutics.

NS: In a strange way, then, Tanabe is very romantic, but at the same time he has no sense of irony. And that is fatal, I think, even though he was openly hostile to hermeneutics.

RC: Do you see this neglect of materiality or textuality as characteristic of the Kyoto School as a whole? Would you see any exceptions in the Kyoto School?

NS: I do not think that is a characteristic at all because a number of authors such as Kuki Shūzō and Nakai Masakazu were very perceptive about that aspect. We have to keep in mind that the position of philosophy at that time was very different. Recently I was reading a memoir by Maruyama Masao who wrote that he was second in the class at First High School The top student went to the Kyoto School for philosophy. That is to say, at that time only the most brilliant students went to there which meant that the Kyoto School was very closely associated with intellectual elitism. So the kind of students you got in the Kyoto School during the 1930s were, more-or-less, all-A students. As you recall, Takeuchi talked about this type of students in terms of *yūtōsei bunka*, a culture of all-A students when he discussed Japan's modernity. Perhaps Maruyama was trying to rescue the reputation of Tokyo University' Law Faculty where he taught since the label of bureaucratic elitism was usually applied to Tokyo University's Law Faculty rather than the Kyoto School of Philosophy. At any rate, I think this is very much related to the mentality of state bureaucrats. As the universal class of the nation, they were impartial and devoted to its destiny. Tanabe and Miki embodied this bureaucratic elitism. It was extremely difficult for them to get out of this mind-set. It's not a question of knowledge of the social sciences and so forth but, precisely, the lack of irony, such that knowledge production itself becomes fatally dysfunctional despite the fact that the Kyoto School was read in Japan's colonies as well. Hence, these thinkers – and Miki in particular – were very conscientious about integrating minorities into the empire but never seriously entertained the possibility that they might not want to be integrated.

RC: That is interesting since in your writings on the Kyoto School you seem to inherit and incorporate the distinction between two types of subjectivity, *shutai* and *shukan*. Certain Kyoto School thinkers, as for example Nishida, conceive *shutai* as somehow an excess to the system of *shukansei*. So there one could certainly identify a moment of excess outside the system that would have disturbing consequences within the system, within the systematicity of the system. How would you consider that aspect of the Kyoto School in terms of your other point, that they were thinkers of systematicity?

NS: In this respect, I think it's very interesting to read their relation to Heidegger. In fact, both Miki and Tanabe, implicitly or explicitly, wrote articles against Heidegger. His Nazi connections were widely publicized by national papers in Japan. Throughout the 1930s Japanese intellectuals were watching the development of Fascism in European countries such as Italy, Portugal, Germany, Spain and Austria. In the 1930s there were a number of important publications in Japanese by authors such as Tosaka Jun and Shinmei Masamichi on the development of Fascism in Europe. For instance, Miki's *The Logic of the Imagination* is essentially an argument with Heidegger, and Tanabe's *The Logic of Species* started with a critique of Heidegger. The critique centered on the issue that, in Heidegger, there is no social sense or, one might say, materiality in the constitution of subjectivity. That materiality was addressed by Nishida, for example, as a historical body. Intention can never exhaustively regulate the actualization of the subject. The historical material process has to be dealt with in relation to the primordial relations of "you" and "I." From this, Tanabe criticized Heidegger's analysis of auto-affection as simply time that is not mediated by space, meaning that it doesn't accommodate other egos. Tanabe argued that another ego is absolutely essential in the constitution of the sense of "I," since social relation is already involved in apperception. In terms of the question of the state and its violence, however, I don't think Tanabe understood the polysemic notion of the state's relation to the individual at all. This seems to touch on the entire question of nationalism. To the last moment, I think, both Miki and Tanabe were good patriots. But here I want to introduce an injunction: they were not nationalists of folkish destiny like Heidegger; they were essentially philosophers of multiethnic nationalism. That's why both of them kept saying that the ultimate goal of philosophy is to find meaning in something for which you can live and die. In Tanabe's case, the ultimate meaning of one's existence is the state, although not simply the existing state but rather the City of God. Such genuine but at the same time extremely dangerous nationalism was present in their philosophical projects, which I subsume under the name of imperial nationalism. But I cannot formulate any sort of coherent argument about it. That's one of the reasons why I am responding to your question by shifting to regional knowledge, historical knowledge.

RC: How would you respond to criticism of your approach to the Kyoto School that you overlook some of the importance of their philosophical insights in a desire to make a political critique?

NS: I agree that there has been a recent shift in my work away from deconstruction to something historical or regional, but the term "regional" has to be qualified. "Regional" is different from "area" in the sense that the historical has to be regional; "regional" means: if there is a historical statement or *énoncé*, it has to be in relation to other statements, other things. The regional thus implies that historical knowledge is about the statement and its, neighborhood, so to speak. Ultimately, one must examine discourse, for only within discourse can the historical be investigated. But this discourse does not necessarily refer to geographic area. This is where I think I find the shortcomings of history as a discipline. History - intellectual history included - until recently constituted itself as a discipline based on the assumption that a book or certain form of argumentation can be construed within the limits of its own market, culture or nation. My approach is different. I want to find a particular discourse – let me call it "contemporaneity" – which can be dispersed; it can be found in Western Europe or Latin America or East Asia or in a combination of multiple places. 'Contemporaneity' is a modality in which dispersed statements are linked together; it may be construed as responses to the same set of questions or as inquisitives about the historical conditions that have been taken for granted globally. But it's specific; it's historical. And then I want to relate philosophical argumentation to that kind of neighborhood and make it regional. In this sense, I'm not following the orthodox method in the history of philosophy as a discipline. I'm neither a philosopher nor an intellectual historian in that manner.

RC: That explains your difference from philosophy, but it does not really speak to the difference in your approach from area studies, in relation to which your approach is extremely philosophical. When I read your work, I feel that you're making a regional or empirically informed response to philosophy while at the same time articulating a philosophical or more general response to empirical area studies.

NS: That's one of the reasons why I wanted to seek some kind of comparative method to understand, for instance, the minority intellectuals in Taiwan of the 1930s and early 1940s together with the Asian American minority portrayed in *No No Boy*, for instance. I do not think these are two different neighborhoods. They were the "contemporaries." For me, they belong to the same neighborhood. In that sense, I clearly want to move away from area studies and instead inquire into how area is constituted in terms of discourse. What is involved in constituting something like "area" as a geographic domain where knowledge production is restricted? It is a regime of separation, by means of which the position of area specialists is withdrawn from coeval simultaneity. This regime of separation serves to constitute North America as a field separate from the fields for area studies research. This explains why area specialists have insisted on, their separation from, and their refusal to merge with, Asian-American studies. In a sense, I want to create a meta-language of area studies.

JK: It seems to me that the very terms or grammar with which you are working is more the grammar that Foucault tried to produce in *The Archeology of Knowledge* than, say, texts like *Discipline and Punish*, which were very much data-based.

RC: It's interesting that you raise this question because I was thinking of something very similar when I heard Naoki speak just now. In Naoki's essay on *No No Boy*, there is a move away from geographical or regional analysis to something like discursive analysis. I wonder if there's not a tension in terms of Naoki's response to geographic-based scholarship. On the one hand, the response would be Foucauldian: the appeal to discursive analysis allows for a critique of empirical positivities, especially geographic positivities. On the other hand, there is a move away from discursive analysis, in turn, to a more deconstructive, philosophical approach. In *Voices of the Past*, for example, I sense a very interesting and productive tension between those two directions, and I would like to know if, one, you are conscious of that tension and, two, you feel that it needs to be resolved.

NS: What is interesting about Foucault is that his work on bio-power and bio-politics in the late 1970s very much represents a continuation of his earlier discursive analysis, precisely because the central issue he posed was the notion of conduct, or *conduit* in French. *Conduit* should not refer to behavior that is observable; rather it involves a demand that a priest, for instance, have a certain conduct and observe the conduct of the penitent, and then through this he creates conduct, *conduit*, between him and the penitent. This creates a power relation that is in fact a passage. Hence, the proliferation of words like conduct, circuit, and circulation, in Foucault's analysis of power. This passage is neither being – the ontic – nor ought – the imperative – but both. And that is, for Foucault, precisely what "institution" means, I think. The institution is not merely a being; it is always a command at the same time. But, it does not necessarily work in the register of morality, of judiciary, discipline, or of delinquency. It evolves and transforms, and each time it changes, the surface in which it is inscribed also changes. He really opened up a new dimension of analysis which represented a critique of social scientific knowledge, and that's one of the reasons why he could maintain a meta-level against the notion of truth. For Foucault, the question of description and being combined or connected to the notion of adequacy itself can be analyzed through the notion of conduct. My analysis takes place at that level.

JK: Your more recent work has emphasized systems as necessarily tied to a certain form of ethics. It seems that you are pursuing this through the dual notion of conduct, which is actually one and the same, conduction as well as well as orchestration. Isn't this conjunction of systems and ethics the site of subjectivation?

NS: Yes, that's why Foucault said that the subject is constituted in conduct. This actually represents a very brilliant critique of negativity.

RC: Can you explain that?

NS: It's a very good critique of Tanabe too, because negativity is central in Tanabe's formation. Negativity means that the subject is formed when you realize something against which you can form yourself: Hegelian negativity. Foucault said no, it is through conduct – that is, by doing something, such as confessing – that the subject is posited. So doing something and the formation of the subject itself are, in a sense, on the same level. Therefore, you don't need to rely upon the logic of negativity, i.e., only when you find something that you have externalized in opposition to yourself can you constitute your own self. No, you don't need to go through that. It's basically a Nietzschean critique of Hegel.

JK: And this is actually the debate that we need to shorthand: the debate between Hegel and Spinoza.

NS: Well. Perhaps, that is one of the reasons why Tanabe was so hostile to Spinoza, too.

JK: Because Spinoza understood ethics as being not governed necessarily by an "ought" but by the creation of systems, systems that create other systems – in other words, that create power.

NS: For Tanabe death is absolutely central. For Spinoza, death is not. That is why Tanabe insists that only through death and resurrection is social transformation is possible. Spinoza carefully avoided this type of teleology. So that is the dimension I want to move into, but I do not know to what extent I will be successful.

JK: This is a new move. You're raising the discussion around post-humanism to another level, it seems, by articulating that there is no human being outside of conduct, *conduit*, in the same way – perhaps not *exactly* the same way, but in a way that is similar – that Spinoza understood how power relations are constituted.

RC: Let me ask a question about the division in your work between theory and practice, or *shukansei* and *shutaisai*. While I agree with the importance of that move, it seems that you sometimes typify that division along the lines of certain individuals. For example, when you criticize Watsuji Tetsurō in his travels across Asia, you say that he typifies a theoretical attitude. In contrast to this, there are certain figures, both actual and fictional, that you positively evaluate because they typify an attitude of praxis. Now this move from a conceptual understanding of the distinction between theory and praxis to an empirical typification of these notions seems to me unwise.

NS: First of all, apologies. Perhaps you're referring to one of my texts where I adopt Luke Gibbons' argument, and Gibbons relied upon Avishai Margalit, who is basically a follower of John Rawls. I found that kind of argument very powerful precisely because Margalit captured the core issue that I wanted to discuss concerning the status of minorities. Although I wanted to gradually develop a minoritarian politics, it is important to remember that a minority is not a type that can be determined in the coherent system of classification because essentially everybody is a minority member. A minority in this case is a person or group of people whose membership within the national community is potentially a target of suspicion, which means potentially everybody. In other words, a minority is a person or group of people who could be the target of discriminatory violence when a set of conditions is fulfilled. In the United States, the Japanese during World War II were definitely a minority. Jews in Christian societies in Europe and the Americas in the 1930s were minorities as well. Resident Koreans in Japan are no doubt a minority in this sense. And, today in the U.S. and Europe, not only the Arabs but the Muslims have become the targeted minority. There are many minorities in this sense. Here there are two directions of analysis. One concerns the objective approach, that is, an inquiry into what those historical conditions are how those people are identified. The aesthetic moment is very important. And why there is always a need for discriminatory violence and why there is complicity of the nation-state with colonial relations, etc. The United States is a very good example because one can clearly see the co-existence of colonial relations and nation-state formation. If you drive just one hour from Ithaca, you can see an Indian reservation just outside of Syracuse. That kind of reality has been somewhat erased in Britain or Japan, except in places like Okinawa. The second direction is subjective. The minority status determines both scope of a person's wish for recognition and his or her modes of participation in the national community. But it is almost impossible to predetermine who minorities are since everything depends upon historical experience. Nobody is born a minority, as brilliantly demonstrated by James Baldwin. Baldwin wrote that a person around the age of ten or so suddenly realizes that he or she is a minority – "I saw the hell" – and thereafter life completely changes. Essentially, being a minority is defined as a particular modality of anxiety. Usually a minority is a person or people who wish to escape that predicament. They feel that they are lacking in something and therefore seek to be normal. The remedy to be offered is usually recognition, which is then constantly sought after. This is the theme of *No-No Boy* and much of the Japanese language literature written by Taiwanese intellectuals under Japanese colonial rule . Luke Gibbons captured this process very well in reference to the history of the Irish, the British Empire and the United States; and he explained it in the vocabulary of Margalit. I was very impressed by Gibbons, so I simply adapted his approach.

I do not view being a minority as something exceptional; rather it is related to the basic manner in which the national subject is constructed. In fact, the construction of the national subject is inseparable from the positing and creating of the minority. Without creating minorities – people are anxious about their own normalcy – it is impossible to create the nation-state. This is the general problem of imperial nationalism in particular. In my own case, I have been fortunate enough to live in the United States where I am very much involved in the tragedy or tragicomedy of minority desire. This predicament helped me to understand the imperial nationalism of prewar Japan. Postwar Japan completely erased that kind of imperial nationalism. But being in the United States, in fact, sharpened my sensitivity to the work of subjective technology. Then when I read prewar texts, I saw that this problem was everywhere. From this I write a minoritarian politics in the modality of contemporaneity. The basic premise is that a minority does not represent a lack and so one does not seek normalcy. Every notion of the human being as normalcy must be viewed with suspicion. The human being is, in fact, always defined in conduct, in the Foucauldian sense. Recognition is not a remedy, nor is national identity. I admired certain attempts, such as John Okada's in *No-No Boy*, to depict the situation of the minority through the novelistic imagination. I also very much respected Foucault and Jean Genet and wanted to relate minoritarian politics and a reading of the minority to a critical reading of Tanabe and the philosophy of the Kyoto School, as these latter in fact reinforce this status. Theirs is precisely a majoritarian politics. That is how I wanted to approach it, though I was not satisfied with Margalit at all. That is clearly not my kind of philosophical argumentation.

RC: That's interesting because one has to walk a fine line between various types of discourse in order to make a political intervention into colonial politics. One does have to speak in a certain voice and that voice, at certain moments, sounds like an anthropological voice, and I see you doing that when you refer to Margalit and the importance of self-respect as opposed to self-esteem, which is simply another form of Hegelian recognition. So there you are very strategically miming an anthropological discourse, but only as a stage in order to make an intervention. By remaining at a philosophical level, one runs the risk of becoming unable to respond to very specific historical cases of violence.

NS: Exactly. I see your point. I was very dissatisfied but just could not find a better form of analysis.

RC: You mentioned the notion of ethics, and it seems to me that this notion is formulated in your work more or less as follows: thou shalt resist identification. I have two questions here. One, what would be the basis of that sort of ethics? And second, how possible is it? For example, Derrida's critique of the notion of ethics in Levinas relates to an excessive privileging of alterity, which however can only be spoken of in terms of a certain kind of propriety. What's at stake is a dialogue between alterity and ownness in which ownness comes to be threatened or transgressed but is never not there. In the critique of identification, it seems to me that one must also take into account this necessary moment of ownness.

NS: To approach this problem, particularly in the general logic of national identification, I wanted to introduce "co-figuration" as a term in order to differentiate the positing of the other and the self in terms of figures, that is to say, schemata. "I" am always posited in relation to some image of another. But in fact social relations cannot be reduced to that image of "own" and "other." That relation I call translation. So I wanted to see how co-figuration takes place, that is, how one's image is posited as if it were one's own self. That is the whole process of identification. But identification is never the positing of myself; rather it is a moment of positing the other. I wanted to rescue something taking place beyond the representation of self and other. In that way, I could conceptually delimit notions such as identification. That's one of the reasons why I am so interested in the question of translation. Eventually, I probably have to develop this argument in such a way that self-identification is based upon the translation of the self to itself. I'm working on that.

RC: There still remains the question of what would this ethics be based. How did you arrive at this notion of ethics as a kind of imperative to resist identification?

NS: I learned that from Nietzsche. That is, the imperative is never known, but somehow you act, and therefore you have an imperative. In which case, one would say the imperative is usually misconstrued. That is, you act as if there's an imperative.

JK: So moral action or ethical action presents itself as if it were teleologically structured. In other words, temporality presents itself as a future, but in fact it's not.

NS: It's what a transcendental analysis of moral action necessarily leads to.

RC: Getting back to the distinction between the West and non-West, we mentioned Derrida and especially his critique of the notion of western metaphysics, which he of course inherits from Heidegger. You've made very critical remarks on the very notion of Western metaphysics. Derrida's use of this notion was different from Heidegger's. For example, with Derrida there's much more of a geopolitical critique of the West and the West's colonial violence, which is absent in Heidegger. Nevertheless, he still holds on to the notion of the West. Could you talk about your criticism of this notion of Western metaphysics? It seems to me that your *Voices of the Past* can be read as a response to this notion in that you showed that metaphysics existed as much outside the West as within it, and also that the deconstruction or dismantling of metaphysics took place just as much outside as within the West.

NS: The first thing is that, when I criticize the West as a notion, marker or figure, I'm not saying that the West doesn't exist or that it's illusory. It's institutionally constituted. Therefore, if you deny it without due process, you will overlook some violence that can be addressed only by using the West. At the same time you really have to understand its behaviors precisely because there are many different contexts or registers in which it works. One of the most important registers is that it is, in fact, integrated into fantasy formation. And it is important to show that, by appealing to the West, you may well fall into exactly the same kind of rhetoric you find in Husserl, It goes something like this. "You are Europeans and therefore you have to be proud of the moral burden you are expected to shoulder since you are expected to be better than non-Europeans. Yet, you are not fulfilling this mission entrusted to European humanity. Thereby you are risking the danger of degrading yourselves down to the level of 'ethnic types.' You are betraying yourself. "By" ethnic types, "Husserl meant non-Westerners such as Indians and Chinese. Of course, Husserl's focus was Europe and we are talking about the West. The transition from Europe to the West requires a certain historical consideration, but in this context, I will simply speak as if Europe and the West were synonymous.. This kind of rhetoric is very closely related to the whole fantasy about the West, which is exactly what Derrida wanted to criticize. This is part of the colonial fantasy that constitutes the main texture of modernity. This is why colonial modernity is not found only in colonies or former colonies. I am not sure whether Derrida was entirely free of this Western exceptionalism. However, I am not advocating the simple destruction of one's civilizational conceit, for many could be easily driven to utter shamelessness when they are deprived of this kind of self-esteem. Recent neo-racisms and neo-fascist movements in Europe, North America, Australia, and Japan amply testify to this surge of shamelessness in former colonizer societies. So there should be a different way of criticizing this. Now I'm thinking about the implications of universalisms in understanding something like the West, sexism, racism, and of course capitalist universality. We really have to understand how the West behaves. At the same time, there has to be a certain way of talking about various sides and different regions without falling into the hierarchical arrangement of universality and particularity. We really have to propose different ways of handling texts, and not necessarily texts in the narrow sense, but textualities. That is what I want to do. I do not want to be simply negative about the West.

RC: Let's turn to the subject of 9/11. What effects do you see 9/11 having on Asian studies or area studies?

NS: It showed to what extent area studies has been insulated from contemporary issues. Yet the whole incident is very symbolic in many ways. This is why I wrote about the similarity between the United States' reaction to 9/11 and the onset of fascism in the 1930s in Japan in a volume of positions: east asia cultures critique, which you edited, Richard. For example, Ward Churchill's dismissal from the University of Colorado called to mind the infamous the Kyoto Imperial University Law Professor, Takigawa Yukitori, incident of 1933 in Japan, where Takigawa was fired by the the minister of education at that time for similar reasons. This shows that there are so many different ways to talk about the comparative realities between Asia, or some parts of Asia, and North America or Europe. So in a sense 9/11 and its aftermath provides us with opportunities understand the formation of area studies because we were in a similar situation to the Japanese intellectuals of the 1930s. Undoubtedly this is related to what I suggested above in terms of contemporaneity. We really need a general investigation of how nationality works in places like the United States today.

RC: It was rather astonishing for me to speak with other Asian studies scholars in the wake of 9/11, as it seemed that they saw this event – in the case of American nationals – as American citizens first and foremost apart from their study of Asia. The reason for that was simply the difference in content between Asia and the Middle East. That is, the area linked to 9/11 is different from the area of their own field of study, but what seems crucial here is that knowledge production generally begins as a response to crisis. So for example, the war with Japan really spurred on the creation of Japan studies in the US just as 9/11 will, I believe, mark the formation of Middle Eastern Studies in the US in a very dramatic fashion. This structural similarity seems to be lost on many Asian studies scholars in the United States.

NS: That lack of reflexivity is amazing when you think about it, but even that is part and parcel of area studies. In addition, I think, sooner or later number of crises will come, as it really marked the end of American hegemony in East Asia. Ten years ago American democracy carried some weight in East Asia, but today does not. Some intellectuals in East Asia called it a paper tiger. You cannot find many intellectuals in East Asia today who really respect or are committed to the notion of American democracy. I know leftists and Marxists in particular ridiculed this notion for a long time, but it did not really destroy respect or envy for American democracy even among leftist intellectuals in East Asia. Yet the behavior of the American government since 9/11 has really dispelled any illusion about it. About two months ago Wang Hui told me that one of the most important consequences of 9/11 is that Asian intellectuals now truly understand what was meant by American democracy.

RC: Geopolitically, I think this is one of the positive consequences of 9/11. And it's not as if this violence is suddenly revealed to exist now in the wake of 9/11. It has existed for a long time, but just in disavowed or repressed form.

NS: That's the way that American hegemony worked until then, but this is really a period where Pax Americana is no longer a given. I do not think the United States can recover it the prominence it used to enjoy.

RC: This might be a good segue into the question of the nation state and its gradual overcoming. One can see this not only now in certain forms, for example certain economic blocks, but indeed throughout the entire twentieth century. We can see Japanese imperialism as a response to that growing demand; meaning that, in order to counter the hegemony of the West, empire building had to be aggressively initiated. But now, in the post 9/11 world, what forms do you see as competing with, or potentially threatening to, the sovereignty of the nation state? Do you see any of these forms as being in some sense more hospitable or receptive to foreigners than the form of the nation state?

NS: Postwar history is very symbolic in this sense. Already in the 1910s, particularly in 1919, the Wilsonian doctrine of self-determination was announced. It upset a lot of people because it marked the beginning of the whole process of discussing whether or not the nation-state was the most appropriate political form. Even in the U.S., the Wilsonian doctrine could not possibly be accepted by the majority of Congress mainly because the U.S. would become fragmented if the self-determination of the nation were pursued literally. Most of the empires of the time, the Japanese, British and French immediately saw that. That was one of the reasons why, on March 1, 1919, the demonstration demanding Korea's independence erupted, leading to bloody oppression by the Japanese colonial government. That was an independence movement within the empire. Such movements could occur immediately everywhere in the empire. This explains the great hostility on the part of the Japanese State to the idea of ethnic nationalism. Intellectuals in Japan were generally very hostile to the idea of nationalism in the sense of *minzokushugi*. In the 1920s, they really repressed *minzokushugi* nationalism of that kind. In this respect, Watsuji Tetsurō was an exception in his equation of ethnicity to nationality as well as in his embrace of the Nazi notion of the purity of the race.. It's very difficult to find the kind of ethnic nationalist who affirmed the integrity of the ethnic nation and tried to build the nation-state upon on that basis during the interwar period. Watsuji was probably one of the very few in Japan at that time. However, after the war you find an amazing proliferation of those nationalists, and understandably so. They thought that because Japan had lost its colonies under had U.S. occupation, it was now possible to create a nation-state on the basis of ethnic unity.

But there are two very important issues here. First, when you talk about modern sovereignty, it usually assumes, for instance, the integrity of territory, and also popular sovereignty – that is to say, the nation should vote and decide. According to this principle, a parliament must be formed. Hence the sovereign must be the people. The case of postwar Japan is very interesting because the old notion of sovereignty was completely undermined. When the United States began its occupation in 1945, most leaders at that time, including Truman and MacArthur, assumed that eventually Japan would resume sovereignty, meaning that US troops would withdraw from Japanese territory. That never happened. Before the Second World War, this kind of infringement of state sovereignty was usually called extraterritoriality. In fact, extraterritoriality continues even today. There are US bases in Korea today, for example. Until the 1970s, Taiwan had many American bases, while the Philippines had huge US airbases and naval ports until the late 1980s. In this respect, it seems that the national sovereignty is not operative after the Asia Pacific War. Furthermore, the nation state's sovereignty no longer seems to be valued because, at least in the case of Japan and countries affiliated with the US collective security system in East Asia, there is really no independence from the US in terms of economic policy, military policy or diplomacy. But this cannot be viewed as an abnormalcy. What is significant is that the conception of national sovereignty underwent some drastic revisions in East Asia as well. In general, no country today can act independently as far as economic policy is concerned.

The only area where a country can sustain the appearance of sovereignty is in the domain of social welfare. Even social welfare is collapsing everywhere, which means that the nature of state sovereignty or popular sovereignty is radically changing, and today is very different from the kind assumed in the concept of international law in the nineteenth century. Whereas both Japan and Korea are both modern nation-states, in nineteenth century vocabulary they are more like colonies. Yet they enjoy a certain appearance of sovereignty. Both countries are deeply immersed in bio-politics, but bio-politics in the sense that the state is in charge of managing its population. The most fascinating recent illustration of this recently concerns state control over the import of American beef into Korea, and Japan. In order to let people lead a secure life, the state interferes and controls. The same logic is used in immigration. Militarily and economically, these states have little sovereignty, but whatever little sovereignty they may have is increasingly confined to very specific areas such as immigration and food import. I don't think the control of American beef itself is a trival issue, but rather an indication of a new form of state sovereignty. At the same time, social welfare is collapsing. In the recent article that Jon Solomon and I wrote for *Traces*, we argued that the old function of state sovereignty was to control class conflict within domestic society and translate class conflict within domestic society into international competition, promoting exports, seizing extra territories for surplus domestic population, and so forth. This function is already substantially replaced by something like border control against immigrants – or, even, in fact, criminalizing immigrants. For this purpose, terms like "terrorist" have been very effectively used. In this sense, then, I think there is a fundamental change in that notion of sovereignty and that it is taking place even in the United States.

JK: You said something very interesting in terms of the way that sovereignty can, at least, "appear." Appearance seems to be very important here since national sovereignty can never be instituted, but the appearance of sovereignty can. Specifically, on this issue of immigration one thinks of the many images of walls and barriers that are going up, when in fact these are not actually effective in any way, and everyone knows this. What is important rather is the appearance.

NS: Hence it serves as a displacement for the internal barriers of class. In fact, the nation state has never been a homogeneous entity. It is not that you simply have a border separating foreigners from national members. No, there are so many barriers within the domestic sphere already. But the state cannot admit this, so it has to create the pretense of holding onto the notion of the border. But today the border is very porous. Thus the state constantly evokes the use of violence to expel these immigrants in Europe, Japan, and the United States. Typically, in Japan there is a great fear of an invasion of North Koreans once that regime collapses.

RC: Let's touch upon your notion of the scheme of co-figuration. One can see traces of that notion even as early as *Voices of the Past*. In your critique of the Hegelian notion of recognition, you describe two entities making an image of one another in order to reflectively form a self-image. Yet this image is not simply philosophical for you. It also responds to certain geopolitical and, especially in the field of Asian studies, institutional demands.

NS: When I introduced the term co-figuration, of course I was struggling with the question of translation, since this question became such an important issue in my reading of eighteenth century Japanese texts. There the essential question was how people could recognize something like the Japanese language. Of course it was clearly obvious that only when they posited something like the Chinese language did it become possible for them to think about something like the Japanese language. Then in order to show that it was absolutely necessary to think about the process in which Hegelian recognition takes place – and later that viewpoint very effectively showed me how the institution of area studies, cultural anthropology and indeed all disciplines in which scholars deal with so-called "foreign cultures" work – I wanted to find out how the notions of foreign culture and unified identity could be conceived. In anthropology today, no serious scholar will use this term "culture" so carelessly, but in area studies it still has currency. Co-figuration helps us understand not only the institutional moment when two cultures are posited, but also why the area specialist cannot escape from that particular way of conceiving the exotic object of inquiry. What is at stake here is that it's not about the area that is the object of inquiry, but rather the scholar's own relation to that object. By positing co-figuration in this way, I was able to discover dimensions that escape that regime. Many sorts of political actions and political negotiations are thus revealed. There are very interesting possibilities here, since if you don't fashion yourself as an entity according to the regime of co-figuration, you might find all sorts of ways to establish new social relations. I owe to Deleuze the use of a term like representation, for this really helped me understand that translation is not representation. Such understanding allows one to open up new fields of inquiry outside the regime of co-figuration. That's the basic approach that I call the heterolingual address. The critique of Hegelian recognition was a way to thematically posit some of these questions.

JK: To get back to the issue of ethics, it seems that the heterolingual address would be one of your core ideas.

NS: Yes.

JK: There's a very interesting question emerging around ethics. I'm thinking in particular about Germany right now, where there's intense interest around two different kinds of objects. One is the animal as the Other, where, if one takes a certain notion of ethics seriously, absolute openness, then one cannot treat animals as so radically other that they cannot be addressed in our language. There's a lot of criticism about that. And then there's a form of intellectual ethics that takes the critique of humanism to such an extreme that it is, strictly speaking, not ahuman but inhuman or antihuman. Specifically, I'm referring to inquiries that take as their primary object of inquiry things like highways, the internet, roads, postal systems, and telegraph systems – types of networks, basically. These are two very interesting tendencies within a certain intellectual community that understands the dangers of humanism.

NS: This second approach seems very important, for it is uncertain what is meant by face-to-face contact. Does this refer to the actual presence of another human? If so, what is meant by this presence? In fact, Itō Jinsai already dealt with this issue in terms of the question of shame, for shame is always related to the presence of other humans. People don't mind being naked in front of cats, for example, but they feel ashamed of their nakedness in front of certain kinds of people. In the past, the master was not ashamed to be naked in front of his servants. Notions such as face-to-face contact and human presence open up fascinating questions regarding what we mean by the human.

Index

Derrida, Jacques 42–3, 134, 145, 150–1,
217, 235, 243–4
Descartes, René 180
Disney films 81
Dodd, Stephen 23
Dower, John 76–80
dream images 93–4
Drucker, Peter 166
Du Bois, W.E.B. 224–5
Dulles, John 226
Durkheim, Émile 197–8

economic ethics 14, 157–69
Eisenstadt, Shmuel 193
Eisenstein, Sergei 81, 84, 88
Engels, Friedrich 178
English language 36–7, 54
Enlightenment philosophy 215
Erasmus 183
Eurocentrism 42, 127, 134, 206
exploitation 123

F+f formula 29
Fabian, Johannes 181, 207
Fanon, F. 178–9
feminism 43, 46, 54
Ferguson, James 129
Foucault, Michel 13, 73, 88–9, 95, 119,
123, 139, 152, 154, 205, 223, 237–41
Freud, Sigmund 93–4
Fujitani, Takashi 224
Fukumoto, Kazuo 230
Fynsk, Christopher 141

Gadamer, Hans-Georg 10, 53–5, 64
Gallicchio, Marc 232
Genet, Jean 241
Gibbons, Luke 239–40
Girard, René 22–3, 25
globalization 91, 127, 184, 188
Goody, Jack 198
Gottl-Ottlilienfeld, Friedrich 164–5
Gramsci, Antonio 121
Greater East Asia Co-Prosperity Sphere
74, 80
Guattari, Felix 35, 37, 109, 186, 188
Guénif-Souilamas, Nacira 187

Hall, Stuart 121–3
Hardt, Michael 11, 93, 122, 128
Harootunian, Harry 195
Harvey, David 115, 127
Haver, William vii, 11–12; *author of
Chapter 6*

Hegel, G.W.F. (and Hegel-ianism) 8, 45,
67, 74, 76, 114, 146, 225, 230–1, 235,
240, 242, 248–9
Heidegger, Martin 146, 183, 230, 237, 244
Heinlein, Robert 75
hermeneutics 52, 54, 56, 69
heterolingual address 10, 12–13, 16, 69,
99, 124, 135, 141–4, 153, 220–1, 249
Hirohito, Emperor 97–100
historicization of culture 1–2
historiography 201–4
Hitler, Adolf 97, 99
homolingual address 10, 12–13, 69,
122–7, 134, 141–3, 220–1
Hozumi Shichirô 164
human relations management 172
humanism 183–9, 229, 240, 249
Husserl, Edmund 227–8, 230–1, 244

"I", use of 57–61, 65, 147, 151
Ignacio de Loyola 16, 216, 218–19
imaginary people of the
West (IPW) 182–3, 189
immigration policy 185, 248
imperialism 15, 164, 180–2, 232,
246
industrialization 178, 181–2
intellectuals, role of 152–4
invisibility, concept of 92–3, 96–7
Iraq 127
Ishikawa Kôji 165
Itô Jinsai 247
Iwasaki Minoru 157, 171

Jakobson, Roman 40–1, 61–2, 143–7,
150–3
Jameson, Frederic 37, 217
Japan studies 223–4, 228, 232, 245
Japanese language 63–4, 224
Japanese national identity 163, 233
Jaspers, Karl 193
Jauß, Hans-Robert 205
Jesuitism 16, 212–20
John III of Portugal 216
Johnson, Ollie 81

Kamei Hideo 22
Kant, Immanuel 4, 26, 60, 159, 215–19,
230–4, 245
Karatani Kôjin 22–3, 36–7
Keizai Dôyûkai 172
Kierkegaard, Søren 231
Kim, John Namjun vii, 10; 223 *et seq;
author of Chapter 3 and co-editor*

For Product Safety Concerns and Information please contact our EU
representative GPSR@taylorandfrancis.com
Taylor & Francis Verlag GmbH, Kaufingerstraße 24, 80331 München, Germany